CULTURE WARS

Culture Wars

THE STRUGGLE TO DEFINE AMERICA

James Davison Hunter

BasicBooks
A Division of HarperCollins*Publishers*

Part of this book was originally published in an article by the author in *The Brookings Review,* Spring 1990, pp. 20–27.

Library of Congress Cataloging-in-Publication Data
Hunter, James Davison. 1955–
Culture wars: the struggle to define America / James Davison Hunter.
p. cm.
Includes bibliographical references and index.
ISBN 0-465-01533-6
1. United States—Civilization—1970– 2. Culture conflict—United States. 3. Pluralism (Social sciences)—United States. I. Title.
E169.12.H77 1991 91-70065
973.92—dc20 CIP

PRINTED IN THE UNITED STATES OF AMERICA
Designed by Ellen Levine
92 93 94 NK/RRD 9 8 7 6 5 4

For my children,
Kirsten, Colin, and Whitney

Contents

II THE NEW LINES OF CONFLICT

III CULTURAL WARFARE

IV THE FIELDS OF CONFLICT

Preface

A European friend of mine recently observed that Americans typically conduct their lives in private and with little controversy. He did not mean to deny that such issues as abortion, gay rights, funding for the arts, women's rights, child-care policy, church and state litigation, multiculturalism, and court-packing are followed in the press and even debated passionately among American families, friends, and coworkers. But, my friend asked, do these culture wars have practical relevance for them? The answer will no doubt become more apparent to him as his stay in the United States lengthens. Eventually, he will see that these issues frequently seem abstract to people only until a part of their own lives intersects an issue of the culture war: a daughter or a friend wants an abortion, a marriage ends in divorce, a cousin comes out of the closet, the local school teaches values they deeply disagree with, they can't find decent day care for their kids, art at a local gallery is censored, a local activist burns the American flag at an antiwar rally. All of a sudden, what had long been confined to the abstract becomes very real. Not only their passions but their very life commitments are drawn into a public controversy much larger than their personal troubles—controversies that seem to have a life of their own. As we will see, the contemporary culture war touches virtually all Americans; nearly everyone has stories to tell.

The idea of a culture war taking place in America will be familiar to some; the term has of late become a topic of conversation in certain circles. The idea has come into circulation as people have reflected on the similarities and dissimilarities between our own time and circumstances and that of the German *kulturkampf* of the last decades of the nineteenth century. At that time the term described the political fallout from Bismarck's efforts to unify the disparate Prussian empires into a unified nation-state. On the surface, the dispute pitted Protestants against Catholics over the religious content and character of public education. Such an issue seems innocuous enough from the vantage point of the late twentieth century. But more was involved than meets the modern eye. Education was a symbol of German unity and national identity. German Protestants and Catholics were battling over the moral character of the nation—as it would be passed on to future generations in the schools.

The culture war in America today is of a fundamentally different cast. Education is just one of the areas of cultural cleavage and is probably not the most divisive. The antagonisms no longer arise between Protestants and Catholics but, as we will see, among a very different and historically unlikely configuration of cultural players. Yet like the *kulturkampf* a century ago, the specific issues being debated today, while important on their own, are really about something deeper and more significant. This book is mainly concerned with understanding and interpreting both the surface issues and the underlying realities of the contemporary culture war, as well as its historical significance and political implications.

I have been helped at all stages of creating this book by many, many people. My first debt of thanks goes to Robert Lynn, Craig Dykstra, and James Wind, and the Lilly Endowment which they most ably serve, not only for generously providing the resources to carry out this project but for their probing, challenging, and supportive engagement with me on the ideas of this book. With the support of the endowment I was able to draw on the assistance of several graduate students for different aspects and stages of the project. It was both fun and stimulating in this regard to work with John Rice, James Hawdon, James Tucker, Beth Schwieger, Tracy Fessenden, Karen Marsh, Jim Nolan, and Leslie Gunning.

Several colleagues read all of the manuscript in various draft stages and offered invaluable comments. I am especially grateful to Ken Myers, Gianfranco Poggi, Paul Kingston, Robert Wuthnow, Peter Berger, William Lee Miller, Jesse Pitts, Jeff Hadden, John Seel, and Os Guinness. Throughout the course of the project, I also received strategic insights and advice from Steven Tipton, Michael Aeschliman, Michael Cromartie,

George Weigel, Richard Neuhaus, Donald Black, and Mark Lupher. Many of the individuals I have acknowledged here would undoubtedly take issue with me on at least some part of the book, but their willingness to engage me in civil and substantive debate has made the writing of this book, from beginning to end, a joy.

In addition to these I am indebted to Susan Arellano, formerly at BasicBooks, for her intellectual insight and editorial support. The book is markedly the better for it. My appreciation also extends to Martin Kessler at BasicBooks for shepherding this project through to the end.

Last, but not least, I am abidingly grateful to my wife, Honey—a truer companion there never was—and to my children, who challenge me, entertain me, and always bring me down to earth.

I

INTRODUCTION

PROLOGUE

Stories from the Front

DISPATCH: 7 NOVEMBER, SAN FRANCISCO

San Franciscans will go to the polls today to vote on Proposition S, a referendum that, if passed, would allow unmarried couples to register their "domestic partnership" with the city clerk and would grant hospital visitation and bereavement rights to registered city employees. The proposition would primarily benefit the city's large gay and lesbian population, who are forbidden by state law to marry. Most of the city's political leadership endorsed the proposal earlier this year, but before the law could take effect, a petition circulated against it gathered 27,000 signatures, enough to take the issue to a citywide vote. Many of the proposition's supporters view today's vote as a test of San Francisco's reputation as "an island of civility," as the late Representative Phillip Burton called it. Yet opponents, including the Archdiocese of San Francisco, believe that the proposition would undermine the sanctity of the nuclear family. The size of the turnout could be critical to the outcome of the measure, particularly in an off-year election in which low voter turnout is common.

Chuck McIlhenny

Issues like Proposition S move Chuck McIlhenny to anger—one might be tempted to say a holy and righteous anger. A forty-three-year-old pastor of a small Presbyterian church not far from the Golden Gate Bridge, he helped lead the challenge to the "domestic partners" ordinance passed by the San Francisco Board of Supervisors earlier that year. He was not the only one angry enough to act against the proposal; a large coalition of Evangelical Protestants, ethnic Roman Catholics, black Pentecostals, and older citizens from various parts of the city were also moved to work day and night against it.

In Chuck's view, the domestic partners legislation was cleverly presented to the public as a means of providing hospital visitation rights to a live-in lover, whoever he or she may be. But this, he says, "was all a ruse—nothing but an emotional red herring." The real, not-so-hidden agenda was to give legal recognition to homosexual unions. Therein lay the problem. To Chuck, the bill represented an effort "to redefine the marriage relationship and therefore the family itself," and was therefore nothing less than "a fundamental attack upon Christianity, a fundamental attack upon the traditional, biblical family and marriage ideal."

As a committed Evangelical Christian trained for the ministry at the Reformed Episcopal and Westminster seminaries as well as at the Moody Bible Institute in Chicago, Chuck looks to the Scripture as the final source of authority on all moral and religious matters, including this one. Some issues may be open for debate because Scripture does not say much or is altogether silent. But on the issue of homosexuality, Chuck maintains, there is no skirting the matter. "In Scripture," he argues, "you have clear and explicit statements prohibiting homosexuality. Nowhere in the Bible does it explicitly and literally state, 'Thou shalt not commit abortion,' but you do have those explicit prohibitions against homosexuality." While part of the strategy for mobilizing the opposition to the proposition was to argue that it was financially unfeasible, Chuck admits that these arguments were somewhat disingenuous: "Ultimately the reason we rejected it was for moral and scriptural reasons. . . . It is a reinterpretation of God's creation ordinances." But can one forbid "sin" among people who make no pretense to be bound by the faiths that call it sin? "Christian morality," Chuck responds, "is not sectarian. . . . The Ten Commandments, for example, contain universal principles of morality and that is how I appeal to them. I say, 'Hey, listen, Jesus didn't argue against rape. There's nothing against rape in the New Testament. Does that mean that rape is fine?' I don't know of anybody who would say it is."

Although political initiatives such as the domestic partners bill raise Chuck's ire, they no longer surprise him. Over the past sixteen years he has become a veteran of such struggles. When he arrived in San Francisco at the age of twenty-six, however, these kinds of concerns were far from his mind. He had been working as an assistant pastor at a church in Long Beach, California, when the pastorship of a small Orthodox Presbyterian church in the Bay Area opened up. Chuck was ambivalent about taking the position; his heart was really in teaching, not in parish ministry. In the end, though, he took the job, thinking that he would stay at the church for a year or so. Perhaps, he thought, the position would be a stepping stone to another job and another city where he would fulfill his dream of teaching.

But something happened in Chuck's ministry that he never anticipated. In one of those early years, his church hired a new organist. The man who took the job was a friendly, competent musician who publicly professed faith in Christ. After three months, however, the church learned that the new organist was a homosexual. This in itself was not necessarily a problem; if the man confessed his sin and turned away from his homosexual lifestyle, he could stay. We are all sinners, after all. Yet the organist had no intention of changing his life, and that proved to be the rub. The teachings of the church would not allow anyone deliberately and openly "living in sin" to be an active part of the church community. It was not an easy decision for a thirty-one-year-old to carry out, but Chuck was obligated by his faith and by his loyalty to the church community. He had no choice but to let the organist go.

As it turned out, this event was the beginning of a long, intense, and divisive legal battle. The organist and his supporters charged discrimination on the basis of sexual orientation, while Chuck's side invoked the First Amendment of the Constitution to defend a religious community's right to order its affairs without government interference. Two full years, tens of thousands of dollars, and a good deal of planning and worrying went into the battle in the courts. In the end, much to Chuck's relief, the church won the case.

The legal obstacles he had to deal with in this dispute were in some ways minor, however, compared to the other kinds of problems he had to face. "When the case hit the front page of the local and regional newspapers," he reminisces, "we received so many death threats that we had to leave the city." Chuck and his family had never confronted anything like this before. What else could they do? But their intent was not to stay away permanently. After the publicity died down, Chuck was back in San Francisco, ready to carry on. But for Chuck McIlhenny, both his life and his ministry would never again be the same. From that point on, the man who was to become known as "the iron fist of orthodoxy" became an outspoken critic of homosexuality in San Francisco.

His public visibility, he says, emerged not because he deliberately sought out the spotlight but rather because the media sought him for his outspoken views on homosexuality and his compulsion to tell the truth as he saw it. The consequences of his willingness to take a public stand were devastating, however, for with each radio interview, television appearance, city council testimony, and other public statements he made, violence would follow. Through that year and the years that followed, the windows of Chuck's church were repeatedly smashed, his own car windshield destroyed, graffiti spray-painted on the outside walls of the church, and the church sign repeatedly destroyed. "People," he says, "will come to our house during the day, sometimes in the middle of the night, and scream at us, or they'll park their car in front of the house and blare their horn for minutes on end." Three years after the lawsuit, on a day in early June, his church and the manse next to it where he and his family lived were firebombed. Luckily, no one was hurt in the incident.

Chuck McIlhenny is a man of conviction and resolve, but his involvement in these local disputes has taken a toll. Is it any wonder? Most of his marriage has been lived in the shadow of these trying circumstances; his children, too, have faced these pressures virtually all of their lives. Still the family stays together, trying, as he puts it, to "hang tough." And somehow they do. One day a group of people demonstrated on the street in front of his house, some chanting epithets, some, he says, screaming. Without any prompting, Chuck's thirteen-year-old son put his arm around him and said, "I'm with you, Dad." Expressions of family togetherness such as these, Chuck says, make the trouble a lot easier to face.

One of the ways he and his wife and their three children have learned to stay together through the notoriety as well as the danger of maintaining their witness in that city is by immersing themselves in the stories and truths of the Bible. As Chuck puts it, they "read tons of Scripture." He says that the Psalms of the Old Testament are especially helpful "because they talk about persecution like ours." He also reads and rereads the Gospels, and the book of Acts "because it describes the experiences of other Christians in situations like ours." Not only this, he owns a copy of the original eight-volume edition of *Foxe's Book of Martyrs,* a history of Christian martyrdom written in the mid-sixteenth century, which lends him solace but which he also finds depressing. Then, too, the family is sustained by a number of support structures. One of the most important is a private Christian school, sixteen miles away from home, where he and Donna send their kids. Not only are the headmaster, teachers, and students all supportive, but, as Chuck says, the school gives his children "total relief from living here for at least ten hours a day." The protection in this case is as much physical as it is moral.

With all of this, one might well wonder why Chuck and his family stay in San Francisco. Wouldn't it be easier for them to go to Waco, Texas, or Greensboro, North Carolina—any city or town where they would not have to face these problems? In fact, he was recently asked to pastor a small church in New Zealand. Wouldn't that do?

Apparently not. They stay in San Francisco first and foremost because they believe that they are called to minister in that community. Yet they have less spiritual reasons as well; Chuck admits that the city has simply grown on them. Over the years, a once new and unfamiliar neighborhood has become *their* neighborhood; why should they leave? A measure of this evolving commitment is seen in the fact that while Chuck and his family used to escape San Francisco at every opportunity, they now have friends and family come to stay with them in the city. "We want to show that this is not a house of terror but one of security," he says. "We want to show that the Lord is our safety and that this neighborhood is our home and here you will have security."

Chuck's commitment to the city and his neighborhood is also reflected in a story he tells of a minister he encountered a few years back. The fellow was an evangelist from the nearby coastal town of Monterey, who boasted that he was going to come into San Francisco "to clean it up"—to fight the prostitution, pornography, and homosexuality. An affable sort, Chuck made him an offer: "You can come and live with me," he said. "As a matter of fact, we can work together. Bring your children with you." The evangelist admitted that he didn't really want to live in the city. Chuck's response was to the point: "Then keep your mouth shut! If you ever want to change San Francisco, fine—come on, move into the city, list your name in the phone book, and we'll do it together." But the evangelist demurred, and that was the last time Chuck ever heard from him. For Reverend McIlhenny, words are fairly cheap. One has to live out one's beliefs in a commitment to the place where one lives.

The focal point of Chuck's commitment to neighborhood and city is his unwillingness to see it taken over by what he regards as immorality. "Unlike other cities," he maintains, "the fight between a biblical morality and the new morality is crystal-clear in San Francisco. The line is drawn real sharp." Thus, for him, the idea that San Francisco could be considered an "island of civility," as described in the opening "dispatch," is a monstrous and mean-spirited joke. "I like to describe San Francisco," he observes, "as the city that leads the way of secular humanism. If you want to see a *godless city*—in its governmental, political, and social dimensions—this is it." Homosexuality, he claims, "is just the tip of the iceberg." Immorality is institutionalized at every level. It is, he says, "part of the *zeitgeist*," or spirit, of the times.

Chuck recognizes that San Francisco is unique in many ways, yet at the same time he believes that what is happening there is symptomatic of a problem unfolding in America as a whole. He frames this assessment in terms of his view of American history. Unlike some other Fundamentalists, he does not believe that America was ever really a Christian nation; Christianity was never institutionalized in the structures of government. "Still," he says, "the Lord has blessed our nation over the centuries because our cultural heritage was Christian." This will not be the case for long, he hastens to add, "particularly if America continues to follow the lead of San Francisco in rejecting that heritage." One of the ways America is abandoning that heritage, he argues, is by rejecting the original Christian meaning of the concepts of freedom and justice. "We will rue the day when we took the Declaration out of its Christian moorings." Thus, for him, both the political and spiritual task for Americans is to return America to its Christian roots. "What are my alternatives?" he asks. "Do I want a godly society or an ungodly society? If I want a godly society then I must advocate godly candidates. . . . I want a Christian society, so I'll advocate Christians running for office."

Chuck hesitates to predict the future. But if the outcome of the conflicts he has found himself embroiled in, as well as those facing America as a whole, is unclear, the stakes of the conflict are very clear. Those stakes, he claims, are nothing less than the life and death of our society. "The homosexual issue," he says, "is a secondary issue. The real fundamental issue is a secular humanism which rejects Christ and the Scriptures as your basis to society. And the ultimate end is always death—death to a society." For Chuck, it is a bitter irony that Christianity is often presented as "a social pathology"—for example, as perhaps the main hindrance to dealing effectively with the AIDS problem. In fact, Chuck is "more convinced than ever that . . . it is the Gospel alone that will stem the tide" of these moral trends.

Richmond Young

They live in the same city, but otherwise, Richmond Young and Chuck McIlhenny have little in common. One point of agreement, ironically, would be the political significance of the domestic partners referendum. Both men believe that the bill was ultimately designed to give official recognition to gay and lesbian relationships. But while homosexuality is so deeply and morally repugnant to one of them, it is a natural and appropriate form of human relationship to the other. So, too, while official recognition of such a relationship represents government support of immorality to one, it implies a movement toward greater equality and justice under the law to the other. "Some people," Richmond says, "want to think of gays as lonely, isolated, and unable to form stable relationships. One of the things I want people to understand is that gay people do form lasting relationships where they honor each other's feelings. The domestic partners law was just a mechanism to allow people to show that." He agrees at one level, then, with those who say that the referendum is "an effort by lesbians and gay men to find acceptance as part of a family." This was not, he says, an effort to redefine the family in a proactive way, as Chuck believes; it was more an effort to recognize and reflect in law the more inclusive and flexible way in which the family has actually evolved in our contemporary society. To this end, Richmond Young worked the precincts of San Francisco trying to get out the "Yes" vote on Proposition S.

In a city the size of San Francisco, it is not surprising that the two men do not know each other personally. Richmond does know Chuck by reputation, however, and his opinion is not at all flattering. "Reverend McIlhenny," he says, "can't be characterized as anything else but an antigay bigot. He's not a homophobe. Homophobia is a word that's been used so often that people have forgotten what it means, which is an irrational fear of homosexuals and of homosexuality. . . . I wouldn't say that about McIlhenny." Richmond readily admits that Chuck McIlhenny's opposition to homosexuality stems not from a desire for power, which he says drives some of his opponents in the Bay Area, but rather a bigotry "rooted in ignorance." He believes, too, probably incorrectly, that Chuck's hostility toward homosexuality "would lose a lot of its force if [he] would understand what it is like to be gay and what gays were like as people. It's interesting," he remarks, "we think of this kind of bigotry and homophobia as something that takes place in cities like Houston or Memphis or in the hinterlands of the country where people don't know any gays. But we have it only a few blocks away."

Richmond Young is thirty-eight years old and an editor at a legal publishing firm. His roots in San Francisco are about as deep as any Californian's can be; his family arrived in 1856. Some of his ancestral attachments to the city are fairly prominent. One grandfather was a superior court judge; the other was president of the San Francisco Bar Association. Richmond traces his political roots to the legacy of his maternal grandfather (the judge), who was an early-twentieth-century progressive—a "classic middle-class reformer," as Richmond describes him. His grandfather's legacy influenced the formation of his own political ideals, ideals that crystallized during his involvement in the antiwar protests of the 1960s. Even as a teenager, Richmond walked the precincts for Eugene McCarthy. It was when he was in his mid-twenties, however, that he became politically active on behalf of gay rights issues. He had known he was a homosexual since he was nineteen, but had repressed the inclination for seven years. Then the "Briggs Initiative," requiring the dismissal of homosexual teachers from public schools, was introduced into the state legislature. "It was time," Richmond says, "to come out of the closet and to fight the discrimination."

Adding to this complex portrait is the fact that Richmond Young is also an adult convert to Catholicism. He was twenty-nine years old at the time. "One night," he recounted, "I had a sudden impression or realization of the reality of Jesus and of God. It came over me like a sudden revelation, and I do think it was the same experience that other people describe as being born again." Richmond Young's conversion gives him another ironic point of agreement with Chuck McIlhenny. Richmond turned to Catholicism rather than Protestantism, however. "My lover at the time," he says, "was a devout Catholic." Through him Richmond met people "whose Catholicism was an integral part of their lives—not just a sterile set of doctrines." He had philosophical and theological reasons for becoming a Catholic as well, one being that, as he puts it, "Catholics don't believe in the inerrancy of the Bible." Richmond's view of Catholicism as a universal church also led him to feel that Catholicism "was more accepting of deviations or differences than Protestantism. The church," he explains, "has always been a part of the history of the world. It never set itself apart. Its sins are also mankind's sins."

Yet the Catholic church does oppose homosexuality, as resolutely as do Evangelical churches like Chuck's. How then does Richmond reconcile his sexual orientation with his newfound Catholic faith? He argues that the Church may be a vehicle of divine grace, but the Church itself is not a divine institution. It is a human institution, and like any human institution, it makes mistakes. Richmond believes, therefore, that the traditional Catholic opposition to homosexuality results not from divine revelation but from an unthinking accommodation to prevailing cultural opinion. As he puts it, "On the matter of sexuality, the Church reflects ancient prejudices designed to control people—to make them more dependent on the Church—rather than the true teachings of Jesus." The teachings of the hierarchy on homosexuality, then, really don't apply. Homosexuality, he concludes, is not a sin at all. "Jesus," he reflects, "wasn't interested in what people did in bed but with whether people deal with others in a loving and compassionate way. In the end, Christ will judge us on the basis of our actions toward others."

One sees a certain symmetry between Richmond's religious faith and his political ideals. Central to his religious faith is the belief that "Jesus came to offer liberation for anyone who would listen." But in his view, the liberation Jesus brings is not a personal liberation from the "sin of homosexuality," as Chuck would have it, but rather the liberation of individuals to live according to the dictates of personal conscience and style, and the liberation of society as a whole from the prejudices and intolerances that keep it from being genuinely free. Says Richmond, "I see Jesus recognizing everyone's radical equality."

The ideals of liberation and equality that he sees embodied in the life of Jesus provide a theological foundation for his views of politics and national life. The same themes are pronounced. "The essence of Americanism to me," he contends, "is contained in the words of the Declaration of Independence, particularly in the lines that say, 'We hold these truths to be self-evident, that all men are created equal, and are endowed by their creator with certain inalienable rights: life, liberty, and the pursuit of happiness.' That, to me, expresses the essence of Americanism. It's what America is. We're not really much else except for that. I mean, everything else is sort of decoration. Our other accomplishments are not all that different from other countries. But our essential Americanism and what sets us apart are contained in those words."

It is in the context of this political philosophy that Richmond sees both his own struggle as a politically conscious homosexual and the struggle of the larger gay and lesbian community. He puts it this way: "Rights always have an existence, but our perception of their existence and what kinds of rights people are seen to have are determined by our historical circumstances. I believe that as we grow in understanding and knowledge we develop a fuller understanding of the concept of rights, and as a consequence, the list of things that qualify as rights expands. The men who wrote the Declaration of Independence, for example, originally only applied its principles to white males who owned property and who belonged to established churches. Since then, however, the whole doctrine of who has access to civil rights has continued to broaden. I think of gay people as those who stand in the line with many others who are waiting to have their claim on that part of the Declaration of Independence recognized. We're just the latest to get in line for that."

All of this quite naturally leads Richmond Young to a very different view of San Francisco than the one held by Chuck McIlhenny. In sharp contrast to Chuck's view of the city as a cesspool of moral decay, Richmond says, "I like to think of San Francisco as the vanguard of fulfilling the Declaration [of Independence]. San Francisco has a reputation of tolerance, and a history of enjoying and reveling in eccentricity. That's just part of the common experience and identity of the city." How then does he explain the tremendous political power of the Roman Catholic hierarchy and the Evangelical churches, both in the Bay Area and in the country as a whole? "I'd like to think it is their last spasm before they go into final decline," he says, laughing. "At least I hope it is!"

DISPATCH: 7 MAY, NEW YORK

Hundreds of people gathered in front of an abortion clinic in midtown Manhattan today to protest abortion. Many of the demonstrators were native New Yorkers, but they were joined by hundreds of others who had come from as far away as California, Texas, and North Carolina—a total of thirty-five states. What made today's rally unique was that the protest involved civil disobedience—a "rescue," as the leaders of the demonstration put it. The locations of the clinics to be picketed were kept secret right up to the time of the protest in order to maximize the surprise and effect of the action. By sitting, standing, or marching in front of the clinic, the picketers created a human barricade, preventing anyone from going in or leaving. According to a spokesman, this was the protesters' objective—to prevent this clinic and every other one they visited from conducting abortions for one full day. Despite the protesters' prayers and hymns, the air was thick with tension. Pro-choice advocates who had learned of the demonstration argued, chanted, and carried their own placards. Tempers flared on both sides until police finally arrived and carried away the protesters. Eight hundred people were arrested, including four rabbis, several Evangelical Protestant pastors, and half a dozen Roman Catholic leaders.

Yehuda Levin

One of the protesters arrested that day was Yehuda Levin, an Orthodox Jewish rabbi from Brooklyn. It was the first time he had participated in a "rescue," but as someone whose thinking on abortion had crystallized over the previous several years, he felt it was time to express his opposition to the practice through this kind of action. Though he would become involved in other rescue activities later that summer in Atlanta, the events of 7 May remained fixed in his memory: the crowd, the police, the arguing and shouting, the confusion, being carried onto a police bus with dozens of others and being booked at the local station. Maybe he remembered that particular day so well because he was pictured on the front page of *Newsday* the next day, holding a sign that read, "New York Rabbis Condemn Abortion."

As a Jew, Yehuda opposes abortion for reasons different from those of the Catholics or Evangelicals who participate in the "rescues," yet his are no less binding. The ultimate reason he opposes abortion, Yehuda says, is that God opposes it. "The Torah tells us that feticide is prohibited," he explains. "It's not only prohibited, it's equated with a capital offense. That really is the beginning and the end of the subject." At a more philosophical and theological level, he argues that the very first commandment is to be fruitful and multiply. In this, God offers to humankind a partnership in creation—the act of producing children. "When a person destroys that seed," Yehuda says, "they are in effect rejecting this partnership. . . . To destroy this seed is to abrogate the covenant, and that's one of the most serious infringements of our tradition there is."

Thinking back, he says, he never could have imagined himself in this situation ten years earlier, as he was finishing his rabbinic training. "I had little knowledge of *Roe v. Wade,*" he admits, "no idea of how many abortions were being performed every year in America and scant knowledge of what abortion was in the first place. It was beyond my purview." Indeed, Yehuda's whole world had been that of Orthodox Judaism—the community of other believers, the yearly traditions and daily observances, and the yeshiva. As he put it, "I had very little contact with the Gentile world. I was living in a ghetto without walls. You see, it is inbred within our community that what goes on in the outside world is *meshugah* [crazy]. Just look at what the newspapers report or see what the billboards advertise. So if it is *meshugah,* why should we bother with it." At the age of twenty-four, however, Yehuda's awareness of the world outside of his religious community began to grow. "I began to learn up front," he says, "that a war was being waged between those who were concerned with traditional morality and those who wanted to break down as many barriers as possible."

This realization would be the beginning of a new chapter in Yehuda's life. Not long after his graduation from rabbinical school, he was invited to give the invocation at a March for Life rally in Washington, D.C., where he met the famous pro-life activist Nellie Gray and several members of Congress and saw over 100,000 people show their support for "the sanctity of human life." "It gave me a tremendous jolt," he says, "to see and encounter so many Gentiles with deep moral sensibilities that were akin to mine. They were fighting the *meshugah.*" This experience and a few others like it made Yehuda realize—indeed, in his view, divine providence was leading him to see—that "the Orthodox were not a dynamic force in this struggle—but should be." The latter belief spurred him to speak out publicly about the evil of abortion in America and about the general moral decline that had brought this to pass. It also prompted him to run for Congress against the Democratic incumbent, Stephen Solarz. With no political organization and no experience, Yehuda not only obtained the Republican nomination (despite being a registered Democrat) but by his count acquired 35 percent of the vote as the district's Right to Life candidate. (It happened to be the district with the single highest concentration of Orthodox Jews in the country.) A year later, Yehuda's conviction moved him to run for mayor of New York City. He claims he had no illusions about winning, and indeed, he gained no more than 1 percent of the vote. His goal was not to win but to distance traditional Jews from the liberal incumbent, who to most people seemed "the quintessential Jew." "I felt I had an obligation to demonstrate clearly," he says, "that we did not countenance many of the things that the mayor was doing."

For Yehuda, abortion is merely one symbol of a larger pattern of moral decline in America. "Obviously," he says, "society is heading down a very, very dangerous road." The source of the problem is clear: "We have got to be blind not to see a parallel between the decline of religion and religious values . . . and all the other things that are happening today." He insists that he is not a crusader, that he never set out to become involved the way he has, but that he came to see that he had a "religious obligation," as he put it, to take the message of God's righteousness "to the middle of the city" (a reference to Lot and his family in the biblical story of Sodom and Gomorrah). As for Chuck McIlhenny, the scriptures of Yehuda's religious tradition not only shape his views on moral issues like abortion, but also compel him, perhaps even against his personal inclinations, to take a public stand on behalf of what he believes to be God's created purposes for human society, including the protection of unborn children.

His aggressive and even confrontational style of "going to the middle of the city" has made Yehuda not simply a curiosity but a serious annoyance to many of his fellow New Yorkers. His personal abrasiveness, some have said, is legendary. He tells, for example, of the time he and a number of other clergy marched into the office of the chair of the Board of Education to demand a meeting, in response to a newly initiated sex education curriculum that they considered "totally devoid of values." Even Yehuda admits that his methods have been excessive from time to time, but he considers his actions to be consistent with his passionate stand on the issue of values and morality. The host of a local television show once observed that it seemed rather inappropriate, even "undignified," for a man of the cloth to do the things he did. "What is it to me," Yehuda came back sharply, "if I lose some of my dignity. You tell me, what does it take to get *you* upset? Do they have to rape your wife and daughter in Central Park? Is that when you start screaming?"

Hostility toward Yehuda's actions has come not only from non-Jews but from members of the broader Jewish community in New York. Outside of the Orthodox and some parts of the Conservative movements in Judaism, his views on abortion, and on moral decline in America more generally, are not widely held. But to Yehuda, his liberal Jewish opponents do not really qualify as Jews. "If we were to give them a test," he says, "use any standard recognized by the most uneducated, uninitiated Gentile as to what would constitute Jewish affiliation—Sabbath observance, eating kosher, frowning on adultery, the Ten Commandments—these people would not match up in any way. So therefore I think that they are practicing a religion which is not Judaism. They certainly are not practicing Judaism as it was practiced by their grandparents." One particular experience a few years back crystallized Yehuda's feelings toward such people, perhaps indelibly. He tells the story this way: "I was at the annual New York City Council hearings on gay rights when roughly fifty Hasidic Jews came in. All were dressed in their long gabardine coats and black hats, beards and side curls. Some were wearing sackcloth. All of a sudden, a number of militant homosexuals stood up, raised their hand in a Nazi-style salute and began to chant, 'Sieg heil! Sieg heil! Sieg heil!' Everyone in the room was paralyzed. How could they accuse us—those who suffered and died in the Holocaust—of being Nazis? Was it just because we are morally opposed to homosexual license? In the midst of this, I stood up and yelled above the chanting at the head of the City Council—who happened to be a liberal Jew—and [who was] not responding at all, 'Have you no pride as a Jew? These are your people! Are you going to say nothing! Aren't you ashamed of yourself?' The city councilwoman in charge finally stood up and gaveled the room to order—but did so without giving but a word of chastisement for what they had done. This was horrifying to me. It showed me that liberal Jews are more concerned with appeasing the forces of immorality than they are of representing or defending their own people." To Yehuda, politically and religiously liberal Jews have "painted a black eye" on the Jewish community. Thus, besides giving witness to religious and moral truth, he also sees his role as "clearing the record on where the Jewish community stands and to be a voice amongst other voices in the center of the city crying out against injustice and immorality."

"To be a voice amongst other voices . . ." While Yehuda has been alienated from many in the broader Jewish community, over the years he has found himself making common cause with others outside of Judaism—namely, many Catholics and Fundamentalist Protestants. These are the others whom he sees crying out against injustice and immorality. One of the women participating in an ad hoc counterprotest on the day of the rescue, Yehuda recalls, spoke harshly to him about just this. "You're a Jew," she screamed at him. "How can you stand with these Nazis? They'll get you next." In his own mind, he could stand there in common cause with the Evangelicals and Catholics because he and the larger Orthodox Jewish community "very much shared the values and concerns of those in the Christian community who were fighting to maintain those values."

Does he mind practicing Christians having such an influence on American public life? Not really, he contends, particularly if the alternative is a completely secular society. In the rabbinic tradition, Yehuda responds with a parable: "In Europe at the time when Jews were third-rate citizens, it was not uncommon for them to get bloodied and beaten up—and they didn't have much recourse in a criminal justice system.

This kind of thing happened a lot when they traveled and often it was the Gentile wagon drivers themselves who perpetrated these crimes. So how did a Jew know what was going to happen to him when he traveled? Rabbinic legend has it that the Jew should watch the wagon driver closely as he passed a church. If the driver made the sign of the cross the Jew should continue on his journey; if he didn't make the sign of a cross, the Jew should ask to be dropped off right there. Why? It was believed that if the driver manifested enough of a religious feeling to make the sign of the cross—even though making the sign of the cross is not exactly the Jewish thing to do—the odds were he would be safe. If the driver didn't show any religious devotion, the risk of being manhandled later on in the journey was much greater. That's my attitude toward the idea of a Christian majority in America. . . . When you have a secular society, you have the rapists and the muggers and the family breakers and you have what is happening today. . . . Quite frankly, it would be better if we did things separately, the way we've always done them. But we can have a greater impact sometimes if we work together. . . . We traditional Jews appreciate any positive efforts on the part of the Christian clergy and leaders to protect moral standards. . . . We may not be as strong as the more liberal segments of the Jewish community, but we stand with [the Christian leadership] to the best of our abilities."

Bea Blair

For Bea Blair, the event that took place on that morning in early May and others like it were actions she has come to expect. For her, the so-called rescue was not about saving babies, but, as she put it, about "denying women the right to health care"—in some cases the right to get an abortion, in others, the right to something as innocuous as contraceptives, or as "pro-life" as infertility treatment. More than this, the "rescue" represented the adoption of certain terrorist tactics by the "anti-choice" movement to further their ends. Thus, Bea rejects the claim of Rabbi Levin and others in the pro-life movement that their protests follow in the tradition of Martin Luther King, Jr.'s civil rights movement. "Martin Luther King and his followers never screamed and yelled at people," she says. "They were sitting, they were quiet, and they never interfered with other people's rights." She recognizes that the anti-abortionists have probably not killed anyone, but explains that in these rescues, they scream at people entering the clinic, calling these patients murderers. "If the right-to-life movement sees itself as nonviolent, then Operation Rescue really gives the lie to that."

Though echoed by many others, Bea's opinions on the abortion issue carry a particular authority, for she is an ordained Episcopal priest. As president of a New York chapter of the Religious Coalition for Abortion Rights, she leads a group of religious leaders and laity from a wide array of denominations—Protestant, Catholic, Jewish, and humanist—who believe that there is a religious pro-choice position. Their chief goal is to make the case that the pro-life movement does not have a monopoly on the abortion issue—that in fact, one can be religious and pro-choice at the same time.

As an Episcopalian, Bea does not believe that abortion is murder because she does not believe that the fetus becomes a person until it is born. "The fetus is life," she explains, "and it is human, but it is not a person—just as an acorn is not an oak tree." She comes to this view in part because, unlike Yehuda Levin or Chuck McIlhenny, she is not a scriptural literalist. Scripture, she contends, is not a document frozen in time: "The Bible is a history of our growing understanding of God. It needs to be read, listened to, and studied in its context." So too, in the context of modern society, "people have to interpret the Scripture or the traditions for themselves." Nevertheless, Bea points out that "there are passages in the Bible that support my point of view on abortion. . . . The book of Genesis in the Old Testament reads that 'God created Adam from the dust of the earth and breathed the breath of life into him and Adam became a living person.' From this text, she explains, "it is clear that when the person starts to breathe, that is when it is real."

Bea's belief that abortion is morally acceptable, and even appropriate at times, should not imply that she believes it is always an easy decision. Often, she says, "it is the lesser of two evils. Yet if a woman really believes that this is the right thing to do, then I don't believe that an outside authority should interfere. The decision is hers and hers alone."

Bea's beliefs about abortion as well as her involvement today is part of a certain fabric of social concern that has given form to her life. She was raised in Washington, D.C., where her father was a pediatrician, a man whom she still remembers getting up in the middle of the night to care for his patients. Her mother was also socially active on the liberal side of social issues, at one point even working with Margaret Sanger, the founder of Planned Parenthood. Bea's great aunts were also, in her words, "strong female figures." Indeed, her heroines growing up were

Margaret Sanger and Eleanor Roosevelt. In her years as a mother and wife in Rochester, New York, she experienced "the joy of having children who were wanted," but during that time she also worked at a Planned Parenthood clinic, where she saw, in her own words, "how devastating it was when a child was not wanted." "In the early years before *Roe,*" she explains, "all we could do was to make contraceptives available. But it was clear that contraceptives didn't always work and that we needed a safe alternative." Even then, she participated in the effort to liberalize abortion law.

After twenty years of marriage, four children, and nine grandchildren, she divorced her husband and moved to New York City. There she worked for Planned Parenthood and later for the National Abortion Rights Action League (NARAL), where she served as executive director. After several years in this position, she resigned to attend General Theological Seminary, also in Manhattan. After her studies she took the post at the Religious Coalition for Abortion Rights.

Bea sees her work on abortion as serving the larger causes of freedom and justice in America, ideals to which she is deeply committed. Two basic moral principles inform this commitment. One is "the belief that nobody should come between a person's conscience and their God." How a person lives is a private matter and should not be hindered by constraints created by others. This was one of her chief complaints about traditional marriage. As she put it, "you can't be happy living your life through somebody else." For Bea, the right to live your own life as a free agent, without having someone else's opinions and decisions imposed on you—whether through marriage or through childbearing—is a basic principle of liberty. A second principle is a sense of fair play: the belief that each person, regardless of his or her personal circumstances, should stand on level ground. The matter for her is particularly acute in the issue of abortion. "It seems so obviously and enormously unjust to have laws restricting or forbidding abortion," she says. "The people who suffer are the poor and the young and the uneducated and even the rural who can't get the service, not the rich, educated, and often white women, and that's just unfair." In Rochester, she says, the wealthy women would fly to Puerto Rico or England for an abortion, while the poor never had that recourse, and went instead to back-alley abortionists. "You know," Bea says, "laws will not stop abortion. They just make them dangerous, even fatal, for women, and to me, that is so obviously unjust."

In the contest over abortion as with so many other family issues, Bea feels, those who bear the brunt of societal constraints and inequities tend to be the women. In her view, "a strong anti-women feeling" underlies not only the anti-abortion movement but the larger effort to defend the traditional family. "It really punishes women," she says. "The anti-choice forces deny women their role as moral decision makers, deny the right of women to follow their own conscience." She argues that this can even be seen in their language. When Yehuda Levin speaks, for example, of "God's partnership with mankind," he linguistically affirms that women are not included, that they are just the tools of a male partnership with God. When he speaks of the scriptural passage "he who sheds the blood of man within the man" to justify his opposition to abortion, he again denies the unique role of women. Her opponents' imagery is suspect as well, Bea claims: "Anti-abortion activists often portray the fetus as a born baby and the mother as a faceless human form, as though she were merely a 'container.' "

Such a view is so contrary to Bea's ideas of what America is all about. "This country," she says, "was founded by people who didn't want one group imposing their ideas on another group." For her, what is ultimately at stake in the battle over abortion are certain key values that are rooted in American history and identity. As she put it, "equality, liberty and privacy—these are basic American values and I think they have to be extended to everyone." In this task, religious organizations like her own play an important role. "If you can move the church on these issues," she says, "then you've really moved justice and equality in the right direction." It is for this reason that Bea celebrates the development of a theology of liberation: a theology whose agenda is to reject societal dominance by a white, male establishment and to empower the other voices that have been silent and silenced for so long.

Bea's reflections on these matters and on her own involvement in them convey a sense of larger purpose. The central motif in her thinking about most issues is the family. "In a family," she says, "we are concerned chiefly about the welfare of our young children, our parents when they are old, and other family members who have needs. The same should be true in the nation as a whole. We need to take care of the health care needs, housing needs, and educational needs of everyone, especially the poor and dispossessed." Her views on abortion fit into this motif. Just as a couple should not have more children than they can adequately care for, she explains, we should think about the nation and world this way as well. Like Yehuda Levin, she quotes Genesis, but sees an entirely different ethic therein. "The Bible," she says, "tells us to be fruitful and multiply. But the population of the world is already more than the earth can handle. We should take care of the ones who are here, then, before we multiply much more."

DISPATCH: 16 JULY, HAWKINS COUNTY

Closing arguments were heard today in a lawsuit that has been billed by some as "Scopes Trial II." The case was triggered when a group of Evangelical Christian parents in Tennessee strenuously objected to their children's required reading material in public schools, which, they say, clashed with their religious beliefs. When the schools would not yield on the matter, the parents took them to court. Attorneys for the parents contend that it is a violation of the rights of children to force them to read anything that they find religiously offensive. The parents specifically object to schoolbooks that they believe contain themes of feminism, occultism, "situation ethics," and anti-Christian bias. Spokespersons for the schools' defense, however, describe the suit as an assault on the basic American principle of high-quality, nonsectarian public education.

Mae Duggan

Make no mistake, she sympathized with the parents involved in the suit. Yet, as she reflected on the news story, she concluded that they had taken the wrong approach. In the final analysis, Mae Duggan felt that the parents' argument addressed only one symptom of a larger problem, not its cause.

No, Mae Duggan was not from Tennessee, not an Evangelical Protestant, and not in any way associated with the lawsuit in Hawkins County. Yet in the thirty years she has worked with the Citizens for Educational Freedom (as a founder and now president), she had observed similar cases around the country, even in St. Louis, Missouri, where she has lived all her life. The real problem is, she says, that "we are all paying taxes to support a government monopoly in education. We have no real choice in how we educate our children." Instead of trying to force the public schools to offer more choice in readings, she says, "the Tennessee parents should have challenged the monopoly itself. . . . To truly satisfy the parental right to have their children educated in ways that do not undermine the morals they teach at home, we need diversity in education." As she points out, "Grocery stores aren't all the same. We don't all buy the same car. And yet the freedom to cultivate your mind in the way you want and the freedom to develop your soul is more important than the choice we have in buying a car or even a house." The only way to ensure diversity in education, she believes, is to offer choices in schools.

At the heart of the matter is her conviction that the public schools are bound by law to "completely ignore God." Children "are forbidden to pray" in schools, or to "recognize God as the ultimate authority for life." Thus, she maintains, "Parents like us, who insist that our children have a God-centered education," have a double burden, since they end up paying tuition for private education as well as public school taxes. In Mae's view, it is unfair that her next-door neighbors, who are willing to send their children to public school because they "don't care about God-centered education," can afford to "pay their mortgage off a lot faster than we could pay ours off." Tuition costs take a big bite out of family budgets. Pressing the point further, she adds, "We're all forced through compulsory taxation and compulsory attendance to support a [school] system that is oriented to secular humanism. . . . This does not reflect pluralism in America, but in fact supresses a freedom of mind and a freedom of thought."

The answer to this dilemma, says Mae, would be a system of "vouchers," giving all parents their fair share of the tax dollar to spend, as they choose, on a range of schools. The system would be modeled on the G.I. Bill, in which military veterans may use public dollars to go to the colleges of their choice. All the government "needs to do is change the distribution of tax funds. Then if the public school wants to be secular, it can be. But the parents could take the money to choose other schools if they wanted to."

Is this a dodge for creating white segregationist schools, as some of Mae's critics maintain? "That's a joke!" she responds. "In St. Louis, our archbishop integrated the Catholic schools eight years *before* the *Brown* [*v. Board of Education,* 1954] decision . . . so that the poor and the blacks in north St. Louis could get a good education." Mae maintains that it is "the poor and the blacks and the Hispanics" who would benefit most by the voucher system because these people "cannot now choose the schools that would do the most for them." She describes the public school in the ghetto of St. Louis as "horrendous. People are afraid to walk through the building. They use police dogs when the school opens and closes to protect the children from the violence." Mae estimates that about 30 percent of the St. Louis public schoolteachers send their own children to private religious schools. "That tells you something! In Chicago it's more like 40 percent!"

It is impossible to see the world the way Mae Duggan sees it without appreciating the role of the Catholic faith in her life. She was raised in a working-class Catholic home in north St. Louis; both her father and grandfather worked for the railroad. Her mother was a devout woman who believed, as Mae puts it, that "faith is the most important thing in life." As a youngster, Mae attended primary and secondary parochial schools. As a teenager, she was involved in Catholic youth groups, where she learned about the Catholic Church's social encyclicals that propounded such principles as distributive justice. When she married her husband, Martin, it was in the Catholic Church, and when she had children, they too were sent to parochial schools. Her faith, then, has always formed a backdrop for her life.

It was at the age of nineteen, however, that Mae first became aware of the larger significance of her chosen career in elementary education. That year the renowned secular philosopher Bertrand Russell lectured at her city teachers college in St. Louis. As Mae recounts it, Russell argued that there were no absolute moral laws to guide human beings through life. Children, as well as adults, should be allowed to make up their own codes to live by. Teachers, therefore, have no professional responsibility or even incentive to give moral direction to the children they teach. After the lecture, Mae challenged Russell, arguing that there were absolute moral laws even if he didn't know them, and that an eternal God was their author. Moreover, Mae insisted, children could not be expected to figure out on their own what was right and wrong. Teachers were obligated, therefore, as a part of their professional duties, to provide some moral direction.

Mae's faith not only shapes her philosophy of education but it motivates her to become involved in the political task of advocating choice in education as well. "Do you know the 'Our Father?' " she asks. "It says that 'Thy will be done on earth as it is in heaven.' " To Mae, this means we are obligated "not just to save our own soul but to help others live a happy life on earth in preparation for heaven." In this she says her guidance comes from the teachings of Christ. "Christ told us," she explains, "to love God with all of your heart and to love your neighbor as yourself." Part of loving one's neighbor is working toward a good society. But for Mae, a good society cannot exist unless religion pervades all of our social institutions: "George Washington, himself, said that without religion and the recognition of God's laws you can't have a good nation." For Mae, the decisive institution for creating good communities, and ultimately a good society, is education. "The bottom line," she says, "the vehicle by which we transmit our heritage and our culture to the next generation," is education. If our schools don't "train our people to be good citizens—and the word 'good' has 'g' 'o' 'd' in it—we are not going to have a good society."

Thus, in her view, much of the blame for this generation's problems can be traced back to the failure of the schools to provide religious instruction. Homelessness, divorce, and domestic violence are problems that cannot be solved by money or government policies alone, she explains, because they are chiefly "moral problems." These crises, she believes, "derive from the breakdown of the religious training that people had years ago." Yet she insists that she is opposed to having the government promote a specific religion in the public schools. This, she feels, would violate the Constitution. Mae's ideal situation is one where there is choice. Yet she says that even when the public schools required Bible reading and prayer, things were not so bad. "Because of the lack of religious influence for 90 percent of our citizens trained in the public schools," we are experiencing "a breakdown in society."

The seriousness of this situation, in her mind, was demonstrated in the history of recent totalitarian societies. "When the Nazis had taken over Germany and were crushing the people, many Germans left the country because the Nazis were taking their children and turning them into little fascists," she reflects. "And the same was true when the communists took over East Germany; some families who had lots of money in Germany and could have lived a decent life there left because they said their children were being turned into communists. They couldn't put them into religious schools anymore." Mae points out that those totalitarian systems were based upon ultimate but secular philosophies of life. "By contrast," she says, "America is a wonderful country based on the marvelous concept of freedom. Up until now we've done pretty well. But I worry about the future, whether our country is moving toward giving up its freedom as Germany and Russia did under the secular philosophies of Nazism and Communism." Mae sees such a threat developing mainly through the evolution of public education. "Our schools," she explains, "have deteriorated under the influence of John Dewey and his secular humanist philosophy. Dewey said himself he was founding a new religion that would reject the old traditional religions—Christianity and Judaism. In their place he would substitute his secular religion of science and materialism." In her eyes, Dewey's secular religion is identical to the philosophical foundations of Nazi Germany and communist Russia.

For Mae Duggan, then, education carries the public responsibility to help children seek and find truth; it "should not be a superficial experience in which just any old fad goes, but the good teacher should be seeking truth and seeking to impart truth and handing this down as a heritage to her students. And the starting point is a belief that God is truth." Americans are facing, as she sees it, "a war between the God-centered view of life and the secular humanist view which rejects God." In the end, she concludes, "Western civilization is at stake. . . . That's why I think this issue is so important."

Harriet Woods

Like Mae, Harriet Woods is a woman of firm convictions. Both women live in St. Louis, and they have known and respected each other from a distance for many years, they might both say, as "cordial adversaries." But unlike Mae, Harriet Woods would have little sympathy for the Tennessee parents, at least insofar as their request for legal redress was concerned. Her contention is that Fundamentalist parents already enjoy the right to send their children to private schools of their choice. For them to demand that public schools accommodate the individual religious needs of their own children, however, goes too far. "I think that every parent has a right to challenge the public schools. But there is a line between their right to say, 'I'm not going to have my child read this,' and saying 'I want a law to impose my solution on everyone else at whatever cost.' " Harriet suspects that the parents in Tennessee and others like them around the country have a hidden agenda. "What they really want is support for imposing certain values. They say, 'We have a right to impose these values on our own children,' " points out Harriet, "but, in effect, they are saying that they want others to share those values as well." In Harriet's view, what these people really mean when they denounce "secular humanism" is that the public schools should promulgate the values of fundamentalism; "secular humanism" is seen as the absence of those values.

As a former lieutenant governor of Missouri, former state senator, former city council member in University City, twice a candidate for U.S. Senate, and now president of a regional policy think tank, this sixty-three-year-old mother of three has no illusions about the public schools. There are many things that she would change about them. "I'm among those," she says, "who would love to see the whole system shaken up. I think it's bureaucratically burdened and the teacher preparation is far too rigid and methodologically oriented." She also has no objections to the existence of alternative religious schools. In fact, she very much favors some limited parental choice *within* a public school system. But the bottom line, for Harriet Woods, is a strong commitment to the pure idea as well as to the admittedly flawed realities of the public education system. She not only sees the schools as "shaping institutions," but she believes that they provide "the underpinnings for our democratic society." For these reasons, she believes that they deserve all of the support they can get. She says, "Anything that diverts the resources or takes away the better students from public schools has to be really challenged." This is what the Tennessee case and others like it, including ones she has tussled with Mae Duggan over in the past, represent to her.

As to the existence of alternative systems of education, such as Catholic parochial, Hebrew, Lutheran, Evangelical, and private nonsectarian schools, these, she maintains, are fine. "Individuals who want an alternative system are free to go ahead and create them and use them." But they should not expect public dollars to support those schools. "It always surprises me," she says, "that people like Mae expect that government will underwrite alternatives that individuals may choose." The "voucher" system that Mae and others advocate would divert tax dollars from public schools, but, as Harriet points out, this alternative system is not accountable to the democratic process. "When you want to separate the accountability for a system of education from those who provide the dollars for that system, that takes a lot of chutzpah." If education worked the way Mae wanted it, Harriet believes, the consequences would be unsettling not only for education but possibly for American society as a whole. "A voucher system would split it all up. We would go back to where we have a bunch of separate value systems, highly structured, and through them we would negotiate public solutions. That's what many of us see happening if we began to heavily underwrite separate school systems through vouchers." Whereas Harriet sees this as a threat to one of the key institutions of American democracy, Mae Duggan sees it as a fulfillment of the democratic ideals of pluralism.

Harriet's remarkable record of public service and her views of education are not at all serendipitous but are based in and guided by a certain personal code. Speaking with her, one can see that this code is perhaps too informal and unsystematic to call a "philosophy of life." Nevertheless, it is still sharp enough in her mind to provide clear principles that shape both her private and public life. In part, it derives from her childhood rearing in the Reform movement of Judaism. Though she was raised and confirmed in that tradition and remained somewhat observant as an adult (when her children were younger), she says she is not very observant now. The very nature of the Reform tradition, she says, requires less formal structure. She describes the values of that tradition as "humanistic," oriented toward "perfecting oneself in this life and doing justice in this life rather than working toward a reward in heaven." Also important, she says, was the tradition of Socratic reasoning, critical thinking, and logic she learned as a student at the University of Chicago forty years before. The idea that "the unexamined life is not worth living" has motivated her to "constantly look at assumptions, positions, values, and sophistries." This orientation was honed after college in her first jobs as a reporter. "From an early age I was put in the role of the observer, the questioner, the analyst who looks beyond appearances for the truth. I quickly came to see that there are sometimes different truths for different people."

Harriet's private code—which Mae Duggan would, without a pause, call "secular humanism"—forms something of a basis for a more public philosophy whose first principle is a humanistic concern for the powerless. As a public philosophy, her perspective is characterized, as she puts it, by "a combination of pragmatism and optimism. I really do believe," she says, "that the success of our society depends on our ability to negotiate solutions together while reserving some safeguards for the eccentrics or for the minority viewpoints. I don't feel the need for a clearly defined authority pattern, where there is one value that everyone says is the 'right' one." In Harriet's view, "people like Mae" have a deep need to seek absolute authority. "I'm willing to take the mistakes, which are frequent in a democracy, and to take the errors and even the injury—I'm willing to lose elections! What I am not seeking, however, is the right to impose a set of values on everyone else."

The theme of tolerance versus intolerance comes up again and again in her reflections. The tensions she observes over the funding of education reflect tensions in society as a whole. Harriet sees those who oppose abortion rights, for example, as people who "feel their existence depends on preventing other people from making their own decisions." The opposition to the Equal Rights Amendment is another example of a world view that insists on the same kind of hierarchy of authority: where "there is a God at the head of the universe, there is a man at the head of the Church, and there is a man at the head of the family." Private religious schools provide another example. These schools are by their very nature "not open to challenge from the outside"; their reliance on "higher authority," unaccountable to the democratic process, can cultivate a closed-mindedness "that can lead to tyranny." People who stand for such things, she says, are unable to persuade others "by rational argument or by pragmatic results, so their recourse is to impose their own value systems on others, threatening those who object with fears of punishment in the hereafter." This "narrowness," she argues, is the opposite of what our society needs if it is to survive.

At stake in this conflict, in Harriet's mind, "is the survival of our democratic institutions. With all their faults, they have been the breeding ground for a lot of excellence, for a lot of individuality, and indeed, for a lot of freedom for the Mae Duggans of this world to do their thing." It's ironic, she adds, that "at a time when we are applauding the awakening and breaking up of authoritarian regimes elsewhere in the world, . . . there are those who want a government underwriting for authoritarian systems here at home."

DISPATCH: 3 JULY, WASHINGTON, D.C.

Citizens across America were outraged by the Supreme Court decision yesterday ruling that flag burning is not a crime, but a form of expression protected by the Constitution. A few protesters even gathered on the steps of the high court today to burn a mock Supreme Court justice's robe. The decision reverses a Texas ruling that found Gregory Johnson guilty of defiling the U.S. flag when, five years ago, he doused a flag with lighter fluid outside the Republican National Convention and burned it. Members of Congress responded immediately with a resolution expressing "profound disappointment" with the high court's decision. One thing is certain: the new ruling can only deepen the debate about the meaning of the flag. For all Americans, the flag embodies national values: the question that will be debated well into the future is, "Which values?" . . .

DISPATCH: 7 APRIL, CINCINNATI

About 1,000 protesters stood outside the Contemporary Arts Center today chanting "Fascists!" "Gestapo, Go Home!" and "Tiananmen Square!" One person yelled, "Just as totalitarianism is crumbling in Eastern Europe, we have it right here in Cincinnati." The protest occurred as sheriff's deputies and about two dozen Cincinnati police officers entered the Arts Center and shut down the museum on the opening day of an exhibition of Robert Mapplethorpe's controversial photographs. A Hamilton County grand jury indicted the museum and its director, Dennis Barrie, charging them each with two misdemeanor counts of pandering, obscenity, and using minors in pornography. A sheriff's deputy presented Mr. Barrie with a subpoena. . . .

DISPATCH: 13 DECEMBER, CHARLOTTESVILLE

Representatives of the clergy from many Protestant and Catholic churches and Jewish synagogues in Charlottesville, Virginia, filed suit against the city today to prohibit the display of a crèche outside city hall. . . .

DISPATCH: 1 AUGUST, MIAMI

DISPATCH: 16 MARCH, ST. PAUL

DISPATCH: 5 JANUARY, LOS ANGELES

DISPATCH: 11 FEBRUARY, BIRMINGHAM

DISPATCH:

DISPATCH:

DISPATCH:

DISPATCH:

I

Cultural Conflict In America

The various conflicts presented in the prologue, and the lives that give them flesh and blood, will not be totally strange to most Americans. All of these stories, and the particular voices that tell them, relate to larger issues that are widely recounted on the front pages of newspapers and weekly news and opinion magazines, in the accounts and commentaries of television news anchors, and in the topical dialogue of radio talk-show celebrities: "I have 'Alan' from Blue Ash, Ohio, on the line. Our question tonight is, Should there be a Constitutional amendment prohibiting flag burning in America? What is your view, Alan?" The stories themselves and, more importantly, the issues that underlie them are the topics of dispute at the corporate cocktail party and the factory cafeteria alike, in the high school civics classroom, in the church lounge after the weekly sermon, and at the kitchen table over the evening meal. Few of us leave these discussions without ardently voicing our own opinions on the matter at hand. Such passion is completely understandable. These are, after all, discussions about what is fundamentally right and wrong about the world we live in—about what is ultimately good and what is finally intolerable in our communities.

The views of the six people presented in the previous dispatches illustrate only a few of the voices heard in public debate today. Yet their few stories nevertheless show that the debates on these issues are not made up simply of abstract and disembodied statements but express views rooted in real lives unfolding in real communities all across the nation. The voices heard here, as well as those that make up the larger forum of public debate and discussion in America, cannot be easily caricatured; in the details, each point of view is novel, indeed incomparable.

Though these voices are distinctive, they are not, in the end, extraordinary. Indeed, they share much that is common and familiar within American life, echoing thoughts and themes that resonate with many of our own experiences. All six people are basically middle-class Americans who are actively involved in their own neighborhoods and cities. In each case, their involvement is born out of a deep concern for the character of life—first and foremost in the places where they live, but also very much within the country as a whole. Each of them was able to draw out the implications of the particular controversy at hand for the character of life in the nation. In the very best sense of the term, then, each is a responsible and engaged citizen; words and phrases such as truth, justice, the public good, and national purpose have important personal meanings for them.

Looking at their backgrounds and current careers, it would be inaccurate to call any of these people "intellectuals." It is certainly fair to say, however, that they are all philosophically or religiously reflective. All would recognize that their own lives and world views form part of a larger community of moral understanding and commitment that is distinct from yet integrated within their involvement in neighborhood, city, and region. For Chuck McIlhenny, that community of moral commitment is the Reformed wing of Evangelical Christianity; for Richmond Young, it is a Catholic fellowship within a gay subculture; for Yehuda Levin, it is the traditional world of Orthodox Judaism; for Bea Blair, it is the social justice wing of mainline Protestantism; for Mae Duggan, it is, as she put it, "old-fashioned" Catholicism; and for Harriet Woods, it is the policy establishment of secular liberalism. These attachments are singularly important: all six find themselves thrust into controversy and into long-term community involvement not because they are quarrelsome by nature but rather because their prior moral commitments—to what they personally believe is true, just, good, and in the public interest—have compelled them to become involved. Chuck's calling as an Evangelical Christian; Richmond's commitment as a liberal Catholic; Yehuda's obligations as an Orthodox Jew; Bea's responsibility as an Episcopal clergywoman; Mae's commitment to the imperatives of traditional Catholic teaching; and Harriet's allegiances to the humanistic ideals of stewardship to the human family—these commitments oblige them to speak out as they do. Remove these commitments and you take away that which engages them as neighbors and citizens; separate them from these understandings and you take away their hearts and souls.

On his or her own terms, we find each of the six individuals profiled to be reasonable, engaging, and even appealing. In the details of their lives they are so normal and human: they all have great qualities as well as a few quirks, high and noble hopes as well as deep worries, personal triumphs as well as disappointments. Yet this personal and human face of public debate is one we rarely if ever see. In most cases, our sources of information about the controversies of the day are the media of mass communications: the radio and television, the daily newspaper and the weekly news magazine. By their very nature, these media can only give superficial coverage; they are incapable of delving into or rising above the personalities and events of the moment. As a consequence, the individuals who inspire various forms of social action tend to be presented as extremists, demagogues, and even opportunists for their own personal causes and special interests. Angry at what they see as injustice, they have decided to stand defiantly against what seem to be the givens of history. Likewise, the events themselves tend to be presented as flashes of political insanity—spasmodic symptoms of civic maladjustment—against the routine conduct of public affairs. Such events are rarely related to one another, but appear to be merely "disparate" outbursts by disparate (and sometimes "desperate") individuals and groups. Commentators make little effort to explain and interpret these stories and the issues that underlie them, to place them in a broader frame of reference. Those who *do* present events as interrelated often raise the specter of a dark and shadowy conspiracy. Most Americans reply, "Bosh!" to conspiracy theories—and they do so quite rightly. Yet they also, perhaps unwisely, tend to overlook the possibility that these "disparate" events may nevertheless be related to each other in complex and important ways.

The question we face is simply this: What if these events are not just flashes of political madness but reveal the honest concerns of different communities engaged in a deeply rooted cultural conflict? What if the voices of public argument—the McIlhennys and Youngs, the Levins and Blairs, the Duggans and Woodses—are not just the cranky utterances of America's political fringe but the articulation of concerns that are central to the course and direction of the mainstream of American public culture?

The argument of this book is that these voices and events *are* related to each other in complex ways—that America is in the midst of a culture war that has and will continue to have reverberations not only within public policy but within the lives of ordinary Americans everywhere. In understanding the character of this conflict, we will see that important differences often separate the personal from the public. As Chuck and Richmond, Yehuda and Bea, and Mae and Harriet have shown us, the personal disagreements that fire the culture war are deep and perhaps unreconcilable. *But these differences are often intensified and aggravated by the way they are presented in public.* In brief, the media technology that makes public speech possible gives public discourse a life and logic of its own, a life and logic separated from the intentions of the speaker or the subtleties of arguments they employ.

In this book we will also see just how high the stakes of this war are. They reach far beyond the biographies of those who give voice to conflicting concerns, and far beyond the immediate policy outcomes news media accounts describe. *At stake is how we as Americans will order our lives together.*

An Absence of Categories

How are we to make sense of all this? Certainly there are disagreements from time to time about matters of community interest and even of public policy. These are to be expected. Yet a "culture war" in America? The very thought or possibility of a deeply rooted and historically pivotal cultural conflict in America strains our imagination.

Our difficulty in coming to terms with the idea of such a conflict in contemporary America arises largely from the absence of conceptual categories or analytical tools for understanding cultural conflict. We simply lack ways of thinking about the subject. The predominant images of contemporary cultural conflict focus on religious and cultural hostilities played out in other parts of the world: the suppression of the Kurds in Iraq; the struggle of Sikh nationalists to establish their own homeland in northwest India; the political offensive of Gush Emunim, the political organ of Jewish fundamentalism in Israel, in its efforts to maintain the purity of orthodoxy in a pluralistic society; and the continuing hostilities between the Hindu Tamil minority and the Sinhalese Buddhist majority in northern Sri Lanka. As vivid and arresting as these images may be, they are foreign to the everyday experience of most Americans, distant from us both spatially and culturally. Thus, few Americans can relate personally, much less passionately, to the interests and concerns these images represent.

These images should not be seen as so remote, however, for they can provide metaphors for our thinking about religious and cultural conflict in our country. Of course, the particular cast of cultural players on the American scene is different from those found in other countries. Likewise, the character of the actual cultural conflict played out in the United States is very distinctive. Nevertheless, the story underlying cultural conflict in numerous places throughout the world—a story about the struggle for power—resonates with narratives found in America's not-so-distant past. An understanding of that past is essential for coming to terms with the unfolding conflict of the present.

CULTURAL CONFLICT: THE AMERICAN STORY

The memory need only be prodded lightly to recall that Protestant hostility toward Catholicism (and, to a far lesser extent, Catholic resentment of Protestantism) provides one of the dominant motifs of early modern American history.[1] Understanding the American experience even as late as the nineteenth century requires an understanding of the critical role played by anti-Catholicism in shaping the character of politics, public education, the media, and social reform.

Of course, the mutual hostility of Protestants and Catholics had been implacable since the time of the Reformation and Counter-Reformation in the sixteenth century. For their rejection of church tradition and ecclesiastical authority, Protestants were regarded by Catholics as infidels who had abandoned the true faith; for their elevation of "arcane rituals" to the status of scriptural truth and for their elevation of papal authority to the status of the authority of Christ, Catholics were regarded by Protestants as heretics who had perverted the true faith.

Needless to say, these tensions were not only religious or theological in nature. Indeed, the split between Catholics and Protestants during the Reformation generated one of the most enduring and consequential *political* divisions in Western experience. More than a century (between 1559 and 1689) of religious warfare within and among the nations of Western Europe can be attributed to these interreligious hostilities. And even after the age of religious wars had formally come to an end, the political tensions between these religious and cultural traditions continued to affect the institutional fabric of Western life. Prejudice, discrimination, and even physical violence were commonplace for the Protestant minorities in southern Europe (France, Spain, Italy, and Portugal) and the Catholic minorities in the north (Britain, Germany, Holland, and Scandinavia).

America, of course, was colonized primarily by emigrating European Protestants of one stripe or another. It is not surprising, then, that anti-Catholic sentiment emigrated to American shores as well, and became woven into the unofficial political and cultural traditions of the colonists. In fact, anti-Catholicism in America reached something of an apex in the nineteenth century. For one, many of the major urban daily newspapers displayed a prominent anti-Catholic prejudice: the *Chicago Tribune,* for example, played a significant role in inciting anti-Catholic agitation through the 1840s and 1850s.[2] There was also an enormous literature exclusively devoted to discrediting the Catholic presence. Between 1800 and 1860, American editors published at least 25 daily, weekly, or bimonthly newspapers and 13 monthly or quarterly magazines opposing Catholicism, while American publishing houses published more than 200 anti-Catholic books.[3] The most titillating and popular of this literature presented accounts of priests and nuns who had abandoned their faith because of their experiences of torture, mental brutality, and even sexual offense. One of the first and certainly the most famous of these accounts, Maria Monk's *Awful Disclosures of the Hotel Dieu Convent: The Secrets of Black Nunnery Revealed* (1836), sold over 300,000 copies. Others published around the same time included Rebecca Reed's *Six Months in a Convent* (1835), Rosamond Culbertson's *A Narrative of the Captivity and Sufferings of an American Female Under the Popish Priests in the Island of Cuba, with a Full Disclosure of Her Manners and Customs* (1836), Andrew Steinmetz's *The Novitiate, or a Year Among the English Jesuits* (1846), and Josephine Bunkley's *The Testimony of an Escaped Novice from the Sisterhood of St. Joseph* (1856). The Protestant suspicion and fear that fueled widespread interest in these tales formed a pretext for riots in Boston, New York, Philadelphia, St. Louis, Louisville, and other cities east of the Mississippi, as well as numerous attacks on convents, churches, and seminaries (such as the burning of the Ursuline Convent of Charlestown in Boston in 1834, and of St. Michael's Church and St. Augustine's Church in Philadelphia in 1844).[4]

Anti-Catholicism also ignited the great school wars of the mid-nineteenth century, visible in Philadelphia and Boston but particularly in New York, due to the outspoken views of John Hughes, an Irishman and the presiding bishop in that city. Because skills, values, and habits of life are passed on to children in school, it was inevitable that the schools would be an arena of cultural conflict, where the majority would assert its power and minority cultures would struggle to maintain a voice. Despite advocates' claims that the common schools of New York were nonsectarian, the Public School Society of New York retained textbooks that contained numerous overt anti-Irish and anti-Catholic statements. They also maintained the practice of a daily reading and recitation of the (Protestant) King James version of the Bible. When the Public School Society refused to accommodate Catholic interests either by allowing Catholic religious instruction after hours or by providing public funds to be used for the establishment of public schools of a Catholic nature, the Catholic community suffered.

Yet perhaps the most vociferous expressions of anti-Catholicism came from anti-Catholic societies (such as the American Protestant Association, the Christian Alliance, the American and Foreign Christian Union, the American Protective Association, and American Alliance) and anti-Catholic political parties (such as the Native American parties of the 1840s, the Know-Nothing party of the 1850s, and the Republican party of the 1850s and 1860s). Importantly, these organizations were most successful in precisely the states where Catholics were most numerous. Thus, they became significant not only for organizing and voicing both popular and elite resentment against Catholics but for mobilizing electoral opinion against the interests of a rapidly expanding Catholic community that remained both severely disadvantaged and largely powerless.

But Catholics are not the only religious minority that has endured hardship in America. The memory only needs to be prodded a bit further to recall the ways in which interreligious hostility has extended to Judaism. Christianity has long held Jews in the ambivalent status of being both God's chosen people, who had been miraculously sustained throughout the generations, and an unfaithful people who suffered deservedly for their betrayal of the Messiah. This was no less true for the Evangelical pietism that prevailed through the nineteenth century. In America, the remnants of Puritan culture retained a deep sympathy with the "People of the Book" and an identification with the Old Testament imagery of a people "in covenant with God." Still, in their view, the sufferings of the diaspora were the just punishments of a vengeful God for a people who had rebelled against His purposes.

Yet while the religious component was never absent, the secular and specifically economic behavior of Jews received the most vicious exploitation in stereotypes. Jews were portrayed as crude, aggressively greedy Shylocks whose conduct in business was always opportunistic and very often unscrupulous. Jews were the pawnbrokers, petty white-collar criminals, and merchants of the big cities, perennially in pursuit of the bargain and conspicuous in their display of new wealth. Such was the imagery presented in popular dramas featuring Jews (like Melter Moss in *The Ticket-of-Leave Man* [1864], Mo Davis in *Flying Scud* [1867], Dicey Morris in *After Dark* [1868], and Mordie Solomons in *The Lottery of Life* [1867]). Popular novels of the period echoed the theme; at least three of Horatio Alger's stories, for example, contain Jews of this cast as minor characters.[5] The portrait was reinforced throughout dozens of inexpensive and sensationalized dime novels written at the end of the century. Herman Stoll, the unscrupulous German-Jewish Wall Street broker in Albert Aiken's *The White Witch* (1871) and the shady operator Aaron Mosenstein in Aiken's *Dick Talbot and the Ranch King* (1892) are just two examples. Jews were similarly stereotyped in the works of Gilbert Jerome, Prentiss Ingraham, H. P. Halsy, and J. R. Coryell, the author of the popular Nick Carter stories.[6]

Despite the vulgar stereotyping and the popular concern about the "Hebrew conquest of the financial centers of New York," anti-Semitism was never greatly politicized in the way that anti-Catholicism had been. Jews never appeared to present a cultural or demographic threat equivalent to that posed by the Catholics. Nevertheless, various forms of anti-Jewish discrimination did characterize the last two decades of the nineteenth century and the first three decades of the twentieth in particular.[7] For one, quotas limited the admission of Jews to private schools, colleges, and medical schools as late as the 1920s. As an upwardly mobile Jewish population began to migrate out of its ethnic and religious enclaves, restrictive covenants were placed in the deeds of homes, allowing real estate agents to refuse to rent apartments to Jews, and landlords to hang "To Let" signs with the addendum "No Jews." These practices extended to membership in social clubs and to the enjoyment of summer and weekend resorts. At Saratoga, Manhattan Beach, and Coney Island, in the Catskills and other resorts throughout New York and New Jersey, placards were raised that stated, "No Jews or Dogs Admitted Here." In retaliation, Jews purchased several prestigious hotels in most of the resort towns and formed their own elite clubs in New York, Baltimore, Rochester, Detroit, and other major cities. In sum, the discrimination faced by Jews in the last decades of the nineteenth century and the first decades of the twentieth, while in many ways different from that experienced by the mainly Irish Catholics, was no less hostile. The net effect was to exclude and control.

Less visible motifs of cultural conflict in American history include hostility toward Mormons. From the founding of the Mormon Church in 1830, Mormons were subject to harassment and persecution. The governor of Missouri stated in 1838, "The Mormons must be treated as enemies and must be exterminated or driven from the state, if necessary, for the public good."[8] And in several states, mainly in the South, they were. Joseph Smith and his brother were jailed and then killed by a mob in Illinois in 1844; four Mormon missionaries were killed by a mob in Cane Creek, Tennessee, in 1884; and numerous others became victims of murder, beatings, tar-and-featherings, and other acts of violence.[9]

In all of these instances cultural tension arose not simply from academic disagreement over the proper form of ecclesiastical structures or a theoretical argument over doctrinal truths. Rather, America's uneasy pluralism implied a confrontation of a deeper nature—a competition to define social reality. Through the nineteenth and early twentieth century cultural discord was kindled, in general, by two competing tendencies. On one hand, there was the quest on the part of various minority cultures to carve out a space in American life where they could each live according to the imperatives of conscience and the obligations of community without harassment or reprisal. Such a space would provide the base from which to expand their own legitimate interests as a distinct moral community. On the other hand, there was the endeavor of Protestants and a largely Protestant-based populism to ward off any challenges—to retain their advantage in defining the habits and meaning of American culture.

THE END OF AN AGE?

The conflicts involving Protestants, Catholics, Jews, and Mormons are indeed a prominent part of the American heritage, and yet even these experiences are largely removed from contemporary American experience. The reason for this is that all signs would seem to point to a growing sense of tolerance among Protestants, Catholics, and Jews (as well as Mormons and others too).

One series of national surveys conducted between 1966 and 1984, for example, showed that strong prejudicial feeling both for and against different religious faiths declined. Neutrality (or what may actually be mutual indifference) among Catholics, Protestants, and Jews generally increased while antipathy toward various groups declined.[10] Another general indication of growing interreligious tolerance is found in the answers to questions about the suitability of presidential candidates who personally identify with one or another religious tradition. In 1958 one of every four Americans (25 percent) claimed to be opposed to a nominee who was Catholic, but by 1987 that number had decreased to only 8 percent. Likewise, in 1958, 28 percent said that they would not vote for a candidate who was Jewish. By 1987, this figure had dropped to only 10 percent.[11]

The research on anti-Semitism in post–World War II America points in the same direction. Once again, the trends point to a rapid *decrease* in the proportion of the population holding negative perceptions of Jews.[12] For example, non-Jews are now far less likely to believe that Jews "have a lot of irritating faults," or are "unscrupulous," or "more willing than others to use shady practices to get what they want," that they "always like to be at the head of things," or that they are "objectionable neighbors." Non-Jews are also now far less likely to believe that Jews "have too much power," that they "don't care what happens to anyone but their own kind," and that they "are more loyal to Israel than to America."

Even among white Evangelical Protestants, the sector of the population that has historically been most hostile to Jews, anti-Semitic feeling is quite low. According to one survey conducted in 1986 for the Anti-Defamation League of B'nai B'rith, there is no longer any "strong direct evidence" to suggest that "most Evangelical Christians consciously use their deeply held Christian faith and convictions as justification for anti-Semitic views of Jews."[13] Indeed, 90 percent of the Evangelicals disagreed with the statement that "Christians are justified in holding negative attitudes toward Jews since the Jews killed Christ," and less than one in ten agreed that "God doesn't hear the prayer of a Jew." The study concluded that many of the negative attitudes of Evangelicals toward Jews are best interpreted as a measure of "general particularism" than of specific anti-Semitism per se. Indeed, the study further noted that "There is some evidence to suggest that Evangelical Christians may have more positive attitudes toward Jews than [toward] other non-Christians because of the interrelationship between the Christian and Jewish tradition throughout the Old and New Testaments."

The expansion of cultural tolerance, it is important to point out, is not an isolated event. It coincides with the slow but steady expansion of political and ideological tolerance (such as tolerance of communists and atheists), racial tolerance (of blacks and Hispanics), and sexual tolerance (of homosexuals and those cohabitating outside of marriage).[14]

No one would say that interreligious and interideological tension of the kind that prevailed in the nineteenth and early twentieth centuries has disappeared altogether—nor, in all likelihood, will it ever disappear entirely. The voices of prejudice can continue to be heard by those who warn against "the Jewish Menace," or like the leadership of the World Congress of Fundamentalists who claimed in 1983 that the Roman Catholic Church is "the mother of harlots and abominations of the earth."[15] Even so, overwhelming evidence demonstrates that the social ethos of the late twentieth century reflects dramatic change.

Social and historical tendencies as important as these compel us to confront a momentous possibility. The Enlightenment *philosophes* long ago predicted that as societies advanced, modern individuals would outgrow their need for the comfort of religious "superstitions." One of the long-dreamed-for consequences of this would be the end to religiously motivated violence and division in society. If religion was deteriorating, its passions could no longer be linked with the tremendous power of the state. All such conflict would come to an end. Though the Enlightenment thinkers held out this hope universally, they were particularly anxious to see the end of hostilities between Protestants and Catholics and between Christians and Jews in their own societies. It was the political disruption and human suffering generated by these particular cleavages that were most immediate to their own time and experience.

The evidence just reviewed provides still another compelling explanation of why the very idea of cultural conflict in contemporary America is so implausible to most Americans. When we look all around the social and political landscape, we see a general harmony among the traditional faiths of the United States; by and large, Protestants get along well with Catholics, Christians get along better with Jews, and even the small number of religious cults are more of a curiosity than a source of widespread resentment and antagonism. If one can argue anything on the basis of scholarly study, it is that the predictions of the Enlightenment age are coming true after all.

But are they? Is the age of cultural and, in particular, religious conflict in America coming to a close?

The answer must be no. The reason is that cultural conflict is taking shape along new and in many ways unfamiliar lines.

NEW LINES OF CONFLICT: THE ARGUMENT IN BRIEF

Let me begin to make sense of the new lines of cultural warfare by first defining what I mean by "cultural conflict." I define cultural conflict very simply as political and social hostility rooted in different systems of moral understanding. The end to which these hostilities tend is the domination of one cultural and moral ethos over all others. Let it be clear, the principles and ideals that mark these competing systems of moral understanding are by no means trifling but always have a character of ultimacy to them. They are not merely attitudes that can change on a whim but basic commitments and beliefs that provide a source of identity, purpose, and togetherness for the people who live by them. It is for precisely this reason that political action rooted in these principles and ideals tends to be so passionate.

So what is new about the contemporary cultural conflict? As we have seen, the cultural hostilities dominant over the better part of American history have taken place *within* the boundaries of a larger biblical culture—among numerous Protestant groups, and Catholics and Jews—over such issues as doctrine, ritual observance, and religious organization. Underlying their disagreements, therefore, were basic agreements about the order of life in community and nation—agreements forged by biblical symbols and imagery. But the old arrangements have been transformed (a matter we will explore in chapter 3). The older agreements have unraveled. The divisions of political consequence today are not theological and ecclesiastical in character but the result of differing worldviews. That is to say, they no longer revolve around specific doctrinal issues or styles of religious practice and organization but around our most fundamental and cherished assumptions about how to order our lives—our own lives and our lives together in this society. Our most fundamental ideas about who we are as Americans are now at odds.

Because this is a culture war, the nub of political disagreement today on the range of issues debated—whether abortion, child care, funding for the arts, affirmative action and quotas, gay rights, values in public education, or multiculturalism—can be traced ultimately and finally to the matter of moral authority. By moral authority I mean the basis by which people determine whether something is good or bad, right or wrong, acceptable or unacceptable, and so on. Of course, people often have very different ideas about what criteria to use in making moral judgments, but this is just the point. It is the commitment to different and opposing bases of moral authority and the world views that derive from them that creates the deep cleavages between antagonists in the contemporary culture war. As we will see, this cleavage is so deep that it cuts *across* the old lines of conflict, making the distinctions that long divided Americans—those between Protestants, Catholics, and Jews—virtually irrelevant.

At this point let me introduce a critical word of qualification. Though competing moral visions are at the heart of today's culture war, these do not always take form in coherent, clearly articulated, sharply differentiated world views. Rather, these moral visions take expression as *polarizing impulses* or *tendencies* in American culture. It is important, in this light, to make a distinction between how these moral visions are institutionalized in different organizations and in public rhetoric, and how ordinary Americans relate to them. In truth, most Americans occupy a vast middle ground between the polarizing impulses of American culture. Many will obviously lean toward one side while many others will tilt toward the other. Some Americans may seem altogether oblivious to either. The point is that most Americans, despite their predispositions, would not embrace a particular moral vision wholly or uncritically. Where the polarizing tendencies in American culture tend to be sharpest is in the organizations and spokespeople who have an interest in promoting a particular position on a social issue. It is they who, perhaps unwittingly, give voice to the competing moral visions. (Even then, I might add, the world views articulated are often less than coherent!) These institutions possess tremendous power in the realm of public discourse. They almost seem to have a life of their own: an existence, power, and agenda independent of the people for whom they presumably speak.

Polarizing Impulses: The Orthodox and the Progressive

To come right to the point, the cleavages at the heart of the contemporary culture war are created by what I would like to call *the impulse toward orthodoxy* and *the impulse toward progressivism.* The terms are imperfect, but each aspires to describe in shorthand a particular locus and source of moral truth, the fundamental (though perhaps subconscious) moral allegiances of the actors involved in the culture war as well as their cultural and political dispositions. Though the terms "orthodox" and "progressive" may be familiar to many, they have a particular meaning here that requires some elaboration.

Let me acknowledge, first off, that the words, orthodox and progressive, can describe specific doctrinal creeds or particular religious practices. Take orthodoxy. Within Judaism, orthodoxy is defined mainly by commitment to Torah and the community that upholds it; within Catholicism, orthodoxy is defined largely by loyalty to church teaching—the Roman Magisterium; and within Protestantism, orthodoxy principally means devotion to the complete and final authority of Scripture. Substantively, then, these labels can mean vastly different things within different religious traditions.

But I prefer to use the terms orthodox and progressive as *formal properties* of a belief system or world view. What is common to all three approaches to *orthodoxy,* for example (and what makes orthodoxy more of a formal property), *is the commitment on the part of adherents to an external, definable, and transcendent authority.* Such objective and transcendent authority defines, at least in the abstract, a consistent, unchangeable measure of value, purpose, goodness, and identity, both personal and collective. It tells us what is good, what is true, how we should live, and who we are. It is an authority that is sufficient for all time. Thus, as different as Chuck McIlhenny, Yehuda Levin, and Mae Duggan are in their personal faith commitments, all three believe that moral authority comes from above and for all time. This is seen clearly in Yehuda's statement that what the Torah says about abortion is "the beginning and the end of the subject." Chuck and Mae, in their own ways, would say something similar. This fundamental commitment, then, is what these three share in common and one reason why, in the current climate, their voices tend to resonate with each other.

Within cultural progressivism, by contrast, moral authority tends to be defined by the spirit of the modern age, a spirit of rationalism and subjectivism.[16] Progressivist moral ideals tend, that is, to derive from and embody (though rarely exhaust) that spirit. From this standpoint, truth tends to be viewed as a process, as a reality that is ever unfolding. There are many distinctions that need to be made here. For example, what about those progressivists who still identify with a particular religious heritage? For them, one may note a strong tendency to translate the moral ideals of a religious tradition so that they conform to and legitimate the contemporary *zeitgeist.* In other words, what all *progressivist* world views share in common *is the tendency to resymbolize historic faiths according to the prevailing assumptions of contemporary life.* This is seen, for example, in Bea Blair's rejection of biblical literalism and her conviction that, as she put it, "people have to interpret the Scripture for themselves." The same theme is illustrated by stories Chuck McIlhenny tells of ministers he has debated, some of whom, Chuck says, reinterpret Scripture to justify homosexuality, while others recognize what the biblical texts say about the immorality of homosexuality but reject its authority over one's life. From Chuck's point of view, progressivist church leaders base their views on the belief that "the Bible is just a human document, no different from any other book." The general point both Bea and Chuck make here is that the traditional sources of moral authority, whether scripture, papal pronouncements, or Jewish law, no longer have an exclusive or even a predominant binding power over their lives. Rather, the binding moral authority tends to reside in personal experience or scientific rationality, or either of these in conversation with particular religious or cultural traditions.

I have been talking about the contemporary cultural divide in the context of religious communities in order to highlight the historical novelty of the contemporary situation. But what about the growing number of "secularists"?[17] These people range from the vaguely religious to the openly agnostic or atheistic. While they would probably claim no affiliation with a church or religious denomination, they nevertheless hold deep humanistic concerns about the welfare of community and nation. (Of those we met in the prologue, Harriet Woods of St. Louis would most closely match this description. She was raised in the Reform movement of Judaism but has for many years maintained only the loosest attachments to that tradition. Instead, she thinks of herself as a humanist.) Secularists like Harriet are central to this discussion for the obvious reason that their presence and perspectives have become so prominent in American life. How then do secularists relate to the matter of moral authority?

Like the representatives of religious communities, they too are divided. Yet public opinion surveys show that a decided majority of secularists are drawn toward the progressivist impulse in American culture.[18] For these people religious tradition has no binding address, no opinion-shaping influence. Some secularists, however, (particularly many secular conservative and neo-conservative intellectuals) are drawn toward the orthodox impulse. For them, a commitment to natural law or to a high view of nature serves as the functional equivalent of the external and transcendent moral authority revered by their religiously orthodox counterparts.

In sum, the contemporary cultural conflict turns upside down (or perhaps inside out) the way cultural conflict has long been waged. Thus, we see those with apparently similar religious or cultural affiliations battling with one another. The culture war encompasses all Americans, religious and "non-religious," in very novel ways.

Political Dispositions: Cultural Conservatives Versus Cultural Progressivists

The orthodox and progressivist impulses in American culture, as I have described them, contrast sources of moral truth and also the allegiances by which people, drawn toward one or the other, live and interpret the world. They also express, somewhat imperfectly, the opposing social and political dispositions to which Americans on opposing sides of the cultural divide are drawn. Here, though, a word of elaboration.

It nearly goes without saying that those who embrace the orthodox impulse are almost always cultural conservatives, while those who embrace progressivist moral assumptions tend toward a liberal or libertarian social agenda. Certainly, the associations between foundational moral commitments and social and political agendas is far from absolute; some people and organizations will cross over the lines, taking conservative positions on some issues and liberal views on others. Yet the relationship between foundational moral commitments and social and political agendas is too strong and consistent to be viewed as coincidental. This is true for most Americans (as seen in public opinion surveys), but it is especially true for the organizations engaged in the range of contemporary disputes. For the practical purposes of naming the antagonists in the culture war, then, we can label those on one side cultural conservatives or moral traditionalists, and those on the other side liberals or cultural progressives. These are, after all, the terms that the actors in the culture war use to describe themselves. The danger of using these "political" labels, however, is that one can easily forget that they trace back to prior moral commitments and more basic moral visions. We subtly slip into thinking of the controversies debated as political rather than cultural in nature. On political matters one can compromise; on matters of ultimate moral truth, one cannot. This is why the full range of issues today seems interminable.

New and Unlikely Alliances

The real novelty of the contemporary situation emerges out of the fact that the orthodox and progressivist communities are not fighting isolated battles. Evangelical Protestants, for example, are not locked in an isolated conflict with liberal Protestants. Nor are theologically progressive Catholics struggling in isolation with their theologically conservative counterparts in the Roman hierarchy. The contemporary culture war is much larger and more complicated. *At the heart of the new cultural realignment are the pragmatic alliances being formed across faith traditions.* Because of common points of vision and concern, the orthodox wings of Protestantism, Catholicism, and Judaism are forming associations with each other, as are the progressive wings of each faith community—and each set of alliances takes form in opposition to the influence the other seeks to exert in public culture.

These institutional alliances, it should be noted, are not always influential in terms of the joint power they hold. Some of the groups, after all, are quite small and have few resources. But these institutional alliances are *culturally* significant, for the simple reason that ideological and organizational associations are being generated among groups that have historically been antagonistic toward one another. Had the disagreements in each religious tradition remained simply theological or ecclesiastical in nature, these alliances would have probably never developed. But since the divisions have extended into the broader realm of public morality, the alliances have become the expedient outcome of common concerns. In other words, although these alliances are historically "unnatural," they have become pragmatically necessary. Traditional religio-cultural divisions are superseded—replaced by the overriding differences taking form out of orthodox and progressive moral commitments.

These unlikely alliances are at the center of a fundamental realignment in American culture and, in turn, identify the key actors in an emerging cultural conflict. It is in this realignment that we find the real significance of the stories recounted at the opening of this book. Each one illustrated the shifting alliances: at the Police Academy on East 20th Street in Manhattan stood Orthodox rabbis, Evangelical pastors, and Catholic priests, all being charged with disorderly conduct. There in the offices of Bea Blair's Religious Coalition for Abortion Rights and in Mae Duggan's Citizens for Educational Freedom an array of faiths (progressive in Bea's case and orthodox in Mae's case) are represented. There in San Francisco, there in Hartford, there in Cleveland, there in Boise, there in Birmingham, there in towns and cities all across America.

Points of Clarification

The first mistake we should guard against is to view the culture war as merely the accumulation of social issues debated today (such as abortion, values in schools, homosexuality, or the meaning of Columbus's discovery of America). The culture war encompasses these issues, but the source of the conflict is found in different moral visions. For this reason, it would also be a mistake to view the culture war as merely a social referendum on Ronald Reagan, George Bush, or other presidents and their political legacies. If this were the case, the present conflict would simply be a dispute between political "liberals" and "conservatives." The cleavages run much deeper. For the same reasons, it would be inaccurate to describe this as a collision between "religious liberals" and "religious conservatives."[19] Nor is it a clash between what one scholar described as "New Protestants" and "Old Protestants," "New Catholics" and "Old Catholics," and by extension, "New Jews" and "Old Jews."[20] In a similar vein, it would be wrong to confuse the contemporary culture war with the ambitions of Protestant Fundamentalism and the New Christian Right and the backlash it created among such secular activists as feminists in the National Organization for Women (NOW) or attorneys of the American Civil Liberties Union (ACLU). It is true that Evangelical and Fundamentalist Protestants are the most vocal and visible actors on the orthodox side of the new cultural divide and that the secular activists of NOW, the ACLU, or the People for the American Way are among the most visible actors on the progressive side of the divide. But to frame the contemporary culture war in this way ignores the central role played by a wide range of other cultural actors on both sides who are neither Fundamentalists on the one hand nor secular activists on the other. Besides, many of the organizations of the New Christian Right (for instance, such as the Moral Majority, Christian Voice, the Religious Roundtable) have either disappeared from public sight or gone out of business. Yet the cultural conflict continues—and it continues without any sign that it will soon abate.

THE STRUGGLE TO DEFINE AMERICA

RANDALL TERRY (spokesman for the pro-life organization Operation Rescue): The bottom line is that killing children is not what America is all about. We are not here to destroy our offspring.

FAYE WATTLETON (president of Planned Parenthood): Well, we are also not here to have the government use women's bodies as the instrument of the state, to force women into involuntary servitude—

RANDALL TERRY (*laughing*): Oh come on, Faye.

FAYE WATTLETON: —I think that as Americans celebrate the Fourth of July, our independence, and when we reflect on our personal liberties, this is a very, very somber time, in which the courts have said that the most private aspects of our lives are now . . . not protected by the Bill of Rights and the Constitution. And I believe that that is a time for Americans to reflect on the need to return to the fundamentals, and the fundamentals of personal privacy are really the cornerstones upon which our democracy is built.

RANDALL TERRY: I think that to assume or even suggest that the founding fathers of this country risked their lives and many of them died so that we can kill our offspring is pathetic.[21]

Although Randall Terry and Faye Wattleton were debating the morality and legality of abortion, what they said goes far beyond the abortion controversy. First, the contemporary culture war is not just an expression of different "opinions" or "attitudes" on this or that issue, like abortion. If this were all there was to it, the conflict I refer to would be, as someone once suggested, the "politics of distraction"—a trivial pursuit that keeps Americans from settling more important matters.[22] No, the conflict is deeper than mere "differences of opinion" and bigger than abortion, and in fact, bigger than the culmination of all the battles being waged. As suggested earlier, the culture war emerges over fundamentally different conceptions of moral authority, over different ideas and beliefs about truth, the good, obligation to one another, the nature of community, and so on. It is, therefore, cultural conflict at its deepest level. This is why the differences between Chuck McIlhenny and Richmond Young, between Yehuda Levin and Bea Blair, and between Mae Duggan and Harriet Woods are so intense and seem so unresolvable.

Though the conflict derives from differences in assumptions that are philosophical and even theological in nature, the conflict does not end as a philosophical dispute. This is a conflict over how we are to order our lives together. This means that the conflict is inevitably expressed as a clash over national life itself. Both Randall Terry and Faye Wattleton acknowledge this in their exchange. Hearing them invoke the Bill of Rights, the "founding fathers," "what America is really all about," and so on, we come to see that the contemporary culture war is ultimately a struggle over national identity—*over the meaning of America,* who we have been in the past, who we are now, and perhaps most important, who we, as a nation, will aspire to become in the new millennium. Importantly, Randall Terry and Faye Wattleton are not the only ones who see a larger relationship between a single issue in the culture war and the American character. A well-known photographer whose work has been scrutinized by the FBI claims, "We are not going down without a fight. We're not going to go down without a voice that's saying loudly and clearly, 'this is not what we think America is about.' "[23] A young mother and activist near Sacramento, who protests the content of schoolbooks in California's public schools, said, "The battle we are fighting here is being fought all around the state and around the nation. We as parents get involved because our children are affected but in the end it is our country that is at stake."[24] A video store owner who was prosecuted for violating pornography laws stated, "I feel like I'm fighting for America. I feel like I'm fighting for our rights as Americans. That's what I feel like."[25] And each of the individuals we met in the prologue believes that the battle they wage has consequences for America—its institutions and its ideals. And the list goes on. Arguably, our national identity and purpose has not been more a source of contention since the Civil War.

Though intellectuals and activists of various sorts play a special role in this cultural conflict, it would be very wrong to assume that this conflict is really just the lofty and cerebral machinations of squirrelly academic types who roam the corridors of think tanks and universities. To the contrary, this culture war intersects the lives of most Americans, even those who are or would like to be totally indifferent. This is so because this conflict has an impact on virtually all of the major institutions of American society. As the "stories from the front" suggest, this conflict has a decisive impact on the *family*—not just on the critical issues of reproduction and abortion but on a wide range of other issues such as the limits (if any) of legitimate sexuality, the public and private role of women, questions of childraising, and even the definition of what constitutes a family in the first place. The cultural conflict concerns the structure and content of public *education*—of how and what American children will learn. Also affected is the content of the popular *media*—from the films that are shown to the television shows that are aired to the books that are read and to the art that is exhibited. It has a critical effect on the conduct of *law,* particularly in the ways in which Americans define rights—who should have them and who should not and with whose interests the state should be aligned. Not least, this cultural clash has tremendous consequences for electoral *politics,* the way in which Americans choose their leaders. The contemporary culture war even has a bearing on the way in which public discussion is carried out—in the way people with opposing ideals and agendas try to resolve their differences in the public forum.

Once again, what seems to be a myriad of self-contained cultural disputes actually amounts to a fairly comprehensive and momentous struggle to define the meaning of America—of how and on what terms will Americans live together, of what comprises the good society. The purpose of this book is to explore the nature, depth, and consequences of this struggle. Part II describes the historical and societal sources that have given rise to the new cultural strains as well as the nature and historical significance of the new cleavages that divide American public culture. Part III explores the mechanisms by which cultural conflict is carried out. In particular, this section explores the *nature* of public discussion about national life and purpose, and how the technologies that mediate public discourse aggravate the differences and intensify the polarities. In this way we see how most Americans are eclipsed from public debate. Part IV examines the various fields of conflict—the symbolic territory over which the larger culture war actually takes place. The key areas surveyed are the family, education, media and the arts, law, and electoral politics. Finally, Part V attempts to assess the status of the conflict today and traces the implications of this conflict for the unfolding of American democracy as it embarks upon its third century.

The first task, however, is to explore the general character of cultural conflict. The topic is somewhat theoretical but its implications are far from abstract. From it we will discern the tangible principles by which the contemporary American culture war takes shape.

2

The Anatomy of Cultural Conflict

The idea of "cultural conflict" may sound abstract, but as we have seen, it involves real individuals who are not unlike many people we know, or perhaps even ourselves. Their lives—their thoughts, emotions, beliefs, activities, and relationships, and maybe ours too—are a central part of the way the contemporary culture war unfolds. For a brief time, however, it is appropriate to step away from the gritty details of those lives to see the larger significance. To this end, let us come right to the point: *cultural conflict is ultimately about the struggle for domination.*

Of course, it would be senseless as well as intellectually idealistic to imagine that "class resentment," the antagonism born out of the unequal access to the prerogatives of wealth, does not play a part in explaining conflict of this nature. It would be equally ludicrous to imagine that ethnic and racial suspicion were somehow insignificant factors. So too would it be folly simply to dismiss the passionate convictions and ideals of the people engaged as irrelevant—"epiphenomenal," as the Marxists say—to its course and outcome. But in the final analysis, whatever else may be involved, cultural conflict is about power—a struggle to achieve or maintain the power to define reality.

The power to define reality is not an abstract power. Indeed, as we have seen, nothing less is at stake than a sense of justice and fair play, an assurance that life is as it should be, indeed, nothing less is at stake than a way of life. And because the conflict ultimately involves a struggle for power, a variety of other tangible factors are invariably involved, including money (a great deal of it), reputation, livelihood, and a considerable array of other resources. To be sure, cultural conflict is serious business.

Yet this is only a point of departure. Many questions beg to be answered. Among them: How does such conflict take form? Where does it take place? Who are the principal contenders? And so on. Though these questions need to be addressed in general and somewhat theoretical terms, what we learn by pursuing them is anything but abstract and useless. This venture, in fact, is critical to an understanding of cultural conflict in our own day. The first question to be addressed here concerns the location of cultural conflict in society. Once the context is established, other facets of the present situation will become much clearer.

PUBLIC CULTURE—PRIVATE CULTURE

If cultural conflict is mainly about the struggle for domination, the arena that is principally contested is the arena of "public culture."

Both public culture and, for lack of a better term, "private culture" can be understood as "spheres of symbolic activity," that is, areas of human endeavor where symbols are created and adapted to human needs. At both levels, culture orders our experience, makes sense of our lives, gives us meaning. The very essence of the activity taking place in both realms—what makes both public and private culture possible—is "discourse" or conversation, the interaction of different voices, opinions, and perspectives. Yet, while public and private culture are similar in constitution, they are different in their function—one orders private life; the other orders public life.

First, consider the domain of private culture. Private culture, as one area of symbolic activity, consists of the symbols and meanings that order experience within the realm of personal experience. These meanings encompass people's self-understanding and the relationships they enjoy with close friends, family, coworkers and colleagues, and other acquaintances, as well as to their circumstances and surroundings. But what do these symbols and meanings do? At one level they take the form of the rules and platitudes that guide ordinary people through the routines of everyday life, from the time they wake up in the morning to the hour they retire to bed. These would encompass the unspoken rules about how to adorn oneself for the day, when and what to eat (for example, the virtues of "fast food" or "health food"), how to spend one's leisure time (for example, reading, shooting hoops, meditating, watching television, or quaffing beers with friends), and so on. These symbols and meanings also provide a kind of map that locates one in a larger world of people, places, events, and situations. Such symbols identify, for example, who is significant in people's lives and why. (Some people are significant because they are related to you by blood—a father, mother, sibling, or child; others, because their decisions affect your life, such as a boss, teacher, coach, or politician.) But beyond the more mundane aspects of private life, private culture contains the truths that help a person cope with both tragedy and elation—the inevitable seasons of anxiety, suffering, boredom, and heartbreak as well as those fleeting moments of anticipation, joy, and enchantment that are together part and parcel of human experience. They help explain why, for example, you did not get the job you really wanted ("it wasn't in the cards"), why you must endure the neighbors you have ("this must be a test of character"), or why your brother was killed in a car accident ("it must have been God's will"). The realm of private culture holds the parables and truths that help people make sense of the events that mark the cycle of their lives—birth, adolescence, marriage, childrearing, vocation, old age, and death. These symbols are what help us see, for example, birth as "a miracle," adolescence as "a stage," marriage as "a union," and so on. Not least, private culture consists of the interpretations that allow persons to locate their own biographies and the biographies of those close to them not only in the broader sweep of community and national life but in the wider reaches of human and even cosmic history as well. Interpretations of this kind are heard commonly when people are described as having "made a real difference in this town"; as being "a real saint"; or, sadly, as having "wasted their life away."

Public culture, by contrast, consists of the symbols and meanings that order the life of the community or region or nation as a whole. In modern times the primary locus of collective experience is the nation-state. A person's attachment to the local community or to a regional way of life (such as that linking people to the South, the West, the Midwest, or New England) remains important, to be sure. Ultimately, though, these particular attachments tend to be subsumed by or encompassed within the interests of national life. In this light, public culture in our day and age can best be understood as the repository of the symbols of national life and purpose. What does this mean?

At its most basic and practical level, public culture consists of what could be called the "instrumentality of the state." By this term I refer to the entire range of procedural norms and legal codes that define the acceptable limits of personal behavior and collective action, specify the nature and extent of public responsibility (such as helping the poor, caring for the environment, and assigning municipal tasks of collecting garbage, paving streets), and regulate interaction among different parties in the public arena (in political controversy, legal disputes, and the like).

Public culture, though, is more sublime than this, for it also embodies the symbols of national identity. These symbols express the meaning of citizenship and, therefore, the meaning of patriotism and disloyalty. More important, public culture consists of the shared notions of civic virtue and the common ideals of the public good—what is best for the general happiness of the people and welfare of the republic. Beyond this, public culture is reflected in the shared standards by which the actions of individuals or communities as well as the actions of other nations and communities with whom it deals are evaluated and judged as either good or evil, right or wrong, just or unjust.

Finally, a nation's public culture embraces the collective myths surrounding its history and future promise. These myths are usually constructed through a selective interpretation of our national history, in which certain themes and events are emphasized and others played down. For example, some may stress historical events that show America as a "secular democratic experiment"; others see America as a "Christian commonwealth, a city on a hill." Mae Duggan gave expression to one of these myths when she invoked George Washington's belief that good government cannot exist without religion as its foundation. Bea Blair expressed another interpretation when she claimed that America was "founded by people who did not want one group imposing their ideas on another group." Such myths elaborate the moral significance of the nation's founding in the context of global history; they guide the selection of its heroes and villains; and they interpret the content of the founding documents—its Declaration of Independence, its Constitution, its Bill of Rights. By providing an interpretation of the past in this way, these myths also articulate the precedents and ideals for the nation's future. They set out the national priorities and tasks yet to be accomplished, and they envision the mission yet to be fulfilled.

Ideally, public culture and private culture would seem to complement each other. As spheres of symbolic activity, each provides a context for the other. Public culture functions as a legal and political context for private culture by demarcating the boundaries of permissible personal behavior and even thought. At the same time, personal interests and aspirations rooted in private culture become expressed as political claims in the public realm. For example, a parent's concern about sex education in his or her own twelve-year-old's middle school becomes more general concern with the quality of education in California, where they live, and perhaps the nation as a whole. Or, a woman's own unhappy experience with an unplanned pregnancy may become a more general concern with the politics of reproduction in her city. In this way, private culture provides the context in which public culture becomes a reality intelligible and personally relevant to ordinary people. Public culture becomes a realm that can be understood and influenced, a sphere of activity in which individuals and communities can present and advocate their particular interests, the place in which the various voices of private interest can press their particular claims as public discourse. To the degree that public and private culture interact in this way, the authority of democratic regimes achieves its measure of popular consent. Such is the moral foundation of the modern liberal state.

Of course, this is how political life under democratic rule is supposed to work in theory. While some of the time practical reality "fits" the theory, much of the time it does not. The special language of public discourse, for example, often seems muddled, obscure, and incomprehensible. The impenetrable nature of legal rhetoric and bureaucratic verbiage is well known. These factors are obstacles that private citizens and local communities face in entering public debate. When the obstacles are too great, public culture remains distant and unapproachable; private culture becomes isolated and the voices of ordinary citizens remain publicly silent. When private culture remains estranged from public culture, and individuals and communities retreat from political expression, personal lives become irrelevant to the course and conduct of civic affairs.

Why is all of this important? Because the right to shape the public culture, or at least the right to have a voice in how public culture will be shaped, confers enormous benefits. The essential benefit is the right to pursue individual and community interests. Those who have no voice may be defined as illegitimate—and their interests may be deemed irrelevant. The very survival of minority moral communities is at risk, unless all have the right to help shape public culture. In real life, of course, the many different voices that contribute to the shaping of public culture are not of equal volume or authority. Many voices may be heard, but the historical tendency has been for one voice to dominate. This was certainly true in the case of the Protestant domination in the nineteenth century. In this case and in others, the values and interests of one moral community overshadowed and oftentimes eclipsed those of other communities. This is what social scientists would call "cultural hegemony," and the benefits that accrue to it are nothing less than power and privilege.

It is precisely for this reason that the arena contested in cultural warfare is the arena of public culture. It is where the struggle for cultural hegemony or cultural domination takes place. But in what ways does this struggle work itself out? This will become clearer after exploring the impact of two other aspects of public culture.

Faith and Public Culture

The first aspect concerns the place and role of faith. The term is used broadly here to include any more or less formal system of belief. Traditional theisms (Protestantism, Catholicism, Judaism, and Islam) would all be considered faiths. By this definition it is also possible to speak about secular ideologies, including such comprehensive political philosophies as Marxism, fascism, or humanism, as faiths.

Some may ask, if "faith" is being defined so broadly, why not use the term "ideology" instead? Besides, the word "faith" carries certain religious and sectarian connotations. The reason is this: the term, ideology, is correct and appropriate in what it implies, but its usage in the American scene is off the mark. The main reason is that the American people have never provided very fertile soil for the growth of purely secular political ideologies. Quite the opposite. America, rather, has always been the "fertile crescent" of the industrialized world insofar as the development of religious sectarianism is concerned. Therefore, it is hardly surprising that when secular ideologies have taken root, as in the case of the humanist and free thinking movement after the Second World War, they have usually had a certain sectarian cast.[1] Thus, in the American context, the term "faith"—even with its religious and sectarian connotations—seems more appropriate in capturing the essence of almost everything that passes for belief in America.

But why are these belief systems, which we call faiths, and the institutions that embody them so important to this discussion? The short answer is this: politics is, in large part, an expression of culture (competing values and ideals and, often, interests based in values). At the heart of culture, though, is religion, or systems of faith. And at the heart of religion are its claims to truth about the world.[2] This is it in a nutshell.

The struggle for power (which is the essence of politics) is in large part a struggle between competing truth claims, claims which are by their very nature "religious" in character if not in content. This can be explained a bit more fully.

The first factor to consider is that traditional forms of faith, like any more or less formal system of belief (even secular belief) provides the fundamental link between public and private culture. They do this in part by articulating the relationship between the individual and the larger society and between the community and the nation. Systems of faith or belief, even if just assumed and not fully articulated, locate the individual and community in the larger social order, offering not only moral explanations of where they fit in and why but of where they *should* fit in as well. This is to say that belief systems explain why some people are rich and others poor, why some people suffer and others do not, why some people are loved and appreciated and others despised or ignored, why there is injustice, why there is tyranny, why there is war—explanations for the issues that all individuals and communities confront in their experience at various times and in various ways. Yet these same systems of belief also prescribe principles of action that specify what should be done, if anything, to help the poor, to alleviate suffering, to pursue justice and peace in the larger social order.

At the same time, these faiths lay out the moral significance of different social institutions and institutional arrangements. They set forth the social and moral meaning of marriage and the family, the needs and objectives of education, the principles of law, the role of government, and so on, and the interrelationships of these institutions. Here again, systems of belief not only define "what is" but also "what should be."[3]

Faith and culture, then, are inextricably linked. By elucidating a broader cosmology or world view, faiths not only link the symbols of public culture with the symbols of private culture; they also infuse the symbols of each sphere with universal if not transcendent significance. This capacity is unique to these more or less comprehensive systems of belief. And despite the constraints modern societies have placed upon more traditional religious authority to remain sequestered in the private sphere, the impulse to synthesize and universalize public and private experience remains one of the central and unchanging features of religion in the modern world.

There is a second factor that explains why the belief systems, or faiths, are important to this discussion. Faith is the source of our most deeply held ideals of right and wrong, good and bad, just and unjust. As such, these fundamental assumptions and ideals not only order and guide our passions but they are often the origins and repository of our passions as well. They make risk, sacrifice, and long-term duty and responsibility possible—the kind of commitments we have seen in the lives of Chuck McIlhenny, Harriet Woods, Mae Duggan, and the others. There is no way to account for the extraordinary energy and emotional intensity seen on both sides of the contemporary culture war except to say that the commitments made by the various actors—both religious and secular; orthodox and progressive—are rooted in a sense of ultimate moral truth.

Elites and Public Culture

Given the importance of these universal systems of meaning, the importance of intellectuals and other elites becomes very clear. While ordinary people participate in the construction of their own private worlds, the development and articulation of the more elaborate systems of meaning, including the realm of public culture, falls almost always to the realm of elites. They are the ones who create the concepts, supply the language, and explicate the logic of public discussion. They are the ones who define and redefine the meaning of public symbols. *Public discourse,* then, *is largely a discourse of elites.*[4] This is the first reason why the vast majority of Americans who are somewhere in the middle of these debates are not heard. They have little access to the tools of public culture that elites have.

But it is important to be clear about which elites are most consequential to the shaping of public discourse.

Those who come immediately to mind are the intellectuals, who reside in the halls of academia, devoting their careers to research, writing, consulting, lecturing, and educating young adults. Within the vast realm of higher education, the academics whose work contributes the most toward the establishment of public culture are those in the humanities, social sciences, public administration, theology, and law. Yet as important as university-based intellectuals are to the development of public discourse, their contribution tends to be fairly abstract and distant. A history of public debate among academics alone would amount to an intellectual one, following the relatively obscure personalities and the somewhat rarified fads and fashions of the ivory tower—deconstructionism, neo-orthodoxy, death of God theologies, structuralism, and so on. This is not to suggest that academic developments and debates are in any way frivolous or inconsequential. They are anything but trifling. Nevertheless, discussion at this level of abstraction is rarely accessible to a national audience: the issues that concern these intellectuals have little immediate relevance to the shaping of widely recognized and broadly contended public symbols.

Much more influential than university-based scholars, then, are the more practically oriented "knowledge workers": public policy specialists located in think tanks, special interest lobbyists, public interest lawyers, independent writers and ideologues, journalists and editors, community organizers, and movement activists—the national and regional leadership of grass-roots social and political organizations. Other knowledge workers include the clergy, theologians, and religious administrators of all denominations and faiths. Each of the people we met in the prologue fit into this category: Harriet Woods, the head of a university-based think tank; Bea Blair and Mae Duggan, presidents of different special interest foundations; Chuck McIlhenny and Yehuda Levin, practicing members of the clergy; and Richmond Young, head of Stonewall Democrats, a gay political union. Knowledge elites they most certainly are, yet these are elites who trade in a more common, but also more accessible form of ideas and symbols. Individually or even in small groups the effect of their labors would be negligible. Collectively, however, their efforts constitute the heart of the formation and maintenance of public culture.

The difficulty in real-life situations is that elites of this sort seldom form a unified voice in their articulation of the ideals of public culture. Often they disagree on the meaning of national identity, as symbolized by the flag, or a national monument or ceremony. They also may quarrel over the interpretation of collective myths, particularly the myths of national origin. Not least they contend over the technical use of law in the resolution of public grievances. The academic question that scholars sometimes debate is whether this disagreement is ever significant enough to be disruptive to the larger society. In general, the answer is no. Most of the time such disagreement does not create confusion in the public order but is simply part of the give and take of social life in a democracy. At times, however, this conflict can be very disruptive.

This is particularly true during times of societal change and transition. According to the Italian social philosopher Antonio Gramsci, it is precisely during periods of societal transformation that a significant cleavage forms among intellectuals and other cultural elites.[5] Knowledge workers square off in opposition to each other and their conflict becomes a central part of the drama of social change. Though this is hardly the place to launch into an exhaustive review and criticism of Gramsci's theoretical musings on the subject, one other point is worth adding.[6] Gramsci maintained that the division that evolves among cultural elites generally takes place between those he called "traditional" and those he called "organic." The labels are not well chosen but they are very suggestive. "Traditional" intellectuals or traditionally oriented cultural elites present themselves as heirs to the truths of the past. Their legitimacy derives from their appeal to historical continuity. "Organic" intellectuals, by contrast, present themselves as the new and dynamic sources of progressive social reform. Increasingly, they become polarized to the point of an all-out contest over the nature and content of the public order.[7] The end of the struggle, according to Gramsci's model, is either the restoration of the old hegemony or the establishment of a new hegemony in the realm of public culture.

As we will see, these ideas are immensely relevant to understanding the contemporary American situation.

PUBLIC CULTURE IN CONTEMPORARY AMERICA

America has always been a nation given to public idealism. Unlike the nations of Europe, its identity was never rooted in millennia of tradition. America compensated for this lack of a long national history through the construction of great myths about its origins and even loftier visions of its calling in the future. Among the Puritan settlers America was seen as a "new Jerusalem," a "city set upon a hill," and its citizens, a "people set apart for a special purpose." The millennial hope for America continued to be voiced throughout the nineteenth century, not only by Protestants who believed that America would be the nation from which Christ's kingdom would be established, but by Catholics and Jews who also believed that America was a land of real spiritual promise.[8] Even in secular political discourse, America has long been portrayed in the most moralistic of terms. Every war in its history has been framed as a moral crusade—to defeat the "harlot of Satan" (the French and Indian War), to eliminate monarchical rule (the Revolutionary War and the War of 1812), to eliminate slavery (the Civil War), to make the world safe for democracy (the First World War), and to resist totalitarian expansionism (the Second World War, the Korean War, and Vietnam) and the expansionist exploits of dictators (the Persian Gulf War).[9] Politicians and other national leaders continue to speak of America as a "model of democracy and freedom to the nations of the world" and the leader in "a new world order." Whether about foreign affairs or domestic politics, then, public debate in America has never been framed merely in terms of a competition of different interests but as a struggle between good and evil. Even through the clamorous confusion of political discourse today, the echoes of American exceptionalism can still be heard; the high-minded imagery about its national character and purpose remains plain to see.[10]

One of the reasons for the persistence of this public idealism is related to the "religious" quality of the arguments. Religious ideals and symbols continue to hold a very prominent place in this debate; traditional religious elites continue to play a prominent role in shaping the arguments voiced on both sides of the cultural divide. Yet if there is one aspect of the contemporary cultural conflict that is striking, it is that the distinction between what is "religious" by conventional or technical terms, and what is not, has become very blurred and, finally, rather beside the point. The reason is that public discourse over the various issues of the culture war is almost always framed in rhetoric that is absolute, comprehensive, and ultimate—and, in this case, it is "religious" even when it is not religious in a traditional way, or when those who promote a position are hostile to traditional forms of religious expression.

In light of all of this, one would be hard pressed to argue that we Americans have become any more or any less idealistic about our nation. Even so, the nature of the public argument of late has been transformed. The volume of the debate is louder, the pitch more shrill, and, more important, the substance of the argument and the players who champion particular positions have also changed.

Why This Is Occurring Now

This raises the question of why a cultural conflict of such dimensions is taking place today. As with most things in life, the answer is not simple and straightforward. In fact, a full explanation would require a separate volume. By way of a brief answer, let it be said that the last decades of the twentieth century constitute, as Gramsci would have put it, a time of societal change and transition. Perhaps the central factor in stimulating this change was the transformation of our economy from an industry-oriented to an information-oriented system after the Second World War. We have seen a huge expansion in the number of people who derive their livelihoods from the economics of knowledge, information, ideas, and the like. A central part of this transformation has been the expansion of higher education. The institutions of higher learning have grown prodigiously, as have the number of people who have access to the worldview-changing experiences of university life. These societal changes have been firmly established since the 1960s. These, in turn, have had their own consequences, one being the economic and political empowerment of women. All these changes in the structure of our society contributed to the undermining of previous agreements about how Americans should order our lives together. The present culture war has evolved in this context as a struggle to establish new agreements over the character and content of American public culture. In Gramsci's terms, it is the leadership of the orthodox alliance who play the part of traditional intellectuals and the leadership of the progressivist alliance who play the part of the organic intellectuals, both struggling to establish their own interpretations of the American past and to articulate an agenda for the American future.

Motives and Resources

It should be clear from the outset that this struggle is not between those who sincerely advocate "truth" and those who either unwittingly or cynically pursue misrepresentations. Neither is it between those who selflessly champion the "best for America" and those who selfishly desire to exploit the blind faith and goodwill of its people to their ultimate ruin. Rather, this dispute is between groups who hold fundamentally different views of the world. On all sides the contenders are generally sincere, thoughtful, and well meaning, but they operate with fundamentally opposing visions of the meaning of America: what it has been, what it is, and what it should be.

It should also be clear from the outset that although this struggle is joined at the cultural level, more is involved than just symbols found randomly throughout the population. To be specific, orthodox and progressive alliances tend to be located in the social world in relatively distinct ways. Consider the profiles of the six individuals we encountered in the prologue. All were middle-class Americans. That is true, as far as it goes. In general, however, the progressive alliances tend to draw popular support from among the highly educated, professionally committed, *upper* middle classes, while the orthodox alliances tend to draw from the *lower* middle and working classes. The association is anything but perfect, yet it generally holds, even in the profiles. Having said this, it still would be a mistake to reduce the conflict to the artifacts of "warring material interests" between the lower middle and upper middle classes. Such a view is rooted in traditional Marxist categories that simply do not apply to this situation—or to anything else anymore! This is not a struggle over scarce economic resources, nor is the exploitation of the working classes even an issue. Again, Gramsci is closer to the truth in showing that the conflict is primarily among different kinds of intellectuals and knowledge workers—who may very well have identical educational credentials and class backgrounds. In this light, perhaps the most Marxist observation one could make is that this is a conflict over "the means of cultural production." The end, however, is to have the power to define the meaning of America.

In all of this, the language of confrontation, battle, even war, then, is not merely a literary device but an apt tool to describe the way in which the many issues contested in American public culture are being settled. It is no surprise that many of the contenders on all sides of the cultural divide use the very same language to understand their own involvement. The National Organization for Women, for example, has a "War Room" in its national headquarters in Washington, D.C., a windowless room with charts, maps, a conference table, and a dozen or so telephones.[11] Both sides of the new cultural divide could agree with the editor of *Publisher's Weekly* who declared that the controversy over the arts and publishing was a "war"—"a war that must be won."[12] So, too, activists on both sides of the cultural divide could agree with James Dobson of Focus on the Family, who announced, "We are in a civil war of values and the prize to the victor is the next generation—our children and grandchildren."[13] Another activist observed that this "is a war of ideology, it's a war of ideas, it's a war about our way of life. And it has to be fought with the same intensity, I think, and dedication as you would fight a shooting war."[14]

As with military campaigns, cultural warfare is always decided over the pragmatic problems of strategy, organization, and resources. Class position becomes a factor as does the favoritism of the state. Even more basic are such resources as money, the control over the media and other reality-defining mechanisms of society, and popular approval (or at least the perception of popular approval). The factions with the best strategies, most efficient organization, and access to resources will plainly have the advantage and, very possibly, the ultimate victory.

II

THE NEW LINES OF CONFLICT

3

The Historical Roots of the Culture War

All human experience has context. There are always preconditions and prior circumstances—there is always a history. And invariably, the larger context is a complex reality that defies simple explanation. Yet to even attempt to understand a facet of social life without at least partially reconstructing both the institutional and historical setting within which it is rooted would be folly. Our understanding would be flawed from the outset.

The contemporary culture war is no exception. It would be frivolous to imagine that this conflict emerged spontaneously out of social and historical chance. Yet most discussions of the tensions in American society fail to consider the historical context. The truth of it is that the contemporary culture war evolved out of century-old religious tensions—through the expansion and the realignment of American religious pluralism. It is out of the changing contours and shifting balance of pluralism that the key actors in the contemporary culture war emerge.

THE EXPANSION OF PLURALISM

The Early Expansion

The story of American religious pluralism begins in the colonial period through the early decades of the republic. In this historical context there was both unity and diversity. Though limited by the boundaries of Protestant faith and culture, the colonies themselves nevertheless exhibited a tremendous diversity: Congregationalists in Massachusetts, Connecticut, and New Hampshire; Anglicans in Virginia, Georgia, and the Carolinas; Baptists in Rhode Island; Anglicans and Catholics in Maryland; Anglicans, Dutch Calvinists, and Presbyterians in New York and Maryland; and Pennsylvania, as the New England consensus had it, was nothing less than "a swamp of sectarianism." The Second Great Awakening, coming on the heels of the republic's founding, only intensified the denominational diversity within the Protestant community. Religious sectarianism became widespread with the flourishing of the Campbellites, Stoneites, and Disciples, not to mention the Baptists and Methodists in the southern territories and the western frontier, the growth of the Shakers in New York and Massachusetts, and Unitarianism and Wesleyan revivalism under Charles Finney in the Northeast.

Yet the depth of dissension within the Protestant community should not be glossed over. Baptists distrusted Episcopalians, Congregationalists feared Presbyterians, Lutherans avoided Methodists and Quakers, "Old Lights" continued to resent "New Lights," and each denomination and faction was certain that its own version of the Reformation was the correct one while all the others were at least partially mistaken.

Still, a kind of "balance" was achieved in that sectarian division. The overwhelming majority of Americans were self-consciously rooted in variations of Reformed theology. Partly as a consequence of this, there was widespread agreement on, among other things, the evils of both Catholicism and infidelity, as well as an understanding of the spiritual mission of the nation—to be an exemplar of Christian (Reformational) virtue among the nations of the world in preparation for the coming Kingdom of God. Within this context there was also the balance of competing sectarian interests. No one denomination could press its own particular advantage without being directly challenged by the interests of other denominations. Thus, a measure of cultural consensus really emerged. All other differences aside, America was, in this *cultural* sense, a Christian, which again meant Protestant, nation.

The extent of the quasi establishment of a "common Protestantism" through the first half of the nineteenth century is rarely disputed and need not be described here.[1] In principle, however, it involved the accommodation of denominational differences and rivalries in the common effort to establish a Christian (Protestant) land. The practical outcome in many regions was not far from this ideal as Baptists, Presbyterians, Methodists, Episcopalians, Christian Disciples, Lutherans, and others came together to forge a vision that would inform all of the major institutions of public life. The symbols and language of Protestant culture permeated republican political rhetoric and informed the conduct of electoral politics (in which anti-Catholic propaganda and parties provided rallying points). It influenced the formation and execution of law (seen clearly in the enforcement of blasphemy law and the like). It provided the vision for popular education: both the establishment of the common school and later the public school (where the moralistic schoolbook *McGuffey's Reader* became a staple of instruction and the reading of the King James version of the Scriptures a source of devotion) as well as the expansion of denominationally founded and governed colleges and universities. It offered the institutional mechanisms for the allocation and administration of public welfare. And finally, Protestant culture provided an agenda for social reform (as seen, for example, in the powerful initiatives of the temperance movement). It was, then, largely through the language and ideals of common Protestantism that the legitimating myths of institutions and society were formed and articulated.

But the "pan-Protestant" hegemony over American culture did not remain unchallenged. From the 1830s onward came a massive influx of Catholic and Jewish immigrants whose net effect was to severely upset that "balance."

In the 1830s, for example, 600,000 Catholics arrived on American shores. Through the 1840s, 1,700,000 additional Catholics came; as many as 2,600,000 more immigrated during the 1850s. Nearly half (43 percent) of these were Irish; roughly one-fourth (26 percent) were from Germany; one-sixth (17 percent) were from England, Wales, and Scotland; and the remainder were from Italy and Eastern Europe.[2] By 1880 there were 6,259,000 Catholics in the United States. The growth in the Catholic presence through the heart of the nineteenth century was, then, remarkable. Indeed, at the time of the first census in 1790, Catholics comprised only about 1 percent of the total population. Less than a century later (by the 1880s) they comprised up to 12 percent of the population. By the 1920s, 17 percent of the American population was Catholic, the single largest denomination in the country.

The massive immigration of Jews did not start until nearly fifty years after the first wave of Catholic immigrants arrived. In the late 1830s there were probably fewer than 15,000 Jews in a total American population of 15 million—barely one-tenth of 1 percent of the population.[3] By the 1880s, when the first surge of German Jewish (Ashkenazim) immigrants arrived, the number of Jews had increased to roughly 300,000.[4] By the mid-1920s, the number of Jews had jumped to 4 million—from only about one-half of a percent of the American population to a full 3 percent, all in the course of four decades.

These Catholic and Jewish immigrants were not immediately diffused through the larger population and territory. Because of their pride in national heritage and culture, their often observable non–Anglo-Saxon characteristics, and their concern to maintain the theological and religious distinctives of their faith, there was a strong rationale (not to mention outside pressures) for concentrating their numbers in homogeneous communities. This they did in the largest cities of the Northeast and Midwest: New York, Boston, Philadelphia, St. Louis, Chicago, Baltimore, Worcester. In New York, for example, the proportion of the foreign-born grew from 11 percent in 1825 to 35 percent in 1845 to more than half of the city's residents by 1855 (and more than half of these were Irish Catholics).[5] The highly visible immigrant concentration in these centers of industry, commerce, and opinion formation created the impression that their impact in American life was even greater than their numbers alone would allow. It was no wonder, then, that many Protestants believed that "their" world was being threatened. In reality, it was. It is in this context that one can understand the legacy of anti-Catholicism and anti-Semitism described in chapter 1.

Eventually, though, accommodations slowly evolved. Open, government-tolerated discrimination gradually ended. The crust of old prejudices slowly softened. In short, as pluralism expanded in this way, so did institutional and individual tolerance. By the middle of the century Will Herberg, in his famous book *Protestant, Catholic, Jew,* could observe that American culture had become a roughly comparable amalgamation of Protestant, Catholic, and Jewish influences.[6] No one would deny the Protestant tilt of this consensus. Even so, the Catholic and Jewish communities had become large and formidable participants in American cultural life whose claims in public discourse could no longer be denied. Even the idea of returning to a more or less exclusive Protestant control over American culture was becoming less and less plausible and desirable in Protestant communities.

A New Consensus

What was happening, in fact, was that a new pluralistic "balance" was being forged around a broader Judeo-Christian consensus. New competing sectarian interests were an important factor in achieving this balance, to be sure. Yet, above this was the continued, tacit acceptance on the part of all of the major players of a public discourse informed by, among other things, the suppositions of a biblical theism.

The role of biblical theism as a cultural cement in American public life requires some elaboration. Even in the middle of the nineteenth century when anti-Catholic and anti-Semitic sentiment was strongest, biblical theism provided the primary institutions and ideals through which an expanding and increasingly diverse immigrant population (Protestant, Catholic, and Jewish) adapted to a new life in America.[7] As Rabbi Solomon Schechter declared at the dedication of the Jewish Theological Seminary of America in 1903, "This country is, as everybody knows, a creation of the Bible, particularly of the Old Testament."[8]

At one level, biblical theism provided the language in which differences could be talked about. Thus, for example, although much of the anti-Catholic hostility was born out of economic rivalry and ethnic distrust, it took expression primarily as *religious* hostility—as a quarrel over religious doctrine, practice, and authority. So too the latent and overt hostility of Protestants toward Jews was often legitimated through the language of religious antipathy.

At a more profound level, however, biblical theism gave Protestants, Catholics, and Jews many of the common ideals of public life. Chief among these were the symbols of national identity. As Timothy Smith has argued, the migration and resettlement of bonded groups in the new land made the biblical imagery of the Exodus seem to be a metaphor for the American experience as a whole.[9] The linking of the American purpose with the Kingdom of God was, in reality, a prominent theme not only for the English Puritans, Scottish Presbyterians, the Dutch Reformed, and the French Huguenots, and all of their descendants, but for immigrant Mennonites, German and Scandinavian Lutherans, German and Russian Jews, and Irish and East European Catholics as well.

Related to this were the ideals of progress. The millennial and messianic promises of the Hebrew and Christian Scriptures provided the common symbols of hope for the future. This became particularly clear at the end of the nineteenth century as the traditional ethical idealism common to each of these faiths matured as denominational ideologies and as programs of public welfare. Reform Judaism and religious Zionism, Catholic triumphalism and the Protestant social gospel movement all espoused the ideals of social progress, all believed in the continuous unfolding of the will of God in human history, and all maintained a deep sense of their own particular place in this drama.

Thus, though based in sectarian commitment and overwhelmingly Protestant in character, the assumptions of biblical religion were sufficiently diffuse in public culture to allow for the participation of other biblical traditions, even during the middle to late nineteenth century. Through the end of that century and up to the middle of the twentieth, these biblical suppositions became even more diffuse. Nevertheless, the limits and boundaries of religious and cultural pluralism continued to be defined by what remained a deeply biblical, albeit no longer Protestant, culture.

Pluralism After the Second World War

After the Second World War, the balance represented in the new consensus was once more upset. Among the most important contributing factors has been the further expansion of pluralism.

Traditional Faiths

Between the mid-1920s and the mid-1940s the size of the Catholic community remained fairly stable vis-à-vis the larger population. After the war, however, it continued to expand. In 1947, about 20 percent of the U.S. population claimed to be Catholic. Twenty years later, in 1967, that number totaled roughly 25 percent and, by the mid-1980s, Catholics were 28 to 29 percent of the population.

The Jewish picture is slightly different. Leading up to and during the Second World War, a second major wave of Jewish immigrants swelled the size of their community to roughly 5 percent of the total population. A considerable portion of these were Orthodox Jews from Germany and Eastern Europe. Some of the new immigrants did not stay long but went on to Israel after its founding in 1948. It is partly for this reason that in the postwar period the numbers of Jews relative to the larger population declined to approximately 2.5 percent.[10]

Also within the biblical tradition are the Mormons, whose numbers have grown rapidly.[11] Between 1830 and 1880 the number of Mormons in North America had increased from 1,000 to 110,000. In 1890 the Mormon Church forbade polygamous marriages, which then allowed Utah to be admitted as a state (in 1896). At that point much of the legal and social opposition to the Latter Day Saints receded and their numbers expanded dramatically. In the century following (up to 1991), the number of Mormons grew to 4 million, or 1.6 percent of the population.

Though minority faiths expanded numerically in this way, these developments were rather uncontroversial. These groups were part of the larger biblical tradition and by this time they were all well established in American society—in part because a substantial number of their adherents had become assimilated into the middle classes.[12] The more controversial developments were to take place in other quarters.

New Faiths

Religious and cultural pluralism expanded after the war, as religious traditions native to Asia and the Middle East began to appear in the United States in greater numbers. For example, in 1934 there was only one mosque in the United States and fewer than 20,000 Muslims. By 1988 there were 600 mosques or Islamic Centers and more than 4 million adherents nationwide.[13] These figures make Islam the eighth largest denomination in the United States—even larger than the Episcopal Church, the Presbyterian Church, U.S.A., the United Church of Christ, or the Assemblies of God. Just over half of these Muslims are recent immigrants from all over the world, particularly Pakistan, India, Turkey, Egypt, and Iran. The remainder are indigenous to America in the movement formerly known as the Black Muslims. Some speculate that soon after the turn of the century, the numbers of Muslims will surpass those of Jews, making them the second largest body of religious believers after Christians.

The growth in the size of the Hindu community is more difficult to assess because Hinduism tends to be a family religion in which a great deal of worship takes place in the home. Even so, estimates placed the number of Hindus in America in 1940 at about 150,000. By the early 1990s, this figure had grown to about three-quarters of a million, with forty Hindu temples. Like Hinduism, Buddhism has no central bureaucracy, no single leader for its many different schools; worship is very often a private matter and, therefore, a difficult phenomenon to track. The introduction of Buddhism to America came as early as 1893 with the World Parliament of Religions in Chicago. At that time and throughout the twentieth century, virtually all of the Buddhist immigrants were of Japanese ancestry. By 1909 there were just over 3,000 Buddhists in America. The number of Buddhists gradually increased until 1960 when, over the following decades, Buddhism experienced the most dynamic growth in its history in America. One of the largest of the Buddhist schools is the Buddhist Church in America (the Jodo Shinshu sect), which claimed in 1988 to have one hundred churches and 100,000 members. In 1960, it could claim only 20,000 members. The other Buddhist presence is the Nichiren Shoshu sect, which in the same year claimed to have forty-six community centers, six temples, and 500,000 members. For Islam, Hinduism, and Buddhism the greatest concentrations of adherents are found in metropolitan areas, but in Hawaii, Buddhism competes with Catholicism as the dominant religion.[14]

Apart from the natural influx of non-Western religious faith through immigration, pluralism expanded through the indigenous adoption of exotic "new religions" by young people in the quest to find alternatives to traditional faith. Many were inspired by the faiths and meditative practices of Central and East Asia. Zen Buddhism, Transcendental Meditation (TM), Rajsneesh, International Society for Krishna Consciousness (better known as the Hare Krishna movement), Meher Baba, the Healthy-Happy-Holy Organization (or 3HO), and local yoga groups were all highly visible in the 1970s. They received wide attention in the media but their actual attraction depended greatly on the demands placed on adherents. Because of advertisement, short courses, and the few requirements placed on practitioners, TM and yoga had much greater appeal in the general population. According to a Gallup survey conducted in 1976, as many as 4 percent of all Americans claimed to participate in TM and 3 percent claimed to practice yoga techniques.[15] By contrast, the quasi-orthodox Buddhism of Hare Krishna and 3HO (which combined Sikh doctrine with the meditative techniques of kundalini yoga) had together, at their peak in the mid-1970s, as many as one hundred local centers of activity but probably less than 10,000 members nationwide.[16]

Also novel to the postwar period were new sectarian expressions of traditional faiths. Some of these were variants of Protestant faith such as The Way, the Children of God, the Local Church, the Fundamentalist Army, and the Christian World Liberation Front. Others, such as the charismatic movement, were Catholic in orientation (at least at the start). Still others were quasi-Christian movements, such as the Korea-based Unification Church (or the Moonies) under the leadership of Sun Myung Moon.

Perhaps the most important sector of the "new age" religious phenomenon included the various organizations that constituted the human potential movement. While the neo-Christian and the more exacting

Eastern religious groups lost much of their popularity by the end of the 1970s, the spiritualism of the human potential movement displayed enormous staying power. The message of human fulfillment was packaged and repackaged through numerous techniques of self-analysis, massage, encounter sessions, sensitivity training, pyramids, crystals, and the like. It was marketed through dozens of organizations such as the Inner Peace Movement (which, by 1972, had established 590 centers in North America), Scientology (with 28 centers and 2,000 members in the early 1980s), Erhard Seminars Training or *est* (which processed nearly 20,000 people in its first three years of existence in the early 1970s, and 500,000 by 1984), Lifespring (which, through its five-day sessions, "trained" more than 250,000 people by 1987), Psychosynthesis, Rolfing, Arica, and Silva Mind Control, among others. In sum, as many as 3,000 local centers of new religious activity were established in the 1960s and early 1970s. While hundreds of these became defunct through the 1980s, hundreds of others replaced them. According to public opinion surveys of the period, as many as 10 percent of the population actually became involved with them in one way or another. In cities such as San Francisco and Boulder, Colorado, between one-fifth and one-fourth of the residents participated.[17]

Secularists

Perhaps the most unnoticed but most momentous way in which religious and cultural pluralism expanded in the postwar period can be found in that part of the population claiming no particular religious faith, those individuals that social scientists call *secularists.* In public opinion surveys, these are the people who respond "none" when questioned about religious preference. Compared to the rest of the population, secularists are disproportionately well educated and professional and are found most commonly in the larger cities of the Northeast and West. Even though they do not claim to adhere to any particular religious tradition, it would be completely unfair to say that they live without any moral commitments and ethical ideals. Fundamentalists are totally wrong, then, to describe secularists as "amoral." It is equally wrong to argue that the secular or secularists are somehow ethically neutral, as in the myth that the institutions and people of science or the modern state are impartial on issues of value. Though oftentimes the principles are implicit and unarticulated, secularists do maintain and live by latent value orientations. These are articulated in various ways and (again) sometimes they are not expressed at all. But in most cases, these values and ideals could be described loosely as "humanistic"—an ethical orientation in which human well-being becomes the ultimate standard by which moral judgments and policy decisions are grounded, and the paramount aim to which all human endeavor aspires. Particularly prominent in this general orientation are the ethical themes of autonomy and freedom, especially as expressed in the notion of individual or minority self-determination.

However one is to finally characterize the latent moral ideologies of the secularist population (and more will be said in the next chapter), it is, in the broader picture, a relatively distinct realm of moral conviction. What is significant about the secularists is that they represent the fastest-growing community of "moral conviction" in America. In 1952, secularists comprised only 2 percent of the population. Through the early 1960s their number remained fairly constant, so that in 1962, secularists still constituted only 2 percent of the population. Yet through the rest of the 1960s and after, their growth was dramatic. By 1972, secularists comprised 5 percent of the population. By 1982 they reached 8 percent and by the end of the decade, they made up approximately 11 percent of the population.[18] The most significant factor accounting for this growth was the expansion of higher education in the 1960s and 1970s, an institution that is well known for its secularizing effects on young adults.[19]

Toward Realignment

In one way, the postwar expansion of pluralism seems to be a natural evolution of a long process: since its founding, American culture has become increasingly inclusive of other, even "alien," cultural traditions. In this light, one could view the expansion of pluralism in the second half of the twentieth century as simply "the next stage" in the long journey toward total inclusiveness. The reality, however, is more profound than that.

The most recent expansion of pluralism signifies the collapse of the longstanding Judeo-Christian consensus in American public life. As it has been argued, however much Protestants, Catholics, and Jews, through the last half of the nineteenth century and first half of the twentieth, distrusted each other socially, even competed with each other economically, politically, and religiously, there remained a certain agreement about the *language* of public debate. The symbols of moral discourse, informed as they were by biblical imagery and metaphor, were symbols understood and even advocated by each tradition. With the expansion of pluralism in the second half of the twentieth century, that agreement has largely disintegrated. But the significance of the trend toward expanded pluralism does not reside in this disintegration alone but rather in its consequences: in the wake of the fading Judeo-Christian consensus has come a rudimentary *realignment* of pluralistic diversity. The "organizing principle" of American pluralism has altered fundamentally such that the major rift is no longer born out of theological or doctrinal disagreements—as between Protestants and Catholics or Christians and Jews. Rather the rift emerges out of a more fundamental disagreement over the sources of moral truth.

But this is getting ahead of things. To understand the nature and extent of contemporary cultural conflict, it is necessary to explore some of the historical and institutional preconditions of this realignment.

CENTURY-OLD FAULT LINES

With the tremendous rivalry and antagonism among religious traditions in the late nineteenth century, it would have been impossible then to have anticipated the kind of changes in the cultural landscape that were to take shape a century later. Yet fissures emerged within each of the distinct traditions of Protestantism, Catholicism, and Judaism that were not only remarkably parallel in character but were also nearly simultaneous in the closing decades of that century. These fissures would evolve into the major fault lines over which the contemporary culture war is now fought. What shape did these fissures take and how did they develop?

Of the fractures taking shape in the three historic faiths, those that occurred in Protestantism are the best known, but in all three cases, breaks appeared as each community struggled to cope with the intellectual and social dilemmas posed by life on the verge of the twentieth century: labor struggles, public health issues, and rising crime and poverty, all problems that had been brought about by industrialization and urbanization. Deep ethnic distrust and political instability had been the fruit of the rapid immigration and the slow assimilation of foreign populations. The credibilty of religious faith had been weakened by higher criticism, historicism, and the advances of science. Interestingly, the way in which each community of faith responded organizationally varied considerably. In Protestantism the fissures were reflected within denominational structure, seminary education, and lay attitudes. In Catholicism, they were reflected almost exclusively in the opinion and policy initiatives of U.S. bishops. In Judaism the ruptures took shape in the formation of new denominational structures. Organizational differences aside, the substance of the response in each tradition was remarkably similar.

Progressivist Initiatives

By the 1870s and 1880s, it became clear to many leaders of all faiths that the problems posed by modern industrial capitalism were unlike any that had been confronted before. The effort to respond to these solely by attempting to evangelize the unsaved and to curb the vices of intemperance, prostitution, and profanity, as held by pietists in the Protestant tradition, was quickly recognized as inadequate. New and creative strategies were needed.

In Protestantism the intellectual and programmatic response came in the social gospel movement. Over the late nineteenth century, its advocates slowly came to reject an individualistic explanation of the afflictions of modern life in favor of a more "structuralist" explanation. It was not so much sin and personal moral failure that were to blame for human hardship as it was the brutal power of contemporary social and economic institutions. The only lasting solution would be found through institutional measures of redress. It was here in addressing the problems of labor, the demand for industrial education, the expanding requirements of poor relief, and the necessity of a spirit of Christian communitarianism in public life that the modern church could most effectively serve the cause of Christianity. By the 1890s an enormous literature advocating the tenets of the "social gospel" was being published and distributed. Prominent in this work was the manifesto "The Social Creed of the Churches," published in 1908. Translating these tenets into programmatic agenda was the motivation for new organizations, such as the Brotherhood of the Kingdom, the Department of Church and Labor of the Presbyterian Church's Board of Home Missions, the Methodist Federation for Social Service, and the Commission on the Church and Social Service.

A significant corollary of the social gospel movement (and in many ways a component of it) was a new spirit of denominational cooperation. This was reflected in such bodies as the Evangelical Churches of Christendom (1900), the National Federation of Churches and Christian Workers (1901), and the Federal Council of Churches (FCC, 1908). The first two groups failed not long after they were founded, but the FCC endured both as an effective ecumenical agency and as an important symbol of the ecclesiastical spirit of the age. At one level the FCC represented a concern to develop interdenominational toleration as an end in itself, but above all it represented the recognition, throughout the Protestant world, that if churches were to effectively address the problems of an industrial age, they would have to face them together.

Innovations were also being pursued among Protestantism's intellectual elite. At root was the need to reconcile traditional Christian theology with the discoveries of modern scientific inquiry. The challenge posed by Charles Darwin and Thomas Huxley was only one of many. Other intimidating tests came from breakthroughs in astronomy, psychology, sociology, and philosophy, which demanded that traditional interpretations of the Bible be reconciled with the methods of modern intellectual investigation. Historicism and higher criticism were powerful intellectual movements in European scholarship, and as they filtered into the discourse of the American academic community they could not be ignored. The net effect of all these pressures was something of a synthesis of old and new, a novel and bold "resymbolization" of the traditions. The most important reworking of the traditions involved the deemphasis of the supernatural and miraculous aspects of biblical narrative and an almost exclusive emphasis upon its ethical aspects. Such theological innovations not only allowed the mainline Protestant churches to keep pace with the intellectual currents of the period but they also provided much needed intellectual legitimations for their new programs of social activism as well.

Within Catholicism, liberal or progressivist initiatives came in the 1890s primarily in the form of new attitudes and policies articulated by particular bishops in the American hierarchy. In part, the new social approaches were associated with the rights of labor, particularly in the support for the Knights of Labor, a Catholic precursor of the labor union. The desire to cooperate with Protestants in the realm of education also played a role. But the movement that came to embody these progressive Catholic ideas more prominently than any other was the Americanist movement. Among its heroes were Father Isaac Hecker (founder of the Paulist Fathers), Archbishop John Ireland, John J. Keane (rector of the Catholic University of America), and Bishop Denis O'Connell, among others.

At the heart of the Americanist movement in the Catholic hierarchy was the desire to integrate the U.S. Catholic Church into the mainstream of modern American society. The Americanists sought to phase out what they considered unessential Romanist traditions and to present the Catholic faith in a positive light to a Protestant society. They hoped to eliminate the "foreign" cast of the church by Americanizing the immigrant population (through language and custom) as quickly as possible, by celebrating and promoting the principles of religious liberty and the separation of church and state, and by helping to foster American-style democracy globally. By the mid-1890s the Americanist movement acquired a more universal appeal by associating itself with the progressive views of biblical, theological, and historical scholarship emanating from Europe. This association was built upon mutual affinities: the Americanists' praise of religious liberty and the European modernists' advocacy of subjectivity in theology; the former's praise of democracy and scientific progress and the latter's program to reconcile the Catholic Church with the modern age.[20] The modernist movement within American Catholic scholarship was fairly modest at the beginning of the twentieth century. A journal of Catholic modernist thinking, the *New York Review,* was founded in 1905, and a few scholars published articles advocating the compatibility of evolution and the official teachings about the doctrine of creation, or the use of higher critical methods of biblical interpretation. The heart of Catholic modernism was in Europe. Yet whether European or American, the progressive theology of modernism was associated with, and found support in, the Americanist movement. As will be seen, such a rapprochement was to have serious consequences for the direction of the American Catholic Church within that very decade.

The progressivist impulse in Judaism had its origins as early as the German Enlightenment of the eighteenth century. The inchoate movement was small and somewhat formless through the first half of the nineteenth century, but with the immigration of German Jews to America after the 1850s, the ideas that would lead to Reform Judaism flourished. The earliest reformers had no intention of establishing a new denomination but, rather, aspired to shape the religious ethos of all Judaism. Indeed, the Union of American Hebrew Congregations (1873); the rabbinical seminary, Hebrew Union College (1875); and the Central Conference of American Rabbis (1889) were all founded to serve the needs of Judaism as a whole. Even before the turn of the century they provided the institutional nucleus of what was to become just one branch of American Jewry, the Reform movement.

As with the Catholics, accommodation to American life and purpose was perhaps the dominant inspiration behind progressivist Jewish thought. To that end, the worship service was shortened, the vernacular was introduced, the use of the organ was sanctioned, and the segregation of men from women in all aspects of the worship service was ended. More important than these modifications, though, were the theological accommodations. There was a decisive move away from traditional belief and ritual observance toward ethical idealism.

These theological alterations became crystallized first in a series of resolutions drawn up by progressives in Philadelphia in 1869 and then more formally in the Pittsburgh Platform of 1885. In these documents progressives maintained that a rabbinical Judaism based on ancient law and tradition had forever lost its grip on the modern Jew. The only viable course, therefore, was to reinterpret the meaning of Judaism in light of new historical developments. The entire range of traditional rabbinic beliefs and practices were abandoned. The first to be rejected was the traditional conviction that Torah or Jewish law was unalterable—that it was somehow sufficient for the religious needs of the Jewish people at all times and places. Accordingly, the doctrine of bodily resurrection was declared to have "no religious foundation," as were the concepts of Gehenna and Eden (hell and paradise). Repudiated as well were the laws regulating dress, diet, purification, and the excessive ritualism of traditional worship. And not least, the messianic hope of a restored Jewish state under a son of David was also disavowed.

In their stead was the affirmation of the universalism of Hebraic ethical principles—the idea that Judaism was the highest conception of the "God-idea." Having abandoned any conception of Jewish nationalism, the mission of Israel was now to bring the ethical ideals of the Jewish tradition to the rest of the world. Remarkable for the historical context in which they were made, the documents even extended the hand of ecumenical cooperation to Christianity and Islam. As "daughter religions of Judaism" they were welcome as partners in Judaism's mission of spreading "monotheistic and moral truth." In large measure the ethical truths they desired to proclaim could be translated into a language that harmonized with the Protestant social gospel. As stated in Principle I of the 1885 Pittsburgh manifesto, Reform Jews would commit themselves "to regulate the relations between rich and poor" and to help solve the "problem presented by the contrasts and evils of the present organization of society." To leave absolutely no doubt about the rightness of their cause, the authors of the Pittsburgh Platform threw down the ultimate challenge to their nonprogressive rabbinical counterparts:

> We can see no good reason why we should ogle you, allow you to act as a brake to the wheel of progress, and confirm you in your pretensions. You do not represent the ideas and sentiments of the American Jews, [in] this phase upon which Judaism entered in this country, you are an anachronism, strangers in this country, and to your own brethren. You represent yourselves, together with a past age and a foreign land. We must proceed without you to perform our duties to God, and our country, and our religion, for WE are the orthodox Jews in America.[21]

The boldness and enthusiasm (even if not the audacity) expressed by these Reform rabbis in their campaign of change in Judaism was remarkable but it was not isolated. It was in large measure shared by progressives in both Protestantism and Catholicism as well. From the circumstances around them, it seemed as though the flow and momentum of history was on the progressives' side and thus the future would be theirs as well.

Orthodox Reactions

Given such reformist pluck it would have been odd not to expect strong counteraction within each tradition. In all three traditions leaders, who were equally articulate, vocal, and powerful, were convinced that the the progressive changes being advocated represented nothing short of apostasy. They rose up to defend the faith as it had been inherited from generations past.

The protest launched by the defenders of orthodoxy within Protestantism centered upon the defense of Scripture. By demonstrating that the Bible was the Word of God, inerrant in all of its teachings, they felt confident that they would have an adequate foundation to reject heresy and to prevent the ordinary believer from straying into impiety and irreligion.

Accordingly, dozens of Bible institutes and colleges all across the country were founded, including the Moody Institute (originally founded for urban ministry in 1886), the Bible Institute of Los Angeles

(1913), St. Paul Bible College (1916), Faith Baptist Bible College (1921), Columbia Bible College (1923), among many others. Annual Bible conferences also came to serve this purpose—the Niagara Bible Conferences, the American Bible and Prophetic Conference, the Northfield Conferences, the Old Point Comfort Bible Conference, the Seaside Bible Conference, among others. A flurry of new periodicals defending the orthodox cause were published—*Bible Champion,* the Baptist *Watchman, The Truth, The King's Business, Prophetic Times, Waymark in the Wilderness,* and so on. Perhaps the most daring effort to defend the orthodox faith was the publication and sweeping distribution of *The Fundamentals* in 1910. This twelve-volume work included over ninety articles systematically cataloguing and defending the major doctrines of the Christian faith, discrediting the Mormon, Roman Catholic, Christian Science, and spiritualist heresies, summarizing all of the major archaeological evidence that confirmed the truth of the Old Testament stories, and refuting the methods of higher criticism. Finally, in the effort to stem the pernicious influence of the "Bible-denying" Darwinian theory of evolution in the public schools, thirty-seven anti-evolution bills were submitted to twenty state legislatures between 1921 and 1929.

In the American Catholic hierarchy, the situation was different. Orthodoxy within Catholicism has always been defined more by fidelity to the teachings emanating from the Holy See than it is by adherence to specific doctrinal positions. Thus, intervening within any intra-Catholic tensions in America was the presence of the Vatican itself. By the end of January 1899, Pope Leo XIII made his views known. His opinion came in the form of an apostolic letter, *Testem Benevolentiae,* and though he was not totally condemnatory, his censure was still broad and effective. In the eyes of the Vatican, the Americanists' idea of presenting the truths of the Catholic Church "positively" in a Protestant context was seen as the watering down of doctrine, their praise of religious liberty was perceived as the praise of religious subjectivism, and their desire to accommodate the Catholic Church to American democratic institutions (the separation of church and state) was viewed as a desire to deny the temporal powers of the papacy—to introduce democracy into the Church.

The papal condemnation of Americanism was significant for many reasons but one of the most important is that it proved to be a precursor to the denunciation of modernism in American and European Catholic scholarship as well. The Vatican viewed the two movements as allied and therefore it moved quickly to quell the latter in the manner it had silenced the former.[22] In 1907 Pope Pius X condemned the modernists, in his *Pascendi Dominici Gregis*, for promoting subjectivist tendencies in theology as well as for adopting some of the principles of the Americanists. In 1908, the modernist periodical *The New York Review* ceased publication, almost immediately after a few of its articles had come under the critical scrutiny of Rome. In 1910, also due to the direct mediation of the Holy See, an associate professor of biblical studies at Catholic University was dismissed for disagreeing with the ordinary Magisterium—he had rejected the Mosaic authorship of the Pentateuch.[23]

The character of the traditionalist reaction within Judaism was different still. Historical Judaism in the United States and Europe was, very simply, "Orthodoxy." Up to the mid-1800s the Orthodox had no real self-image of themselves as a movement within American Judaism—they *were* Judaism in America. There were, of course, those who attempted to modify and modernize the traditions, but plainly they were not in good standing with the conventional and taken-for-granted understandings of Jewish faith and life. But the pronouncements of the Philadelphia and Pittsburgh platforms forced the traditionalists for the first time to think of themselves and struggle to survive *self-consciously* as the defenders of the true faith.

All traditional Jews interpreted the Pittsburgh statement of 1885 as an insult and immediately proceeded to sever their relations with the Union of American Hebrew Congregations. Likewise Hebrew Union College was declared unfit to educate the next generation of rabbis. But beyond this, the response varied. The most orthodox and observant Jews found themselves a beleaguered and ghettoized minority, with few adherents and little resources. Of approximately 200 major Jewish congregations in existence in the 1880s, only a dozen of these, representing between 3,000 and 4,000 people, remained strictly Orthodox.[24] The larger portion of traditionalists pursued compromise. These traditionalists remained committed to traditional practices and teachings—to the foundation provided by biblical and Talmudic authority—but they were also committed to the political emancipation and Westernization (and therefore, deghettoization) of Jewish experience. They recognized that this would entail modifications to orthodoxy, but they were persuaded that these changes should only be made according to Talmudic precedent and with the consent of the whole community of believers.[25] In 1886, one year after the publication of the Pittsburgh Platform, the Jewish Theological Seminary in New York was founded and with it, the Conservative movement in American Judaism was formally launched.

By 1913, after the founding in 1901 of the Rabbinical Assembly of America (the national association of Conservative rabbis) and the establishment of the United Synagogue of America in 1913 (a national union of the Conservative synagogues), the Conservative movement had become a powerful force in American Judaism.

The Aftermath

In the years to follow, no formal resolution of the tensions among progressive and traditionalist forces in all three faiths evolved—at least not one that was satisfactory to all parties. After the widely publicized trial of John Scopes, the biology teacher who defied Tennessee's anti-evolution law in 1925, traditionalist forces in Protestantism (Fundamentalists, as they were now called) had been widely discredited. The progressive forces in Protestantism (no longer referred to as modernists but simply called mainline Protestantism) held a position of undisputed domination for the first fifty years of the twentieth century. In Catholicism, the actions of the Vatican effectively put to rest most progressive tendencies until the 1940s: critical scholarship and liberal social planning in the Catholic Church simply came to an end. Not until the Second Vatican Council in 1965 did the progressive forces in the American hierarchy regain a prominent role in guiding the course of Catholicism. In Judaism, the progressive forces of the Reform movement retained sway. It is true that the Conservative movement was, through the twentieth century, the fastest-growing denomination in American Jewry, but on the whole, it evolved ideologically more in the direction of the Reform than in the direction of classic orthodoxy. Besides, with the revitalization and growth of the Orthodox Jewish movement in the years preceding and following the Second World War, a new public standard of traditionalism in Judaism was defined. In the public eye, Conservative rabbis could no longer publicly claim to be the exclusive heirs to historical Judaism. In short, the locus of orthodox tendencies in Judaism shifted to a revived Orthodox movement.

Though not politicized, by the 1950s the essential lines of division between orthodox and progressive forces in America's main faiths had been drawn. Not only had the particular ideological positions been roughly demarcated but so too had the institutional apparatus of intra-religious conflict: within Protestantism in the division between Fundamentalist and Evangelical denominations and mainline and liberal denominations; within Judaism in the continuum between the Orthodox/

Modern Orthodox movement and the Reform movement (with Conservatism somewhere in between); and within Catholicism in the development of different and opposing religiopolitical coalitions in the larger Catholic community.[26]

It is important to recall that up to this point, the divisions in all three faiths continued to emanate from the liturgical and theological program of modernism. With the further expansion of pluralism and the collapse of the Judeo-Christian consensus in public culture, the issues that would divide progressive and orthodox forces in the major religious traditions in the decades to follow would become far more extensive.

Although the arena of the conflict would become more extensive, it is still quite possible that these internal tensions would have remained at a fairly low intensity had it not been for two other changes in the composition of American religious institutions. The first was the waning of denominational loyalty; the second was the proliferation of parachurch organizations. Let us first examine the weakening of denominational boundaries.

THE WANING OF DENOMINATIONAL LOYALTIES

While there was no satisfactory resolution to the issues that first factionalized Protestantism, Catholicism, and Judaism, it could be said that the progressive and orthodox principals within each always implicitly understood the limitations of their quarrel. However deep the theological and ideological divisions were *within* each faith community between the 1880s and the 1960s, they never were more consequential than the ideological divisions that still existed *between* faith communities. No matter how complex and intense their internal disagreements might have been, Protestants, Catholics, and Jews retained a very clear theological and ideological distinctiveness.

What is more, a number of empirical studies of the postwar period confirmed the seemingly inviolable nature of lines separating Protestant, Catholic, and Jew. Perhaps the most famous of these was the 1958 public opinion survey of the residents of the Detroit metropolitan area. The study, titled *The Religious Factor,* found that vast differences still existed among Protestants, Catholics, and Jews not only in terms of their relative socioeconomic positions but in terms of their broader view of the world. Religious tradition was the source of significant differences in their general political orientation and commitment to civil liberties (such as freedom of speech and desegregation), not to mention the differences in voting behavior and in attitudes toward the exercise of governmental power (to set price controls, establish national health insurance and medical care, lessen unemployment, and strengthen educational programs). The religious factor also had a marked effect on the public's views of morality (such as gambling, drinking, birth control, divorce, and Sunday business), and on their views of the role of the family. Finally, religious difference had consequences for economic aspirations and attitudes toward work (as seen in their various views of installment buying, saving, the American dream, and the like).[27] In the mid-1960s, Rodney Stark and Charles Glock collected and analyzed national and regional data and discovered similar denominational differences in religious commitment. Religious knowledge, belief, experience, ritual commitment, and devotion all varied considerably depending upon denominational affiliation.[28]

Yet within two decades of these studies, new evidence was showing a certain reversal in these trends: people were becoming less concerned about denominational identity and loyalty.[29] At one level this change was seen in the marked decline in popular anti-Semitic and anti-Catholic sentiment. But an increase in *positive* sentiment appeared too. Surveys of the period showed that the majority of people of all faiths (up to 90 percent) favored more cooperation among local churches in community projects, in promoting racial tolerance, in sharing facilities, and even in worship.[30] The weakening of denominational boundaries extended to the relations among denominations with the Protestant community as well. According to Gallup surveys conducted from the mid-1970s to the mid-1980s, the overwhelming majority of Protestants had mutually positive feelings toward those belonging to the major denominations.[31]

The waning of denominational loyalty was reflected in people's attitudes but it was confirmed increasingly in their behavior. Since mid-century, Americans of every faith community have become far more prone to change denominational membership in the course of their lives.[32] The evidence on interreligious marriages is also suggestive of this pattern. For example, the proportion of Jews marrying non-Jews increased from 3 percent in 1965 to 17 percent in 1983. The proportion of interreligious marriage between Catholics and Protestants and of different denominations within Protestantism is considerably higher.[33]

As denominational affiliation has weakened so too have the effects of denominational identity upon the way people actually view the world. The 1987 General Social Survey showed no significant differences among Protestants, Catholics, and Jews on most issues, including capital punishment, tolerance of communists, gun control, interracial marriage, welfare, and defense spending. And there was no significant difference between Protestants and Catholics on the abortion issue. What is more, the only significant differences among Protestant denominations exist according to their general location on the ideological continuum between orthodoxy and progressivism.[34]

What accounts for the lessening of denominational loyalty and its fading social and political effects is not a deep mystery. In brief, the social characteristics that had previously distinguished the adherents of different faiths have become less pronounced. Catholics, for example, have made tremendous strides in occupational and educational achievement since the early 1960s. By the mid-1980s Catholics were just as likely to hold a professional position as Protestants. (In 1960, they were only 80 percent as likely.) Likewise they were also more likely to have been to college than Protestants (whereas three decades before they were only 70 percent as likely). As a consequence of their socioeconomic mobility, Catholics moved out of their ethnic enclaves in big cities—they became "suburbanized." A similar pattern of mobility can be seen among Baptists, Lutherans, and other sectarian Protestant denominations. On the other hand, unlike the Catholic population, Jews in the United States historically (certainly since the early twentieth century) have always been disproportionately better educated, professional, and well off. But like the Catholics, they were socially distinguished by their ethnic solidarity. In 1952, for example, nearly two-thirds of all American Jews lived in New York, New Jersey, and Pennsylvania. Yet the proclivity to cluster together regionally has decreased dramatically: in 1980, just over one-third of all Jews were located in these states.[35]

Whatever the cause, the reality is fairly clear: denominational loyalty receded considerably as a vital element of the religious landscape. It is only against this backdrop that one can see the changing place of para-church organizations in religious experience. For here we see something of an institutional inversion: while denominations have become *less* important for the religious life of the republic, para-church organizations—independent organizations often drawing support from a broader inter-denominational base on behalf of a particular political, social, or spiritual mission—have become *more* important. This is particularly true insofar as they provide the primary institutional framework within which an even broader and more portentous cultural realignment takes form.

RELIGIOUSLY BASED SPECIAL AGENDA ORGANIZATIONS

Of course, para-church and special agenda associations have long played a conspicuous role in the course of American religious life. In the nineteenth century alone numerous pan-denominational organizations were established to promote a particular mission. There were, for example, societies concerned with the calamitous effects of alcohol, such as the American Temperance Society (1826, which claimed 8,000 local organizations and 1.5 million members), the Women's Christian Temperance Union (1874), and the Anti-Saloon League (1895). Other associations were devoted to providing at least a basic education to all children, such as the American Sunday School Union (1824), the American Educational Society (1826), and to a certain extent, the American Tract Society (1823). Important organizations tried to counter the effects of industrialization upon the family, such as the White Cross Society (1883), Mother's Congress (1896), and the National League for the Protection of the Family (1896). Finally, organizations were committed to social service, such as the Young Men's Christian Association (YMCA, 1851), and the Salvation Army (1880).[36] Toward the end of the nineteenth century, Catholics also developed their own para-church organizations, such as the Knights of Columbus (1882), the Catholic Workman (1891), and the Daughters of Isabella (1897).[37] Among Jews, such groups included B'nai B'rith (1843), the Jewish Chautauqua Society (1893), the Jewish Labor Bund (1897), and the National Council of Jewish Women (1897).[38]

Thus, the existence of extraecclesiastical organizations is by no means novel. What is novel, however, is their growth in number, their increasing variety, and their rising political impact.[39] According to figures aggregated by Robert Wuthnow, this is particularly true for a certain type of para-church organization, the "special agenda" groups. Of these, no more than a few dozen existed in the 1860s. In 1900 less than 150 were operating. By the end of the Second World War, 400 had come into being. But in the roughly forty years between 1945 and 1987 approximately 500 more new "special agenda" religious organizations had been founded and were in operation.[40] Notably, all of this growth corresponds to an equivalent growth among other, nonreligious voluntary associations—in 1880 and in 1980, those devoted to religious concerns comprised about 5 percent of all such groups. But when compared to trends for religious denominations, the para-church or special agenda organizations have come to greatly outnumber denominations. And while membership in the mainline religious denominations has remained fairly stable since the mid-1960s, membership or involvement in the special agenda associations has increased substantially.

The vast variety of special agenda organizations is almost unfathomable. Umbrella agencies of interdenominational cooperation provide the bureaucratic mechanisms for both communication and the coordination of statements and activities among various (mainly Protestant) denominations.[41] Special agenda structures oriented toward the service and development of various faith communities have immense numbers and diversity.[42] The third and most important category of special agenda organizations includes the wide variety of religiously based public affairs organizations, political lobbies, and associations concerned with promoting particular social or political agenda in the public domain.[43] As one would expect, these organizations range considerably in size and budget. As a general rule, the closer they are to Washington, D.C., or New York City (where most of the special agenda organizations are located), the larger and better funded they tend to be.[44]

Special Agenda Organizations and Cultural Realignment

On its own terms, the expansion of these special agenda structures after the Second World War would seem a rather benign development. But *when coupled with the weakening of denominational ties, this expansion has actually encouraged the deepening of century-old intrafaith divisions.* Why? Because most of these groups are decidedly partisan both in nature and in agenda. More to the point, most of these organizations coalesce fairly tightly around opposing ends of the new cultural axis: orthodoxy and progressivism. This means that they increasingly provide the institutional framework within which a larger cultural realignment develops—the institutional setting within which a new and larger cultural conflict takes shape.

Illustrations abound. In Protestantism, the championing of orthodoxy or cultural conservatism by groups such as the Moral Majority, Christian Voice, the Religious Roundtable (which became the Roundtable), and the like in the 1980s are well known.[45] Dozens of other, less visible organizations also champion either part or all of the cause (especially such issues as abortion and pornography). The Christian Action Council (1975), for example, organizes Evangelical Christians who are "committed to the principle that law and public policy in our country should be in harmony with the fundamental biblical principles of the Judeo-Christian civilization."[46] In a similar vein, the American Coalition for Traditional Values (ACTV) was founded in 1984 to unite Evangelical leaders in common cause "to restore traditional moral and spiritual values" in all sectors of U.S. society—government, schools, mass media, and the family. As with the Coalition on Revival (1990), Concerned Women for America (1979), the American Constitutional Rights Association (1979), the Christian Heritage Center (1964), the National Reform Association (1864), the National Pro-Family Coalition (1980), the Christian Law Institute (1972), Christian Family Renewal (1970), and other general interest Protestant groups, the moral rhetoric employed is very similar. Similar too is the practical agenda pursued: they oppose the Equal Rights Amendment, gay rights, liberal pornography laws, and abortion on demand; they support tuition tax credits, a voluntary prayer amendment to the Constitution, and a strong national defense.[47]

The progressivist agenda in Protestantism is also well represented by these associations. Largely because the denominational structures of the mainline Protestant establishment already endorse a more or less liberal social and theological program, the special agenda groups on this side of the cultural divide tend to proliferate around those issues not perceived as being adequately advocated by these bodies. Gay rights and needs, for example, are advanced by such groups as Integrity, a gay and lesbian organization for Episcopalians founded in 1975. With 2,500 members and nearly twenty-five local or regional affiliates, it is a relatively small organization but it is vocal. It maintains a speakers' bureau, sponsors conferences and a biennial convention, conducts seminars for the clergy and lay people, and publishes a newsletter. Integrity pursues clear objectives: to "minister to the spiritual needs of gay men and lesbians and to work for the full participation of gay people in both the church and the larger society."[48] Similar gay activist groups can be found among Lutherans, Presbyterians, Quakers, American Baptists, Pentecostals, Unitarians, and members of the United Church of Christ.[49] Women's rights are also energetically promoted by progressive Protestant groups.[50] Pacifism and peace initiatives are pursued as well.[51]

In Protestantism the division between progressive and orthodox is seen *within* denominations; progressive interests are generally pursued by the denominational leadership and culturally conservative interests are generally promoted by local ministers and the laity. This is particularly true for the mainline Protestant churches. One of the more interesting cases is the 3 million member Presbyterian Church, U.S.A.[52] The Presbyterian Lay Committee, Presbyterians United for Biblical Concerns, Presbyterians for Democracy and Religious Freedom, and Presbyterians Pro-Life are all special interest groups that emerged since the mid-1960s. All are registered within the denomination but since their inception, they have aggressively challenged official church stands on theological, moral, and political issues. Especially outspoken is the Presbyterian Lay Committee founded in 1965, which has built a reputation around its unqualified criticism of the denomination's drift to the "theological and political Left." Its bimonthly magazine *Presbyterian Layman* is distributed free to over 620,000 members of the denomination, making it the single largest Presbyterian publication in existence.[53]

An analogous situation can be found in the 9.6 million member United Methodist Church (UMC). On one hand, progressivist ideals are preserved through the general boards of Church and Society, Discipleship, Higher Education and Ministry, and the General Commission on the Status and Role of Women, as well as by such special interest caucuses as the Methodist Federation for Social Action and the homosexual group Affirmation. On the other hand, there is a sizable grass-roots (and Evangelical) protest against denominational policy and drifts. The UMC's Evangelical caucus is called Good News (also known as the Forum for Scriptural Christianity) and was founded in 1966. Also part of the orthodox protest within the United Methodist Church is the group Methodists for Life (1978) a pro-life organization "opposed to abortion and to the Methodist church pro-abortion policy." But perhaps the most symbolic protest against progressivist tendencies in the denomination was launched in the closing months of 1987. Then, forty-eight local United Methodist ministers from eighteen states drafted the Houston Declaration in protest of the denomination's inclinations "to abandon the truths and traditions of the historic Christian faith." These ministers had numerous complaints but chief among them was the drift toward incorporating practicing homosexuals into the leadership of the UMC and toward abandoning the names "God, Father, Son, and Holy Spirit" in church liturgy. Not surprisingly, the document generated considerable reaction, both for and against. One theologian-minister called it "clearly heretical."[54]

After the 1960s, similar trends developed in the Episcopal Church.[55] The Lutheran Church, the United Church of Christ, and the Disciples of Christ also experienced divisions.[56] In a spirit of collective protest, in fact, renewal leaders within each of these denominations (plus the Presbyterian Church, U.S.A., and the United Methodist Church and, significantly, the Roman Catholic Church) drafted the "DuPage Declaration: A Call to Biblical Fidelity" on 20 March 1990. This declaration was comprised of eight affirmations and eight corresponding denials ranging from the language of the Godhead to the nature of Scripture and of Christ, from the limits of legitimate sexuality and the sanctity of human life to the global mission of the church. In each of these areas they affirmed a thoroughly traditional and pietist interpretation of these issues and deliberately repudiated a humanistic and liberally politicized position.

Curiously, these divisions have also emerged within the so-called Evangelical denominations. The Lutheran Church–Missouri Synod split in 1976 over precisely these issues. More significantly (because of its size), the Southern Baptist Convention was all but torn in two through the 1980s in a bitter struggle between the "fundamentalists" and "moderates" over these kinds of issues.[57]

As in the previous half century, the divisions in Catholicism continued through the 1980s to be reflected in the church hierarchy—with Joseph Cardinal Bernardin of Chicago and the U.S. Catholic Conference usually on the progressivist side and John Cardinal O'Connor of New York, in large part because of his vocal opposition to abortion, leading the cause of Catholic orthodoxy.

The cultural divide in Catholicism has gone far beyond disagreements among cardinals, however. Where the hierarchy has remained more intransigent in its orthodoxy, special interest groups have evolved to press the progressive agenda. Thus, for example, on the issue of abortion, Catholics for a Free Choice (1972) and (to a lesser extent) the Committee of Concerned Catholics (1986) defend the rights of women to choose in both childbearing and childrearing. On the issue of women's rights, Catholic Women for the ERA (1974), Priests for Equality (1975—2,300 member priests and 1,200 "supporters"), the Women's Ordination Conference (1975—2,000 members, 100 local affiliates), the Women of the Church Coalition (1977—2,000 members), and the U.S. section of St. Joan's International Alliance (1965) support the complete equality of women in the church and in the larger society. This would encompass the ordination of women into the priesthood and the elimination of sexism from the structures and understandings of the church, including the liturgy. On the issue of homosexuality, Dignity (1968—over 5,000 members and 120 local affiliates) and New Ways Ministry (1977) maintain that gay and lesbian Catholics are members of Christ's mystical body, and therefore it is their right to participate fully in the sacramental life of the church. Other organizations, such as the Quixote Center (1975), press forward the range of progressive Catholic agendas from women's and gay rights in the church to aid to Nicaragua.

Conversely, on issues where the Catholic hierarchy has taken on a more progressive stand, special interest groups (largely lay) have surfaced to defend the traditionalist position.[58] The Catholic Traditionalist Movement (1964), Catholics United for the Faith (1968), Catholics for Christian Political Action (1977), the American Catholic Committee (1982), the Society of Traditional Roman Catholics (1984), and, perhaps most important, the Catholic League for Religious and Civil Rights (1973)—with its approximately 30,000 members (mostly lay people) and fourteen local affiliates—are representative of Catholic orthodoxy. Several important periodicals, *Crisis, National Catholic Register, The Interim, Challenge, Fidelity,* and *The Wanderer,* all stand in general opposition to women's rights, gay rights, a revised sexual ethic, theological modernism of any kind, and every other major progressive interest.[59] All of these would give spirited assent to the passage from Nehemiah used as the epigraph for *Fidelity* magazine: "You see the trouble we are in: Jerusalem is in ruins, its gates have been burnt down. Come, let us rebuild the walls of Jerusalem and suffer this indignity no longer."

The Jewish situation more closely resembles the Protestant case in that the cultural realignment largely takes on denominational form. Yet because of the very small size of the Orthodox community and the political liberalism that has long been a prominent tradition in American Jewish experience, the cultural divisions are not quite so prominent or even so politicized as they are in Protestantism or Catholicism. Still the rifts are visible. Though not by any means uniform, as Samuel Heilman makes clear, there is a strong voice of opposition within the Orthodox Jewish community against abortion rights (such as Orthodox Jews for Life), the liberalization of the role of women, gay rights, and pornography, and a strong voice of approval for tuition tax credits for private religious education, and even a creationist view of the origins of humanity.[60] It is noteworthy as well that the Conservative Jewish movement experienced a schism in 1990 along these precise cultural lines—in the formation of the Union of Traditional Judaism. The progressively oriented Jews who dominate the Reform and Conservative movements tend to stand on the opposite sides of many issues. Consider the 1984 New York congressional election between the liberal incumbent Stephen Solarz and his politically conservative challenger Rabbi Yehuda Levin. In the election, the Jewish vote was split. The larger Jewish community supported Solarz. Yet, as we have seen from Levin's story in the prologue, numerous Orthodox rabbis and believers prominently and defiantly rejected Solarz's bid as a demonstration of their broader opposition to gay rights, abortion, pornography, and an isolationist foreign policy, championed by the incumbent.[61]

Corresponding to the divided sentiment are opposing para-church organizations. On the politically conservative side would be the National Jewish Commission on Law and Public Affairs (1965), whose members represent the observant Jewish community on legal, legislative, and civic matters. The National Jewish Coalition (1979) is organized around the goal of promoting Jewish involvement in Republican politics. There is also the government affairs office of the Agudath Israel, which promotes the policy perspectives of orthodoxy.[62]

On the progressivist side are such general interest organizations as the Religious Action Center of Reform Judaism (1961) and New Jewish Agenda (1980). More focused associations include the World Congress of Gay and Lesbian Jewish Organizations (1980), the Jewish Peace Fellowship (1941), and the women's organizations Ezrat Nashim (1972) and the Task Force on Equality of Women in Judaism (1972). As in Protestantism and Catholicism, the list goes on.

While this overview makes no pretense to being comprehensive, it does serve to highlight several new realities. The first is that the polarities existing for a century within Protestantism, Catholicism, and Judaism have evolved well beyond disputes over theological modernism. The disputes over the meaning of biblical authority (in Protestantism), over loyalty to Rome (in Catholicism), or over the inviolability of Torah and traditional ritual observances (in Judaism) remain important, that is certain. But now the conflict in each tradition has extended beyond the realm of theology and ecclesiastical politics to embrace many of the most fundamental issues and institutions of *public* culture: law, government, education, science, family, and sexuality.

Second, this overview serves to show the institutional embeddedness of the current conflicts. Opponents on whatever side and in whatever faith are not simply discontented; their discontent is organized, directed, and cumulatively speaking, very well funded. A cultural conflict this extensively entrenched will not simply fade away. Apart from the ideological passions that are at play, too much is at stake institutionally for that to happen.

THE REALIGNMENT OF AMERICAN PUBLIC CULTURE

Surveying religiously oriented public affairs organizations illustrates the wide scope and deep institutional embeddedness of the division between the orthodox and progressive within religious traditions. It also illustrates the way in which the polarities within each religious tradition mirror each other across religious traditions. Progressive circles within Protestantism, Catholicism, and Judaism, on the one hand, express virtually identical ideological concerns and programmatic interests. So too the orthodox within each of these traditions also display virtually indistinguishable anxieties and agendas.

Given this pattern, it is not at all surprising to see these organizational affinities reflected in the attitudes and opinions of the activists themselves.[63] A survey of the leadership of the three major faiths conducted in 1987, for example, documented just this—that two fairly distinct cultural orientations take shape across religious tradition on the basis of theological commitment.[64] The theologically orthodox of each faith and the theologically progressive of each faith divided consistently along the anticipated lines on a wide range of issues. Take the issue of sexual morality as an illustration. The orthodox wings of Protestantism, Catholicism, and Judaism were significantly more likely to condemn premarital sexual relations and cohabitation as "morally wrong" than each of their progressive counterparts.[65] The orthodox were also between two and three times more likely than progressives to condemn the viewing of pornographic films as morally wrong.[66] The same is true in their attitudes toward family life. For example, when presented with the statement, "It is much better for everyone involved if the man is the achiever outside the home and the woman takes care of the home and family," Evangelical Protestants were three times as likely to agree, conservative Catholics were twice as likely to agree, and Orthodox Jews were nearly five times as likely to agree as their progressive counterparts.[67] This distribution of opinion was seen again and again on issues pertaining to the locus of authority in the family and the proper roles of women and men.[68] Not surprisingly, this pattern was generally reflected in the opinion of these leaders when asked about three divisive family policy issues: support for the Equal Rights Amendment (ERA), the morality of abortion, and homosexuality.[69] Lest one imagine that this range of views was unique to the private matters of family and sexuality, the range was equally evident in how they identified themselves politically.[70] Ideologically the same patterns held. For example, the survey showed that by a margin of about 2 to 1 in the Protestant and Catholic leadership and 1.5 to 1 in the Jewish leadership, progressives identified themselves as Democrats. Even more telling, progressives in Protestantism were 6 times as likely, in Catholicism were 7.5 times as likely, and in Judaism were nearly twice as likely as their more orthodox counterparts, to describe their political ideology as liberal or left-wing.[71]

As one might expect, this cleavage in political opinion takes concrete form in the orthodox and progressivist views of capitalism and of America's role in international affairs. For example, the orthodox and progressivists differ in often dramatic but also predictable ways over the fairness of big business to working people; the best ways to improve the lot of the poor—economic growth or redistribution; and whether the United States would be better off if it moved toward a more socialist economy.[72] Likewise, they differ in their views of the role of U.S. multinational corporations in the Third World, Europe's neutrality in the East-West conflict, the nuclear freeze, the use of sanctions against the South African government for its policies of apartheid, the creation of a Palestinian homeland, and so on.[73] This survey made it clear, in sum, that the relative embrace of orthodoxy was the single most important explanatory factor in sorting out variation in elite political values. Indeed, it accounts for more variation within and across religious tradition than any other single factor, including people's social class background, race, ethnicity, gender, the size of the organization they work in, and the degree of pietism by which they individually live.[74] Other recent empirical studies have shown identical patterns.[75]

The New Ecumenism

What all of these events graphically illustrate is that the impulse for alliance building among the progressives of different traditions and among the orthodox of different traditions goes beyond mere ideological affinity. These affinities express themselves institutionally as a "new ecumenism"—a new form of cooperative mobilization, in which distinct and separate religious and moral traditions share resources and work together toward common objectives.

Through the better part of the twentieth century, ecumenism was a movement primarily within the mainline Protestant bodies, whose central concern was to join distinct Christian denominations through cooperative effort. In many cases there was an effort to actually unify denominations. This was understood in sociological terms as a bureaucratic strategy designed to defend the organizations involved against a hostile secular environment.[76] Ecumenism, as it was argued, reduced the number of "competing units," allowing those that remain to compete more effectively for adherents. Under earlier circumstances ecumenism indeed functioned in that way.

Yet if the structure of religious pluralism has changed, then the nature and structure of religious cooperation must be changing as well. Ecumenism can now be understood as a much more encompassing social process. The associations being formed across traditions among the orthodox and among the progressive are not designed so much to maintain or win adherents against the onslaught of secular modernity but to marshal resources against each other and, more important, against the larger cultural forces that each side represents. The new ecumenism, then, represents the key institutional expression of the realignment of American public culture and, in turn, it provides the institutional battle lines for the contemporary culture war.

The clearest ways in which this new ecumenism takes tangible expression is in the joining of forces on behalf of a particular issue or event. When the Civil Rights Restoration Act was being decided in early 1988, for example, it generated organized and coordinated support from the National Organization for Women, the National Education Association, the American Federation of Teachers, the U.S. Conference of Bishops, the National Abortion Rights Action League, the National Gay and Lesbian Task Force, and a host of mainline Protestant organizations. It was opposed by Agudath Israel, the National Association of Evangelicals, the U.S. Catholic Conference, the National Right to Life Committee, the American Council of Christian Churches, and the American Association of Christian Schools, among others. So too, in the Act for Better Child Care debated throughout the late 1980s and eventually passed in 1990, the National Organization for Women, *Ms.* magazine, the Union of American Hebrew Congregations, and the United Methodist Board of Church and Society, among others, worked in favor of the measure and squared off against such orthodox groups as Concerned Women for America, the American Council of Christian Churches (as editorialized critically by its own Fundamentalist News Service), and James Dobson's Focus on the Family publication, *Citizen.* The lineup is very predictable at this point: the pattern is seen again and again as policy issues come and go, from the nomination of Robert Bork to the Supreme Court in 1986, to the Housing Now March in 1989, and so on.

Another significant way in which this new ecumenism takes form is within the newly expanded structure of special purpose organizations, especially in the way these organizations relate to each other. In some instances, as a matter of longstanding policy, some groups join other groups in realizing a particular policy objective. The Catholic League for Religious and Civil Rights provides a telling illustration of this dynamic on the side of orthodoxy.[77] The Catholic League was established in 1973 by a Jesuit priest as a Catholic counterpart to the Jewish Anti-Defamation League and the secular American Civil Liberties Union: "To protect the religious rights and advance the just interests of Catholics in secular society."[78] While it claims to be a nonpartisan organization, working to serve the needs of the whole Catholic community, the league tilts decisively toward the orthodox community in Catholicism. In this, it openly supports the work of like-minded Protestants and Jews. Indeed, the league's first major case came in the defense of Dr. Frank Bolles, a Protestant physician and right-to-life activist. (Bolles had been charged by a Colorado district attorney for "harassing and causing alarm" by mailing out anti-abortion literature.) In the first fifteen years of existence, the league also has publicly defended the right of a Jew to wear his yarmulke while in uniform; it supported Reverend Sun Myung Moon, the leader of the Unification Church, in his tax-evasion case; it has publicly "defended the right of parents [Protestant, Catholic, and Jewish] to give their children a God-centered education"; and so on. A similar dynamic operates on the progressivist side of the cultural divide. The Religious Action Center of Reform Judaism, for example, officially serves as a government liaison between the Union of American Hebrew Congregations and the Central Conference of American Rabbis by representing the positions of these groups to the federal government. Beyond this, however, the center cooperates with a wide variety of liberal Protestant and Catholic denominations and organizations on progressive policy concerns, issuing statements in opposition to the nuclear arms race, to U.S. involvement in Central America, to the Supreme Court nominee Robert Bork. In both cases, the alliances formed are built upon a perceived self-interest. Both organizations tend to support groups and individuals of other religious faiths when such support also advances their own particular objectives.

The activists in these organizations communicate with each other, and even draw direct support from each other. For example, in an informal survey of forty-seven of these public affairs organizations, the leadership of all of these groups claimed to be in communication with individuals or groups outside of their own religious or philosphical tradition and most of these had engaged in active cooperation.[79] The public affairs office of the Orthodox Jewish organization Agudath Israel, for example, regularly allies with Catholics on concerns over private education and conservative Protestants on moral issues. The overwhelming majority of these organizations were supported by grass-roots contributions and of these all but one or two claimed to receive contributions from Protestants, Catholics, the Eastern Orthodox Church, and Jews. In the early 1980s, for example, 30 percent of the membership of the Moral Majority was Catholic. Finally, roughly half of these groups sought to make explicit and public their commitment to coalition formation (that is, the larger ecumenism) by deliberately including representation from the range of traditions on their organization's board of advisors or board of trustees. The (orthodox) American Family Association, for example, advertises an advisory board that includes four Catholic bishops and one cardinal, three Eastern Orthodox bishops including the Primate of the Greek Orthodox Church, and dozens of Evangelical and Pentecostal leaders.[80]

The new ecumenism is further seen in the emergence of still other special purpose organizations whose explicit aim is to formally bind together the orthodox of different faiths or the progressives of different faiths to oppose coalitions on the other side. Such groups seem to develop with greater facility on the progressive side of the cultural divide. Bea Blair's organization, the Religious Coalition for Abortion Rights (discussed in the prologue), for example, was founded in 1973 to consolidate the efforts of the various independent pro-choice organizations. By 1988, it had thirty-one member groups, including such diverse ones as the American Jewish Congress, Catholics for a Free Choice, the American Humanist Association, the YWCA, the United Methodist Church, and the Women's League for Conservative Judaism. The Religious Network for Equality for Women was founded in 1976 as a coalition of forty-one Protestant, Catholic, Jewish, and humanist groups committed to education and advocacy on behalf of the cause of "economic justice for women." Among its members were associations representing Episcopalians, Catholic nuns, Baptists, Conservative and Reform Jews, Quakers, Unitarians, Presbyterians, Methodists, Lutherans, and Mormons. An equal amount of diversity is represented in other coalitions for women's issues (such as Church Women United [1941] and the Panel of American Women [1957]), in the gay rights movement (such as the Lesbian and Gay Interfaith Alliance and the National Gay and Lesbian Task Force), in antinuclear and pacifist groups (such as the Fellowship of Reconciliation [1915], Clergy and Laity Concerned [1965], the Interfaith Center to Reverse the Arms Race [1980], the Religious Task Force [1977], and Action Against Armageddon [1984]), in groups concerned with foreign policy (such as Coalition for a New Foreign Policy [1976], the Inter-Religious Task Force on Central America [1980], the Interfaith Center on Corporate Responsibility [1974]), and in organizations generally committed to both countering the agenda of the religious right and advocating liberal conceptions of public life—such as People for the American Way [1980], National Impact [1969], Network [1971], the Interchange Resource Center [1978], and the Washington Interfaith Staff Council (WISC).

The number of formal coalitions drawing together orthodox patterns is far fewer in number primarily because of their commitment to the primacy of theological distinctiveness. A few do exist: one of the most important is the Center for Pastoral Renewal, which actively seeks to draw together theologically conservative Catholics, Evangelical Protestants, and Eastern Orthodox leaders for the purposes of forging a new orthodox ecumenism. The center sponsors annual Allies for Faith and Renewal conferences in which orthodox Christians of all confessions come together to work through common problems. The independent periodical *Touchstone: A Journal of Ecumenical Orthodoxy* works toward the same goals. The Coalitions for America, organized through Free Congress, draws together politically conservative activists, whether religiously oriented or not, on numerous issues, from abortion to national defense. Through the 1980s the National Pro-Family Coalition was active: this was a coalition of numerous "pro-family, pro-decency, pro-morality, and pro-life organizations" all committed to achieving a "just and humane society functioning in accordance with the moral imperatives of the Judeo-Christian ethic."[81] And Americans for Educational Choice, an organization closely affiliated with Mae Duggan's Citizens for Educational Freedom, is made up of theologically orthodox Protestant, Catholic, and Jewish organizations committed to educational choice through tuition tax credits or vouchers.

It is important to note that these coalitional organizations on both sides of the divide vary considerably in their size, scope of activity, and ability to actually unify member groups. A few, like the World Congress of Gay and Lesbian Jewish Organizations, and the National Coalition for Public Education and Religious Liberty, have a staff of two to four people and a budget under $50,000 and their actual political engagement barely reaches beyond the letterhead on their stationery. Others, such as the Liberty Lobby, Clergy and Laity Concerned, Concerned Women for America, and People for the American Way, have a staff of twenty to fifty or more, budgets of a half a million to 10 million dollars, and are efficiently administered. They carry enormous social power.[82] Yet what is relevant here is neither the size nor effectiveness of the organizations but their very existence. Their very presence on the political landscape aptly symbolizes the nature and direction of a major realignment in public culture.

Justifying the New Alliances

It is essential to note that the realignment of public culture does not take place without tension. For example, the memory of anti-Catholicism and anti-Semitism remains in the minds of many Catholics and Jews, refreshed periodically by incidents of interreligious prejudice. Suspicions on all sides linger. Yet insofar as the resolution to the issues of contemporary public debate (abortion, the role of women, the changing structure of the family, homosexuality, nuclear proliferation, the "failures" of public education, the meaning of the "separation between church and state," and the like) is not forthcoming, the pressures for interreligious realignment in public culture mount. At the same time, the pressure to tolerate or overlook existing tensions also rises.

Yet it is not enough to simply tolerate the tensions. Given the long history of interreligious antagonism, realignment must be justified. On the progressivist side, such explanations are linked to basic concerns for survival. As a publication of the Union of American Hebrew Congregations in 1983 put it, the "renaissance of interreligious communication and cooperation . . . emerges out of profound concern with the moral and social issues of the 80's which uniquely threaten our physical and political survival. The nuclear arms race, the suffering engendered by a rate of unemployment unsurpassed since Depression Days and radical attempts to eradicate First Amendment Constitutional protections; almost every social issue, every social welfare concern is being addressed by interreligious coalitions of decency."[83] A spokesman for the progressively oriented Washington Interreligious Staff Council agreed: "Different communities of faith converge because they share the same conception of the common good."[84]

Interestingly, on the orthodox side, the justification for interreligious cooperation is also linked to survival. A statement made in 1986 by the Fundamentalist writer Tim LaHaye is illuminating in this regard. Despite basic theological differences, he begins, "Protestants, Catholics and Jews do share two very basic beliefs: we all believe in God to Whom we must give account some day for the way we live our lives; we share a basic concern for the moral values that are found in the Old Testament." LaHaye continues,

> If religious Americans work together in the name of our mutually shared moral concerns, we just might succeed in re-establishing the civic moral standards that our forefathers thought were guaranteed by the Constitution.
>
> I realize that such statements may cause me to lose my fundamentalist membership card, but I really believe that we are in a fierce battle for the very survival of our culture. . . . Obviously I am not suggesting joint evangelistic crusades with these religions; that would reflect an unacceptable theological compromise for all of us. [Nevertheless], all of our nation's religious citizens need to develop a respect for other religious people and their beliefs. We need not accept their beliefs, but we can respect the people and realize that we have more in common with each other than we ever will with the secularizers of this country. It is time for all religiously committed citizens to unite against our common enemy.[85]

In 1984, the Evangelical activist Franky Schaeffer observed that

> our backs are against the wall and we are facing an aggressively secularistic society whose powerful elements are deliberately attempting to eradicate what little remains of orthodox religious influence in society. The majority of Christians are either asleep or simply do not care. The minority of activist believers no longer have the luxury of concentrating solely on denominational and church affairs and petty theological differences. *The time has come for those who remain to band together in an ecumenism of orthodoxy.* Unlike liberal ecumenicism which is bound together by unbelief, this ecumenicism is based upon what we *agree* to be the essence of the Christian faith, including an orthodoxy of belief in social concerns and priorities.[86]

It is not just the Protestant fundamentalists who feel these pressures to cooperate.[87] As the director of the public affairs office of Agudath Israel argued, "Joint efforts with Catholics and Protestants do not mean that we Jews are endorsing their theology." He said, "We can overlook our religious differences because politically, it makes sense."[88] A spokesman for the Catholic League maintained, "The issues are too important to have a denominational focus."[89] Rabbi Joshua O. Haberman similarly noted, "As a Jew, I differ with a variety of Bible-believing Christians on theology, our nation's social agenda, and matters of public policy. I am, at times, repelled by fits of fanaticism and a narrow-minded, rigid dogmatism among fundamentalist extremists. Yet far greater than these differences and objections is the common moral and spiritual frame of reference I share with Christians, including fundamentalists. The Bible gave our nation its moral vision. And today, America's Bible Belt is our safety belt, the enduring guarantee of our fundamental rights and freedoms."[90]

The moral reasoning employed by both sides of the cultural divide to legitimate these alliances, then, is very much alike. In brief, though the alliances being formed among the orthodox or among the progressives across religious tradition are historically "unnatural" they have become pragmatically necessary. In the end, they are justified by the simple dictum that "an enemy of an enemy is a friend of mine."

THE COLLAPSE OF THE OLD DIVIDE

The divisions among Protestant, Catholic, and Jew have had such a significant place in Western civilization for so many centuries that it is difficult to imagine pluralism (at least in this context) in any other way. These formal divisions (and to a lesser extent, those ecclesiastical divisions within these faiths) remain the significant ones in the popular imagination, the relevant ones for public policy, and the decisive ones in intellectual circles, particularly in modern social science. They remain part of the taken-for-granted scenery of public life in America and Europe.

The ways in which scholars conceptualize pluralism is especially interesting, for here we see that the habits of social science are as difficult to break as any. With a few exceptions, social science has continued over the past two decades to measure religious and cultural pluralism in a manner that reifies, as it were, the divisions among the major religious traditions as the correct way to think about cultural pluralism in America. Based upon this methodology, social science has also gradually documented religion's declining significance as an explanatory variable. Whether one is a Protestant, Catholic, or Jew simply does not mean very much when attempting to explain variations in people's attitudes or values. As a result, the larger social scientific community has come to assume that general religious preference may be irrelevant or "epiphenomenal." Indeed, in many recent empirical investigations, formal religious variables have not even been included as a part of the research strategy. They just do not make any difference anymore.

Old habits die hard but die they must, for the evidence strongly suggests that the significant divisions on public issues are no longer defined by the distinct traditions of creed, religious observance, or ecclesiastical politics. These do remain strong sources of personal meaning and communal identity, but their consequence for public culture has dwindled substantially. In other words, it is increasingly difficult to speak of the Protestant position or the Catholic position or the Jewish position (or, for that matter, the Mormon or Buddhist position) vis-à-vis American public culture. Meanwhile, other kinds of differences have expanded: increasingly, the politically consequential divisions are those that separate the orthodox from the progressive *within* religious traditions. And orthodox and progressive factions of the various faiths do not speak out as isolated voices but increasingly as a common chorus. In this, the political relevance of the historical divisions between Protestant and Catholic and Christian and Jew has largely become defunct.

Yet I want to stress again that the lines separating orthodox and progressive, or conservative and liberal, are not, in reality, always sharp. Some notable ideological cross-currents flow against the larger cultural tendencies. First, even if their numbers are relatively few, one cannot ignore the presence on the public scene of, among others, pro-life feminists and libertarians, Mormon and Pentecostal homosexuals, Evangelical Christian pacifists, and secularists (even atheists) who are politically conservative, and Fundamentalists who are socialists. Second, and even harder to ignore, are the myriad individuals that define themselves more or less in the middle of the ideological spectrum. Although some may lean ideologically toward the orthodox camp while others lean toward progressivism, no one can fairly describe them as extremists. Third, groups and individuals on the orthodox side have sharp disagreements with others on the orthodox side, and the same is true for the progressivist side. And fourth, there are some who would certainly be classified as being on one side of the cultural divide or another but they wish to fight their battles alone—they choose not to be aligned at all. All of these realities cannot be disregarded. Yet recognizing the existence of these counterintuitive developments cannot negate the broader tendencies in the realm of public culture. The dominant impulse at the present time is toward the polarization of a religiously informed public culture into two relatively distinct moral and ideological camps.

4

Competing Moral Visions

The realignment of public culture takes institutional form in a shifting configuration of religious and political associations and organizations. This is the lesson of the preceding chapter. At issue are two *relatively* distinct and competing visions of public life. To identify the predominant and polarizing tendencies as "orthodox" and "progressive" suggests a great deal about the nature of these visions. Knowing something about the specific political agenda pursued by either side reveals even more. But to truly understand the depth of contemporary cultural conflict and its historical significance, it is essential to probe more thoroughly into the perspectives on public life being advocated.

Yet, does it go too far to suggest that both sides of the cultural divide represent something as coherent as "perspective"? Certainly there are no comprehensive philosophical treatises articulating in full measure the nature and profile of these visions. There are no modern manifestos declaring a coherent system of programs and goals. What actually exists in public discussion are, very often, nothing more than jumbled accumulations of pronouncements, accusations, appeals, and partisan analyses. It would be foolish to deny the complexity of the divisions, the subtleties and ambivalent moral commitments in the hearts and minds of ordinary Americans. As I have emphasized from the start, Americans find stances across a wide spectrum of values and perspectives. Despite this complexity, it is possible to discern certain cultural tendencies. That is to say, all of these pronouncements, allegations, complaints, and appeals seem to reveal broad, yet still distinct and opposing cultural impulses. These impulses, I would argue, have come to be rather strong in public discourse mainly because they have been embraced and promoted through the elites and institutions of special interest organizations. As such, they are suggestive of more comprehensive visions of public life—public philosophies whose general contours can be roughly sketched out as ideal types.[1]

COMPETING PHILOSOPHIES OF AMERICAN PUBLIC LIFE

As we learned in chapter 2, one of the chief tasks of a public philosophy centers around the problem of national identity—deciding who we as a nation have been, coming to grips with who we are now, and defining what we should aspire to become in the future. Often the mechanism for articulating our public philosophies (and thus the meaning of national identity) is nothing more than a simple narrative—chronicles that begin with an account of the nation's mythic origin and end with a vision of its future. The impact of these stories is critical. When they are intelligible, credible, and compelling to those who hear them, not only do they inspire a sense of cohesion within communities but they provide a ready justification for the nation's conduct in world affairs—for only actions consistent with a nation's self-conception (what it has been and what it aspires to be) will be an appropriate field of national endeavor.

The general public philosophies that have evolved on either side of the cultural divide have been presented many times in recent years and therefore require neither an exhaustive review nor a detailed analysis. But a brief overview of the opposing ideals of national identity and purpose will offer a beginning point for considering the underlying cultural differences that split these new coalitions of conviction.

History As Ideology

The Orthodox Vision

The most effusive interpreters of the mythic origins of the republic on the side of cultural conservatism are the Evangelical Christians. Theirs, of course, is not the only version. Orthodox Catholics and Jews tell the story from a different angle, one that tends to emphasize the generally religious rather than the specifically Christian nature of the story. Intellectually oriented neo-conservatives stress the generally moral rather than religious nature of the story. Yet all of these versions would have at least a distant resonance with the Evangelical account, particularly in how each of these would understand the republic's founding ideals.

The Evangelical Protestant account of the nation's founding has a very long history, to be sure. Indeed, many of the earliest stories were fashioned by Protestant leaders who lived through the events of those years, some who actually participated in shaping those events—John Witherspoon, John Adams, Timothy Dwight, Patrick Henry. Through the nineteenth and twentieth centuries, much the same story was retold, if not by Evangelicals, then by kindred spirits, through song (such as "The Battle Hymn of the Republic," written in 1862), literature (from the fiction of Herman Melville to the poetry of Walt Whitman), political oratory (from Abraham Lincoln to Woodrow Wilson), and sermon (as in the revivalism of Billy Sunday). Present-day Evangelicalism, then, is the contemporary bearer of a story that claims a very long past.

We were introduced to the Evangelical account by Chuck McIlhenny at the opening of this book when he described the Christian heritage that was the context for the nation's founding. It is a start. The larger account varies in detail from Chuck's, but through linking the nation's birth to divine will, the story, as told by some of the most vocal and visible of contemporary Evangelical spokespeople, has a rough coherence. To them, America is, in a word, the embodiment of Providential wisdom. Evangelical journalist Rus Walton put it very simply when he wrote that "the American system is the political expression of Christian ideas."[2] In *The Light and the Glory,* Peter Marshall and David Marvel contended that a divine call upon America can be traced from the very earliest events in the nation's history (including the spiritual calling that Columbus himself received to seek undiscovered lands) to the present, and that this call is still valid today.[3] Another Evangelical author observed that "God's hand was in the founding of this country and the fiber of Christ is in the very fabric of America."[4] According to another, our "civil government is ordained of God [and] . . . America was founded upon Christian principles,"[5] upon the idea that America is "the greatest Christian nation the world has ever known."[6] Arguing more in line with the sensibilities of their new partners in the culture war, Fundamentalist writer Tim LaHaye contends that "it is improper to say that America was founded on Christian principles, for that would unnecessarily exclude the Jewish community. America was founded on biblical principles, all of which are found in the Old Testament."[7] A similar appeal comes from the Religious Roundtable, which asserts that the United States was "born and built upon basic principles of righteousness" and for this reason "has been blessed and exalted in her short 200 year history like no other nation in history."[8] This assertion garners support from orthodox Catholics. As Mae Duggan puts it, "the founders of our nation, George Washington, James Madison, and even Thomas Jefferson (who did not have any church affiliation), believed that government must be based on God; that governmental structures must have an authority greater than itself, which is God. This is the meaning of our motto, 'In God We Trust.' "

For many, however, the rhetoric goes beyond generalities. Many in the Evangelical camp further contend that the founding documents themselves reflect the hand of divine providence. Argues LaHaye, "The last six commandments of the Decalogue, dealing with man's treatment of his fellowman, and the civil laws of the Old Testament formed the basis for our laws and our Constitution."[9] The Evangelical writer and attorney John Whitehead argues that "the concept of a secular state was nonexistent in 1776 as well as 1787, and no less so in 1791 when the Bill of Rights was adopted." At the framing of the Constitution, Whitehead maintains, the American population "lived under laws that were either written directly from the Scriptures or influenced by them."[10] Whitehead is not alone. "The Founding Fathers," John Eidsmoe writes, "were Newtonians. They believed in absolute, unchanging, God-given laws of science—as well as moral laws. When Jefferson spoke of the 'laws of nature and of nature's God' in the Declaration of Independence, he used language both Christians and Deists would approve. . . . To the Founding Fathers, law was God-given, absolute, unchanging and revealed to man through Scripture, nature and conscience."[11] Still others have gone so far as to call the Constitution and the Bill of Rights "divinely inspired."

The genius of the "American experiment," from this perspective, was the creation of institutions that would guarantee both freedom and justice. Freedom and justice, however, are cast in a particular way within this mythic tradition.

The meaning of freedom, as it is emphasized within the various orthodox communities, is the freedom enjoyed by a society when it does not live under despotism; the freedom of a *society* to govern itself—what philosopher Charles Taylor has called "civic freedom."[12] It is precisely for this reason that the contrast between the United States and its European allies (or the "free" world) and the Soviet Union and the former communist bloc played such a key part in the Evangelical and even conservative Catholic world view. Their definition of freedom made that contrast important.

This definition of freedom also naturally highlights the importance of economic self-determination, as in "free" enterprise. Conservative Catholics have not championed this notion so much in part because of Rome's longstanding concern for the interests of organized labor. *The Spirit of Democratic Capitalism,* a book by Catholic scholar Michael Novak, is a notable exception to the rule. But among the more vocal public theologians within the Evangelical tradition, the celebration of capitalism—the freedom to pursue economic gain without government interference—is virtually unqualified.[13] Jerry Falwell repeatedly claimed that "God is in favor of freedom, property, ownership, competition, diligence, work and acquisition. All of this is taught in the Word of God, in both the Old and New Testaments." Therefore "people should have the right to own property, to work hard, to achieve, to earn, and to win."[14] Elsewhere Falwell has written that "the free-enterprise system is clearly outlined in the Book of Proverbs in the Bible. Jesus Christ made it clear that the work ethic was a part of His plan for man. Ownership of property is biblical. Competition in business is biblical."[15] In a similar vein, religious broadcaster Pat Robertson has contended that while "communism and capitalism in their most extreme, secular manifestations are equally doomed to failure, . . . free enterprise is the economic system most nearly meeting humanity's God-given need for freedom. . . . Capitalism satisfies the freedom-loving side of humanity."[16] Such theologies have even been translated into practical, profit-oriented seminars. At the Marriott Hotel, Anaheim, California, in 1981, Evangelist Bill Bright (founder of Campus Crusade for Christ) and Texas billionaire Nelson Bunker Hunt led a three-day financial seminar in which participants were instructed in the biblical foundations of free enterprise and economic success. As one participant enthusiastically stated, "God is an all-time Capitalist, not a Socialist."[17]

Underlying the reverential endorsement of capitalism among these Evangelicals is the conviction that economic and spiritual freedoms go hand in hand, that one is impossible without the other.[18] Some trace the relationship to the Old Testament land laws that linked private property to the freedom from state coercion, especially from taxation.[19] Others see a less complicated connection: the relationship between investing and taking profits is essentially the same as that between giving and receiving, between sowing and reaping. According to Bill Bright, this is one of the laws that "rule the universe."[20] This dynamic requires economic freedom. As the economist (and professed Evangelical) George Gilder put it: " 'Give and you'll be given unto' is the fundamental practical principle of the Christian life, and when there's no private property you can't give it because you don't own it." For this reason, he concludes, socialism is "inherently hostile to Christianity and capitalism [is] the essential mode of human life that corresponds to religious truth."[21]

Just as a particular understanding of freedom is emphasized in the communities of cultural conservatism, so is a particular definition of "justice." Justice is generally defined in terms of the Judeo-Christian standards of moral righteousness. As R. J. Rushdoony makes clear, justice can only be understood in terms of the law, which in its highest form is "theocentric and is a manifestation of the nature and life of the ontological Trinity."[22] A just society, therefore, is a morally conscientious and lawful society. When its people abide by these standards it is also an ordered society. The Old Testament is often quoted in this regard: "Righteousness exalts a nation," "By justice a king gives a country stability," "When the righteous thrive, the people rejoice; when the wicked rule, the people groan," "Evil men do not understand justice, but those who seek the Lord understand all things," and so on. In this view, the moral fiber of American life is built upon standards of biblical morality. As a pamphlet from Christian Voice proclaimed, "The mandate from our Heavenly Father is to make sure government is faithfully meting out justice and punishing what is wrong and rewarding what is right."[23] Freedom, justice, and America's biblical culture are seen as intimately linked. Summarizes LaHaye, "In truth, what has granted more freedom for the longest period of time . . . to the largest number of people, while at the same time producing the greatest wealth for the most people, can be traced to . . . our Bible-based form of government and our unique Bible-based educational system."[24]

This vision of America's past contains an implicit vision of America's destiny. In language reminiscent of nineteenth-century exceptionalism, a pamphlet published by Students for America announces that "America has a unique mission to extend the boundaries of liberty and righteousness."[25] But from the conservative Evangelical perspective, the only hope for achieving this end is for the United States to stay the course. If change is necessary, it should only be undertaken to more perfectly fulfill the ideals established at the nation's founding. So warns Pat Robertson: "Either we will return to the moral integrity and original dreams of the founders of this nation . . . or we will give ourselves over more and more to hedonism, to all forms of destructive anti-social behavior, to political apathy, and ultimately to the forces of anarchy and disintegration that have throughout history gripped great empires and nations in their tragic and declining years."[26] Along the same lines, evangelist Jimmy Swaggart has asserted, "We believe the salvation of the United States of America is still the old-fashioned principles laid down in the Word of Almighty God."[27] And from Jerry Falwell comes the argument that "only by godly leadership can America be put back on a divine course."[28]

The Progressivist Vision

Those on the progressive side of the cultural divide rarely, if ever, attribute America's origins to the actions of a Supreme Being. The National Education Association, for example, insists that "when the Founding Fathers drafted the Constitution with its Bill of Rights, they explicitly designed it to guarantee a secular, humanistic state."[29] Some professional historians, as Garry Wills points out, have added to this myth in the name of objective scholarship. He notes that Henry Steele Commager's *The American Mind,* for example, contends that the American mind has been from the outset pragmatic, optimistic, and secular, with little regard for the forces of religious or artistic irrationalism. Arthur Schlesinger, Jr., also argued that secularity was the dominant trait of American society. "The American mind," he says, "is by nature and tradition skeptical, irreverent, pluralistic and relativistic"; elsewhere he says, "Relativism is the American way."[30] The premise of the progressivist account, then, is a rejection of the particularistic loyalties of the orthodox in favor of what one secular tract called "eternal verities"—universal ethical principles in part derived from the nation's religious and humanist traditions. A placard seen at an anti–Moral Majority demonstration in St. Paul, Minnesota, read, "God loves the world—not just America." As another put it, "America is not a Christian nation but one in which many Christians happen to live. America and every nation on earth is called by God to seek justice and serve the common good of humanity, not as special privilege, however, but as special responsibility."[31]

Accordingly, the founding documents of the republic take on a different understanding from that maintained by cultural conservatives. The Constitution and the Bill of Rights, for example, are not seen as reflecting absolutes either given by God or rooted in nature; instead the founders gave us a "living Constitution," one that cannot be straightjacketed, forever attached to the culture of an agrarian, preindustrialized society, but one that grows and changes with a changing society. Law in a democratic society is one of the highest expressions of human rationality and must evolve as society evolves and matures. The ideals that it serves are also the ideals of freedom and justice.

In this progressivist vision, freedom and justice are understood in fundamentally different ways than they are on the orthodox side of the cultural divide. Here freedom is defined largely in terms of the social and political rights of individuals. This is what Charles Taylor has called "liberal" freedom (as opposed to "civic" freedom, mentioned earlier). It is, Taylor says, "freedom in the 'negative' sense, a condition in which the individual is granted immunity from interference by others in his life, either by state or church or by other individuals."[32] This perspective was reflected in the views of all the progressivists we met in the prologue: Richmond Young's concern with the rights of homosexuals, Bea Blair's concern for "reproductive rights" and the rights of women, and Harriet Woods's concern for the freedom of inquiry in public schools. The logic is unambiguous. As one religiously based women's rights newsletter stated simply, "Being oppressed is the absence of choice."[33] It is in this light that one can understand the high tribute given to "pluralism" and "diversity." As Norman Lear of People for the American Way argued, "First and foremost among our shared values is a celebration of diversity and respect for the beliefs of others."[34]

It is not surprising that the founding myths advanced in progressivist circles tend to focus on the struggle of the founders to establish and preserve "pluralism and diversity." The names of Roger Williams, George Washington, John Adams, Tom Paine, James Madison, and Frederick Douglass are commonly invoked as champions of these principles. A People for the American Way publication maintained, "Throughout our history, American men and women have fought hard to make this country a better place. They fought for fair representation. Open debate. A healthy respect for diverse public opinion. . . . [Thus,] America is the freest . . . nation on earth. A legacy left to us by the Founders of our country."[35] A pamphlet put out by the Religious Coalition for Abortion Rights justified its position by stating that "fortunately, the framers of this country's Bill of Rights understood and cherished diversity."[36]

Justice, on the other hand, tends to be understood by progressivists in terms of equality and the end of oppression in the social world. This is the theme of "fair play" that Bea Blair emphasized in her story.

Whether it is the case for women, blacks, Hispanics and other racial minorities, homosexuals and lesbians, refugees, Palestinians, the black majority in South Africa, or the poor and laboring classes, justice means greater equity and thus the elimination of repressive relationships. Political rights are a part of the equation, but almost invariably economics becomes perhaps the central part of the equation. It is in this light that, for example, the progressive journal *Christianity and Crisis* described the "minimum wage" as a "minimum justice."[37] The Religious Network for Equality for Women identified support for the Equal Rights Amendment, a comprehensive jobs program, affirmative action, an earning-sharing provision within Social Security, and so on, with "God's call for justice."[38] *Sojourners* magazine called its commitment to speak on behalf of the poor and oppressed a "commitment to justice," and Clergy and Laity Concerned described their opposition to "workfare, plant closures, family farm loss, etc." and their "stand in solidarity with the poor" as efforts to promote justice.[39] Peace with Justice organizers in 1988 identified "people of color, women, children, the hungry, the poor, small farmers," and the like as "victims of injustice."[40]

Those who hold the progressivist vision generally maintain that America's enormous wealth and power in the world have inevitably created equally huge inequities. The responsibility of the American people and their government is equally great. "Social justice," they maintain, "may no longer be a fashionable concept. But, justice and empathy are not fads. They are a matter of faith. And, a matter of action." The calling, then, becomes clear: as stated in a National Impact pamphlet, the goal is "to move our government toward compassionate and sensible public policies."[41] Such sensibilities are shared among virtually all activists on this side of the cultural divide.

Clearly, then, within each of these opposing public philosophies, the words "freedom and justice" carry enormous symbolic weight. Both sides explicitly link these words and their broader vision of the public order to either scriptural referents or other universal ethical standards. But the meanings of the terms on either side of the divide are almost precisely inverted. Where *cultural conservatives* tend to *define freedom economically* (as individual economic initiative) and *justice socially* (as righteous living), *progressives* tend to *define freedom socially* (as individual rights) and *justice economically* (as equity). These differences naturally account for the different meanings each side imputes to the founders and their struggle to build a republic. Both biblical *and* Enlightenment themes are present in the historical record. Yet in public discourse, each theme is accentuated by opposing sides at the expense of the other. However true or false the account may be, history tends to be reduced to ideology, a means through which the social and political interests of each side of the cultural divide are legitimated.

PUBLIC PHILOSOPHY AND NATIONAL PRIORITY

Anything but abstract and inconsequential, both of these rival philosophies of public life translate into practical standards for evaluating America's identity and priorities in the global order. This became amply apparent in the Religion and Power Survey conducted by the Opinion Research Corporation in 1987.[42] The survey found that Protestant, Catholic, and Jewish leaders on both ends of the new cultural axis generally agreed that America bore tremendous responsibility in world affairs. Virtually all were prone to agree that the United States is not "pretty much like other countries" but "has a special role to play in the world today."[43] Leaders of all faiths were strongly disposed to affirm that "the United States should aspire to remain a world power" and not "a neutral country like Switzerland or Sweden."[44] But opposing factions sharply disagreed as to how the United States should actually carry out that responsibility. When asked, "How much confidence do you have in the ability of the United States to deal wisely with present world problems?" progressives in all three faiths were at least twice as likely as their more orthodox counterparts to say "not very much" or "none at all."[45]

The same kind of division was exhibited among the orthodox and progressives when asked to make moral assessments of America's place in the world order. The overwhelming majority of the orthodox in Protestant (78 percent), Catholic (73 percent), and Jewish (92 percent) leadership circles said, for example, that the United States was, in general, "a force for good in the world." By contrast, the majority of the progressives in Protestantism and Catholicism (51 percent and 56 percent, respectively) said that the United States was either "neutral" or "a force for ill."[46] The contrast was even more stark when respondents were asked to assess how America treats people in the Third World. Progressives, particularly Protestants (71 percent) and Catholics (87 percent), were much more likely to agree that America "treats people in the Third World unfairly." The majority of the orthodox in each tradition claimed just the opposite.[47]

Opposing perspectives of America's moral status in world affairs became apparent when respondents were asked to compare the United States and the Soviet Union. A plurality of all religious leaders characterized the competition between the United States and the Soviet Union as a struggle in power politics, as opposed to a moral struggle, yet the more orthodox Catholics and Protestants were three times more likely (and Orthodox Jews over twice as likely) to say that it was a moral struggle.[48] Ideological disparities between orthodox and progressive were even more dramatic, however, when asked which was the greater problem in the world today: repressive regimes aligned with the United States or Soviet expansion? The majority of progressives within Protestantism (61 percent), Catholicism (71 percent), and Judaism (57 percent) claimed that it was the repressive regimes aligned with the United States; the majority of the orthodox in these three faiths (Protestants—84 percent, Catholics—64 percent, and Jews—87 percent) identified Soviet expansion as the greater problem.

The results of a survey of the political opinion of Christian theologians conducted in 1982 reveal similar divisions in perspectives on domestic spending.[49] Nearly two-thirds (63 percent) of the progressives compared to under one-fifth (19 percent) of the orthodox claimed that the government was spending too little on welfare. Eighty percent of the progressives said that the government was spending too little on national health compared to just 52 percent of the Evangelicals. Likewise, nearly nine out of ten (89 percent) of the progressives agree that the government was spending too little on protecting the environment; just half (50 percent) of the orthodox Protestants felt the same way. Almost nine out of ten (87 percent) of the progressives complained that the government spent too little money on urban problems compared to 56 percent of the orthodox. And roughly six out of every ten of the progressives (59 percent) claimed that too little was spent on foreign aid; just one out of every four (24 percent) of the orthodox agreed.

MORAL AUTHORITY AND THE REALIGNMENT OF PUBLIC CULTURE

My main point thus far is to demonstrate that the opinions of elites reflect different and, in many cases, opposing visions of national identity and public life. They differ, then, in their public philosophies.

Yet even this does not quite capture what is fundamentally at issue here. The basic distinction I have insisted on bears repeating. To explain the nature of the emerging cultural realignment solely in terms of the differences in political philosophy as reflected in public opinion is to risk arguing that the primary contenders in the cultural conflict are really nothing more than political "liberals" and political "conservatives." The inadequacy of these terms which I suggested earlier, is immediately apparent. To conceptualize the problem as a political squabble, as some have proposed, is to suggest that the new and opposing alliances in American public life operate on the *same* plane of moral discussion.[50] Such a view would imply that each side shares the same ideals of moral community and national life, but that they simply envision different strategies for getting there. As we have observed, the orthodox tend to be conservative and the progressive tend to be liberal but those tendencies, I contend, are merely the *political manifestations of still deeper commitments.* In reality orthodox and progressive alliances do not operate on the same plane of moral discourse.

Others would argue that differences in political philosphy are reducible to social rank. Those holding orthodox commitments can be found among the disenfranchised lower middle class, the old petite bourgeoisie, who have incurred losses in power and privilege through the political and economic changes of the past decades. By contrast, this theory holds that progressivist commitments can be found among the rising "new class" of knowledge workers, the "new bourgeoisie," who have turned their control over cultural capital to social and political advantage. In its more simplified formulation, public philosophy is merely a reflection of class interests. But what this perspective fails to see is that the "new class" of knowledge workers is divided within itself. Traditional family proponent James Dobson of Focus on the Family, for example, is every bit as much a knowledge worker or symbol specialist—and therefore a member of the new class—as is Planned Parenthood's Faye Wattleton.

Political formulations of the debate, then, seem inadequate. Though there are clearly political manifestations of this dispute, the dispute is more than political. Likewise, while each side betrays certain social characteristics, the cultural controversy is much more than a reflection of competing class interests. There is, then, a more vital cultural dynamic involved in generating this cultural realignment. In this sense, the conflict is prepolitical and it precedes class. What ultimately explains the realignment in America's public culture are *allegiances to different formulations and sources of moral authority.*

Sources of Moral Authority

To speak of moral authority is to speak of the fundamental assumptions that guide our perceptions of the world. These assumptions provide answers to questions about the nature of reality—what is real and what isn't. For example, is there a spiritual as well as a physical and material realm of existence? Does God exist? If so, what is God's nature? Is God an active agent in human affairs or a distant ideal of human aspiration? These are also the assumptions that define the foundations of knowledge—how we know what we know. Upon what do we ground our knowledge of the world, our understanding of truth, and our conception of moral and ethical behavior? Does our knowledge derive from divine revelation, through the analysis of empirical evidence, or through personal and subjective experience? These assumptions act as a lens that highlights certain aspects of experience as important or unimportant, relevant or irrelevant, good or bad, and right or wrong. These generally unspoken assumptions are the basic standards by which we make moral judgments and decisions.

The point needs to be made that all individuals ground their views of the world within some conception of moral authority. Not only those who are religious in a traditional sense, but also those who claim to have no religious faith at all base their views of the world in unprovable assumptions about "being" and "knowledge." To imagine otherwise would be philosophically naive. It is precisely for this reason that the Religious Coalition for Abortion Rights and the Religious Coalition for Equality for Women include in their fellowship such secularist organizations as the American Humanist Association and the Ethical Culture Society, and speak of them literally as "communities of faith."[51] Even average, nonactivist secularists—ordinary people who maintain no religious belief, who worship no deity—live by unspoken assumptions about their world; they too are people of particular, even if implicit, faith commitments.

The view that perhaps comes closest to the argument offered here has been proposed by Richard Merleman. He has speculated that the strains in American culture are those that exist between the "tight-bounded" and "loose-bounded" moral communities within our society.[52] Moral obligation within tight-bounded communities tends to be fixed and rigid, viewed by its members as a "given" of social life. In opposition are loose-bounded communities for whom moral commitment tends to be voluntary, contingent, and fluid—where the liberated individual, not the social group, becomes the final arbiter of moral judgment. Merleman's perspective supports the argument made here; namely, that what finally *unites* the orthodox and the progressive *across* tradition and *divides* the orthodox and progressive *within* tradition are different formulations of moral authority. Here again, in social reality there is complexity and diversity. Even so, certain tendencies and commonalities exist on each side of the cultural divide that can be described in ideal-typical terms. What is the substance of each?

The Orthodox Appeal to Authority

Within communities that hold orthodox views, moral authority arises from a common commitment to transcendence, by which I mean a dynamic reality that is independent of, prior to, and more powerful than human experience. God and the realm God inhabits, for the orthodox, is indeed super- and supranatural. Of course transcendence has a different content and meaning in each tradition. In each tradition, moreover, transcendence communicates its authority through different media: for example, through the spiritual prerogatives of the inerrant Scriptures, both Old and New Testaments; through Torah and the community that upholds it; through the pope and the traditional teachings of the Catholic Church; through the Book of Mormon; and, small though the Unification Church may be, through Reverend Sun Myung Moon and the Divine Principle. Within each faith, the commitment to these specific media of moral authority is so forceful and unwavering that believers in each would consider sources other than their own as heretical.

Yet despite these differences, there are formal attributes to their faith that are held in common with the others. As argued earlier, each maintains a paramount commitment to an external, definable, and transcendent source of authority. For the believers in each tradition, moral and spiritual truths have a supernatural origin beyond and yet barely graspable by human experience. Although the media through which transcendence speaks to people varies (as noted earlier), they all believe that these truths are divinely "revealed" in these written texts and not somehow discovered through human endeavor or subjective experience apart from these texts. This implies that they also share a common method of interpreting their world and their experience. In this case transcendent authority is not just symbolic, but propositional; it is not just representational, but it has objective and concrete agency in human affairs. God, they would say, is real and makes Himself tangibly, directly, and even propositionally known in the everyday experience of individuals and communities. From this authority derives a measure of value, purpose, goodness, and identity that is consistent, definable, and even absolute. In matters of moral judgment, the unequivocal appeal of orthodoxy is to these uncompromisable standards. It is, then, an authority that is universally valid—adequate for every circumstance and context. It is an authority that is sufficient for all time.

Even though Rabbi Yehuda Levin is an Orthodox Jew and even though Orthodox Judaism is so sparsely represented in America, his views of moral truth speak in a general way for others on the orthodox side of the cultural divide—Evangelical Protestants and conservative Catholics. In this, his observations illustrate the argument well. Says Yehuda, "Being Jewish means a total surrender of my intellect to God. In other words, God tells me what's right and what's wrong. I may attempt in a limited capacity to try to understand that, but I have to start off from the point that I am surrendering my personal intellect to God. If something doesn't make sense to me, that has no bearing on the reality of it or my obligation to respond to it. God said I should observe the Sabbath, for example, so I observe the Sabbath. God said, 'Thou shalt not steal' and so I don't steal—not because 'crime doesn't pay,' but because God said not to steal. [Likewise with abortion] I do not need any proof that [the fetus] is human. In fact, if somebody somehow would bring proof positive—scientific evidence—tomorrow that the fetus is just a glob of gelatin or something like that, it would not in one iota change my view on abortion." Levin's general orientation is precisely what Harriet Woods meant when she said that "they [Evangelicals, conservative Catholics like Mae Duggan, and Orthodox Jews like Yehuda Levin] cannot hold people by rational argument or by pragmatic results."

As noted in chapter 1, there are secularists on the orthodox side of the new cultural divide. The philosopher Sidney Hook, a celebrated atheist and conservative, and the political philosopher Leo Strauss (and his school) both come to mind. One may also find in the orthodox ranks many secular neoconservative intellectuals for whom religiously grounded arguments hold aesthetic or even functional appeal, but are not personally or inwardly compelling. One should not gloss over the sometimes deep philosophical disagreements between the religiously orthodox and such secularists, for whom the public pronouncements of Protestant Fundamentalists and of some orthodox Catholics will often seem excessive, even silly. More often than not, however, the crankier voices of religious orthodoxy are tolerated in silence, if only because these secularists recognize them to be fellow travelers working toward a common mission.

What forges their bond with the religiously orthodox is that they too are committed to a transcendent foundation for moral judgment. Theirs, however, tends to be a classic form of humanism, in which a high view of nature, natural law, or the social order itself acts as a functional equivalent to an objective and transcendent authority. What makes their view of nature or the social order "high" is a belief that nature is intrinsically rational, that it reflects a logical order that human beings are able to discern. As such, while truth and the good are subject to the change that affects nature itself, they are relatively durable over time and across societies.

Based upon this general understanding of moral authority are certain non-negotiable moral "truths." Among the most relevant for the present purposes are that the world, and all of the life within it, was created by God, and that human life begins at conception and, from that point on, it is sacred. Another "truth" is that the human species is differentiated into male and female not only according to genitalia, but also according to role, psyche, and spiritual calling. Related to this idea is the belief that the natural and divinely mandated sexual relationship among humans is between male and female and this relationship is legitimate only under one social arrangement, marriage between one male and one female. Homosexuality, therefore, is a perversion of the natural or created order. Building on this is the conviction that the nuclear family is the natural form of family structure and should remain inviolable from outside (state) interference. And this idea encompasses the belief in the inviolable rights of parents—their right to raise their children into their own religious and moral tradition, the implication being that this role should be encouraged and not hindered by a secular, liberal educational establishment.

The Progressivist Appeal to Authority

The progressivist vision of moral authority poses a sharp contrast. For progressivists, moral authority is based, at least in part, in the resymbolization of historic faiths and philosophical traditions. Of course, all religious communities (even the orthodox) resymbolize their traditions, but the orthodox tend to do it unwittingly and as a defensive measure when they feel threatened.[53] In the progressivist alliance, however, resymbolization is accomplished more or less consciously, deliberately, and in a way that is compatible with the spirit of historical change. Consider first the appeal to authority advocated by those who profess a liberal religious faith.

The premise of this resymbolization is usually the intentional rejection of the form and content of orthodoxy. Such a rejection varies in degree and intensity, as one might imagine, but all progressivists maintain to a certain degree that the language and programmatic thrust of traditional faith—at least as appropriated by their orthodox counterparts—is no longer relevant for modern times. Traditional faith must be reworked to conform to new circumstances and conditions; it must respond to new challenges and needs. What compels this rejection of orthodoxy is the conviction that moral and spiritual truth is not a static and unchanging collection of scriptural facts and theological propositions, but a growing and incremental reality. Faith should continually develop, in part because the object of faith (or at least our understanding of it) is continually developing.

There is, therefore, no objective and final revelation directly from God, and Scripture (of whatever form) is not revelation but only, and at best, a *witness* to revelation. The moral and spiritual truths of religious faith can only come to human beings indirectly and they can only be understood and expressed in human (which is to say, historical and institutional) terms. Thus, moral and spiritual truth can only be conditional and relative. This orientation is well illustrated by the views of both Richmond Young and Bea Blair. Richmond chose to embrace Catholicism in part because he believed that the Catholic Church was not bound by the doctrine of the inerrancy of Scripture. What is more, the Magisterium in his view may be an agent of divine truth but in the end is a human and therefore fallible institution. A similar attitude about the humanity of Scripture is taken by Bea Blair. She "of course" is not a "literalist." Scripture, she says, "must be interpreted," not taken at face value. In a negative way this view is acknowledged by the progressivists' adversaries as well. Yehuda Levin's complaint about liberal and secular Jews like Harriet Woods is that "they do not consider themselves bound by the sources. They do not give any legitimacy to the Talmud, they are not bound by the code of Jewish law or the Halakah or even bound to what Maimonides, the greatest formulator of classical Judaism, says or anything else for that matter. They make up the rules as they play the game. I don't think they can deny this." This is also the criticism that Chuck McIlhenny directed at the liberal churchmen and women who supported the domestic partners proposal in San Francisco. "They reject what the Bible says about itself. They say it is not inspired, that it's just a human book like anything else."

For this reason the legacy of faith for progressivists becomes valuable not as the literal account of historic personalities and events in relation to God, but primarily (and perhaps only) as a narrative that points to ethical principles that can be applied to contemporary human experience. In the case of scriptural hermeneutics, what is important in the scriptural accounts of God's dealings with His people is not whether they literally occurred but what they symbolize about human relationships today.

To say that the progressivist wings of Protestantism, Catholicism, and Judaism have largely rejected the absolute authority of their traditions is not, therefore, to suggest that their traditions have become in any way irrelevant or socially impotent. The traditions still provide a powerful sense of continuity with the past, inform a style of communal worship and interpersonal solidarity, and guide their communities in the search for universal ethical principles—principles that have as their ultimate end the fulfillment of human needs and aspirations.

We can see a deep affinity between the cultural hermeneutics of liberal religious belief (Protestant, Catholic, or Jewish) and of civic (or areligious) humanism. Both activist humanists (as found in such groups as the American Humanist Association, Ethical Culture, and the Council for Democratic and Secular Humanism) and the larger, nonactivist, secularist public reject the validity of any traditional religious symbols and rituals. They also tend to be particularly hostile toward orthodox religious belief.[54] But there are important positive affinities between religious and secular progressives as well. Like their counterparts during the classical era, the Italian Renaissance, and the French Enlightenment, the contemporary expressions of areligious humanism also maintain the fundamental conviction that moral truth is perpetually unfolding; that moral truth is a human construction and, therefore, is both conditional and relative; and that moral truths should reflect ethical principles that have the human good as their highest end.

In sum, within the broader progressivist alliance (both religious and secular), moral authority emerges primarily if not exclusively within "this-worldly" considerations. The inner-worldly sources of moral authority may vary in at least two ways. First, the progressive conception can be based in what could be called "self-grounded rational discourse."

In intellectual terms, this is the tradition of "Enlightenment naturalism"—of Thomas Hobbes, the Enlightenment encyclopedists, Baron D'Holbach, John Dewey, Willard van Orman Quine, Wilfrid Sellars, and others.[55] Here, in principle, moral positions and influence are justified solely on the grounds of evidence about the human condition and the coherence and consistency of the arguments adduced. Not only are the nature of reality and the foundations of knowledge established by the adequacy of empirical proofs uncovered and the quality and coherence of the logic applied, but in this frame of reference, autonomous rationality and the empirical method become the decisive criteria for evaluating the credibility and usefulness of all moral claims as well. In the more extreme scientistic formulations, it is argued that there is no reality except that which science has shown to exist; no truth except that which is established by the scientific method. Such claims are common in debates (often in the context of a lawsuit) over medical policy, educational policy, or other forms of public policy, where the ethics of a particular action—say in the area of genetic therapy, or in the value of educational curricula, or in the promotion of child-care regulations—depend upon scientific proof that people are helped, or at least not hurt, by that course of action. If expert knowledge—from, say, educational or family psychologists—can show that a course of action has no untoward psychological effects on people, then that action is morally permissible.

On a second and very different plane of moral reasoning, the progressivist conception of moral authority may be based in personal experience. This is probably the dominant basis of moral reasoning on this side of the cultural divide. In intellectual terms, this is the tradition of Enlightenment subjectivism—of Kant, Existentialism, and the various streams of Heideggerian hermeneutical philosophy such as found in Wittgenstein and Richard Rorty. In this case, experience is ordered and moral judgments are made according to a logic rooted in subjective intuition and understanding. (The premise here is that by virtue of our symbolic activity, we human beings are responsible for the way the world is.) The moral logic of this position, as it translates into popular culture, has been described in numerous ways by social scientists in recent years, perhaps most commonly as liberal or expressive individualism. This concept implies a moral pragmatism centered around the individual's perception of his or her own emotional needs or psychological disposition. In this situation, reason linked with a keen awareness of subjective orientation provides the ultimate crucible for determining what is right and wrong, legitimate and illegitimate—and ultimately what is good and evil. The cliché that beauty lies in the eyes of the beholder is expanded and elevated to the status of a fundamental moral principle—that what people view as ultimately true, morally good, worthwhile, artistically pleasing, sensually pleasurable, and so on, resides wholly in the private whim or personal perspective of individuals. Private perspectives are inextricably bound to the individual's unique collection of experiences. In some ways, biography is the main foundation of truth.

As with orthodoxy, a list, if you will, of specific precepts tends to emanate from the progressivist conceptions of moral authority. Among the most relevant here are the assumptions that personhood begins at or close to the moment of birth, at least until science can prove otherwise. Likewise, until science can prove otherwise, male and female are differentiated solely by biology; other differences are probably human constructions imposed through socialization and reinforced in human relationships by powerful and sometimes oppressive institutions. So too, human sexuality is based in biological need. The forms in which those needs are met are historically and culturally variable and completely legitimate as long as those forms reflect a positive and caring relationship. Homosexuality, then, does not represent an absolute and fundamental perversion of nature but simply one way in which nature can evolve and be expressed. As one gay activist put it, we should "appropriate our sexuality not as something biologically necessitated, or as socially coerced, but as a freely chosen way of expressing our authentic humanness in relation to the special others with whom we wish to share our lives."[56] In like fashion, marriage and family structures are historically and culturally varied. Their form, by and large, depends upon need and circumstance.[57]

In sum, the orthodox communities order themselves, live by, and build upon the substance of a shared commitment to transcendent truths and the moral traditions that uphold them. The very identity of these communities is "bound tightly" around that tradition.[58] Moral authority on the progressivist side of the cultural divide tends not to be burdened by the weight of either "natural law," religious prerogative, or traditional community authority. Rather, as Merleman put it, it is a "loose-bounded" authority, detached from the cultural moorings of traditional group membership. As such it carries few, if any, of the burdens of the past. Memory does not inhibit change: authority is distinctly forward-looking, open-ended, and malleable. Thus, this is a form of moral authority that is uniquely shaped by and oriented toward legitimating the prevailing *zeitgeist* or spirit of the age.

Moral Authority and Political Expedience

The orthodox and progressivist conceptions of moral authority and the range of specific assumptions that follow from them are obviously more complex than the rough sketches presented here. Nonetheless, what is important is that they bear on political philosophy and practice in direct ways. The most obvious way is with regard to controversial issues of the day: abortion, the ERA, gay rights, educational policy, and the like. The assumptions and the interests of each alliance preclude or endorse the specific proposals from the outset. Moral logic reflects those interests and assumptions. Thus, for example, abortion is murder and must be stopped if human life is defined as beginning at conception. Legalized abortion is morally acceptable and therefore a viable public policy if life is defined as beginning with the first breath at birth or perhaps the third or even second trimester of pregnancy. By a similar logic, homosexuality is a perversion if the only legitimate sexuality is between a man and a woman. Homosexuality between consenting adults is acceptable and sodomy laws anachronistic if we assume that there are many justifiable ways of satisfying human biological needs. Equalizing the role of women will be undesirable if it appears to threaten the "traditional" patriarchal family structure. If the "bourgeois family" is regarded as just one possible familial arrangement (and one that tends in practice to be oppressive), legislation on behalf of the rights of women will seem both fitting and desirable. Similarly direct correspondences between assumptions and policy positions can be found vis-à-vis the day-care debate, the eugenics controversy, euthanasia, the many issues that make up the disputes over religion and public education, and a host of other issues.

But the relationship between moral authority and political expedience goes beyond the predictable responses to policy issues. It is often asked how, for example, a fundamentalist view leads to opposition to America's relinquishing control over the Panama Canal, or how being a liberal Catholic leads one to support the proposition of "comparable worth." On the face of it, having certain religious commitments does not seem to have anything at all in common with certain specific political commitments. Yet seemingly strange patterns of alliance constantly surface in political life. Perhaps the best answer to questions like these is simply to say that there is a loose affinity between religious orientation and political opinions. Specifically, there seems to be a loose affinity or "isomorphism" between religious conservatism and political preservationism on the one hand, and between religious and even secular liberalism and political reformism (if not radicalism) on the other.[59] These general affinities lead people of particular cultural orientations to not-so-predictable political commitments. This might help explain why, for example, the religiously orthodox tend to be more disposed toward a strong military and an aggressive foreign policy. The religious self-identity of the orthodox groups draws much from America's role as a world power (for example, by checking "godless" communist expansion, by defending Israel, and so on). Religious interests are at least indirectly tied to America's geopolitical interests. This isomorphism also partially explains the opposing relationships between religion and capitalism, particularly in Protestantism: the religious individualism of Evangelical Protestantism and economic individualism mirror each other in much the same way as religious communalism (as expressed in the ethical tradition of the social gospel) and economic collectivism. It might also explain why *both* orthodox and progressivist camps (correctly) accuse each other of supporting policies that engender the intrusion of the state into private life. The enactment of law that endorses a shifting cultural climate will be perceived as an intrusion by those who resist the present cultural changes; the reversal of these laws or the attempt to prohibit their enactment will be perceived as an intrusion by those who approve of these changes and whose interests are served by them.

IN SEPARATE WORLDS

The central dynamic of the cultural realignment is not merely that different public philosophies create diverse public opinions. These alliances, rather, reflect the *institutionalization and politicization of two fundamentally different cultural systems.* Each side operates from within its own constellation of values, interests, and assumptions. At the center of each are two distinct conceptions of moral authority—two different ways of apprehending reality, of ordering experience, of making moral judgments. Each side of the cultural divide, then, speaks with a different moral vocabulary. Each side operates out of a different mode of debate and persuasion. Each side represents the tendencies of a separate and competing moral galaxy. They are, indeed, "worlds apart."

The Interminable Character of Moral Debate

As a consequence of this mutual moral estrangement, concessions on many policy matters become a virtual impossibility. The abortion debate exemplifies this most poignantly, particularly in the voices of those who care most passionately about the outcome. No one on the pro-life side of this controversy doubts that "God's gift of life begins at conception." How do we know this? "The Bible clearly states that life begins at conception."[60] Thus, the Old and New Testament texts are copiously cited. But what is more, modern science also demonstrates that there is life in the womb. After all, "The unborn child has a beating heart at 24 days, brain waves and unique fingerprints at 43 days, a complete skeleton and reflexes at 6 weeks," and so on. Abortion, therefore, could never be anything else than the "killing of innocent life." For this reason, "the abortion of the 22 million fetuses between 1973 and 1988" is nothing short of "mass genocide." The moral choice, then, is clear: one is, as a Methodists for Life brochure put it, "either for life or against life; for Jesus or against Jesus."[61]

The moral logic is fundamentally different on the pro-choice side of the controversy. Arguments also grounded in theological and scientific insight show that there is "an important distinction between potential life and actual life" and that fetuses "are not of equal moral value with actual persons."[62] After all, "The biblical characterization of human being is that of a complex, many-sided creature with the god-like ability and responsibility to make choices. The fetus hardly meets those characteristics."[63] On this side too, as the Religious Coalition for Abortion Rights makes clear, abortion is a religious issue. Not only do different faith traditions hold different theological and philosophical beliefs about "personhood," they also hold different ideas about when abortion is morally justified. The bottom line, according to the Religious Coalition for Abortion Rights and other progressivist groups, is simply this: "If abortion is a religious issue, and religious theologies differ, and each denomination counsels its members according to its own theology, wouldn't a law prohibiting abortion violate religious liberty? Exactly. . . . The issue of abortion is a crucial test of religious liberty—one of the cornerstones of democracy."[64]

The reality of politics and public policy in a democracy is, for better or worse, compromise born out of public discussion and debate. But such discussion would seem to be unattainable when the moral language employed by opposing sides is so completely antithetical. One can easily imagine an Evangelical Protestant, charismatic Catholic, Hasidic Jew, or a Mormon asking rhetorically: "How can murder be a First Amendment right?" One could also imagine a liberal Protestant, liberal Catholic, Reform Jew, or secularist asking just the opposite: "How can the exercise of basic First Amendment rights be called murder?" Political resolution seems sociologically impossible when the moral languge for talking about mutual problems is so contrary.

This problem is also crystallized within the debates about homosexuality. For the orthodox communities, homosexuality is "the zenith of human indecency"—a sin "so grievous, so abominable in the sight of God that he destroyed the cities of Sodom and Gomorrah because of [it]."[65] For most progressivists, homosexuality is "not unscriptural" but simply an alternative sexual lifestyle; one other way in which loving relationships can be expressed.[66] Once again each employs a fundamentally different moral vocabulary to understand this behavior. For one side, homosexuality is sin; for the other, homosexuality is "just one type of human behavior"—the only sin is the "sinful discrimination against lesbians and gay men."[67] As a consequence, any mutually agreeable resolution of policy, much less cultural consensus, is almost unimaginable.

Virtually the same moral impasse has been reached in discussions about war, inequality, pornography and obscenity, euthanasia, the use of fetal tissue for medical research, and other controversies. All of these disputes, as Alasdair MacIntyre has described them, are characterized by an "interminable character."[68] True, not all of these issues are equally polarizing. Nevertheless, the existence of common moral ground from which to build and resolve differences appears to be equally elusive in every case.

The moral arguments on either side of these disputes appeal with equal facility to the evidence of science (as, for example, in discussions about human biology), the precedents (or lack of precedents) from social history, and the legitimations of theology and biblical textual analysis. At least from a lay person's point of view, the logic of the competing claims is equally rigorous. But in the end, whether concerned with abortion, homosexuality, women's rights, day care, or any other major moral or political issue of the day, the tools of logic and the evidence from science, history, and theology can do nothing to alter the opinions of their opposition. Because each side interprets them differently, logic, science, history, and theology can only serve to enhance and legitimate particular ideological interests. The willingness or unwillingness of opposing groups to have a "dialogue" about their differences is largely irrelevant. Even a spirit of compromise maintained by either side would be irrelevant. *In the final analysis, each side of the cultural divide can only talk past the other.*

The orthodox and progressivist impulses provide the foundations not only for competing moral visions, then, but for competing dogmas. This is true because what both sides bring to this public debate is, at least consciously, non-negotiable. What is ultimately at issue, then, are not just disagreements about "values" or "opinions." Such language misconstrues the nature of moral commitment. Such language in the end reduces morality to preferences and cultural whim. What is ultimately at issue are deeply rooted and fundamentally different understandings of being and purpose.

To put this in the terms proposed by the French sociologist Emile Durkheim, what is ultimately at issue are different conceptions of the sacred. For Durkheim, the sacred was not necessarily embodied in a divine or supernatural being, the sacred could be anything that was viewed as "set apart" and "exalted"; anything that provided the life-orienting principles of individuals and the larger community. To know the nature of the sacred in each moral community is to know the source of their passion, the wellspring of their fervor. The reality, as Durkheim pointed out, is that communities cannot and will not tolerate the desecration of the sacred. The problem is this: not only does each side of the cultural divide operate with a different conception of the sacred, but the mere existence of the one represents a certain desecration of the other.

The Historical Significance

Needless to say, this cultural realignment has tremendous historical significance. Few would disagree that the rise of Christianity as a world religion between the first and third centuries, and the success of the Protestant Reformation in the sixteenth century created the most fundamental cultural divisions in the history of Western civilization: those that divide Christian from Jew and Protestant from Catholic. As described earlier, the historical effect of these divisions was not only "religious" or cultural but manifestly and irrefutably political as well. They have been at the root of centuries of prejudice and discrimination. They have been at the heart of social strife and even war.

But if the organizing principle of American pluralism is shifting in the direction described here—so that progressively oriented Protestants,

Catholics, Jews, and secularists share more in common with each other culturally and politically than they do with the orthodox members of their *own* faith tradition (and vice versa)—then the practical effects of the birth of Christianity and the Reformation have, at least in the U.S. context, become both politically and culturally defunct.

If the organizing principle of American pluralism has shifted in these ways, then, it is because another world-historical "event" has become paramount. Yielding to the temptation of hyperbole, it could be said that the politically relevant divisions in the American context are no longer defined according to where one stands vis-à-vis Jesus, Luther, or Calvin, but where one stands vis-à-vis Rousseau, Voltaire, Diderot, and Condorcet, and especially their philosophical heirs (including Nietzsche and Rorty). The politically relevant world-historical event, in other words, is now the secular Enlightenment of the eighteenth century and its philosophical aftermath. This is what inspires the divisions of public culture in the United States today.

This, of course, is a caricature of our situation. Virtually everyone, nowadays, is influenced by the profound philosophical reorientation of the Enlightenment with its rejection of otherworldly "superstitions" and its emphasis on societal progress through human mastery over nature and rational judgment. Even the most Bible-believing Evangelical, the most Rome-bound Catholic, and the most observant Orthodox Jew has been influenced in subtle even if unacknowledged ways. What really divides our culture is the matter of priority—the sources upon which different moral communities rely *most* in establishing their own sense of right and wrong. Clearly there are people at each extreme, particularly those who act as voices for opposing communities. There are also, as we recognized in chapter 1, many people somewhere in the middle, who draw in varying degrees from both Enlightenment and biblical sources of moral understanding. (The fate of the "middle"—the majority of Americans—will be discussed in chapter 6.) Still, as a historical event, the Enlightenment has become an increasingly prominent source of division in American public life. The division is certainly "religious" or cultural, but it has unmistakably political consequences too. Already these have begun to take expression as new forms of prejudice, discrimination, social strife, and political conflict.

III

CULTURAL WARFARE

5

The Discourse of Adversaries

The demand for moral clarity in the larger public order issues from a wide variety of sources. First, there is a certain requirement for commonly held ideals to sustain national identity. There is also a practical need for a universal system of law and justice. Not least is a strong public desire for a common heritage within which to educate succeeding generations of children. All of these factors, as well as others, create extraordinary pressure to find and maintain commonly held symbols—the symbols that make collective life possible.

As has been seen already, the realignment in American public culture entails a deep division that centers around what those symbols will be and the way they are to be interpreted. It goes without saying that this realignment involves more than a passive ideological gerrymandering—the redrawing of ideological boundaries and affinities around different political and even philosophical issues. The realignment has brought about not only subterranean friction in public culture but open conflict. But what is the nature of that conflict? How does it take form and expression? This chapter examines the tone and the temper of the conflict; so doing will make it possible to see more clearly what is ultimately at stake in the realignment of American public culture.

DISCREDITING THE OPPOSITION

The struggle to institutionalize a particular vision of national identity and purpose is always an effort to gain the widest public approval possible—in a word, to achieve legitimation. Basically, two strategies, one negative and the other positive, are involved in the struggle. The *positive face* of moral conflict is expressed through constructive moral reasoning and debate, as opposing factions articulate their ideals for "the way things should be." By grounding the "rightness" or legitimacy of their claims in logic, science, humanitarian concerns, or in an appeal to tradition or God, each side endeavors to persuade its opponents, as well as all others who might listen, of the superiority of its claims. Such is the ideal of civility in public discourse.

Yet the contemporary cultural conflict poses a special dilemma. Given the incompatible nature of the polarizing cultural impulses, positive moral argument is simply insufficient as a way of achieving any real advantage over the opposition. In other words, because each side operates out of a fundamentally different conception of moral authority, because each side uses a radically different measure of moral sensibility, because each side employs a markedly different kind of moral logic, neither side will ever be able to persuade the other of the superiority of its own claims. Positive moral argument may have some sway over the ambivalent, but by itself it would not go very far toward inaugurating a new moral crusade; alone it could never have much effect on shifting the weight of popular opinion in favor of one cause and against its opposition.

As a consequence, the struggle to gain legitimation requires something besides positive moral persuasion. Inevitably it entails the existence of an enemy to stand against. This is the *negative face* of moral conflict: the deliberate, systematic effort to discredit the opposition. In the culture war, this negative aspect of the conflict has taken on a life and force of its own; indeed, neutralizing the opposition through a strategy of public ridicule, derision, and insult has become just as important as making credible moral claims for the world that each side champions. Arguably, this negative persuasion has become even more important, for in public discourse, "dialogue" has largely been replaced by name calling, denunciation, and even outright intolerance. In the words of the old adage, the contemporary culture war has become a contest that will determine "not who is right but who is left."

Historical Antecedents

Just as the divisions in contemporary public life have certain precedents, so too the hostility shared by each side of the contemporary cultural divide is not entirely novel. In 1927, for example, the president of the Science League of America wrote a spirited polemic on the relationship between Christian Fundamentalism and modern science, and declared that "in the United States today there exist, side by side, two opposing cultures, one or the other of which must eventually dominate our public institutions, political, legal, educational, and social. On the one side we see arrayed the forces of progress and enlightenment, on the other the forces of reaction, the apostles of traditionalism. There can be no compromise between these diametrically opposed armies."[1]

The clash to which he was referring, however, was already more than a century old. Indeed, antecedents to the contemporary antagonism appeared soon after the founding of the new republic, in the antagonism between Evangelical pietists and organized deism, in the Evangelical-based hysteria over the so-called conspiracy of the Illuminati.[2] Similar hostility arose in the Evangelical-based, anti-Masonic movement of the early to mid-1800s.[3] Bitter precursors to the contemporary secular resentment against orthodoxy also existed through the early nineteenth century.[4] The belligerence was mutual. Other, more comparable precedents to our present situation occurred in the late nineteenth and early twentieth century.

Against "Infidelity"

Hostility toward religious infidelity and irreligion was voiced by Protestants and Catholics alike. Although Protestants and Catholics recognized the prevailing influence of Christianity, it was considered that there was already enough sin in American society and the situation would only get worse if atheism were to prevail.[5]

From the perspective of many traditionalists, the further introduction of sinful ideas was precisely what happened in the last decades of the nineteenth century and first decades of the twentieth century in the contest between science and faith, between the evolutionary and creationist views of human origins. The organizational efforts by Protestant Fundamentalists (and some Catholics) to dam the flow of these intellectual currents made the contest a national issue.[6] Behind these efforts was a profound hatred of modernism in all of its forms.

In 1926 the Bible Crusaders of America formed: its special mission was to "combat Modernism, Evolution, Agnosticism and Atheism." This was only one of many such groups, such as the World Christian Fundamentals Association (1919) and the Defenders of the Christian Faith (1925). The religiously orthodox were engaged in nothing short of a "relentless warfare [with] Evolution and Modernism."[7] The intensity of rancor felt by Fundamentalists toward those who propagated modernist ideas was expressed sharply by one clergyman from North Carolina when he called them "jackass preachers without faith," a "gang [that] consists of newspaper editors and scientists, who *should be exiled out of our country* for insulting the high moral standard of the creation of human life, Christianity and civilization, for they are not one hundred percent American, but an insane set of ignorant, educated fools, who insist on lowering their own organic life to that of a monkey or animal. Take a jackass, a hog and a skunk and tie them together and you have a scientific evolutionist or a Modernist."[8] An editorial published in the *Los Angeles Examiner* in 1923 voiced similar views: "Take the evolutionists, infidels and no-hell teachers out somewhere and crucify them, head downward, and we will have a better country to live in and, instead of these evolution and easy-way ideas, teach people the Word of God to go by, and all will be well."[9]

Why such animosity? For one, such intellectual currents, especially the ideas of evolution, were seen as "utterly false." As one clergyman put it, "Scientific statements on the descent of man and survival of the fittest are simply camouflage for infidelity."[10] Because the liberal view of Scripture and of religious tradition was false it was also, in the words of a resolution made by a Baptist congregation in Arkansas in 1926, "dangerous, deceptive and destructive to the cause of Christianity."[11] Two weeks before the Scopes trial in Dayton, Tennessee, the author of the state bill outlawing the teaching of evolution stated a similar opinion in the *New York Times*:

> I regard evolution to be the greatest menace to civilization in the world today. It goes hand in hand with modernism; makes Jesus Christ a faker; robs the Christian of his hope and undermines the foundation of our "government of the people, for the people and

> by the people." People are free in this country to worship God as they please but they are not free to do everything that the devil wants done.[12]

A Lutheran pastor went even further in describing the ill effects of modernist thinking, when he declared that

> liberalism wrecked Eden's happiness and perfection; it condemned Jesus to the death on the cross; it fought the spread of Christianity from the start. Less than 400 years after the first Pentecost, liberalism nearly succeeded in destroying the soul of Christianity. It came down like a blight on the fruits of the Reformation; it has caused in part the large number of divisions by which the visible church is rent. It is the source of present-day crime waves.[13]

Animosity toward liberal and secularistic tendencies in religion and academia remained clamorous through the 1920s, and continued through the 1950s, though as American Fundamentalism retreated from public visibility, so too its hostility toward the forces that had caused it fell from public attention. There were a few exceptions, of course. In the 1920s and 1930s, Gerald B. Winrod accused modernists of "shar[ing] more basic principles with atheism than with orthodox Protestantism."[14] In the 1930s, Billy Sunday denounced modernists as "evolutionary hot-air merchants." And in the 1940s, James M. Gray of the Moody Bible Institute argued that modernism was a prelude to "the red doctrine of the Third International."[15] Reverend Carl MacIntyre, the founder of the antimodernist American Council of Christian Churches (1941) and ally of Senator Joseph McCarthy, relentlessly attacked liberal Protestantism through the 1940s and 1950s. "A man who calls himself a modernist," he wrote, "is not a Christian." Modernists "are infidels, and must be forever tagged as such." Pointing to the leaders of the "liberal" Presbyterian Church, U.S.A., he claimed, "These men are not Christians. . . . They are no more Presbyterian than the Devil himself." The Federal Council of Churches, he said, promoted "apostasy." For MacIntyre, modernism was nothing short of "paganism," a "treason to the cause of Christ." Thus, the struggle between Fundamentalism and modernism was really "the struggle between belief and unbelief—between [true] Christianity and paganism." Through vigilance, "the stealth and stupidity of [the] enemy [would] be exposed."[16]

The language and themes of malice toward "infidelity" and "irreligion," then, have been persistent within the Evangelical wing of orthodoxy. But the champions of Enlightenment rationality never suffered silently. Progressive voices within organized religion and the voices of more militant secular rationalists reciprocated throughout the decades.

Against "Theocracy"

Although organized deism as a self-conscious movement declined in the 1800s, the legacy of Enlightenment rationalism continued during the late nineteenth century through the efforts of the Unitarians, the Universalists, a few obscure free thought magazines, and mavericks such as Robert "Pagan Bob" Ingersoll.[17] Until he retired in 1899, Ingersoll was one of the greatest orators of the Gilded Age, especially noted for his diatribes against traditional religion. Ingersoll, a great admirer of Thomas Paine, accused organized and orthodox religion of keeping people both physical and mental slaves to a dead dogma.[18] Speaking to established religion, Ingersoll wrote,

> You have imprisoned the human mind; you have been the enemy of liberty; you have burned us at the stake—wasted us upon slow fires—torn our flesh with iron; you have covered us with chains—treated us as outcasts; you have filled the world with fear; you have taken our wives and children from our arms; you have confiscated our property; you have denied us the right to testify in courts of justice; you have branded us with infamy. . . . In the name of your religion you have robbed us of every right; and after having inflicted upon us every evil that can be inflicted in this world, you have fallen upon your knees, and with clasped hands implored your God to torment us forever.[19]

In contrast, Ingersoll claimed, "The doubter, the investigator, the Infidel, have been the saviors of liberty."[20]

The unbroken thread of liberal and secularist criticism of orthodox religion escalated as the Fundamentalist-modernist controversy emerged in the early twentieth century.[21] By this time its popular base of support was widening. No longer the fulminations of freethinkers and Unitarians, such criticism of authoritarian religion became the stock of nearly all progressively minded intellectuals. By the time Sinclair Lewis had published his tale of the odious preacher Elmer Gantry in 1927, the images of the hypocrite, the swindler, the charlatan, and the bigot had already become an established part of the Fundamentalist stereotype.

But the public image of Fundamentalists portrayed by modernists and secular intellectuals went beyond this as well. All Southern conservative Protestants came to be identified as "religious zealots," even "barbarians"; their culture came to be linked with "militant ignorance"; and their worries about cultural change were viewed as a "sinister movement" marked by a "propaganda of intolerance, hatred, bigotry and violence" within which lay the potential for "another bloody, terrible Inquisition."[22] In *The War on Modern Science* (1927), Maynard Shipley wrote,

> The forces of obscurantism in the United States are in open revolt. . . . The armies of ignorance are being organized, literally by the millions. . . . If the self-styled Fundamentalists can gain control over our state and national governments—which is one of their avowed objectives—much of the best that has been gained in American culture will be suppressed or banned, and we shall be headed backwards toward the pall of a new Dark Age.[23]

The prospects were "alarming." He wrote, "If the Fundamentalist forces can gain control of our political and judicial institutions, our country will ere long be converted into a relentless Fundamentalist theocracy, under which religious and academic freedom will eventually be totally suppressed."[24] The "peril to our modern civilization," though, was not just a possibility for the future. It was a present danger. As another individual announced (referring to the effects of the Scopes trial), "The church is the Rock of Ages blocking the road to enlightenment. We must make our schools safe from theocracy."[25] Another modernist preacher put the matter even more bluntly: "Religious zealots barricade the road of progress, put out the eyes of intelligence, mutilate learning and nail reason to the cross."[26]

Yet in the works of the literary and social critic H. L. Mencken, Fundamentalist bashing became something of an art form. For him, the ultimate enemy of American civilization was the Puritan; he wrote to a colleague in 1916, "My whole life, once I get free from my present engagements, will be devoted to combatting Puritanism."[27] Mencken called Fundamentalists "yokels," "half-wits," "hillbillies," "peasants," "gaping primates," "anthropoid rabble," "morons," and "Babbitts." He called their ministers "shamans," "militants," "inquisitors," "one-horse Popes," "amateur Messiahs," "the most ignorant class of teachers ever set up to guide a presumably civilized people," and their beliefs "nonsensical," "degraded nonsense," "malignant imbecility," a "childish theology" that was "cunningly rolled in sugar and rammed down unsuspecting throats." His attacks on William Jennings Bryan, the champion of Fundamentalism at the Scopes trial, were particularly savage.

> If the fellow [Bryan] was sincere, then so was P. T. Barnum. The word is disgraced and degraded by such uses. He was, in fact, a charlatan, a mountebank, a zany without shame or dignity. . . . [At Dayton] he seemed only a poor clod like those around him, deluded by a childish theology, full of an almost pathological hatred of all learning, all human dignity, all beauty, all fine and noble things. He was a peasant come home to the barnyard. Imagine a gentleman, and you have imagined everything that he was not. . . . [To his Fundamentalist followers], he was the peer of Abraham. . . . Bryan made the grade. His place in Tennessee hagiography is secure. If the village barber saved any of his hair, then it is curing gall-stones down there today.[28]

Of course, this attack was not leveled so much at Bryan himself as it was at what Bryan represented. Mencken's venomous satire reflected the judgment of an entire generation of progressively oriented church people and secular intellectuals.

As Fundamentalism retreated from public visibility beginning in the late 1930s so too did the counterattacks. Yet the animosity lay just beneath the surface of public dialogue. The mainline periodical *Christian Century* tended to ignore much of Fundamentalism, but when it did address such issues, the journal claimed that dispensationalism was not only "pagan" and "extremist," but also a "neurotic" movement allied with "reactionary" capitalists.[29] The "emotional fundamentalist Protestantism" that "dominates the Bible belt" was criticized for "aid[ing] the fascist effort." "This type of religion," Harry F. Ward wrote in the *Century,* "thrives on war and the disasters that follow war."[30] Particularly vituperative were the *Century*'s attacks on the Fundamentalism of Carl MacIntyre, who through his "baseless and deliberately deceptive charges" spawned a "hate campaign" against American religion, creating "religious discord and tumult."[31]

A Motif for the Present?

Both sides, then, have long sought to undermine each other's credibility and legitimacy in the public realm. In this legacy there is much that speaks to the present. The contours of past antagonisms parallel today's antagonisms both in terms of the temper of debate and in the substance of the specific criticisms articulated. The fact that the culture bashing was performed by elites and activists on either side and not by the organized laity is also analogous to the present situation. But there is much that is brand new in the contemporary situation. The most obvious novelty is that it is no longer primarily a Protestant phenomenon (fundamentalist versus modernist) or a clash between pietists and the deistic and atheistic humanists. The base of active involvement is much wider. And the range of issues has broadened. It is more than a debate about science, more than a debate about drink, more than a debate about the uses and meaning of the Bible. These are no longer the ultimate issues. A completely different approach to public life is at stake, as is a fundamentally different structure of moral logic. Greater volumes of material are produced in the effort to discredit the opposition today, and a greater variety of media is available to communicate that message: television commercials, magazines, advertisements, direct mail, and the like. Finally, it is arguable that the complexity and stridency of the antagonism between orthodox and progressivist voices has sharply increased.

THE GRAMMAR OF CONTEMPORARY HOSTILITY

At first glance, the substance and pitch of contemporary public discourse creates an impression that the typical way in which the culturally conservative and progressivist alliances communicate to each other and about each other is through language that is impulsive, if not outrageous. Certainly the images portraying the opposition and the manner in which these images are publicly presented do not appear to be well thought out. A few of the actors contributing to this situation do, of course, come from the fringes of public life and so one is not surprised to hear outrageous accusations and arguments. But much more interesting is the fact that even among organizations and personalities publicly perceived as mainstream liberal (such as People for the American Way or the National Education Association) or mainstream conservative (such as the Catholic League for Civil and Religious Rights), there is a certain unrestrained character in their statements. Whether accusations on either side are the products of a momentary reflex or of careful reflection, one can see the makings of a definable pattern—a pattern of image building and accusation shared by *both* sides of the cultural divide.

Defining the Enemy

The most conspicuous way each side discredits its opposition is by portraying their opponents as extremists. Illustrations abound.

In a speech to incoming freshmen in 1981, for example, the president of Yale University called politically active Evangelical Christians and their "client groups" "peddlers of coercion." In reaction to a threatened boycott by the Coalition for Better Television, the president of ABC News called its advocates "moral zealots."[32] Such epithets are not at all uncommon. As cultural tensions have mounted, voices of the progressivist impulse routinely label their orthodox counterparts as "right-wing zealots,"[33] "religious nuts," "a misanthropic cult," "self-proclaimed moral leaders," "fanatics," "extremists," "moral zealots," "fear brokers," "militants," "demagogues," "right-wing homophobes," "latter-day Cotton Mathers," and "patriots of paranoia."[34] They maintain that their opponents are "anti-intellectual and simplistic,"[35] and that their message is "vicious," "cynical," "narrow," "divisive," and "irrational." The activism of orthodox groups is said to reflect "a narrow, extremist ideology"—and to constitute a "voice of hatred" in public discourse, one that "revels in a rhetoric of condemnation."[36] The movements of cultural conservatism are declared to be "built upon . . . deception, falsehood, character assassination, willful distortion of the truth, and a power-crazed authoritarianism based upon a win-at-any-cost ethic and a total disregard for personal values or religious freedom."[37] An ACLU appeal stated that they are "whipping up fear and hysteria" through a "campaign of fear and intimidation." An Americans for Democratic Action publication stated that so-called New Right groups "deliberately trigger popular waves of irrational fear." And a People for the American Way pamphlet agreed that the message of the religious right brings "fear and distrust into millions of American homes."[38]

Cultural conservatives portray progressivist forces as extremists, too, sometimes employing identical language. Responding to the claim made by People for the American Way, the ACLU, and other progressive groups that their agenda is "non-partisan," Jimmy Swaggart remarked in 1987, "They're about as non-partisan as Joseph Stalin."[39] Progressive activists have been labeled "arrogant and self-righteous," "militant," "deceitful," "treacherous," "masters of deceit." One pamphlet from the Roundtable called them "intellectual barbarians."[40] Their moral commitments have likewise been called "amoral," "anti-Christian," "a godless liberal philosophy," "the regnant evil of our time," and their agenda, "ruthless," "insidious" "a religious evil" associated with, as one Catholic organization put it, "the forces of anti-Christ."

These images of extremism, of course, are imbedded within a theory of the opposition's moral missions. The voices of religious orthodoxy accuse progressivists of promoting the social agenda of "secular humanism," a philosophy that is, for them, "not only the world's greatest evil but until recently, the most deceptive of all religious philosophies."[41] A Fundamentalist newsletter of Decatur, Georgia, called secular humanism "a diabolical religion."[42] Concerned Women of America claimed that "the secular humanists, who deny God and traditional moral values, have almost gained total control of our public policies, our schools, even our law-making institutions and courts—in just one or two generations." In this spirit, the Catholic League for Religious and Civil Rights posed a question in one of its appeals that many Evangelicals and Mormons have asked as well, "Will we passively watch as the Secularists destroy our Judeo-Christian heritage?"[43] Meanwhile, progressivists claim that the orthodox, primarily the Evangelicals, are working toward the "christianization of America." According to statements from the People for the American Way, the Union of Hebrew Congregations, the ACLU, and other groups, foisting a particular and narrow view of Christianity upon national life is one of the expressed goals of the Religious Right.[44]

Both sides contend that they are seriously misrepresented. Many progressivists, for example, dismiss the very existence of an ideology of secular humanism. One prominent Lutheran minister simply summarized it as "the bogeyman of the religious right." The National Education Association called secular humanism a "myth" used as a tool of harassment.[45] People for the American Way and the ACLU consistently maintain that the notion is nothing more than "a convenient label for most of the ills of our society and a catch-all for ideas that don't fit into their narrow sectarian world view."[46] It is seen as a "label used by the Far Right to attack virtually everything that they disagree with about the schools and the society at large."[47] Another called it an imaginary dogma upon which is based a new "witch hunt."[48]

On the other side of the divide, cultural conservatives (mainly Evangelicals but also many conservative Catholics) also maintain that their own identity and mission is deliberately misrepresented. Secularists are said to confuse "Christianization" (or in the particular case of Catholics who oppose abortion, the "Catholicization of public policy") with legal rights of all groups (including religious groups) to participate in democratic exchange.[49] They contend that progressivists simply do not like the agenda they are pursuing. Through the 1980s, leaders in the orthodox alliance repeatedly pointed out that their critics never accused the National Council of Churches or the Reverend Jesse Jackson of mixing religion and politics.[50] A Jewish columnist articulated this complaint in reflecting about the repeated accusations of People for the American Way. Their "concern over the co-mingling of politics and religion is quite selective; it objects to certain sectarian involvement in the political process. But if it's wrong for fundamentalist candidates to claim their positions are divinely inspired, it must be equally objectionable for the Witnesses For Peace to say that aid to the Contras is ungodly." But about this, the author continues, the "guardians of secular government are strangely silent."[51] Another conservative remarked, "Nobody was crying 'separation' [of church and state] when Father Drinan or Jesse Jackson were [politically] active. . . . If it's good for the liberal goose, its good for the conservative gander."[52]

By portraying the opposition as extremist, each side implicitly maintains that the other is a minority removed from the mainstream of American life and that they, instead, represent the interests of the majority. Jerry Falwell spoke succinctly for many in the orthodox alliance when, at the time of his rise to public visibility, he said that "the godless minority of treacherous individuals who have been permitted to formulate national policy must now realize they do not represent the majority." Contrarily, as an appeal from the National Abortion Rights Action League stated, the threat to American institutions was posed by "a small number of dogmatic religious leaders and ultra-conservative politicians" and, thus, "to preserve our own freedoms and our Constitution . . . we must mobilize [the] majority quickly."[53] Other voices attempt to argue for the same reality. Tim LaHaye claimed that "we are being controlled by a small but very influential cadre of committed humanists," while liberal observers Flo Conway and Jim Siegelman maintained that the campaign of "religious and political absolutism" of the right was being "led by a small group of preachers and political strategists."[54] And while David Balsiger of Christian Voice argued that "liberals are not the majority in America, Christians are the majority," Reverend John Buchanan claimed that "Falwell bears false witness against the overwhelming majority."[55]

In making these claims, public opinion data are frequently invoked by both sides. For example, pro-life advocates (correctly) contend that the majority of Americans oppose abortion on demand, while pro-choice advocates (also correctly) contend that roughly "four out of five Americans reject our opponents' goal of outlawing all abortions."[56] On the basis of survey data provided by the Gallup Organization, LaHaye calculates that there really is a moral majority. Not all are "born-again Christians" but they are "religiously or idealistically pro-moral," and they would "vote the pro-moral cause if they saw it clearly."[57] But at the same time, social scientists contend that there really is no moral majority.[58]

Monopolizing the Symbols of Legitimacy

By labeling the opposition an extremist faction that is marginal to the mainstream of American life, each side struggles to *monopolize the symbols of legitimacy*. This is seen most clearly in the effort of each side to depict themselves as defenders of the institutions and traditions of American life while depicting the opposition as the foes. Evidence of this has already been seen in the efforts of each side to appropriate the intentions of the framers of the Constitution and Bill of Rights. It is also seen in the use of the flag, the traditional family, and other positive symbols. It can even be seen in the very names of the contending organizations. Each time the name of one of these organizations is invoked in public discussion this cultural dynamic is conspicuously at play. An exegesis is hardly necessary. The trademark phrases "Christian Voice," "Moral Majority," "Coalition for Traditional Values," "Americans United for Life," and the like imply that those who disagree are in some way against Christianity, against morality, against traditional values, against life, and so on. By the same token, names such as "Americans for Democratic Action," "People for the American Way" (which describes itself as "a national voice for liberty"), the "American Civil Liberties Union" (which describes itself as the "guardian of liberty" and "the organization that protects the Bill of Rights"), the "National Organization for Women," and others suggest that if you do not support their objectives, you do not favor democracy, the American way, civil liberties, women's rights, and so on.

As one might expect, as the attempt to monopolize the symbols of legitimacy becomes more explicit it turns more mean-spirited. Once again there is a remarkable similarity in accusations. On the one hand, one-time presidential contender Pat Robertson has claimed that "the minute you turn the [Constitution of the United States] into the hands of non-Christian people and atheistic people, they can use it to destroy the very foundation of our society and that's what's been happening."[59] On the other hand are the counterassertions of Anthony Podesta (of People for the American Way). Of Robertson himself, Podesta says,

"Beneath the superficial impression of a friendly television personality who loves America, lurks the reality of a fanatic who hates our nation's courts, its public schools, its system of social insurance and even much of its Constitution."[60]

In the same spirit that the president of Americans for Democratic Action called the Moral Majority "enemies of this country," the Christian Voice called the ACLU "anti-American."[61] And when Tim LaHaye asked rhetorically why he opposed humanism so vigorously, he offered two reasons: "I am a committed Christian and I am a committed American. Humanism is viciously opposed to both."[62] Others have submitted the rejoinder that when conservative religious leaders make religiously grounded political judgments and accusations, such activity is not "the American way." Both reserve the moral high ground of the mainstream for themselves and by implication relegate their opposition to the low ground of political and social marginality.

The Specter of Intolerance

The fundamental reason why each side characterizes their rivals as extremists outside the mainstream is because each ardently believes that the other embodies and expresses an aggressive program of social, political, and religious intolerance.

This belief is particularly salient among those holding to a progressivist vision. The Religious Right, according to one direct mail appeal from the ACLU, is "militantly intolerant." "Their leaders," as a People for the American Way brochure claims, "want to silence dissent and exclude from fullest citizenship anyone who disagrees with them." According to the brochure, the Religious Right labels people who disagree as "amoral, ungodly and un-American." In a speech to Yale freshmen, A. Bartlett Giamatti concurred: "Angry at change, rigid in the application of chauvinistic slogans, absolutistic in morality, they threaten through political pressure or public denunciation whoever dares to disagree with their authoritarian positions. . . . They would sweep before them anyone who holds a different opinion." Another critic made a similar argument: "These leaders tolerate no disagreement, they accept no compromise. Those people not sharing their philosophy on family life and on the proper role of government are labelled un-Christian, un-American, anti-family or adherents to the supposed religion of 'secular humanism' which exists mainly in ultraconservative fulminations."[63] Another writer notes that

> such intolerance is not new. Movements committed to the politics of intolerance and resentment are never far from the surface of American life. What sets the moral majoritarians apart, however, are their impressively-funded and highly-sophisticated communications campaigns. Their ability to harness national print and broadcast media for 'religious' programming magnifies the reach and impact of their dogmatic and intolerant messages to an extraordinary degree. People identified through electronic media are then organized into effective state and local organizations through a coordinated program of computerized mailing, newsletters, rallies, conventions and seminars. The moral majoritarians' belief that there is only one self-evident truth leaves no room for debate and discussion.[64]

The fundamental threat posed by the "moral absolutism" and "intolerance" of the culturally conservative is, as it is commonly held, "the imposition of values and beliefs upon others."[65] "The radical right . . . seems less interested in attacking these public evils (social injustices) than in legislating private morality and, by so doing, imposing its standards on all citizens."[66] A People for the American Way brochure summarized: "Their declared goal is the enactment of laws that will prohibit everything which goes against their narrow interpretation of the will of God."[67] Their agenda is seen as an effort to impose intellectual and moral uniformity.

From the perspective of the religiously orthodox, it is the secularists who are intolerant. Within this alliance accusations of intolerance are not vocalized as frequently as they are among progressivists, yet the concept is often used. Cal Thomas, editorialist and former executive for the Moral Majority, remarks, "The great sin in America today is not homosexuality, it's a brand new sin created by the secular elite: intolerance. The sinners are elevated, and those who preach against sin are condemned."[68] The Evangelical legal activist John Whitehead argues, "Humanism, contrary to popular belief, is not a tolerant system. It preaches against religious 'dogmatism,' but imposes its own." Concerned Women for America contended, "Do not be fooled by Planned Parenthood's rhetoric. It does not tolerate any deviation from its tenets. Those who choose not to agree with it are labeled 'zealots,' 'anti-choice,' 'ignorant,' and 'right-wing.' "[69] Such accusations are echoed regularly in everyday political dialogue, demonstrating the abiding conviction that the other side expresses intolerance by seeking to impose its oppositional values upon those who do not want them.

The Totalitarian "Threat"

Given all of this it is entirely predictable that each side would portray the other as an exceedingly dangerous force in American public life. Thus, at the same time the direct mail appeals of the National Abortion Rights Action League claim that the religiously orthodox are "a very real and imminent threat" capable of "wreak[ing] havoc upon millions of American families," Christians Concerned for More Responsible Citizenship argue that progressivists have placed "America [in] . . . the greatest crisis in its history."[70] According to their respective literature, each side has wittingly or unwittingly spawned a political agenda that is antidemocratic and even totalitarian in its thrust.

Norman Cousins voiced the fears of many on the progressivist side when he stated in the *Saturday Review* that religious fundamentalism seeks "to establish itself as a power over government." In a full-page advertisement in the *New York Times* the ACLU expressed it even more boldly: religious fundamentalists, as the ad called them, are "a radically anti-Bill of Rights movement. . . . Their agenda is clear and frightening: they mean to capture the power of government and use it to establish a nightmare of religious and political orthodoxy."[71] The Americans for Democratic Action have been even more specific in saying that this activism represented nothing less than "a cynical and calculated effort to create a colossal new movement, to destroy the Republican and Democratic Parties, and to rule the United States."[72] For the activists of NARAL this is nearly an accomplished reality, for such groups "are now within reach of their goal—control of our nation's political process."[73]

To be sure, the threat posed by the politically active religious orthodox is often associated with the worst instances of political repression. The specters of both fascism and communism are evoked. Almost every progressively oriented special purpose group along with many prominent individuals has characterized the political designs of its opposition as "religious or moral McCarthyism." The People for the American Way has associated the religious right with the neofascist Lyndon LaRouche, the Ku Klux Klan, and the neo-Nazi Aryan Nation.[74] The president of Georgetown University placed the Moral Majority in a long tradition of "rancorous moods" including "Nativism, America First, the Ku Klux Klan, [and] McCarthyism." An editor of a Texas daily associated these "zealots" with such "political bullies" as fascists, socialists, and communist cults.[75] Another editorial likened the pro-life and pro-family movement to the actions of Adolf Hitler and Joseph Stalin.[76] Similar sentiments were expressed by the Americans for Democratic Action (who associated orthodox movements with the Ku Klux Klan and the Nazi party) and by the Union of American Hebrew Congregations (who linked them with the totalitarian vision of George Orwell's novel *1984*).[77] One writer observed that "the new right, consciously or not [were] stealing not only the tactics but the philosophy of Communism. They are poisonous toadstools, which if not plucked and discarded in the bud, could well grow into an American-style totalitarianism."[78] Anthony Podesta, of People for the American Way, agreed that many of the interests desired by the Religious Right "are the guidelines for a frightened totalitarianism, not of a vital, free society."[79]

Conservative activists have also been associated with the political atrocities of religious extremism. In an editorial, the *Chicago Tribune* related activism in the orthodox alliance to the Crusades, the Spanish Inquisition, the "intolerant theocracy" of the Massachusetts Bay Colony, Islamic fundamentalism, and Jewish fundamentalism in contemporary Israel.[80] Anthony Podesta has called Jimmy Swaggart "the Louis Farrakhan [of the Nation of Islam] of the Right, while others have likened Falwell to Iran's now deceased Ayatollah Khomeini.[81] Still others have linked the infusion of religion into the affairs of state (particularly by the pro-life movement and Moral Majority) to "the carnage in Iran, the bloodshed in Northern Ireland, [and] the bombs bursting in Lebanon."[82]

For cultural conservatives, and particularly the religiously orthodox, the situation created by the ascendancy of progressivist values is no less dire. "We are," according to Bill Bright, "in danger of losing our nation by default, and with it our individual freedoms and possibly our lives."[83] The reasons are clear. Although referring specifically to the ACLU, the observation of Christian Voice is commonly applied to all progressivist groups: such activities "pose a serious threat to America's freedoms. . . . [Their] positions [are] anti-freedom, anti-life, anti-moral, anti-Christian, and anti-American." People for the American Way is seen as "a most deceitful organization. Militantly humanistic, it cloaks itself in a mantle of tolerance. Its purpose, it loudly proclaims, is to protect First Amendment freedoms. In reality, the group labors to enact the liberal/left agenda and simultaneously expunge any trace of spiritual influence from the public realm."[84] The same has been said of the National Organization for Women: "Molly Yard and other feminists frequently use terrorist-type tactics when attempting to further their selfish political agenda."[85]

Here too the threats posed by the progressivist agenda are commonly associated with historical instances of political repression, primarily those perpetrated by secular statist policy. In this way progressivists have been accused of using "McCarthy-like fear tactics."[86] Others point out that they use "the same play on words that Communists use."[87] A number of Evangelicals have associated the progressivist agenda with those of totalitarian regimes. John Whitehead, for example, in his book *The Stealing of America,* argues that America may be "on the road to Auschwitz" by elaborating in great detail the "ominous parallels" between pre-Nazi Germany and present-day America. In an earlier book, he made the same association but focused on the anti-Christian nature of the Nazi regime as compared to the anti-Christian nature of the contemporary state.[88] This view is reiterated in the pro-life literature as well. As a Methodists for Life brochure put it, "Apathetic clergy make me understand how Hitler succeeded."[89] Others have associated the political designs of progressivists and the expanding secular state with the images of Aldous Huxley's *Brave New World* and George Orwell's *1984.*

The Temper of Animosity

The rhetoric infused into public discourse by each side is so similar that without identifying the object of derision and aversion, it is nearly impossible to distinguish which of the two coalitions is speaking. In each case the rhetoric is divisive and inflammatory. But what makes contemporary public discourse even more inflammatory is the appeal to sensationalism. Is it really true, as some progressivist voices claim, that "religious fervor now combines with reactionary politics resulting in a type of neo-fascism that threatens the very foundations of American life"? or that "the result of a political takeover by the religious right" might "bring into existence a kind of Christian Nazism (with the Bible as *Mein Kampf*) whose manipulated multitudes goosestep mercilessly over the godless"?[90] Is it really true, as some orthodox voices have claimed, that "those of the humanistic stripe want to see all Bibles banned in America . . . to see all church doors closed"? Or that if nonbelieving politicans are elected it would be necessary to "put your Bible under the mattress, fold up your American flags and throw away all your coins that say 'In God We Trust' "?[91] But sensationalism and exaggeration, regardless of the party and the object of disfavor, always foster fear, mistrust, and resentment. At times this is openly encouraged. As Karen Mulhauser of NARAL wrote in a direct mail appeal, "Constitutional scholars, bishops and rabbis are worried. So am I, and so are thousands upon thousands of your fellow citizens. I hope you too are worried. . . ."

In the end such language may titillate even the most dispassionate of listeners, but it can only lead to one conclusion: the further polarization of public discourse.

The Drift Toward Bigotry

If it is true, as I argued earlier, that each embattled side upholds a different conception of the sacred, it is not surprising that each side lashes out at the other. Humans simply cannot tolerate the desecration of that which is most cherished. If it is true, therefore, that each side of the cultural divide represents a competing dogma, it would be no surprise to find evidence of a certain politics of exclusion—the markings of a social bigotry. And indeed, this is still another way in which each side of the new cultural divide mirrors the other.

The most obvious examples of social bigotry exist in a sector of the orthodox alliance—in that part of Protestant Fundamentalism that retains the strong nativist belief in a Christian America. Some in this grouping have claimed that God does not hear the prayers of Jews. In the early 1980s others within this community even encouraged prayer for the deaths of Supreme Court Justices so that they might be replaced with Justices who oppose abortion. On occasion, books and record albums by secularists are burned. The list of examples goes on. To these people, why should they tolerate sin?

Given their championing of the ideal of toleration, far more interesting is evidence of intolerance in the progressivist communities. For example, at St. Patrick's Cathedral, in New York City, on a Sunday morning in mid-December 1989, thousands of gay rights and pro-choice activists demonstrated outside the church, shouting and raising placards that read, "Eternal life to Cardinal John O'Connor NOW," "Know your scumbags," "Curb Your Dogma," "Papal Bull," and the like. Dozens of protesters went inside during the mass and stood on pews, shouting, waving their fists, and tossing condoms in the air. Other displays of open hatred toward conservative Catholics and Evangelicals by the gay community are not uncommon.[92] In another example, a political cartoon published in 1986 depicted five brains of different sizes. The largest was identified as the "brain of man"; those in the middle were identified as the brain of a Neanderthal, a *homo erectus,* and an ape; and the last, the size of the head of a pin, was identified as the "brain of a creationist." The caption read, "Proof of Evolution."[93] One wonders whether the cartoonist could have replaced "the brain of a creationist" with "the brain of a woman," or the "brain of a black person" with equal impunity. Other political cartoons stereotype Evangelical ministers as snake-handling, money-grubbing charlatans. Would the artists or newspapers take the same liberties in stereotyping, say, rabbis or priests?

The progressivist communities as a whole pride themselves on their cosmopolitanism, and defend the freedom to think and behave according to individual wishes with the provision that the exercise of those rights does not inflict harm on others. The preceding examples demonstrate, however, that these communities are not immune to asserting absolutes of their own. For some in the progressivist alliance, moral ambiguity itself acts as an absolute of sorts. Many on the progressivist side of the cultural divide resent those who claim to speak with moral certainty. Ashley Montagu captured this feeling when he wrote (referring to creationists), "Absolute truth belongs only to one class of humans . . . the class of absolute fools."[94] Yet sometimes the ideal of tolerance assumes a kind of dogmatism of its own. For many progressivists, intolerance is utterly intolerable, and should be met with an equal measure of vehemence. The progressivist communities find it difficult to tolerate positions that are considered choice-restrictive and thus "intolerant." Renowned science fiction writer and humanist advocate Isaac Asimov, commenting on the New Christian Right in the Canadian magazine *Macleans,* wrote: "And it is these ignorant people, the most uneducated, the most unimaginative, the most unthinking among us, who would make of themselves the guides and leaders of us all; who would force their feeble and childish beliefs on us; who would invade our schools and libraries and homes. I personally resent it bitterly."[95]

Liberal tendencies toward absolutism become more clear when we consider the symbol of liberal civility—dialogue. While progressivist groups love to express their penchant for it, there is little indication that they have actually sought dialogue with conservative groups. Most liberals perceive the Christian Right as intransigent in its positions. Yet it is clear that most liberal groups are equally intransigent in their positions. One would hardly expect, for example, the National Abortion Rights Action Lobby to change its opinion on abortion, or the gay rights lobby to change its mind about the rights of homosexuals. In Rabbi Yehuda Levin's words, "What they call liberals are so 'open-minded' their brains are falling out. These people cannot be converted. They cannot be persuaded." One man's experience with progressives at Harvard Divinity School led him to comment, "Tolerance may exist on the denominational levels, but once discussion moves to the oppression of women or the poor, strict standards of acceptability are applied. Tolerance quickly fades if these standards are violated, and the friendly atmosphere of religious pluralism gives way to serious combat."[96]

Former Iranian hostage and American foreign service officer Morehead Kennedy described his experiences at the Peace Institute at the Episcopal cathedral St. John the Divine in New York City in similar terms: "I would have [had] a much easier time denying the Resurrection than I would have questioning the Nuclear Freeze."[97] Absolutism and fanaticism, he concluded, apply not only to the Religious Right but to the Religious Left as well. When progressivist groups call for "dialogue," their objective may not always be "mutual understanding of unreconcilable opinions," but the extraction of compromise from their opponents. As one Fundamentalist minister from Staten Island complained, progressivists are "denying us every right to the pluralism they say we're trying to destroy." Another put the complaint even more sharply. "Religious bigotry and political hatred are what [they are] all about."[98]

The Boundaries of Tolerance

In all of this the nature of tolerance and intolerance becomes very clear.

Most scholars and lay people have attributed attitudes of tolerance to individual factors, such as a person's educational background. The greater the educational achievement one had attained, the more tolerant one would likely be. Under previous cultural arrangements this has been shown to be true. But now our cultural environment has changed in such a way that one can see the *structural* preconditions for tolerance. Tolerance, in this light, may not be so much a function of "enlightenment" as it is a function of the relative sharpness of moral boundaries separating groups. With the realignment of pluralism, the boundaries separating groups has shifted. As the lines dividing Protestant, Catholic, and Jew have become more indistinct, tolerance has increased among the denominations. But as the lines dividing orthodox from progressivists or conservatives from liberals have become clearer and sharper, new bigotries have begun to take shape. Today the chasms are not so much between one alliance that is tolerant (because it is cosmopolitan and highly educated) and another that is intolerant (because it is religiously orthodox and less well educated). Nor are the rifts between those who would guide people toward truth and those who would indoctrinate. Now each side asserts its own parochialisms; each side lives by its own "narrow" dogma. In this light the conflict is in large part about whose definition of moral parochialism (and, therefore, what is tolerable and intolerable) should prevail.

SYMMETRY IN ANTIPATHY

After considering the substance and style of public discourse engaged in by the principle actors in the contemporary culture war, one is tempted to agree with the adage that "the Left is the Right and the Right is the Left."[99] Both ends of the cultural axis claim to speak for the majority, both attempt to monopolize the symbols of legitimacy, both identify their opponents with a program of intolerance and totalitarian suppression. Both sides use the language of extremism and thereby sensationalize the threat represented by their adversaries. And finally, each side has exhibited at least a proclivity to indulge the temptation of social bigotry.

What, then, is the meaning of this rhetoric? Philosophers and social scientists have observed that during times of social fluctuation and cultural uncertainty, communities may unwittingly exaggerate a threat to their existence and well-being. These communities under stress may even *fabricate* such a threat. The process is not mysterious: perceived threats typically engender a sense of cohesiveness among the threatened members. In the act of opposing an adversary—either exaggerated or manufactured—the community expresses a common moral indignation, and asserts its moral authority anew. It is, in effect, saying in one voice, "We are not like you; we oppose what you stand for." Thus, not only is the community drawn together, united as a collectivity, but it is reminded of its heritage, its duty, and its mission to the larger world. The "latent functionality," as sociologists would say, of standing against such an adversary is the ritual reaffirmation of the community's identity in the face of what may be a far greater adversary, its own internal moral disintegration. In the past, under such stresses, religious communities punished agents of "evil," as the Catholic hierarchy punished heretics during the Inquisition in the sixteenth century, and as the Puritans of Salem, Massachusetts, punished "witches" in the seventeenth century. Political parties seek out "subversives," as the Nazis singled out Jews, as U.S. Senator Joseph McCarthy and the Senate subcommittee on un-American activities repressed communists and their sympathizers in the early 1950s, and as Mao Tse-tung and the "Gang of Four" attacked intellectuals and "capitalist roaders" during the Cultural Revolution in China in the 1960s and 1970s.

It is important to stress that willful intention is not really a factor in the emergence of these ideological scapegoats. That is to say, there is usually no cabal consciously and cynically conspiring to induce fearful illusions. There is no calculated manipulation of public sentiment on the part of a secret elite sect. Rather these developments are "systemic," part of a natural collective response to the threat of the community's own structural insecurity and moral instability. These same sociological forces are at play in today's culture war. In the context of America's own declining position in the larger world order, and after several decades of domestic social unease, both the orthodox and progressivist alliances, as relatively distinct sets of moral communities, have struggled to maintain their own cohesiveness and at the same time realize their own political ideals. Indeed, signs of America's failure to compete economically or educationally with the rest of the world—those mediagenic events that remind us of our failure to cope with the drug problem, homelessness, crime, teenage pregnancies, and so on—all these things provide the fertile ground for accusation and counteraccusation in the culture war. By inflating the nature, size, and political power of their opposition, the identity and mission of each alliance has been forcefully reaffirmed. Ironically, by those very same acts, each side has also unwittingly contributed to the invention of precisely that which they fear and oppose so much.

Just because each side of the cultural divide has in some ways fictionalized the threat posed by its opponents does not mean that the conflict is somehow artificial and therefore inconsequential. Quite the contrary. Certainly both power and privilege are at stake. Nothing else can adequately account for the enormous sums of money and profusion of human energy poured into the conflict. The diabolic images fashioned and applied to the opposition are, in a way, merely resources used by either side to draw out the contrasts. This is the mechanism for making broad appeals for financial backing and for galvanizing popular sentiment.

To argue that each side of the cultural divide employs a similar rhetoric is also not to suggest that the two are somehow "morally equivalent." Rhetorical symmetry does not necessarily imply moral symmetry. One might argue theologically, philosophically, or politically that one side is morally superior to the other, but the truth of such claims cannot be established in a social scientific or an ethically neutral frame of reference. Such arguments can only be put forward in language that itself is vulnerable to the polarizing tendencies of the contemporary cultural division.

Sociologically, then, this conflict is not "about" who is right and who is wrong or even who is better or who is worse. As with all other expressions of cultural antagonism, this conflict is "about" the uses of symbols, the uses of language, and the right to impose discrediting labels upon those who would dissent. It is ultimately a struggle over the right to define the way things are and the way things should be. It is, therefore, more of a struggle to determine who is stronger, which alliance has the institutional resources capable of sustaining a particular definition of reality against the wishes of those who would project an alternate view of the world.

It is true that the contemporary culture war is built upon a long history of mutual animosity. Yet the struggle has evolved into something more extensive and more momentous. New and much broader coalitions are involved, a wider range of issues are disputed, a greater volume of information is available, and, as we shall see, new technologies communicate that information. Given the scope of what is being contested coupled with the urgency and shrillness by which each side voices its complaint, it is arguable that in this conflict, the stakes are much higher as well.

6

The Technology of Public Discourse

The impulse toward polarization in contemporary public discourse is undeniable. It is a dynamic that reveals itself with force and severity. But to say that public discussion is polarized is not to say that the progressive and orthodox voices are the only ones. Voices of moderation and restraint do exist. Public opinion research reveals a rich complexity of ideas, beliefs, and commitments among the leadership of the nation's public institutions as well as ordinary citizens. As Cindy Burgess, a farmer from Starbuck, Minnesota, said at the 1990 pro-life march in Washington, D.C., "I'm so sick of being called a religious radical. We're Americans—simple moral people."[1] A pro-choice activist complained similarly, "Just becaue I favor reproductive rights does not make me a murderer." Statements like these are not only honest and discerning but eloquent. Indeed, the number of people who actually hold strongly traditionalist or strongly progressivist positions are in the minority (perhaps 20 percent at each end). And even these so-called extremists do not always fit the caricatures or ideal types very well. The problem is that the complexity of personal conviction and the subtlety of personal opinion are rarely reflected at the level of public discourse. In today's cultural climate, voices of quiet, reflective passion are rarely heard. Even less vocal are those who are ambivalent or apathetic. This is to say that although alternate voices exist, and may even be in the majority, they are, for all practical purposes, *silent* in the broader public discussion. *Without doubt, public discourse is more polarized than the American public itself.*[2]

THE ECLIPSE OF THE MIDDLE

The "eclipse of the middle" can be attributed to several factors. The first we have already mentioned: public discourse is a discourse of elites. Ordinary Americans have no mailing lists and there is no PAC for those who find good and bad on both sides of an issue. Related to this are the issues themselves. In matters of life and death, individual liberties, social oppression, justice and injustice, war and peace, and the like, it is virtually impossible to sustain ambivalence over a long period of time. There is a distinct and forceful sociological propensity to find lasting resolutions.

A third factor is rooted in what may be an anthropologically grounded need we all have to be stirred and titillated (this, in turn, may reflect a human aversion to monotony and boredom). Thus, public debate that is sensational is more likely to arouse and capture the attention of ordinary people than are methodical and reflective arguments. For this reason, the shrill pitch of harsh moral criticism and blunt commentary is much more likely to sell newspapers, build audience ratings, or raise money. The net effect of loud, sensational clamor, however, is to mute more quiet and temperate voices.

Another factor has to do with the level of suspicion in today's public culture. When new or alternate voices are heard, there is a strong inclination to categorize them according to the logic and language of the political polarities: "If they are not for us, then they must be against us." The National Organization for Women, for example, dismisses the very idea of an organization such as Feminists for Life. Said one spokeswoman, "Either they misunderstand the whole issue of feminism, or they are using it for purposes I disagree with—*their philosophy is irrelevant*."[3] In today's climate of apprehension and distrust, opinions that attempt to be distinctive and ameliorating tend to be classified with all others that do not affirm a loyalty to one's own cause. Perspectives that are moderately progressive or moderately conservative or traditionalist tend to be portrayed as extremes.

But there is still another factor that contributes to the polarization of public discourse and the eclipse of the middle. *The polarization of contemporary public discussion* is in fact *intensified by and institutionalized through the very media by which that discussion takes place. It is through these media that public discourse acquires a life of its own; not only do the categories of public rhetoric become detached from the intentions of the speaker, they also overpower the subtleties of perspective and opinion of the vast majority of citizens who position themselves "somewhere in the middle" of these debates.* The categories of public rhetoric are so dominant that someone who favors legal abortion but only in the first trimester is considered "pro-choice." Likewise, someone who opposes homosexuality on moral grounds yet defends the civil rights of homosexuals is still considered a "homophobe." *Middling positions and the nuances of moral commitment, then, get played into the grid of opposing rhetorical extremes.* This chapter explores how this comes to be.

THE MEDIA OF PUBLIC DISCOURSE

The significance of the media is that they define the "environment" in which public discussion takes place. This is important because the environment predetermines much about the actual substance of what is communicated.

A historical comparison is illuminating. In colonial New England, where the only regular medium of public communication was the sermon, churchgoers listened to roughly 7,000 sermons in a lifetime, totaling about 15,000 hours of concentrated listening.[4] Through the late eighteenth and early nineteenth centuries, public discussion continued to be conducted through sermons but also in speeches, lectures, newspapers, religious tracts, and hundreds of pamphlets. Pamphleteering was particularly important. Alexis de Tocqueville wrote in *Democracy in America,* "In America parties do not write books to combat each other's opinions, but pamphlets which are circulated for a day with incredible rapidity and then expire."[5] These circulars written by local, regional, and national elites were disseminated widely through the literate population, an accomplishment made possible by increasing refinements in printing technology. Often these documents were lengthy treatises (such as transcriptions of full-length political speeches) and oriented toward a literate middle-class audience. New printing technology also generated a rapid profusion of newspaper dailies, weeklies, and periodicals, including the penny press. The number of newspapers and periodicals published in America grew from about 7 in 1730 to 180 in 1800 to over 2,500 in 1850.[6] Public lectures also played a central role: the early nineteenth century witnessed the Lyceum movement for public oratory, and by 1835 there were over 3,000 Lyceums in fifteen states.[7]

Even in those days, the rhetoric of public discourse was emotional, passionate, even inflammatory. This was especially true of the penny press of the mid-nineteenth century. But within other forms of public discourse there was the aspiration toward intellectual substance. Speeches, debates, and pamphlets were long enough to develop an argument yet not so long that they would be accessible only to intellectuals. They could be read, studied, and debated by a large and diverse public.

Public discourse continues to be carried on in political, moral, and religious oratory today. Of course, scholarly books, lengthy articles, editorials, white papers, and the like also play a role. Yet in addition to all of these are still other, newer media and formats that not only reach a large audience but do so in a way that substantially eclipses the communicative power of a more labored if scholarly format. These are the media of television commercials and news broadcasts, newspaper editorials and letters to the editor, print advertisements, brochures, direct mail solicitations, and so on. The volume of these media is much greater and their ability to convey images is much more powerful and universal than the penny press ever was. For this reason, their social impact cannot be overestimated. Advocates of various political and social interests rely on these new media, and thus cumulatively these communications technologies have become an increasingly prominent facet of our public discourse.

Still, not all of these are relied upon in the same way. In some cases, the actors and organizations committed to public debate fund the publication of political advertisements to publicize their grievances. Though fairly rare (because they are expensive), the ads themselves become "events" after a fashion. For example, on 7 October 1984, Catholics for a Free Choice sponsored a full-page advertisement in the *New York Times* calling for "a dialogue within the Church on the issue of abortion."[8] Ninety-seven people signed the statement; many were religious women, and a few were priests and religious brothers, making it an act of formal dissent within the American Catholic hierarchy. Between January and February 1989 the National Abortion Rights Action League published full-page ads in twenty-four national and regional newspapers commemorating the sixteenth anniversary of *Roe v. Wade.* These NARAL ads featured a coat hanger, suggesting that women would mutilate themselves in self-inflicted abortions if *Roe* was overturned. Through the spring of that same year, Planned Parenthood had a series of full-page advertisements in *Time* magazine accusing pro-life forces of a "campaign of violence and intimidation" and lies. The ACLU also ran ads in the spring of 1989 in the *New York Times,* the *Los Angeles Times,* the *New Republic,* and on billboards in major metropolitan areas. There have been other examples of groups conducting public discourse through paid political advertisements as well, concerning such issues as U.S. policy in Central America and South Africa, disarmament, church-state relations, welfare reform, blasphemy, and the like.

There are also paid television commercials. People for the American Way, for instance, aired over 2,000 commercials in a single year, "reaffirming the Founding Fathers' dream of a free and tolerant nation."[9] In the same genre, though of a different format, are the religiopolitical oratories of many televangelists. Nearly 40 percent of the U.S. population in 1987 claimed to watch a religious broadcast every month, while 20 percent claimed to watch one every week.[10]

Direct mail solicitations are perhaps the most common of the new communications technologies. The technique was first used on behalf of social and political causes in the early 1950s during the Eisenhower-Nixon campaign. The technique was refined and developed on a much larger scale through the 1960s and 1970s: by the midterm elections of 1982, more than half a billion pieces of politically oriented direct mail were sent to ordinary citizens. The amount of mail has not diminished since then. Even for what direct mailers call a "house list"—people who are known to be loyal contributors to particular organizations—the numbers are quite remarkable. People for the American Way, for example, had more than a quarter of a million people on its house list in 1988; Americans for Democratic Action had 20,000 names; Christian Action Council had 46,000; and Independent Action had nearly 18,000. Jerry Falwell's "Old-Time Gospel Hour," in 1979 alone, had more than 2 million individuals on its mailing list. And the American Family Association has had as many as 3 million names on its direct mail computers.[11]

The implications of these media for the contemporary culture war are tremendous. They define a historically unique "environment" within which public discourse takes place; an environment that establishes novel, perhaps unprecedented rules for the conduct of public discussion. A comprehensive study of all of the newer media of communications, exploring the particular ways that each effects the environment of public debate, is impossible here. For the present purposes, a brief inquiry into just one of the new technologies—direct mail—is sufficient to make a case.

Direct Mail as Public Discourse

The explicit objective of direct mail solicitation is, of course, fund raising. The success of the technique, on the surface, is quite striking: lobbying groups raise millions of dollars annually. Common Cause, for example, is known to raise approximately $8 million a year; the American Civil Liberties Union, $6 million; the National Organization for Women, $10 million; People for the American Way, more than $7 million; and while it existed, the Moral Majority/Liberty Federation took in $10 million a year. The Republican National Committee in election years raises more than $60 million, while the Democratic National Committee raises just under that amount. Some estimate that, cumulatively, the political left and right raise up to $200 million *on each side* annually.[12]

There is another side to this story, however. From the perspective of cost-efficiency, serious problems arise. In a word, there is very little return against the investment. The way in which direct mail solicitation is applied to electoral politics is instructive. Senator Jesse Helms's Congressional Club, for example, a lobby committed to providing financial backing to conservative congressional candidates, raised $9.3 million in 1982 through direct mailings. But out of this, only $150,000 went to House and Senate candidates in that year. The rest of the money raised went to covering operating expenses.[13] Likewise, Senator Ted Kennedy's Fund for a Democratic Majority gave out only 8 percent of the money it raised in 1982. Indeed, one study from 1976 showed that candidates only received nine cents for every dollar spent on direct mail.[14] Much the same dynamic is at play among the social action organizations of the right and left. According to one report, direct mail consumed so much of the resources of one progressive lobby that after giving out the $250,000 promised to candidates, it ended up $328,061 in debt, most of which was owed to its direct mail consulting firm, Craver, Mathews, Smith. The lobby Independent Action spent the entire next year sending out still other solicitations written by the same firm just in order to pay back Craver, Mathews, Smith.[15] Elsewhere it was reported that the U.S. Committee Against Nuclear War raised $1.3 million from a direct mail appeal that appeared to be written on the stationery of a hotel in Hiroshima, from a congressman looking out at "ground zero." As is common in these sorts of mailings, the stationery was counterfeit, the letter was written in Washington, D.C., and 97 percent of the $1.3 million was used to cover the overhead expenses.[16]

Despite the problems surrounding the cost-effectiveness of direct mail, social and political organizations continue to use them. The reason is plain: in the end, making money is not really the point behind the appeals. As the conservative direct mail expert Richard Viguerie put it,

> It is a form of advertising. It is not an evil conspiratorial thing. It is just a fact of life, which I haven't found anybody to deny, that the major media of this country has a left of center perspective. The conservatives can't get their message around this blockade, except through direct mail. It's a way for conservatives to bypass the monopoly the left has on the media. It's a way of mobilizing our people; it's a way of communicating with our people.[17]

Morris Dees, a liberal direct mail consultant (who handled the mailings for George McGovern's presidential bid in 1972), acknowledged the same motive when he called direct mail a technique for "raising the consciousness" of the people.[18]

The capacity of direct mail to "advertise" or to "raise popular consciousness" is vast. For the average organization, the house list (loyal contributors) typically represents under 3 percent of a total mailing list. Therefore, to sustain a house list of 270,000 contributors (the size of the People for the American Way house list), it is necessary to send out over 9 million letters. For the Christian Action Council to sustain a house list of 46,000 contributors it has to mail out over one and a half million letters of appeal. By the late 1980s, the most successful direct mail brokering firm in the country had well over 30 million names of people from which to draw.[19]

Some may doubt the effectiveness of direct mail to really communicate to a large constituency, given the conventional wisdom that "people really do not open and read 'junk mail'." Yet several studies have shown that up to three-fourths of all those who receive politically oriented direct mailings not only open them but actually read them.[20]

The insight of the communications technicians, then, is essentially correct. Direct mail may not be a cost-effective way to raise money but it certainly is a practical and self-supporting mechanism of social and political advertising.

In the broader scheme of things, however, it is even more than this. Direct mail copy can be viewed quite literally as *a form of public discourse;* the letters themselves as a mechanism for communicating publicly about issues of social and political consequence. In this capacity direct solicitations also are instruments of civic education; a device for the prejudicial instruction of large segments of the population in the dynamics of contemporary social and political life. In this view, direct mail (as well as many of the other new forms of media) is anything but superfluous. It makes a very consequential contribution (whether for good or ill) to the reconstruction of public philosophy—to formulation of the myths and ideals of American life.

Direct Mail and the Discourse of Adversaries

Because of its ability to reach so many people, direct mail has clearly become an important new mode of public communication. The medium itself is closely related to the message of what is communicated. Something about the very nature of direct mail exerts a strong influence on the substance of public debate. The *feigned familiarity* (such as personalized address, personalized stationery, "handwritten" enclosures, "penciled" underlining and marginal notes, "personal" memoranda from political, media, and intellectual celebrities, stamps affixed slightly askew), the *sense of urgency* (such phrases as "Express Wire," "Urgent Gram," "Jet Message," "Air Express Urgent Letter" printed on envelopes typically mailed third class), the *appeal to officialdom* (through references to high public office, or a government agency) and the *gimmicks* (such as petitions, questionnaires, maps, clippings, fake honors, membership cards, bumper stickers) are the classic, if farcical, earmarks of direct mail. These features are designed to bestow upon the individual who receives the message a sense of personal obligation to become involved. They provide potential donors with the sense of a direct link between their contribution and real action taken to further a specific social or political cause. An individual contribution of just ten dollars, the reader is encouraged to believe, can influence the very future of the nation, one's community, one's own well-being, and that of one's children. By themselves, however, such features are not what make the medium so consequential for public discussion.

What is most consequential about direct mail is that it uses bald-faced, and rather cynical, manipulation of emotions. "Direct mail," as one consultant put it, "is a medium of passion."[21] The object is to make the reader either indignant or scared. "The message has to be extreme, has to be overblown; it really has to be kind of rough."[22] Indeed, on both sides of the cultural divide there is basic agreement: the more extreme the appeal, the more successful the mail campaign will probably be.[23] The letters are overtly biased since they tend to be aimed at an audience that is already committed. This explains in part the tendency toward sensationalism. In the realm of direct mail, there are no religious conservatives, only Fundamentalists, religious zealots, fanatics, and the like; there are no liberals, only ultraliberals, godless humanists, and so on. In this world, public education is not just teaching secular values but "Your tax dollars are being used to pay for grade school education that teaches our children [that] CANNIBALISM, WIFE-SWAPPING, and the MURDER of infants and the elderly are acceptable behavior."[24]

Going far beyond merely the biased and sensational, every successful direct mail appeal makes effective use of what the technicians in the industry call "the devil factor." In some cases the demonic is embodied in an individual, such as Pat Robertson, the pope, Carl Sagan, Oliver North, Jerry Falwell, Ted Kennedy, or Ronald Reagan. One Moral Majority letter called television producer and People for the American Way founder Norman Lear, "the number one enemy of the American family." In some cases the demonic is embodied in an organization, such as Concerned Women for America, the ACLU, National Organization for Women, Planned Parenthood, and the National Education Association. One mailings consultant was quite forthcoming about it: "You've got to have a devil. If you don't have a devil, you're in trouble."[25] Others in the business agree, "Find . . . a nasty enemy. Tell people they're threatened in some way. . . . It's a cheap trick, but it's the simplest."[26] For example, in 1979, 50,000 letters were sent out to individuals in the pro-life movement calling for the defeat of five pro-choice incumbents in the U.S. Congress and in the process using the words "murder" and "baby killers" forty-one times.[27] Even within direct mail appeals each side "demonizes" the other. A letter from Senator Jesse Helms, for example, attacked Senator Alan Cranston "as the ultra-liberal leader of the peace/freeze movement. . . . Led by the union bosses, they have launched a massive hate campaign against me." To this, Cranston replied with a mailing of his own: "Today Jesse Helms launched a zealous nationwide campaign to defeat me."[28] Extremism seems to feed extremism.

One expert provided this rationale: Why "freight a direct-mail letter with a great deal of doctrinaire political language?" After all, the purpose of the letter is "not to convince [the reader] of anything [but to] motivate the person to send some money."[29] A former employee of Richard Viguerie agreed, "The bottom line in my business is to raise money."[30] As one observer summarized, "The tacit rule among direct mailers is that there are no rules—anything goes in the pursuit of profit."[31]

Two other features of direct mail have a special impact on public discourse. One is the literary quality of the letters. The rule of thumb in the industry is to keep writing to about the sixth- to eighth-grade level. In a society inundated by information, the simple, easily grasped message is the most effective. There simply is no way one can debate the complexities of a social issue or justify an appeal for support with so many people at one time. Political scientist Larry Sabato reports that direct mailers apply the "magic word test" to their letters. "You add up the number of words under five letters in your copy, and if you've anywhere under 65 to 70 percent, you have problems."[32] Another obvious feature is the nearly universal poor quality of the moral argumentation. Documents such as these are not born of careful reflection or concern for evidence. The adage within the industry is, "Push the mail out the door and don't worry about the quality."[33]

Institutionalizing Superficiality

One must not lose the basic point in all of this: direct mail is, in the end, just one interesting and important case. Virtually all of the newer communications technologies tacitly acknowledge the pressures of time and the need to be distinctive in an information-glutted culture. Television commercials are between fifteen and sixty seconds in length, opinion-editorials are usually between 800 and 1,200 words (and letters to the editor are much shorter); print advertisements are usually one page in size, and dominated by large bold-face headlines; and direct mail letters are no more than four double-spaced pages. These media are also driven by market forces. More time, more space, and greater intellectual reflection just do not offer practical economic pay-off. Therefore, these mass communications technologies provide, as Neil Postman put it, "a structure for discourse, which both rules out and insists upon certain kinds of content and, inevitably, a certain kind of audience."[34] By their very nature, then, they must reduce sophisticated moral reasoning to simplifications; they must replace substantive moral argument with sloganeering. In other words, these media *demand* superficiality, which actually institutionalizes the impulse toward polarization in public discourse.

A noticeable sense of discomfort exists on the part of some activists about this institutional compulsion toward both superficiality and immoderation. One former executive of a large special interest lobby conceded that much of the rhetoric was indeed extravagant, if not apocalyptic, but also pointed out,

> When we complained, we were always given to understand that certain immutable laws known only to direct mail copy writers . . .

> govern this arcane field. A softened word here and a modified word there could cost us .005% return. So, we let outrageous stuff go over our good name. I wrote many memoranda internally telling my superiors that we had to cool the claims or I couldn't guarantee religious institutional support from mainline bureaucracies. My job was made far more difficult by direct mail production.[35]

There is, then, a very real sense of the tail of media technology (in this case, direct mail) wagging the dog of organizational ideals and interests.

Television commercials, prime-time debates, newspaper advertisements, and the like suffer from the same tendencies. Social organizations as well as politicians falter or thrive depending upon the discourse of paid political advertisements. Approval ratings and financial contributions soar and plunge as a direct response to the claims and counterclaims of adversaries in thirty-second television spots.[36]

This dynamic even extends to crowd estimates as a form of public discourse. Counting the numbers of people who turn out for demonstrations and rallies has become a politically charged exercise. At a gay rights march in Washington, D.C., in 1987, for example, the National Park Police estimated that 50,000 people demonstrated. Organizers were furious at this official figure and complained, saying that the officials deliberately underestimated the crowd size. (Eventually, the police revised their figures to 200,000.) So too, at the April 1990 pro-choice rally, organizers estimated that 600,000 people came, while police, using aerial photographs, only came up with 300,000.[37] Here again, substantive and nuanced arguments are ignored and forgotten. These factors, which encourage shallow rhetoric and crowd-size controversies, can only intensify tensions that are already quite volatile.

The way in which the contemporary cultural conflict is artificially played up by the newer media of public discourse raises questions about sincerity: Do the activists really mean what they say? On one hand, one is tempted to say that they do not, particularly when we know that many of the activists are capable of reflecting philosophically about their efforts. Yet one cannot simply "explain away" the intensity of the conflict by claiming that it is *only* an artifact of fund-raising considerations or an artifact of the need to capture public attention by shouting louder than the others. Clearly more is involved than an artificially contrived enmity. The enormous sums of money that sustain cultural conflicts boldly testify to this reality, as does the fervor of the activism on each side. Civil disobedience, in the form of an illegal sit-in, a "rescue" at an abortion clinic, the harboring of illegal aliens from war-torn countries, is not taken on as simply an afternoon's entertainment. Real passion inspires these tensions. There is a genuine and deeply felt hostility that is only magnified by the use of certain kinds of media.

In the final analysis, however, the question of motives may be irrelevant. Undoubtedly the cultural division has helped to spawn a superficiality of discourse; at the same time, that superficiality aggravates and deepens the cultural cleavage. Either way we are left with a language and a moral reasoning that are as extreme as they are superficial. But this extremism and superficiality is the only objectification of the debate that really exists, and, like it or not, it is this language and moral reasoning that defines the terms and limits of popular debate.

Here again, the net effect is the eclipse of the middle. The rhetoric required by the new communications technologies simply does not allow for middling positions and the subtleties they imply. Of course, moderate and even dispassionate voices do exist, but they do not have access to the same kind of public platform. It is virtually impossible to translate substantive moral reasoning into a sixty-second commercial, a "sound bite" on the evening news, a full-page political advertisement, a syndicated opinion-editorial piece, or a direct mail letter. The more temperate voices on both sides of the cultural divide are either drowned out by the louder extremes, or they themselves are dismissed as extreme. In the end, much of public discourse is reduced to a reciprocal bellicosity.

IV

THE FIELDS OF CONFLICT

Opening Observations

Cultural conflict may be a struggle to control the *symbols* of public culture, but this does not mean that it only exists in the ethereal realm of philosophical speculation—as a noisy and irritating form of sophist bickering. Cultural conflict, in reality, is much more consequential for a very simple reason. The symbols of public culture are always mediated in the social world by a variety of social institutions. *It is,* therefore, *in the context of institutional structures that cultural conflict becomes crystallized.*

The present contest is no exception. The contemporary culture war rages on a variety of institutional fronts. But five areas in which it rages most intensely are in the realms of the family, education, the popular media, law, and electoral politics. Each of these areas can be viewed as instruments of cultural warfare, to be sure. More important, each of these can be understood as a kind of *symbolic field or territory* for which opposing sides assert their interests through competing claims, seek to extract concessions, and endeavor to minimize their own losses.

But why these institutions? The *family* is an important symbolic territory because the social arrangements and relationships found there are very much a microcosm of those in the larger social order. The way men and women relate to each other, the different levels of status and authority they enjoy (or endure), the place of children, and the nature of legitimate sexuality—all of these, among other matters, have evolved into general social and political issues, but they are perhaps most tangible to ordinary people in the context of their own families and those of their friends. The truth, it would seem, is that on all of these issues it is virtually impossible to sustain a disjunction between public convention and private reality. The sociological tendency is always toward continuity: what is permissible in one sphere cannot be eschewed in the other and vice versa. In this we see that the distinction between public and private culture is ultimately artificial. The boundaries separating the two spheres are porous. What happens in one sphere inevitably has an impact in the other.

Education is a meaningful territory not because of its formal charge to pass on the basic skills and socially relevant knowledge necessary for adolescents and young adults to eventually participate responsibly in society. Rather, education is strategic in the culture war because this is the central institution of modern life through which the larger social order is reproduced. Together, the curriculum, the textbook literature, and even the social activities of the school convey powerful symbols about the meaning of American life—the character of its past, the challenges of the present, and its future agenda. In this way the institutions of mass education become decisive in socializing the young into the nation's public culture. Public education is especially significant territory in this regard, primarily because it reflects the will and power of the state vis-à-vis the nation's public culture.

The *popular media* in its various forms—television, film, art, music, and so on—are salient in part because they reflect the aspirations and ideals of communities and the nation. Naturally, in the present conflict there are sharp disagreements over which aspirations and ideals should be reflected. Perhaps a more pressing reason is the fact that these media comprise the single most important instrument of cultural warfare. The mass media not only reflect ideals but actually define reality in a society—by selecting which events "deserve attention" and are, therefore, "important," and which events are ignored and, therefore, unimportant; by depicting individuals and communities in particular ways; and by presenting what is acceptable and unacceptable.

Law is a decisive symbolic territory because it represents the patronage of the state. It is often said that the ultimate foundation of any social order is violence or the threat of violence enacted by the various mechanisms of the state. The ultimate guarantee that laws will be obeyed, then, is the formidable force exercised by the police, the national guard, the armed services, and so on. The debate over law—which laws will be enacted; whose interpretations will be endorsed—is not simply an esoteric quarrel among highly paid attorneys but a conflict over the ultimate sanction of the state and the rules it will enforce.

Finally, *electoral politics* is extremely significant symbolic territory, but not for the reasons one might think. Quite naturally, most people view electoral politics as the process by which lawmakers and government officials are popularly chosen. It is this, of course, but much more is involved. Electoral politics can be alternatively viewed as a collective ritual regularly enacted whereby certain symbols of national life are either embraced or rejected. Political candidates themselves are central to this process. Candidates may attempt to sway the voting public about their own competence, experience, or integrity, as compared to their opponent's ineffectiveness and corruption, yet ultimately the candidates themselves become symbols of different national ideals, opposing visions of what America is and should be. As we shall see, this is particularly true at the most powerful levels of political appointment. How political candidates define themselves, in their public rhetoric vis-à-vis the larger cultural conflict, becomes a decisive factor in casting their political fate.

Far from placid, then, each of these five spheres of activity is a locus of deep and bitter antagonism between the alliances on each side of the cultural divide. What happens on each of these fronts makes the contemporary culture war both concrete and consequential for the direction of American public life. Moreover, far from just reflecting the natural tensions of a shifting pluralism that will eventually balance itself out, these antagonisms represent the quest of different alliances for cultural domination. But how do these antagonisms actually take shape within a particular institution? The starting point is the family.

7

Family

In many ways, the family is the most conspicuous field of conflict in the culture war. Some would argue that it is the decisive battleground. The public debate over the status and role of women, the moral legitimacy of abortion, the legal and social status of homosexuals, the increase in family violence, the rise of illegitimacy particularly among black teenagers and young adults, the growing demand for adequate day care, and so on, prominently fill the headlines of the nation's newspapers, magazines, and intellectual journals. Marches and rallies, speeches and pronouncements for or against any one of these issues mark the significant events of our generation's political history. One might be tempted, then, to say that this field of conflict is the beginning and end of the contemporary culture war, for the issues contested in the area of family policy touch upon and may even spill over into other fields of conflict—education, the arts, law, and politics. In the final analysis there may be much more to the contemporary culture war than the struggle for the family, yet there is little doubt that the issues contested in the realm of family life are central to the larger struggle and are perhaps fateful for other battles being waged.

Most who observe the contest over the family, however, tend to grasp the controversy as a disagreement over the relative strength of this institution. One observer, for example, has described the controversy as one between optimists and pessimists. Both sides, he argued, agree that the family is changing yet they disagree sharply over the scope, meaning, and consequences of those changes. The pessimists view rising trends in divorce, single-parent families, dual-income couples, couples living out of wedlock, secular day care, and the like, as symptoms of the decline of a social institution. The optimists, on the other hand, regard the changes as positive at best and benign at worst and, therefore, they believe that social policy should reflect and accommodate the new realities. The American family is not disintegrating, the optimists say, but is adapting to new social conditions. The resilience of the family, therefore, signals that the family is "here to stay."[1]

Observations such as these provide interesting perspective and insight on the matter, forcing us to consider the concrete social and economic circumstances of family life. But they miss what is really at stake. The contest over the family, in fact, reflects fundamental differences in the assumptions and world views of the antagonists. The issue, then, is not whether the family is failing or surviving. Rather, the contest is over *what constitutes the family* in the first place. If the symbolic significance of the family is that it is a microcosm of the larger society, as averred in the Opening Observations, then the task of defining what the American family *is* becomes integral to the very task of defining America itself. For this reason it is also a task that is, on its own terms, intrinsically prone to intense political contention.

DEFINING THE FAMILY

But what is new in all of this? The family, as many have observed, has long been a social problem that has engendered heated political debate. One can observe, for example, profound anxiety about the well-being of the family in America and fears of its impending decline well into the nineteenth century. This was a time when industrialization was considered to threaten the cohesiveness of the family by severing its traditional ties to extended kinship, community, and church networks; when urbanization was viewed as threatening the moral development of the young and as brutalizing the integrity of family bonds. As a report to the National Congregational Council put it in 1892, "Much of the very mechanism of our modern life . . . is destructive of the family."[2]

Yet, as tangible as these problems were, there was still a general cultural agreement about what exactly it was that was being threatened and, therefore, what it was that needed defending. The nature and contours of the family were never publicly in doubt. Not so anymore:

as with so many other aspects of American life, the nineteenth-century consensus about the character and structure of family life has collapsed, leaving the very viability of the institution *as traditionally conceived* in question. The divisive issue now is in what form or forms contemporary families will remain viable.

Signs that the family would become an explicit public policy issue subject to polemical controversy appeared before the 1980s. The social science establishment began to raise the issue as a subject of national policy concern as early as the mid-1960s. Research and writing on the problem expanded through the 1970s.[3] The abstract rhetoric of intellectual discourse, however, soon translated into the push and pull of real political debate. In 1973, for example, the United States Senate held hearings on "American Families: Trends and Pressures." "Family experts" offered their views of problems faced by the family and suggested how the government might deal with them. Then in 1977, the Carnegie Council on Children (founded in 1972) published a report recommending that "the nation develop a family policy as comprehensive as its defense policy."[4] In the words of the report, "Our nation's professed belief in the importance of the family has not been matched by actions designed to protect the family's integrity and vitality. Although the sanctity of the family is a favorite subject for Fourth of July orators, legislators rarely address the question of how best to support family life or child development."[5] The call for concerted policy action would soon be answered.

Within the policy establishment itself, there were a wide range of perspectives about what problems actually plagued the family as well as how they should best be addressed. Among these "experts," a consensus was emerging that there was no one family type to which a national policy would be oriented. Rather than viewing families that were not nuclear, patriarchal, or self-sustaining as somehow deviant—families that were caught in what Daniel Patrick Moynihan called, in 1965, a "tangle of pathology"—public policy would now have to recognize a diversity of families. It was generally recognized that families differed in size, economic status, national origin and custom, and, not least, structure and composition.

During the 1980 White House Conference on Families, the quandary over how to define the American family was elevated to a permanent component of the national family policy debate. Indeed, in the early stages of organization and preparation, the conference title itself was changed from the singular "family" to the plural "families" because the organizers could not agree on what the American family was supposed to be.[6]

The conference, promised by President Carter during his 1976 presidential campaign, pledged the power and prestige of the White House to explore the ways in which public policy might strengthen U.S. families. Its outcome was mixed. That the conference succeeded in becoming an event of national scope there is little doubt. Statewide hearings and conferences took place in all fifty states, along with five national hearings, culminating in three White House conferences—in Baltimore, Minneapolis, and Los Angeles. But instead of generating a coherent set of policy recommendations serving to strengthen American families, the primary substantive accomplishment was to further crystallize and politicize, on a national scale, differences of opinion over the nature, structure, and composition of the family.

The polarization was seen in a variety of ways, although the politically progressive leanings of the Carter administration and of the conference leadership guaranteed that most of the protest would come from what was regarded as a newly galvanized "pro-family" movement made up of predominantly conservative Catholics and Evangelical Protestants. Only a few months earlier, conservative Senator Paul Laxalt had introduced the Family Protection Act, which among other things, eliminated the "marriage tax," protected parental rights, required informed consent of parents for minors seeking abortions, and allowed for discrimination against homosexuals in employment.[7] At the Minneapolis conference, 150 conservative activists staged a formal walk-out; dozens of conservatives in Los Angeles engaged in ballot tearing; and in Washington, D.C., less than a month after the Baltimore meeting, an orthodox alliance staged a counter-conference called the "American Family Forum." Of the latter, columnist James Kilpatrick said, "It was as one-sidedly conservative as the Baltimore affair was one-sidedly liberal."[8] Polarization was also seen in the balloting over the conference recommendations. There was little controversy over such issues as child welfare and maternal health, but on such issues as the ratification of the Equal Rights Amendment, abortion policy, and "variant family life-styles," the conferees generally took the extreme opposite positions—either strongly in favor or strongly opposed.[9]

National and regional media reports of the White House Conference on Families reflected the antagonism in the meetings. An article in *Newsweek*, for example, called it "the biggest political battleground between conservatives and liberals since the National Women's Conference in

Houston in 1977."[10] The *Nashville Banner* reported that "during the first three hours of the conference's forums, divorce, homosexuality, violence on television, sex education in public schools, welfare and prayer came up, rose to debate, then fell into the boiling pot of controversy."[11] The *Washington Post* observed the "uproar [created] by the 'pro-life' lobby, the abortion rights lobby, the gay rights lobby, the pro-family lobby and all the rest," and commented that these "single-interest groups . . . approached [the conference] as a forum in which either to press their views or to defend them against assault from other quarters."[12] The *New Mexican* concluded that "the feelings produced by these [meetings] are more appropriate to a buffalo stampede than they are to an enlightened, growing experience."[13] One observer writing in the *New Republic* was not at all surprised. As she put it, the discord generated from the White House conference merely reflected the futility of "construct[ing] a family policy when we have neither a generally accepted understanding of what a family is nor of what such a policy should accomplish."[14]

THE FATE OF THE TRADITIONAL FAMILY

The White House Conference on Families was an important event in the history of the family policy debate in its own right; however, its story is recounted here because it displays the level and intensity of discord over how Americans define the family. Obviously, more is at stake than a dictionary definition of "the family." The debate actually takes form as a political judgment about the fate of *one particular conception of the family and family life.* The rhetoric of the activists, however, misses the mark. Leaders within the orthodox alliance call it the "traditional" family, by which they mean persons living together who are related either by blood, marriage, or adoption. But the family type they envision is "traditional" only in a limited sense. What is in fact at stake is a certain *idealized* form of the nineteenth-century middle-class family: a male-dominated nuclear family that both sentimentalized childhood and motherhood and, at the same time, celebrated domestic life as a utopian retreat from the harsh realities of industrial society. Although such bourgeois families were central in many ways to the flourishing of the early modern society, their fate is now in serious doubt. The political debate asks whether this family type should be preserved or abandoned.

One could make numerous qualifications about the ideological differences that exist among otherwise compatible activists (on either side of the cultural divide). Down to the essence, however, the posture of each alliance is so well known that the presentation of either viewpoint is almost a caricature of itself. Conservative Catholics, Mormons, and Evangelical Protestants generally view the survival of the bourgeois family as essential, not just because it was believed to be established in nature and ordained by God, but because it is believed to foster social harmony. "Much of the conflict in the modern family," wrote one Evangelical, "is caused either by misunderstanding of or by the refusal to accept the role each [family] member was designed by God to fulfill." For this reason, "it is essential to family harmony that the wife submit to her husband's leadership." The writer continued, "The man has yet to be married who wouldn't enjoy coming home each day to a wife with a song in her heart, a thanksgiving attitude and a submissive spirit."[15]

By contrast, the general consensus within the progressivist alliance is that the bourgeois family is not only the symbol but the *source* of inequality and oppression for women in society. "The central values of the modern family stand in opposition to those that underlie women's emancipation," one activist argued. "Where the women's movement has stood for equality, the family historically has denied or repudiated equality. . . . Where the women's movement has called for a recognition of individualism, the family has insisted upon subordination of individual interests to those of the group. . . ."[16] Thus, the demands of progressives are not just for civil rights, "reproductive rights," and equal opportunity for women, but for a fundamentally new conception of the family. "We believe," asserted NOW's founding statement of purpose, "that a true partnership between the sexes *demands a different concept of marriage,* an equitable sharing of the responsibilities of home and children and of the economic burdens of their support." To that end progressive voices call for a change in the nuclear family structure and in society as a whole. The more moderate within the movement call for the reform of the bourgeois family through the equal division of domestic and public labor; the more extreme view the oppression of women as rooted in their biological role in reproduction and demand the total abolishment of all forms of traditional and patriarchal authority. In either case, the net effect within this alliance is to define the family not in terms of a particular configuration of biological relationships but more broadly as companionship. Such a definition recognizes the "validity of different family types" not accounted for by the nuclear family ideal—single parents, nonmarital cohabitation, homosexual and lesbian unions, and so on.

The social and ideological reaction is entirely predictable. Because cultural conservatives assume that the traditional family is mandated by both nature and God, a pluralistic model of family life can only be regarded as organized hostility toward the "traditional" family; "a total assault on the role of the American woman as wife and mother, and on the family as the basic unit of society."[17] And so it is that contenders in this cultural contest square off to determine which definition and ideal of family life will finally hold sway.

POLICY BRAWLS

The struggle to define the American family—whether public policy should embrace or reject the nineteenth-century middle-class family ideal—is practically enjoined not in its totality but in terms of its component parts. The clash, in other words, takes shape over specific concepts that underlie various policy proposals under debate—components that together make up a definition of the American family.

Authority

Families, however they are practically imagined, are a social unit that cooperates to carry out collective tasks—providing for the members' basic material and emotional needs, nurturing children to acceptable levels of social and moral responsibility, and so on. But who is responsible for these tasks and who will have the final say when difficult decisions need to be made? The issue here is one of *authority*. Should it rest with husband and father, as the orthodox and their culturally conservative allies prefer? Or should authority and responsibility be shared on egalitarian principles, as progressives and their liberal allies favor?

The issue of authority is implicit within several policy debates. Perhaps the most important, because it has been debated for the better part of the twentieth century, has been the Equal Rights Amendment (ERA). This amendment to the Constitution initially was introduced in Congress in 1923 through the efforts of the National Women's party. It finally was passed by Congress in 1972, yet it failed to be ratified by a sufficient number of state legislatures by a 1982 deadline. Reintroduced in 1983, the proposal lay largely dormant through the 1980s and early 1990s. Even so, the goal of the ERA has remained a central aspiration of the women's movement and of political progressives in general.

Advocates argue that the amendment guarantees equal protection under the law without regard for a person's gender. Conservatives claim that such protections are already guaranteed under the Constitution and that an amendment would be redundant. The deeper significance of the amendment, however, is symbolic. For progressivists, the Equal Rights Amendment symbolizes the formal recognition by the state (through the instrumentality of law) that women are autonomous from and therefore economically and politically equal to men. For those on the orthodox side, the amendment symbolizes a forsaking of the inherited structure of social relationships in the family and society as a whole. The ERA, claimed one conservative Illinois legislator, was "really an attack on the home. It [was] an attack on motherhood. It says that for a woman to have to be a mother and have to be a housewife is somehow degrading."[18]

Morover, many activists with orthodox commitments may also have mobilized against the ERA because it was viewed as way of "smuggling" legal protection of homosexual rights into a Constitutional amendment. One Fundamentalist opponent to the amendment put it this way: "If effective laws to help women are already on the books, who needs the ERA? Not women as a sex but lesbians and homosexuals need the ERA; and believe me, that's what it's really all about! Homosexuals and lesbians, who number perhaps 6 percent of the population, recognize their unpopular status. They decided early that the feminist movement and the ERA provided them with a handy vehicle to ride piggyback upon 'women's rights' and achieve homosexual rights. Fortunately, citizens who suddenly realized how close we were to the city limits of Sodom and Gomorrah successfully resisted the ERA."[19] Other symbolic issues were at stake as well, such as the role of women in the military and the fate of single-sex institutions (such as Catholic seminaries and Orthodox Jewish schools) which discriminate according to gender for religious reasons. These issues remain key symbolic landmarks on both sides of the cultural divide.

The ERA is, of course, only one of the ways in which the issue of authority in family and society is played out in public policy. The identical arguments emerge in policy debates over such ideas as an "Equal Rights Act" and "comparable worth" or "pay equity."[20] Though the latter issue technically deals with gender bias in wage setting, the symbolic meaning of the proposal is clear. Its advocates contend that the issue involves more than "just money," it involves "the esteem of half our population."[21] Opponents insist that, among other things, pay equity "requires us to close our eyes to innate sexual differences which affect job preferences."[22] The matter of authority is also contested in our very language.

Language is not challenged at the level of federal law, although it is disputed at the level of organizational etiquette. This conflict focuses on the use of gender-specific language, as in the generic use of masculine pronouns (he, him, his) or the generic use of masculine titles (chairman, repairman, garbageman). What for traditionalists is the proper use of the English language is, for progressives, a pattern of speech that denigrates women and linguistically validates male domination. On both sides of the cultural divide, language itself—the ordering of symbols in our society—has become a politicized dimension of the culture war. This reality begins in the conflict over authority but it extends to the issue of abortion, homosexuality, euthanasia, and so on. The battle will be nearly over when the linguistic preferences of one side of the cultural divide become the conventions of society as a whole.

Perhaps this is the reason why the issue of language is so fiercely fought in religious institutions. Churches and synagogues may not possess great political power, but their capacity to legitimate social reality is undeniable. Nowhere is gender-specific language used more authoritatively than in religious and theological discourse. Among progressivists in the churches, the very language of God the Father, Christ the Son, Christ as "bridegroom," and the church as "his bride," as well as the standard references to "God's love for mankind," and so on, gives religious and sacred legitimation to gender-based inequities and even oppression. Granted, the Scriptures were written in the context of a patriarchal society, but progressive revelation, it is held, would never condone such practices for our own day. On the basis of this general rationale, hymn books, prayer books, Sunday school material, and the language of Scripture itself have been revised in order to reflect new realities. In response to such concerns, for example, the National Council of Churches published three sets of highly controversial revisions of biblical passages that referred to God as "Father" and "Mother," inserted women's names that did not appear in the original, and refrained from calling God "Father" or "King," Jesus the "Son" of God or the "Son of Man," and heaven as a "kingdom."[23] The same kinds of linguistic changes were employed in a controversial lectionary sponsored by the National Council of Churches. In this new style of speech and worship, the Trinity would be referred to as "Creator, Redeemer, and Sanctifier," Christ's disciples would be called to be "fishers of human beings," the lineage of the old covenant with Israel would now include the wives of Abraham, Isaac, and Jacob, and every male-specific pronoun would be excised from the text. Battles have been waged over this issue in most if not all the mainline denominations, including the Episcopalians, the United Methodist Church; the Presbyterian Church, U.S.A.; the Evangelical Lutheran Church in America; and the Disciples of Christ. But such innovations, especially the efforts to neuter the language and imagery of God, only deepen the discontent of the more conservative laity in opposition to their more progressive leaders in the denominational hierarchy. For the religiously orthodox, inclusive language in religious, theological, and biblical discourse denies the classical religious understanding of divine revelation. As an orthodox Episcopalian complained (in response to the introduction of inclusive language in Episcopalian liturgy), "When we dehistoricize our faith, when we substitute abstractions and our own ideas for the narrative in which God has made himself known, we evacuate the Gospel of its content and power and replace it with a religion of our own making."[24]

Not surprisingly, the symbolic conflict over authority has led to controversies about the ordination of women. The issue carries more symbolic weight in some traditions than in others. In some, the issue is not controversial at all. The American Baptist Church, for example, has been ordaining women since 1893, the United Church of Christ since 1853, and the Pentecostal churches since their beginning in the late nineteenth century. In others, the symbolic meaning of ordination is enormously consequential, representing (at least in the Christian traditions) nothing less than the succession of Christ's authority in this world. Among those mainline denominations that previously did not ordain women, two major ones began to do so in the late 1950s (the United Methodist Church and the Presbyterian Church, U.S.A. in 1956), and many others began in the 1970s: the Episcopal Church in 1977, the American Lutheran Church and the Lutheran Church in America in 1970, the Reformed Church in America and the Mennonite Church in 1973. The seriousness with which women take this opportunity is reflected in the enrollments of women at seminary. Between 1968 and 1976, the number of women in Protestant seminaries increased from 12 percent of total enrollment to 21 percent.[25] By 1985–86, women made up over one-fourth of the total Protestant seminary enrollment nationally, with their representation in the mainline seminaries much greater.[26] Though the Catholic hierarchy has shown no sign of compromising on the ordination question, the pressure to admit women to the priesthood in America, nevertheless, continues to increase, not only because of the social and political pressure of many progressive Catholic women, but because of the desperate shortage of male priests. But the pressure from

Catholic traditionalists to maintain the status quo is also substantial.[27] In the end, even where the battle over ordination has been resolved, it extends to the sharing of authority in ecclesiastical structure, both at the congregational level (where still very few women act as head minister), and at the denominational level (in the struggle for representation among positions of national leadership). The issue promises not to fade away.

Obligation

Another concept crucial to family life (however it is defined) is that of *obligation.* Of course, in a family there is a mutual obligation to care for and nurture each other. But to whom are we bound in this way? To what extent are we bound and for how long are we bound in this way? The answers to these questions reveal positions on matters of personal autonomy. No matter how tight the family is as a social unit, the family is made up of individuals who have needs and desires apart from the family. So, in addition to the questions surrounding obligation, a further question asks how the need for individual autonomy is to be balanced against the requirement of family obligation. Should the need for autonomy (the obligation to the self) take priority over the needs of the family (our obligation to others) or should personal needs be subordinated to the will and interests of the family?

Consider the matter of abortion. The sociologist Kristin Luker has argued cogently that the struggle over abortion is ultimately a struggle over the concept of motherhood.[28] For pro-life activists, motherhood tends to be viewed as the most important and satisfying role open to a woman. Abortion, therefore, represents an attack on the very activity that gives life meaning. For pro-choice activists, motherhood is simply one role among many, and yet when defined as the only role, it is almost always a hardship. Abortion in this context is a means of liberating women from the burden of unplanned or unwanted childbearing and childrearing.

Luker's argument is certainly true as far as it goes, but beyond the concept of motherhood, abortion also raises issues of obligation and autonomy. Those holding to the orthodox vision tend to believe that family obligation extends not only to the born and living but to the unborn as well. Pro-life activists contend that the unborn have rights that must be protected by others, since they cannot defend those rights themselves. Because historically and religiously, the duty of motherhood is commonly viewed as the protection of children, legalized abortion represents an assault on the mother's principle obligation and her source of identity. Progressivists reject this idea and wonder how we can be obligated to what are, at best, "potential persons." The legal right to an abortion is seen as ensuring that women maintain their individual autonomy from men who might compete with them in the workplace or husbands who wish to restrict wives' freedom by keeping them in the realm of domestic travail. In this view, legislation that restricts access to abortion would, in the words of a statement from the National Abortion Rights Action League, "threaten the core of a woman's constitutionally valued autonomy . . . by violating the principle of bodily integrity that underlies much of the [Constitution's] promise of liberty . . . and by plac[ing] severe constraints on women's employment opportunities and . . . their ability to support themselves and their families."[29]

The same issue of obligation underlies the policy debates over child care. With an increasing number of women in the work force and an increasing number of working women with young children, it is not surprising that child care would become politicized. The question is not really who has the obligation to care for young children. Everyone would agree that it is the parents or those acting as parents. The real question is, what are the legitimate ways that parents or guardians can meet those obligations? Two different understandings of parental responsibility have taken shape. Within the progressivist vision, parental responsibility is principally achieved in meeting the growing economic requirements of raising children at the end of the twentieth century. Besides meeting basic needs, this means making sure that children have the opportunities to develop their full potentials as human beings. As for moral and social development, progressivists tend to believe that the children of dual-career families do not necessarily suffer if some child care is given by someone other than a parent or family member. What matters is the *quality* of time spent with children. But the consensus among cultural conservatives is that children do suffer when others besides family members participate in child care. Parents, they claim, are the ones best suited to socializing the young, particularly when it comes to passing on a moral and religious heritage. "The education and upbringing of children is the primary responsibility of parents. Selfishly or ignorantly surrendering this role would be a grave disservice to our youth as well as our free society. The family must cling to its God-ordained roles or future generations will suffer the consequences."[30]

These opposing views lead to predictable positions on public policy concerning child care. Policies promoting government-sponsored child care for dual-career families are seen as a way to give economic assistance to a growing number of women who have small children and must work, or as an abdication of the parental obligation to provide care and moral instruction to children. In the Act for Better Child Care, for example, we can see virtually all of the dimensions of the culture war. As briefly observed in chapter 3, the act was supported by, among others, the National Organization for Women, *Ms.* Magazine, the Union of American Hebrew Congregations, and the United Methodist Board of Church and Society. The act was opposed by such orthodox groups as Concerned Women for America, the American Council of Christian Churches (and criticized by its Fundamentalist News Service), and James Dobson's Focus on the Family periodical *Citizen*. The bill assumed, according to its critics, that "the federal government is more capable than the parents to determine what is best for the child." Catholic constitutional lawyer William Bentley Ball said that the bill "reads flat out as a secularist prescription for the care of American children."[31]

It is the sense that family obligations are being willfully abandoned that is behind the conservative complaint about the liberalization of divorce law (as in the idea and practice of "no fault divorce") and the concomitant rise in the rate of divorce as well. For many holding to a progressivist vision of moral life, the liberalization of divorce law is simply a means of guaranteeing individual autonomy when the obligations of marriage or of family life become burdensome and oppressive.

Sexuality: The Challenge of Homosexuality

Sexuality, of course, is also at the heart of family life. It is the family more than any other institution that establishes the rules for sexual intimacy—the codes that define the persons with whom, the time when, and the conditions under which sexual intimacy is acceptable. How the family enacts these rules also implies a judgment upon what "nature" will allow or should allow. But what is "natural" in matters of sexuality? The answer goes right to the heart of assumptions about the moral order: what is good, what is right, what is appropriate. Family life, however, is also a "school of virtue," for it bears the responsibility, as no other institution can, for socializing children—raising them as decent and moral people, passing on the morals of a community to the next generation. How parents view nature in matters of sexuality, therefore, is reflected in the ways they teach children about right and wrong. How the actors in the contemporary culture war view nature in matters of sexuality, in turn, will be reflected in their different ideals of how the moral order of a society will take shape in the future.

Perhaps with the exception of abortion, few issues in the contemporary culture war generate more raw emotion than the issue of homosexuality. The reason is plain: few other issues challenge the traditional assumptions of what nature will allow, the boundaries of the moral order, and finally the ideals of middle-class family life more radically. Homosexuality symbolizes either an absolute and fundamental perversion of nature, of the social order, and of American family life, or it is simply another way in which nature can evolve and be expressed, another way of ordering society, and an alternative way of conducting family life.

Both sides of the contemporary cultural divide understand the critical importance of homosexuality for the larger culture war. One apologist for gay and lesbian interests put it this way: "We should see anti-gay fear and hatred as part of a cultural offensive against liberal egalitarian social principles generally. Homophobia is a vehicle for the conservative ideology that links the defense of the patriarchal family with the maintenance of class, race, and gender hierarchy throughout society."[32] To be gay, then, is to share the ordeal of other marginalized people in the nation; to be public about it places one in solidarity with the oppressed and their agenda of social change. Clearly, this is why major gay rights organizations participate in and often officially cosponsor activism on behalf of abortion rights, women's rights, the homeless, and so on. As literature from the National Gay and Lesbian Task Force put it, they are "committed to ending systems of oppression in all forms."[33]

The hostility to gay rights activism on the other side of the cultural divide follows much the same line as presented by Chuck McIlhenny or Rabbi Levin, for whom homosexuality represents an assault on biblical truths. Republican Congressman William Dannemeyer from California, for example, is quoted as saying that the homosexual movement represents "the most vicious attack on traditional family values that our society has seen in the history of our republic."[34] Some in the orthodox alliance have argued that "the family is the fundamental unit of society, for it is the principle of permanence. For most persons it furnishes the primary experience of stability, continuity and fidelity. In this respect, and in many others, it is a school for citizenship. But it can maintain its function over the long run only if we accord it preferential status over alternative sexual arrangements and liaisons." The homosexual movement, therefore, is "destructive of the family and . . . a potent threat to society."[35]

The rejoinder to this orthodox contention is an explicit affirmation of the aim to redefine the family—to proclaim "a new vision of family life." The response of the National Gay and Lesbian Task Force is that "lesbians and gay men are not a threat to families, but are an essential thread in the fabric of American family life." Ours, they contend, "is a vision of diverse family life that is directly opposed to the once-upon-a-time myth promoted by the right wing. Our vision is inclusive, not discriminatory. It is functional, rather than legalistic." Therefore, "threats to the American family do not come from the desire of gay men and lesbians to create loving relationships," but rather "from the right wing's manipulation of ignorance, bigotry and economic injustice. These threats to *our* families must be met with outrage . . . action . . . and resources."[36]

And indeed the gay community has responded in this way within several areas of public policy. Perhaps the most important area over which the issue of the legitimacy of the "gay alternative" is concretely contested is the matter of marriage rights for homosexual couples. Let's be very clear about this: more is at stake here than the emotional rewards of formalizing a shared commitment in a relationship. The practical benefits of marriage are of tangible and often crucial importance to the lives of individuals: marriage partners may take part in the spouse's health plan and pension programs, share the rights of inheritance and community property, make a claim upon a spouse's rent-controlled apartment, and file joint tax returns. These legal and economic advantages were all designed to encourage the economic independence and interdependence of the traditional family unit and indeed, couples in traditional heterosexual marriages have long benefited from them. By the same token, they have been denied to homosexual couples, heterosexual couples living out of wedlock, and living arrangements involving long-term platonic roommates—all of which may involve the same degree of economic and emotional dependence that occurs within a traditional family.

As the contemporary culture war has intensified, the general ambition of gay rights activists has been to push for the legal recognition of homosexual relationships as legitimate marriages or at least as "domestic partners" in order to ultimately secure these economic benefits. This is precisely the conflict we saw between Chuck McIlhenny and Richmond Young in San Francisco at the beginning of the book. While the fifty states have been reluctant to recognize the legality or legal rights of homosexual marriages, a handful of cities such as Los Angeles; New York; Madison, Wisconsin; and Takoma Park, Maryland, do provide bereavement leave for domestic partners who are municipal workers. A few others, such as Berkeley, Santa Cruz, and West Hollywood, offer health benefits for the same. This push has continued in still other cities around the country where laws prohibiting discrimination on the basis of marital status are being examined to see whether they extend to the living arrangements of homosexual couples.

Needless to say, such proposals pose a serious challenge to the traditional conception of marriage and family. The very idea is a "serious blow to our society's historic commitment to supporting marriage and family life," stated the archbishop of San Francisco in response to the domestic partners referendum in that city.[37] Yet even in the gay community there is disagreement about this goal—not because it shares the archbishop's views, but because the legislation does not go far enough. The campaign for domestic partnership or gay marriage is misdirected, argued one lesbian activist, because it tries to adopt traditional heterosexual institutions for gays rather then encourage tolerance for divergent life-styles. "Marriage, as it exists today, is antithetical to my liberation as a lesbian and as a woman, because it mainstreams my life and voice."[38]

The issues of bigotry and discrimination, in the view of homosexuals and of many activists for the progressivist vision, has gone beyond disputes over marriage rights or domestic partners to other areas of policy concern. For example, bigotry has been seen in the battles to either perpetuate or repeal "sodomy laws," as in the 1986 Supreme Court decision *Bowers v. Hardwick,* which upheld Georgia's sodomy law. Such laws (which still exist in twenty-four states), according to gay activists, "define our sexual lives as criminal, unnatural, perverse and repulsive." The perpetuation of these laws they feel, "gives the government's stamp of approval on individual people's homophobia, in much the same way that Jim Crow laws institutionalized racism and the segregation of black people in the American South."[39] The struggle over the passage, in 1990, of the Hate Crime Statistics Act, requiring the federal government to collect statistics on crimes motivated by prejudice based on race, ethnicity, religion, or "sexual orientation" brought gay issues to the fore when Congress passed an amendment to this bill stating that "American family life is the foundation of American society" and "nothing in this act shall be construed" to "promote or encourage homosexuality."[40] The symbolic significance of that amendment was not missed by the gay rights activists, even as they celebrated the bill's passage. Direct mail from the National

Gay and Lesbian Task Force called the act "the most significant lesbian and gay rights victory in the history of the U.S. Congress!"[41] Bigotry and discrimination in economic issues such as employment and housing have been sharply contested in policy debates over the Civil Rights Amendments Act. The original Civil Rights Act of 1964 prohibited discrimination on the basis of race, color, religion, or national origin; the new amendment (originally proposed in 1975) would extend the existing act to include the prohibition of discrimination relating to sexual orientation. In each of these policy areas, what is at stake is a tacit recognition on the part of the government that homosexuality is an authentic manner of life, social relationship, family, and community.

Interestingly, the stakes of recognition and legitimacy are raised to perhaps their highest symbolic level in those cases where the source of "discrimination and bigotry" is the military establishment itself. The military, of course, is an American institution that has long been defined by a rigid organizational hierarchy and by traditional notions of manliness: bravery, platonic bonding, emphatic heterosexuality, and the like. The contrast between U.S. military culture and a subculture that is defined by an intimacy among members of the same sex could not be more stark. The tensions are inevitable. A Naval cadet near the top of his class was expelled just two months before his graduation from the Annapolis Naval Academy after announcing to his friends that he was gay; fourteen lesbians at Parris Island boot camp were discharged from the Marine Corps in 1988; and twelve noncommissioned officers in the Air Force were discharged in 1989 for homosexual activity. These occurrences are not uncommon, for according to Department of Defense figures, an average of about 1,400 gay men and women are expelled from the armed forces every year.[42] Legal challenges to incidents such as these, and to military policy that requires dismissal of gay officers in training from ROTC programs at universities (where the military often acquires more than half of its new officers) point to an intensification of the conflict that will be decisive for the larger controversy.

The other pivotal institutions in which the legitimacy of homosexuality has been contested are the churches. One might imagine that the deep and longstanding hostility of the Judeo-Christian faiths toward homosexuality would encourage homosexual men and lesbians to leave their faiths altogether. But for those who continue to identify with a particular religious tradition, there appears to be little desire to leave. This was certainly true for Richmond Young, whom we met in the prologue, as it is for others. Said one priest, "My Catholicism is a deep part of my identity, as is my sexuality. I do not plan to give up either."[43] Others have echoed this sentiment, "As members of Dignity we are a gay presence in the Church and a Christian presence within the gay community. We are proud that we can bring Christian values and beliefs to the gay community and equally proud that we can bring our gayness before the Church."[44] One lesbian nun spoke for many others of every religious confession when she described herself as "very much of a prophet among my own sisters."[45] The objective is not to be changed by the church but to change the church from the inside. The sense that they are succeeding in this was captured in the words of one layman who lamented, "What in 1963 was regarded as an offense against basic morality and a betrayal of solemn vows is today, alas, too often regarded as a legitimate 'sexual preference,' a 'human right,' and a 'progressive cause.' . . . [Today] those who still think that homosexual acts are sinful are accused of being 'homophobic,' while active homosexuals boldly proclaim their own moral superiority."[46]

The key dispute here is over the moral authority of the churches and of religious tradition. The dominant symbolic issue is ordination: can a practicing homosexual be God's representative here on earth? The answer is unequivocally "no" in religious bodies and organizations in the orthodox alliance. Homosexuality is a sin against God, an open violation of His divine and intended order. Mainline and progressive religious bodies and organizations, however, are much more ambivalent about the issue. Only a handful of denominations, such as the Unitarian Universalists, the Swedenborgians, and regional bodies in the United Church of Christ and the Disciples of Christ openly and officially ordain practicing homosexuals. A few Episcopalian and Lutheran bishops have ordained practicing homosexuals against the official teaching of the denominational hierarchy (actions that always raise the ire of lay people and conservative clergy yet frequently generate little more than a call for censure).[47] The Roman Catholic hierarchy has remained staunchly opposed to the ordination of practicing homosexuals and yet estimates of the number of gay priests in parishes range from 10 to 50 percent.[48] On the one hand, then, official ecclesiastical policy in the mainline bodies has been reticent to bestow its ultimate blessing upon homosexuality. There has been, nevertheless, a strong progressive impulse to support the movement from a distance. At least fifteen denominations or official organizations within denominations representing Protestant, Catholic, and Jewish faiths, for example, have formally endorsed the liberal reform of sodomy laws.[49] The pressure upon denominations to do more than this is not likely to fade away since there is at least one (and often two or three) gay and lesbian rights lobby pressing its agenda within virtually every major denomination in America. Still, orthodox-leaning renewal leaders and their followers in the mainline religious bodies (especially in Protestantism) view policy on homosexuality as *the* "watershed issue"—the issue over which they either stay within the mainline or leave.[50] A tremendous amount of money, people, and resources, therefore, would likely disappear if homosexuality were sanctioned any more than it is.

As the strongest institutional bulwarks of traditionalist ideals of gender roles and sexuality, the military establishment and the churches are barometers of how the conflict over homosexuality fares in the larger social order. As the armed forces and the churches go on this issue, so may go the rest of American society.

What intensifies the struggle over the homosexuality issue is the AIDS crisis in the gay community. The quest for public recognition and legitimacy has become a matter of life and death because along with recognition and legitimacy comes the ability to credibly argue for and expect both public sympathy and increased public expenditure for medical research and health care. Cultural conservatives recognize this as well, many believing that "homosexuals and liberals are using the AIDS crisis to force our children to be taught their ultra-liberal views on sexuality and morality."[51] A measure of the desperation that gays feel is seen in the practice of "outing"—intentional exposure of secret and usually prominent homosexuals (politicians, religious leaders, and the like) by other homosexuals. The rationale is that the gay rights movement needs all the support it can muster. These public figures could be helping the cause but either have chosen silence or have openly worked against the cause in order to protect their careers. They deserve "outing" for their "malicious hypocrisy on matters of life and death."[52]

In Sum

The disputes over the nature and structure of authority, the moral obligations of parenting and marital commitment, the natural and legitimate boundaries of sexual experience, and so on, are all part of the struggle to define the family in its totality. In this struggle, it is important to point out that progressive activists have faced a difficult time shaking the image of being anti-family and anti-children. "Its enthusiasm for abortion and for day care," one observer remarked, "has strengthened this impression, suggesting that here are people who want to prevent children from being born . . . and failing this, to dump children so that mothers can pursue their selfish programs of self-realization." Progressive activists vehemently deny that their agenda is anti-family. They maintain that they desire a much more "inclusive vision of family life . . . of people who love and care for one another."[53] Their insistence on this serves to confirm the argument made here, that each side of the cultural divide simply operates with a different conception of what the family is, how it behaves, and what its place and role should be. Which side is finally tarred with the label "anti-family" will depend on which model of the family finally prevails in public policy.

FAMILY AND NATION

Few would disagree that the family is perhaps the most fundamental institution of any society. This has been acknowledged again and again: from the pronouncement of a Puritan minister from Connecticut, who in 1643 wrote, "The prosperity and well being of the Commonwealth doth much depend upon the well government and ordering of particular families," to the oratory of President Lyndon Johnson, who in 1965 stated that "the family is a cornerstone of our society. More than any other force, it shapes the attitudes, the hopes, the ambitions, and the values of the child. When the family collapses it is the children that are usually damaged. When it happens on a massive scale the community itself is crippled."[54] If this is true, then it is in a government's interest to create a policy that would foster healthy family life. Early on it was believed that a coherent national policy could be formulated that would do precisely that. The policy establishment could have never imagined how naive that belief was.

As it has evolved, family policy has come to mean different things to people involved in influencing that policy. For those on the progressivist side of the debate, family policy is understood to mean economic assistance and social services that would put a floor under family income and lead the way to self-sufficiency. Such policy would be particularly useful in redressing old and ongoing wrongs to blacks, to the poor, and to women. Those on the conservative side tend to view such policies as promoting indolence, promiscuity, easy abortion, and parent indifference to the task of childrearing. They believe that the infusion of public money into social and economic programs would lead to greater family instability. For this reason, the government should leave the family alone. As Phyllis Schlafly said at the White House Conference on Families in 1980, "Pro-family groups don't think the Federal Government has the competence to deal with the family: it aggravates problems rather than solves them."[55]

On the surface, one side would appear to favor government assistance while the other does not; one favors public policy and the other does not. But those who maintain the latter option really argue disingenuously. Because our earlier consensus on what the family *is* has unraveled, the question is not now whether to *have* a family policy but which policy will be adopted. Which vision of the family will enjoy the massive favor of the government? In this light, one can begin to understand that conflict over the family is also a conflict over the power of the state in the service of a still larger vision of reality, a still larger agenda for public culture.

8

Education

When, on the one hand, the president of Citizens for Excellence in Education (the activist wing of the National Association of Christian Educators) mused strategically about getting "an active Christian parents committee in operation in all [15,700 school districts in America], [so that] we can take complete control of all local school boards," and when, on the other hand, the legal director of the American Civil Liberties Union asked for financial support for its "longstanding effort to protect nonsectarian education from the meddling of the fundamentalist right," there is all but a formal declaration of war over the public schools.[1]

One might point to the infamous Scopes trial of 1926, which pitted the legitimacy of teaching evolutionism against creationism as conflicting theories of human origins, as the start of it all. Indeed, that particular issue has been contested with slight variations many times since—in Tennessee, Louisiana, California, and elsewhere. But the creation-evolution debate is really only one component of a much more comprehensive conflict that has taken shape over the content of public education. In 1974, for example, a member of the board of education in Kanawha County, West Virginia, the wife of a Fundamentalist minister, took exception to the content of some new books under consideration for public schools. Her complaint was that the books were both anti-Christian and morally flawed. When the books were finally adopted by the board's majority against the wishes of Fundamentalist parents and local clergy, a massive protest ensued which included a boycott of the school and even the firebombing of the classrooms. Other real-life illustrations of the larger conflict over the schools abound—in issues dealing with prayer, equal access for Bible-reading and prayer clubs, the moral content of textbooks, public funding for religious education, and the like.

The reason that the contemporary culture war extends to the realm of education is not difficult to divine. The education of the public at every level—from elementary school through college—is not a neutral process of imparting practical knowledge and technical skills. Above and beyond that, schools are the primary institutional means of *reproducing community and national identity* for succeeding generations of Americans. This is where we first learn and where we are continually reminded with others of our generation—through courses on history, geography, civics, literature, and the like—what it means to be an American. Thus, when the meaning of our identity as Americans is contested, as it is in the contemporary culture war, the conflict will inevitably reach the institutions that impart these collective understandings to children and young adults.

THE "SCHOOL QUESTION"

It is because of the intrinsic link between public education, community and national identity, and the future (symbolized by children) that the institutions of education have long been a political and legal battleground.[2] In the mid-1800s, for example, there was also a struggle over the moral content of public education. At the time, what was commonly and perhaps understatedly referred to as simply the "School Question" reflected the major cultural divisions of the time—antipathy between Protestants and Catholics. How that struggle unfolded is a story instructive for our own time, for it reveals the dynamics, the passions, and the political stakes involved in the present battles over education.

Lessons from the Past

As the number of Catholic immigrants in the United States continued to swell through the early decades of the nineteenth century, they began to press for an educational system that would meet the needs of their young. The public and state-supported education that existed was simply not adequate. The "common schools," as they were then called, promoted religious instruction, but of a decidedly nonsectarian, Protestant cast. Schools required the use of the (Protestant) King James Bible (instead of the Douay Bible—an English translation of the Latin Vulgate edition); instituted Protestant hymns and prayers; and permitted anti-Catholic passages in textbooks and library books. The so-called nonsectarian schools, Catholics argued, were in reality very much sectarian, but of a wider denominational cut. As Bishop Francis Kenrick of Philadelphia put it, "[The schools are] founded on a Protestant principle, and the books, even if free from direct invective against Catholics, which is not often the case, are all of a Protestant complexion." The Catholics wished to respond simply by establishing their own system of education. In New York they were somewhat successful in that endeavor, but in Philadelphia Catholics were almost wholly dependent upon the common schools. In both situations, however, the situation was viewed as unfair. If public funds were to be made available for what was, in effect, Protestant education, these funds should also be made available for Catholic education. Otherwise, the public schools should become more genuinely pluralistic, allowing Catholic children to use the Catholic Bible and Protestant children to use the Protestant Bible. As Bishop Kenrick argued, the "religious predilections of the parents [should] be respected."[3]

The efforts of Catholics under the leadership of Bishop Kenrick and Bishop John Hughes of New York either to acquire some portion of the public aid given to public education for Catholic purposes or to pluralize the existing public schools gained some hearing initially. Ultimately, however, their bid failed in the face of a strident and organized Protestant backlash, not only from the anti-Catholic Know-Nothing organizations but from the mainstream Protestant press itself. The public schools, claimed the *North American,* had been "planned by Protestants, directed by Protestants, and almost wholly supported by Protestants." The *Presbyterian* concurred: "Protestants founded these schools, and they have always been in the majority." The implication was that their views should therefore prevail. Similar convictions were voiced in the *Baptist Record,* the *Episcopal Recorder,* and Congregationalist and Methodist journals. Their sense of entitlement over the public schools ultimately betrayed a resentment against Catholicism that was not always gracefully disguised. As one Baptist weekly, the *Watchman,* sneered, "If the children of Papists are really in danger of being corrupted in the Protestant schools of enlightened, free and happy America, it may be well of their conscientious parents and still more conscientious priests, to return them to the privileges of their ancestral homes, among the half-tamed boors of Germany."[4]

But the expanding Catholic community was not deterred in voicing its complaint. One bishop in Illinois described public schools as "seminaries of infidelity, and as such most fruitful sources of immorality." Even the papal authorities in Rome became involved. In 1875 the Congregation of the Propaganda, which was responsible for overseeing the Catholic Church in America, issued a statement directing parents to send their children to Catholic schools along with a warning to the American Catholic bishops that they would be "recreant to their duty" if they failed to provide such schools. The logic behind this decree was rooted in the conviction that "evils of gravest kind are likely to result from the so-called public schools," which are "most dangerous and very much opposed to Catholicity." For this reason many leaders in the Catholic hierarchy continued to press for a system of education similar to those existing in European countries "where," as an archbishop from Cincinnati explained, "the rights of conscience in the matter of education have been fully recognized."[5]

Over the long term, the efforts to secure public funds for Catholic education failed. The well-intended efforts to consolidate public and parochial school systems in a just manner failed too. Often, attempts at compromise resulted in an absence of religious instruction rather than a choice between Protestant and Catholic forms. Catholics, as a consequence, were portrayed as the enemies of Bible reading and true Christian morality. The reality, however, was that the Catholics did not reject either Bible reading or moral instruction. Both were central to their theory and practice of education. Catholics opposed secularism as much as Protestants did. The issue was always *which* Bible and *whose* religious instruction. Nevertheless, the Protestant conviction prevailed that the moral and religious foundations of public education were being undermined. The National Teachers' Association (which soon became the National Education Association) at its annual convention in 1869 articulated the dominant Protestant view in two ironically posed resolutions. One stated that "the appropriation of public funds for the support of sectarian institutions is a violation of the fundamental principles of our American system of education." Another stated that "the Bible should not only be studied, venerated, and honored as a classic for all ages, people and languages . . . but devotionally read, and its precepts inculcated in all the common schools of the land."[6] The irony, of course, was that the educational establishment rejected public funds for sectarian education yet that establishment itself was thoroughly sectarian, albeit of the dominant Protestant variety. For Protestants, the common school was one of the chief mechanisms for maintaining their cultural domination. By contrast, the Catholic quest for public funding for parochial schools or for an equitable arrangement in the common school system represented a formidable challenge to that domination.

The Present Struggle

Not only did the Protestant domination over public education dissipate through the first half of the twentieth century but so did the Catholic parochial alternative.[7] The older struggle faded away, but not because the "School Question" had been resolved. Rather, it was because the changing structure of American pluralism made the old antagonism obsolete. Thus, in our own time we see that *the institutions of public education continue to mediate cultural conflict, but the character of the "School Question" has altered to conform to the contours of the contemporary culture war.* The cast of players has changed completely, yet the stakes have remained the same: power over the public schools.

The significance of the public schools to the larger culture war is not small. Actors on both sides of the cultural divide have placed the battle over public education at the center of the larger conflict. An observer of the Kanawha County incident (mentioned earlier) stated, "This country is experiencing a religious crusade as fierce as any out of the Middle Ages. . . . Our children are being sacrificed because of the fanatical zeal of our fundamentalist brothers who claim to be hearing the voice of God. . . . In this religious war, spiced with overtones of race and class, the books are an accessible target."[8] From the opposite point of view, a spokesman for the National Association of Christian Educators claimed that

> there is a great war waged in America—but not on the battlefield of conventional weapons. This battle is for the heart and mind and the soul of every man, woman, and especially child in America. . . . The combatants are "secular humanism" and "Christianity." Atheism, in the cloak of an acceptable "humanitarian" religious philosophy, has been subtly introduced into the traditional Christian American Culture through the public school system. The battle is for the minds of our youth.[9]

Clearly, both caricature the nature of the conflict, yet they do correctly perceive the lines of contention, namely that the alliance of moral traditionalists has become the challenger to a new hegemony, maintained by those it would call "secular humanists."[10]

Conservative Complaints

Orthodox Catholics have long been the most perceptive and articulate on this issue. As early as the 1950s, Catholic educators decried the "problem of secular humanism" in schools. Such a perception, for example, was central to the founding of Citizens for Educational Freedom, a parents' rights educational organization founded by Catholics in St. Louis in 1959. According to one of its founders, a shift occurred: "For a century we opposed the public schools because they were Protestant institutions but now we oppose them because they are secular humanist. They reject any absolutes in morality."[11] This view has been amplified by the conservative Catholic scholar James Hitchcock, who in his book *What Is Secular Humanism?* argued: "Far from being neutral, the American government is now in the position of favoring unbelief over belief and irreligion over religion." Other conservative Catholic organizations, such as the Catholic League for Civil and Religious Rights and such conservative Catholic publications as *The Wanderer* and *Fidelity* have followed suit, openly protesting the way in which "secularists destroy our Judeo-Christian heritage" through sex education programs, "values clarification," and the like.[12] "Our public schools," wrote the president of the Catholic League, "have become 'mission schools of Secularism.' "[13]

Orthodox Jews have not been silent on this issue either. Agudath Israel, representing Orthodox Jewish interests in public policy, for example, explicitly states its opposition to sex education programs, the teaching of evolution, and any other efforts by government "to impose religiously objectionable curricula or other education requirements" particularly upon religious schools.[14]

Though Evangelical and Fundamentalist Protestants have offered subtle analyses of the problem, generally the voices that are heard from these quarters tend to be the most desperate. Presidential hopeful Pat Robertson, for instance, spoke for many of his constituents when he claimed that the American government was "attempting to do something that few states other than the Nazis and the Soviets have attempted to do, namely, to take the children away from the parents and to educate them in a philosophy that is amoral, anti-Christian and humanistic and to show them a collectivistic philosophy that will ultimately lead toward Marxism, socialism and a communistic type of ideology."[15] Never one to mince words, Jimmy Swaggart concluded similarly that "the greatest enemy of our children today in this United States . . . is the public school system. It is education without God." "If the educational system in America in our public schools and our universities," he elsewhere stated, "went totally, absolutely bankrupt tomorrow, it would be the finest thing that ever happened to this country."[16]

Importantly, these views represent more than the early morning crankiness of a few leaders in the orthodox alliance; in fact they have broad-based appeal. In a national survey conducted in late 1987, over two-thirds (69 percent) of the Evangelical respondents familiar with the term agreed that "public schools [were] teaching the values of secular humanism" compared to only one-quarter (27 percent) of those identified as secularists (those without religious preference). An even greater number of Evangelicals (82 percent compared to only 21 percent of the secularists) described its "impact on this country" (presumably in large part through the public schools) as "bad." Among the Evangelical clergy, the assessment was even more uniform. Ninety-one percent agreed that public schools were teaching the values of secular humanism and 94 percent viewed its impact as bad. Likewise the majority of conservative Catholics were disquieted by the public schools as well. The majority of both liberal and traditional Catholic priests (80 percent), for example, agreed that the values of secular humanism were being taught in the schools. Some 87 percent of the traditionally oriented priests argued that its impact was bad, compared to 67 percent of the more liberally oriented priests.[17]

How do the culturally conservative identify the sources of secular humanism? Many fix the blame on the various Supreme Court rulings prohibiting prayer or a moment of silence in public schools. Bill Bright, the founder of Campus Crusade for Christ, for one, called the 1963 ruling against prayer in the public schools "the darkest hour in the history of the nation."[18] Sympathetic with this perspective was a book published by Concerned Women for America, which provided "irrefutable evidence of what has happened to America since school prayer was removed in 1962." According to their research, "removing prayer and the acknowledgment of God from our classrooms has been the *primary cause* of the devastatingly serious decline in the lives of students, their families, the schools, and our nation." For instance, "premarital sexual activity has increased over 200%; pregnancies to unwed mothers are up almost

400%; gonorrhea is up over 200%; suicides have increased over 400%; divorces are up almost 120%; single parents are up 160%; unmarried couples living together have increased over 350%; [and] adultery has increased from 100% to 250%."[19]

Others have maintained that the problem stems directly from the political activism of the National Education Association (NEA). The NEA has been called everything from a "lobbying group for liberal causes," to a "propaganda front of the radical Left"—"an organization more interested in indoctrinating our nation's youth with social ideas than in promoting education interests."[20] "The teachers who are teaching your children," according to Pat Robertson, "are not necessarily nice, wonderful servants of the community. They are activists supporting . . . one set of values and a number of the values which they espouse are: affirmative action, ERA, gun control legislation, sex education, illegal teacher's strikes, nuclear freeze, federal funding for abortions, decriminalization of marijuana, etc."[21] According to a Focus on the Family publication, a recent president of the NEA is reported to have said that "instruction and professional development have been set on the back burner to us, compared with political activism."[22] Yet it is precisely this orientation toward political engagement and the belief that a large part of the organization's multimillion dollar budget goes toward political lobbying rather than educational reform that so infuriates their opposition. "The NEA," stated one outspoken critic from New Jersey, "has no business passing resolutions and engaging in activism on foreign policy, abortion, gun control, Supreme Court nominees, birth control, nuclear weapons, and so on."[23]

Some see the textbooks as the source of the problem. Studies have shown that the role of religion in American life and history has received rather short shrift in public school history and social science textbooks. The 1985 analysis by Paul Vitz for the National Institute of Education, titled "Religion and Traditional Values in Public School Textbooks: An Empirical Study," was the first to show this. Other studies, such as one sponsored by People for the American Way (titled "Looking at History") and another sponsored by Americans United for the Separation of Church and State, came to the same results. The Vitz study summarized that

> public school textbooks commonly exclude the history, heritage, beliefs and values of millions of Americans. Those who believe in the traditional family are not represented. Those who believe in free

> enterprise are not represented. Those whose politics are conservative are almost unrepresented. Above all, those who are committed to their religious tradition—at the very least as an important part of the historical record—are not represented.[24]

Needless to say, findings like these are red meat to the lions of conservative political activism. Mel and Norma Gabler, the founders of the conservative textbook-watchdog organization Educational Research Analysts, have come to the conclusion that "until textbooks are changed, all these rising rates of crime and illiteracy and vandalism and promiscuity, VD, and so forth, they'll never be solved as long as we're teaching our children the present value system, because the schools are teaching values diametrically opposed to the values upon which our nation was founded."[25]

Still another source of the problem is found in curricular programs that "foster moral relativism." The indictment of sex and family life education is unequivocal from conservative Protestants and Catholics: "Sex education becomes [a] 'how-to' course without fixed moral values."[26] Such classes "undermine religious belief about sexuality in a passive way."[27] "Most sex education is really contraceptive education," says another conservative, "something which always ends up with more pregnancies, illegitimacy, abortion, cervical cancer, divorce, living together, single parenthood, VD and sterility."[28] The same judgment is leveled against values clarification programs: they smuggle "into the classroom, under the cover of neutrality, an outlook of ethical relativism which encourages a subjective, self-centered attitude in students. By presupposing that the individual—liberated from the influence of family, society and religion—is the final judge of his own personal 'values,' values clarification effectively assumes the role of an antinomian secular 'religion.' "[29] According to some, "the ultimate end [of these programs] is to instill the idea that all values are relative, the result of mere personal choice."[30] Values clarification "threatens to imprison" students "within walls of egotistic subjectivity, to drown them in a flood of feeling."[31] If the affront to the integrity of their world is as deep and as comprehensive as they say, there can be little surprise that the orthodox alliance would respond with a call to arms.

Progressive Responses

The response among progressivists to these claims reveals the sense of bewilderment and hostility we have come to expect in our examination of the culture war. Charges about the existence, not to mention the adverse effects, of so-called secular humanism are unequivocally rejected: "They [the conservative alliance] want to rid the public schools of everything about contemporary life they object to by labelling it secular humanism."[32] From the progressivist perspective, secularism in the schools is nothing more than nonsectarianism; humanism (in the values clarification and sex education curriculum) is nothing more than the celebration of individual autonomy and responsibility. Together, these emphases are seen to reside within and indeed to extend the traditions of individual liberty and pluralistic diversity. Therefore, as one People for the American Way statement put it, "To use secular humanism as a means to closing the minds of our schoolchildren is an attack on the principles and future of our nation."[33]

But the progressivist response goes beyond dismissing what they see as a phantom secular humanism. The policy initiatives of voluntary prayer, "creation-science," "release-time programs," the opposition to "morally objectionable" books, and the like, represent a concrete effort by the "fundamentalist right" to "impose their own religious beliefs on the educational system"(the ACLU),[34] to "commingle theology and public education" (the National Association of Education),[35] to " 'Christianize' every child's schooling" (PAW),[36] and so on. Here again, progressivists see a denial of the liberal ideal of democratic and pluralistic expression in the activism of their opponents. Through the political actions of these conservatives, argued a spokesman for People for the American Way, "students would no longer be exposed to materials which accept ambiguity, encourage independent thinking, and question the dogma of religious fundamentalism or ultraconservatism. If successful, the movement would smother the kind of creativity and advanced scientific understanding needed in today's and tomorrow's society."[37] Others concur. The religiously orthodox "oppose teaching children to think critically and independently, to understand different views and beliefs, and to appreciate the diversity of our society."[38] In the end, the effect of such actions can only be, as another observed, to "weaken the public schools and ultimately destroy them."[39]

The debate between the cultural conservatives and cultural progressivists on these issues both intensifies and is intensified by the largely secular argument about quality in education and the means for achieving quality. The movement to return to a core curriculum (such as the "back to basics" campaign), the drive to improve flagging national achievement test scores, the concern to produce more literate and more productive graduates, all build upon and support the criticism that public education is a failing institution.

Whose Pluralism?

The voices of progressivist moral commitment, then, defend the educational status quo in terms of the preservation of pluralism. Ironically, conservative voices advocate the breakup of the status quo by the very same terms. For cultural conservatives, it is not they who stand for moral and religious uniformity in the public schools, but their opponents. Literature from all sectors of the traditionalist alliance consistently maintains that the public schools already exist as a government monopoly—one that is "protected by discriminatory tax distribution" and whose administrative and instructional policy is primarily determined not by parents and local school boards but by the institutional and political interests of national educational elites, principally the National Education Association. As a result, a "monolithic set of values" incorporating "one-worldism, situation ethics, sexual permissiveness and 'creative learning' " is seen as "imposed upon our nation's youth."[40] As a conservative Baptist from Portland, Maine, observed, "You can't put a child in a classroom thirty hours a week and have that child not adopt the philosophy [of humanism] being taught."[41] From the orthodox perspective, then, public education as it currently exists does not serve the interests of pluralism. Just the opposite. "The state-monopoly over education," a Citizens for Educational Freedom brochure states, "is harmful to quality and equality in education. It eliminates viable alternatives in philosophy, values curriculum and methodology, reduces fiscal accountability, and destroys competition. In our generation, the sad results can be seen in the declining educational standards and achievements."[42]

In the view of virtually all conservative organizations, genuine pluralism in education can only be based upon the concept of parents' rights. In the words of Mae Duggan, whom we met in the prologue, "Parents' rights are God-given human rights. The child doesn't belong to the State. It is the parents who have the primary right and responsibility for educating their children. This is even affirmed in the United Nations Declaration of Human Rights [1948]. It says that 'Everyone has a right to education; that education shall be free and compulsory; and parents have a prior right to choose the kind of education that shall be given their children.' "[43] The problem, as Mae Duggan points out, is that a government monopoly cannot repond to the rights of parents to educate their children in the moral universe of their particular choice. It is the logic of parents' rights and the pluralism that parents' rights implies that necessitates, for the conservatives, the breakup of the public school monopoly.

The Challenge of Alternatives

The growing bulk of church-state litigation concerning the pedagogical aim and curricular content of public education is only the most obvious challenge to the existing conditions. But the effort to break up the present public school monopoly also takes form in the pursuit of alternatives to public education.

An interesting alternative promoted among a growing number of those under the orthodox umbrella is the home schooling movement. Within the world of home schooling, a minority of parents are committed to nonsectarian or secular home education; the overwhelming majority are found in the communities of religious orthodoxy (roughly 90 percent). Of these, most (roughly 75 percent of the total) are Evangelical Protestants but the balance are either conservative Catholics or Mormons.[44]

How substantial an alternative is home schooling? By the late 1980s less than 2 percent of the total school-age children were being educated at home by their parents. But this relatively small percentage masks the prodigious growth of the movement. In Colorado alone the number of state-approved home schoolers grew from 54 during the 1980–81 academic year to 835 during the 1987–88 academic year.[45] This pattern is found in most other states as well. Indeed, national estimates suggest that the actual number of children in home instruction has grown from about 15,000 in the early 1970s to approximately 700,000 in 1990.[46] The movement is also supported by a growing institutional base. The Home School Legal Defense Association (founded in 1983), for example, serves as a clearing house of information and legal advice for the parents of home schoolers who are prosecuted for violating compulsory education laws. Through the 1980s, its own membership doubled every thirteen months. There are also a growing number of organizations (nearly 150 by 1990) providing home curricular materials, support, or services.

A more substantial challenge to public education is the private religious school. Catholic Mae Duggan, Evangelical Chuck McIlhenny, and Orthodox Jew Yehuda Levin represent the growing number of parents who have chosen this option. By the late 1980s, roughly 14.5 percent of all school-age children attended private schools, up from 12.5 percent in 1970.[47] The greatest growth since the 1960s, however, has been in the Evangelical camp. Between 1965 and 1985, enrollment in non-Catholic religiously affiliated schools (of which Evangelical schools are the major share) has grown 149 percent, with enrollments accounting for roughly 2.5 million students. The number of elementary and secondary schools educating these children has grown to about 18,000.[48] The same kind of growth, but on a much smaller scale, can be seen among (primarily Orthodox) Hebrew day schools. Thus, for example, just after the Second World War there were only 30 Orthodox day schools but by the late 1960s their number had increased to 330 (with an enrollment of 67,000) and by 1983 this figure jumped to over 500 with an enrollment of close to 100,000.[49]

The figures on the growth of these schools only show that private religious education is an increasingly viable alternative to public education. It is an increasingly strong alternative, however, because its grass-roots advocates and a widening base of political leadership (primarily in the Republican party) support their indirect funding through a policy of government vouchers and/or tuition tax credits. Organizations as diverse as Agudath Israel (Orthodox Jewish), the Alliance for Catholic Defense, the National Association of Evangelicals, the Eagle Forum, the Association for Public Justice, the Catholic League for Religious and Civil Rights, the Heritage Foundation, and the American Association of Christian Schools both endorse and work in coalition on behalf of a public policy that would provide a parental choice of schools without the loss of tax benefits. Though their constituency would not benefit directly from a voucher system, even the Home School Legal Defense Association is a member of this coalition. The reason: "Anything that contributes to the demonopolization of the public school establishment, and to parental choice is good for children."[50]

One of the benefits of such a system, in the view of the orthodox, is that it would imply the recognition that education can never be neutral—that all education presupposes moral judgment of one kind or another—and that it is the parents' right to choose in which religious or philosophical value system to educate their children. Second, the system as it presently stands is socially elitist, for only wealthy families can exercise their right to select schools. Therefore, a policy of vouchers would be more democratic and egalitarian, for it would enable the poor and minorities to elect a program of education most suitable to their needs and cultural and religious values. Finally, a voucher policy would improve the quality of public education, for it would rest upon the principles of free market competition. Schools, in other words, would become accountable to parents for the quality of their educational product and services. "How hard," one activist asked rhetorically, "would Safeway try to please you if it were the only place you could go for food?" In sum, the orthodox insist that "a dual system of government and non-government operated schools is essential to a free, pluralistic society."[51]

For the National Education Association, the American Civil Liberties Union, the American Jewish Committee, and the host of other more politically liberal organizations, alternative education (whether home schooling or private religious education) is a legal right that should not be denied anyone, yet they uniformly oppose a voucher or tuition tax credit program. Such programs, especially voucher systems, they say, would potentially violate the constitutional prohibition against the establishment of religion by providing indirect subsidy to religious organizations. Moreover, such programs would provide government support for religiously oriented institutions "in the guise of aiding disadvantaged students."[52] In reality, progressivist groups argue, these programs, "could lead to racial, economic and social isolation of children." This would be a consequence of the affluent and better-educated parents choosing first and best, leaving the underfunded and undervalued schools for the less educated and poor parents.[53] The program might also generate schools of particular racial or ethnic characteristics, providing the basis for racial or ethnic or even class discrimination and segregation. Finally, government aid to private schooling in either of these forms could either weaken or destroy public education by, in effect, defunding public education. Resources that could be provided for the improvement of the public schools would be siphoned off, leaving public education impoverished. The National Education Association's policy statement on vouchers summarized it this way: "For all the rhetoric in which they are cloaked, vouchers are a cruel hoax on America's schoolage children and their parents. Disguised as educational reform and parental 'choice,' vouchers are really a matter of 'chance' and a diversionary tactic to shift the public focus from the most critical issue of the day—adequate funding for high quality public education for every child in this nation."[54]

Needless to say, the arguments invoked on either side of the voucher and tuition tax credit issues are both more complicated and passionate than those sketched here. Yet the cultural intent of each position is clear: both sides are attempting to speak on behalf of the poor and disadvantaged in society; both in turn speak on behalf of pluralism; and thus both in effect are striving to speak on behalf of a vision of the common good. One need not doubt the sincerity of those on either side of this public debate. Voices from both sides can and should be taken at their word. Yet two observations should be made. The first is that *pluralism,* the decisive word that links all other concerns together, is conceptualized in very nearly opposite ways. For the orthodox, genuine pluralism only exists when there is respect for the integrity of diverse even if exclusive religious and moral commitment. For progressivists, pluralism can only exist when there is an acceptance of all religious and moral commitments as equally valid and legitimate; as simply different but equally authentic ways of articulating truth. The second observation is that the debate over how the interests of democratic pluralism can best be served through educational policy conceals a deeper issue—the issue of who controls the institutional mechanisms of cultural reproduction.

CONTENDING FOR THE IVORY TOWER

In considering education as a field of conflict, the focus thus far has been on mass education at the primary and secondary levels. Higher education is at least as important a symbolic territory, yet it presents a very distinct set of circumstances. In the first place, mass education is compulsory for all children regardless of class or background; higher education is voluntary and tends to serve the upper and middle classes. Public education at the lower levels is also designed to provide a basic proficiency and competence capable of making nearly anyone economically self-sufficient. By contrast, college or university education (at least in principle) is oriented toward endowing an elite with tools of leadership. The struggle over the ivory tower is significant for the contemporary culture war for the simple reason that its outcome will ultimately shape the ideals and values as well as the categories of analysis and understanding that will guide the next generation of American leaders.

Yet one might well wonder what there is to talk about here, since most people would regard higher education in America as a bastion of liberal secularity. The point is well taken. The cultural ethos of the modern university clearly favors a progressivist agenda. The progressivist hegemony over the university, however, is by no means unchallenged. Moral and political traditionalists are far from conceding the contest.

The Battle Within the University

Consider the following event: On a spring day at the University of Massachusetts, the university's chapter of Young Americans for Freedom (YAF) held a rally celebrating "straight pride." Roughly 150 students waved American flags and held pro-heterosexual and anti-homosexual placards. Within a very short time, however, the rally disintegrated into shouting and shoving matches between various protesters and counter-protesters. One of the leaders of the YAF chapter, Bible in hand, was unswayed by the arguments and epithets leveled against him. "I'm against homosexuality because I think it is perverse," he said. "It goes against God's law. I don't want my tax money subsidizing a gay week," he added, referring to the fact that the Lesbian, Bisexual, and Gay Alliance is an officially recognized university group and a recipient of student fee funds.

Not many days after this rally, a counter-rally was sponsored by the university's Lesbian, Bisexual, and Gay Alliance. About 200 people from the ranks of the administration, faculty, and student body turned out to decry "homophobia" on campus. The event also provided an occasion for the Alliance to issue a list of eleven requests, including, among other things, more education about "oppression and diversity" on campus. In the background, a handful of students from YAF shouted, raised posters, and waved American flags.[55]

Conceding the contest? Not likely. Indeed, events such as this one are part and parcel of semester life on college and university campuses around the country and are perhaps the most visible way in which the culture war takes shape in the ivory tower. Of course, gay rights is only one of the issues under debate. Abortion, apartheid, animal rights, and almost every other issue of the larger cultural conflict are also battled out in this way: protest spawns counter-protest, rally spawns counter-rally, and in the editorial pages of student newspapers, accusation spawns counter-accusation. The culture war within universities is at least as polarized as it is in "the real world" and, moreover, it is anything but over.

The Struggle Over "Academic Freedom"

Yet one would be mistaken to view cultural conflict on the university campus as just a microcosm of the larger culture war in America. The battles here have their own distinct character, one that centers on the ongoing struggle to define *in practical terms* the mission of the modern university itself. That mission *in ideal terms* remains what it has always been: to be a sanctuary in which knowledge and truth might be pursued—and imparted—with impunity, no matter how unpopular, distasteful, or politically heterodox the process might sometimes be.[56] Again, the conflict comes in translating the ideal into the practical. Surely everyone in the university would embrace the ideals of "academic freedom" and "open-minded inquiry" as principles to guide academic life. They are not, then, just the lofty, self-important, and ultimately hollow words invoked at commencement addresses. In historical practice, the ideals of "free and open inquiry" have always been delimited by certain philosphical and political boundaries. Depending on the historical and regional context, academic establishments have always established certain limitations on what is appropriate to teach, to study, to research, and publish, the violation of which could mean professional censure or at least professional obscurity. One need not dig far into the historical record to see that university life in America, particularly before the Civil War, emphasized not so much free inquiry but theological orthodoxy and orthodox classicism, less "freeing" the mind than disciplining and channeling the mind within the bounds of the prevailing moral philosophy. "Modern" thinkers such as Shakespeare, Cervantes, Montesquieu, Kepler, and Harvey were largely absent from the curriculum at this time. In this context it is easier to understand how in 1832, after a member of the Jefferson Society at the University of Virginia made a public speech in favor of the emancipation of slaves, the faculty reacted by ruling that "there should be no oration on any distracting question of state or national policy nor on any point of theological dispute." Such activity was simply out of bounds for a university community. Lest one think that such constraints existed only in antebellum America, consider also the fact that as late as 1936, twenty-one states plus the District of Columbia required loyalty oaths of their teachers.[57]

When conflict arises along these lines, it is because the ideas and actions of one group test the implicit boundaries of inquiry and expression considered appropriate by another group. In our own time, those boundaries shift according to where one stands in the contemporary culture war. In reality, then, the culture war in higher education centers on what the boundaries of academic freedom should be. Implicit in this is a battle to define the content of knowledge and truth.

All of this takes form in a number of ways, as we shall see, but the heart of the matter can be witnessed in the debate over curriculum—particularly, the manner in which the curriculum is determined. Those on both sides of the cultural divide would agree that when the process of curriculum formation is politicized, academic freedom is threatened. Predictably, each accuses the other of doing just that.

Conservative Challenges

In the view of most progressives, the forces of traditionalism and moral orthodoxy present the chief threat to academic freedom in the curriculum. Accuracy in Academia (AIA), an organization founded in 1985 to document and oppose political bias in the classroom, is considered to be one such group. As AIA's existence became publicized, rumors surfaced that it sent student "spies" armed with tape recorders into lecture halls to root out Marxists and feminists. The reaction in universities and other academic organizations was predictably hostile. The American Sociological Association, for example, passed a resolution stating it was "profoundly disturbed by organizations such as Accuracy in Academia, whose objectives represent *a serious threat to academic freedom by isolating particular perspectives as being illegitimate lines of intellectual inquiry.*"[58] In a joint statement made by nearly a dozen student, faculty, and university associations, the feeling was similar: "The presence in the classroom of monitors for an outside organization will have a chilling effect on the academic freedom of both students and faculty members."[59] For progressives, this is not the way universities work; the academic mission and ideas are clearly subverted by such activity. The response of AIA was to dismiss these accusations outright. "Academic freedom," a spokeswoman said, "permits professors to research whatever they please but it does not give them the license to give biased lectures in the classroom. Academic freedom does not extend to political indoctrination!"[60]

A controversy such as this is fairly infrequent, in part because organizations like AIA are few in number, tend to be small, and offer little more than a symbolic challenge to the academic establishment. One university chancellor called AIA a "useful irritant."[61] Because a progressivist vision tends to dominate the university, the most persistent accusations that academic freedom is being challenged (if not directly subverted) come from the other direction, from those who would challenge that domination. Here, the controversy surrounding AIA and its alleged threat to "academic freedom" becomes very instructive, for the accusations leveled by traditionalist and conservative voices in these cases echo those usually leveled by progressivists. The argument, however, is considerably more complicated, and requires some elaboration.

Multiculturalism as Credo and Program

The politicization of the curriculum by progressivists, their critics contend, takes form chiefly in the debate over the issue of the diversity of knowledge in the academy. In the current jargon, the debate is over the virtues of "multiculturalism." The argument goes something like this: The existing curriculum is politicized by virtue of the fact that its principal works have been composed almost entirely by dead white European males. White male literary critics canonize white male novelists; elite white male historians document elite white male history; white male psychologists test white male sophomores; and so on. Thus, progressivists argue, only a small part of human experience has really been studied—a part intrinsically contaminated with racism, sexism, heterosexism, and imperialism. Knowledge, in a word, is inherently biased. The solution today, therefore, is to be more inclusive of different experiences, perspectives, and truths, particularly those that have been ignored or silenced in the past—the voices of women, the poor, minorities, and others disenfranchised from the prevailing power structures.

The two-year-long debate over the Western Culture program at Stanford University in the late 1980s is something of a parable of how the controversy over multiculturalism is articulated. At Stanford, a group of students called for the abolishment of the Western Culture program. In its place they proposed a course that would emphasize "the contributions of cultures disregarded and/or distorted by the present program." A task force was appointed by the administration to evaluate the existing program and the proposal to diversify. After much political debate and pressure, the committee finally came to the conclusion that a new "Culture, Ideas and Values" course emphasizing "diversity" should replace the course on Western Culture. This conclusion evoked a strong political response from both sides, especially those who favored the idea. Rallies and demonstrations were held in support of the proposal ("Hey, hey, ho, ho, Western Culture's got to go"); a faculty senate debate over the proposal was disrupted by students chanting, "Down with racism, down with Western Culture, up with diversity"; and members of a student group called Rainbow Agenda staged a sit-in in the office of the president of the university, demanding, among other things, adoption of the task-force proposal. The proposal was adopted, and not long after, still other new course requirements for undergraduates emphasizing racial, ethnic, sexual, and gender-based diversity were established.

The situation at Stanford is just the most publicized case of a debate that has been repeated in different ways at most colleges and universities across the country—Columbia, Chicago, Brown, Pennsylvania, Michigan, Minnesota, and Indiana, among others. At the University of Wisconsin, students are required to take ethnic studies courses but are not required to study Western civilization or even American history. Similar measures have been enacted at Dartmouth, Mount Holyoke, and the University of California at Berkeley.[62]

The debate over multiculturalism takes even more controversial form in curricular and extracurricular programs, some mandatory, that are designed to "increase sensitivity" to racial and cultural diversity in the university community.[63] Here, too, opponents of multiculturalism claim that academic life has been politicized. Dozens of universities, for example, have introduced regulations against what the National Education Association has called "ethnoviolence," including "acts of insensitivity."[64] The University of Michigan, for example, adopted a six-page "anti-bias" code (later found to be unconstitutional) that allowed for the punishment of students whose behavior "stigmatizes or victimizes an individual on the basis of race, ethnicity, religion, sex, sexual orientation, creed, national origin, ancestry, age, marital status, handicap, or Vietnam-era veteran students." Likewise, the University of Wisconsin made subject to disciplinary sanctions those students who engage in "certain types of expressive behavior directed at individuals and intended to demean and to create a hostile environment for education or other university-authorized activities. . . ." Students Toward a New Diversity at the University of Virginia introduced a proposal to the Board of Visitors stating among other things that the university should "discipline a student, faculty or staff member when that individual intentionally uses racist or discriminatory comments, slurs, ethnocentric or sexual invectives, epithets or utterances to directly attack an individual or an identifiable group of individuals rather than to express an idea or opinion." The number of these sorts of cases is considerable and, in many cases, the rules have been enforced. A student at the University of Connecticut was ordered to move off-campus and was forbidden to return to university dormitories and cafeterias after putting up a jesting sign on the door of her dorm room saying that preppies, bimbos, men without chest hair, and "homos" should be shot on sight. A student from Brown University was expelled for shouting insults while in a drunken stupor against blacks, homosexuals, and Jews. And students were required to take down flags displayed in their dorm windows during the Persian Gulf War. The university's rationale, according to one university spokeswoman, was that "we have a big population to be sensitive to. . . . This is a very diverse community, and what may be innocent to one person may be insulting to another."[65] The purpose of such rules in student conduct codes, according to their proponents, is to ensure that the university becomes an institution that serves and respects all people. "Racial epithets and sexually haranguing speech," as one Stanford law professor put it, "silences rather than furthers discussion."[66]

One of the most far-reaching ways the curriculum has accommodated the pressure to diversify is seen in the range of new disciplinary programs that emerged since the 1970s: women's studies, black studies, Hispanic studies, gay studies, and so on. These correspond to an aggressive campaign of affirmative action. Proponents feel that in order to ensure that new perspectives are presented fairly, it is essential that university recruitment be extended to those who can best identify with those perspectives—faculty recruited from the ranks of women and people of color. Here, too, advocates promise that the ultimate outcome of these "re-visions" will be a fuller and better liberal arts curriculum—"a more inclusive version of human knowledge."[67]

Affirmative action as a means to promote this kind of diversity extends to student admissions.[68] Admissions committees at nearly all American colleges and universities have changed their policies in order to encourage a greater representation of blacks, Hispanics, and Native Americans. The changes require a double standard when it comes to demonstrated academic ability. In the Ivy League schools, white students must have a grade-point average of close to 4.0 and SAT scores of at least 1,250 to get in. Many of these schools, however, will admit minorities with a grade-point average below 3.0 and SAT scores under 1,000. The same is true at elite state schools like the University of California at Berkeley and the University of Virginia. At the former, a student with a GPA of 3.5 and SATs of 1,200 will most definitely be admitted if he or she is black and will be most unlikely to be admitted if white. At the latter, black freshman enrollment doubled in five years in the 1980s in response to an order of the court. According to one report, the university complied by accepting more than half of all black applicants compared to about one-fourth of all white applicants, even though the white students often had better academic credentials. In 1988, for example, the average SAT score of white freshmen was 246 points higher than that of the average black student. The word "qualifications," one professor put it, is a code word for whites.[69]

The institutionalization of the ideals of multiculturalism in academia is carried out by still other means as well. Not all but many professional organizations in academia, for example, go beyond serving the professional needs of their members to acting as political lobbies. Of the hundreds of resolutions passed by the American Psychological Association since the early 1950s, for example, over a quarter have dealt in one way or another with issues relating to the culture war; most of these have been passed since the mid-1960s and most favor the progressivist position. For example, the association has passed resolutions endorsing a legal right to an abortion; opposing apartheid in South Africa; calling for an immediate halt to the nuclear arms race; favoring handgun control; opposing discrimination against homosexuals, women, and racial and ethnic minorities; and supporting the passage of the Equal Rights Amendment.[70] Much the same can be said for the American Sociological Association, which has passed resolutions opposing the intent of the "so-called Family Protection Act," encouraging the end of U.S. aid to El Salvador, opposing the overturning of *Roe v. Wade,* opposing discrimination against homosexuals, favoring total divestment from South Africa, favoring the boycott of Gallo wine, and on and on. Moreover, the public image and identity of many of these professional organizations *as political organizations* is made even clearer by their policies not to hold their national or regional conventions in states that have refused to ratify the ERA or that still maintain antisodomy laws.

The Critique of Multiculturalism

The multicultural credo and program, critics say, is a sham. The "diversity" its advocates celebrate, they say, is not a true diversity. After all, its advocates rarely if ever propose courses in Irish Catholic, Greek American, Asian American, Jewish, or Protestant Fundamentalist studies. Rather, their idea of diversity is defined by political criteria—namely, the presumed distinction between "oppressors and oppressed." Programs such as women's studies, black studies, Chicano studies, and the like, therefore, are better subsumed under the heading of "oppression studies." The classes taught in these programs, critics claim, have more to do with "raising consciousness" than expanding students' knowledge. The whole idea behind multiculturalism is "to give an academic gloss to an implied power struggle and to organize the academy on a political basis without seeming to do so." "When the children of the sixties received their professorships and deanships," another observer concluded, "they did not abandon the dream of radical cultural transformations; they set out to implement it. Now instead of disrupting classes, they are teaching them; instead of attempting to destroy our educational institutions physically, they are subverting them from within."[71]

Even those who are willing to accept the challenge to open up university education to a broader range of cultural experiences complain bitterly about the methods used to bring this goal about. Consider the remarks of William J. Bennett, at the time Secretary of Education, about the Stanford affair: "Stanford's decision . . . to alter its Western Culture program was not a product of enlightened debate, but rather an unfortunate capitulation to a campaign of pressure politics and intimidation. . . . In the name of 'opening minds' and 'promoting diversity,' we have seen in this instance the closing of the Stanford mind. . . . The methods that succeeded in pushing CIV through the faculty senate have shown that intimidation works—that intimidation *can* take the place of reason. The loudest voices have won, not through force of argument, but through bullying, threatening and name-calling. That's not the way a university should work."[72] Another embattled dean complained that while the problems of injustice based on gender, race, and class are profound, pervasive, and indefensible, to institutionalize them in university life through "a Puritan style of reform" is simply incompatible with the life of the mind.[73] The net effect of such programs and policies, still another argued, is not the encouragement of open inquiry on campus but attitude adjustment, if not ideological indoctrination.

Counter-Charges

The progressivist response to this long series of accusations is that the curriculum in particular and academic life in general has always been politicized. The Western Civilization course at Columbia University, for example, which became a model for others in the country, is said to have evolved out of the War Issues course offered during World War I, which had the ideological mission of inoculating young people against Bolshevism and other subversive doctrines and making them "safe for democracy."[74] Defining civilization at that time was very much a political act. On a more contemporary note, one student critical of the Stanford Western Civilization course put it this way: this is "not just a racist education, it is the education of racists."[75] In the final analysis, say those holding to the progressivist vision, the public should not be misled. The critics of the multicultural innovations in the university are themselves motivated by political ideals—the same repressive assumptions that undergird the university system and American society as a whole. A best-selling work like Allan Bloom's *The Closing of the American Mind* was popular not because it treated the esoteric philosophy of Socrates, Heidegger, and Nietzsche with great refinement, but because it provided intellectual legitimation for a populist and conservative critique of progressive change in the university.[76] So, too, E. D. Hirsch's book *Cultural Literacy* was wildly successful not because of his educational theory but because of his endorsement, cataloguing, and packaging of what were in effect "the eternal verities" of Western civilization. And then there are *The Dartmouth Review* and over sixty other similarly oriented college publications that very often derive their funding from outside the university—from Washington- and New York–based conservative foundations.[77] Who, progressivists would ask, can deny the politicizing effects on the university of these?

Freedom and Repression in Academia

The ideals of academic freedom and open-minded inquiry in the university have always been embedded in a social and historical context. However exalted these ideals have been in times past, there have always been certain unspoken limits on what topics could be studied and boundaries on the methods used in researching them. In our own time, the battles in the ivory tower center in many respects upon whether to retain an older agreement or to establish a new agreement about what is appropriate for the life of the mind. Clearly, representatives from each side of the cultural divide fervently believe that they properly uphold the principles of academic freedom—and that it is the other side that has politicized and thus tainted the atmosphere of academic inquiry. Unfortunately, what is for one side the pursuit of serious scholarship is for the other a sign of academic repression. Once again, the culture war yields little or no middle ground. This debate too has an interminable character.

The Battle Between Universities

There is another important element to this story. As with mass education at the primary and secondary levels, one way the traditionalists and the religiously and morally orthodox have responded to the threat posed by the growing domination of university education by their opponents has been to set up their own alternatives. Within the safety of their own colleges and universities, the minds of young men and women would be challenged and shaped but within the boundaries of their religious and moral traditions.

Most Evangelical colleges and universities were established in the mid-nineteenth century as a response to the secularization of still an earlier generation of Protestant universities. Institutions such as Wheaton College in Illinois (1860), Taylor University in Indiana (1846), Houghton College in New York (1883), George Fox College in Oregon (1891), Gordon College in Massachusetts (1889), among others, were established to carry forth the beacon that was seen to have flickered out at Harvard, Yale, and dozens of other mainline denominational colleges. Lutherans began establishing colleges and universities during the same period: 29 of the 34 Lutheran colleges and universities, 13 of the 19 Lutheran seminaries, and 9 of the 20 Lutheran junior colleges in America were founded before 1900. The initial spurt of Catholic institutions of higher learning were also founded at this time. Of the nearly 200 Catholic colleges and universities, 73 were founded before 1900 and an additional 61 were founded in the next twenty-five years. And finally, 7 of the 10 major Jewish colleges were founded before 1925.

Over the twentieth century, this broad range of institutions has met with mixed success in maintaining its ideal of an alternative vision for higher education. The pressures to accommodate to the ethos of modern secular learning have always been subtle but they have steadily increased over the decades. Particularly since the 1970s, these institutions have been caught between a growing pressure to accommodate further, thereby losing their institutional distinctiveness, or to struggle even more vigorously to hold fast to their founding ideals. The seventy member institutions of the Christian College Coalition continue their efforts to be an alternative to the secular liberal arts, but many of them have capitulated to secularizing tendencies that they have either ignored or been unable to recognize. By virtue of the subject matter, the large network of Bible colleges (which number well over one hundred) have been far more successful than their liberal arts counterparts. Among the Lutheran and Catholic schools, the general tendency has been that the smaller colleges have been more successful at maintaining their educational and religious distinctiveness than the larger ones.

The tensions within the Catholic community have been particularly sharp. Orthodox Catholic publications continually rail against the liberalizing trends within various Catholic universities. Theology professors abandoning God and undermining the faith of their students, the adoption of a radical menu of curricular offerings, secular sex education in the dormitories, softening faculty and administration views on abortion and homosexuality—such developments have led orthodox Catholics to wonder whether Notre Dame, St. Louis University, Catholic University, Fordham, and many other Catholic colleges and universities are still Catholic.[78]

Orthodox communities have been led to two kinds of institutional responses. One has been to defend the traditions by cutting losses with the larger universities and starting anew. As Evangelical colleges and Bible schools were founded in response to secularism in the older denominational colleges in the nineteenth century, so too a new cycle of orthodox and traditionalist colleges and universities have now been founded because of the perceived vacuum of colleges to carry the true traditions on to the next generation. Thomas Aquinas College in Santa Paula, California, is a case in point. It was founded as a Catholic "great books" liberal arts alternative in 1971 because of, as its founding statement claimed, "the growing tendency of Catholic colleges to secularize themselves—that is, to loosen their connection with the teaching Church and to diminish deliberately their Catholic character."[79] Though not oriented toward the "great books," the identical sentiment gave birth to a decidedly orthodox Catholic alternative, Christendom College in Front Royal, Virginia, in 1977. On the conservative Protestant side as well, several colleges emerged as a direct or indirect response to the contemporary culture war: Liberty University (1971) associated with the Reverend Jerry Falwell's ministry, Regent University (1977) formerly Christian Broadcasting Network University associated with the Reverend Pat Robertson's ministry, and Oral Roberts University (1965).

The other response to the threat of secularism within religious colleges and seminaries has been to "purify" existing colleges and seminaries by purging those professors who have failed to prove their allegiance to the traditions. This is precisely what happened in the mid-1970s at Concordia Seminary of the Lutheran Church-Missouri Synod, and in the seminaries of the Southern Baptist Convention in the late 1980s and early 1990s. In these cases, the struggle was bitter but the traditionalists eventually won.

In the effort to create or maintain a distinct alternative to secular higher learning, the state has not played a neutral role but has exerted pressure to accommodate to secular and often progressivist public policy. In the case of the Fundamentalist Bob Jones University, the federal government (through the Internal Revenue Service and then the Supreme Court) threatened and eventually took away the school's tax-exempt status as an educational institution because the university prohibited, on the basis of biblical injunctions, interracial dating and marriage. An attorney for the university argued in 1983 that the government's position would mean that "religious bodies, if they are to enjoy tax exemption, must lock-step themselves to public policy even if it violates their conscience and doctrine."[80] The same kind of pressure was exerted in the 1980s in the case of Grove City College, a small Presbyterian liberal arts college in western Pennsylvania. Though it had never been accused of discriminating on the basis of gender and though it never directly received federal funding, when the administration refused to fill out a federal form (Assurance of Compliance with Title IX), the government threatened and (through the Civil Rights Restoration Act), eventually cut off federal funds to students attending the college. Another example of the power of the state over schools attempting to maintain a religious distinctiveness occurred at Georgetown University, the oldest Catholic university in the nation. The contest involved two gay student organizations that sued the university for denying them the right to receive funds for campus activities. After eight years of pitched legal battles, a Washington, D.C., Superior Court and Court of Appeals ruled that Georgetown University had violated the city's Human Rights Act by discriminating against people for reasons of sexual orientation, despite the Catholic Church's strong theological opposition to homosexuality.

In the final analysis, the effort to establish a network of alternatives to secular higher learning continues to renew itself. On their own terms, such institutions would not seem to provide much of a challenge to the secular and progressivist establishment universities. They are relatively small and low in prestige—mere Davids in the shadow of a Goliath. Yet in fact, a huge number of leaders within the orthodox alliance—who work for all aspects of the culture war, not just education—are educated through this network. Like the boy David, neither these individuals nor

David, neither these individuals nor the institutions that train them have any intention of stepping away from the fight.

A TRAIL OF IRONIES

If education is a symbolic territory over which opposing sides compete for advantage, the terrain is vast and perhaps it is impossible to gain a sense of direction for the whole battle. An observation about the battles at the lower levels, however, may offer a useful insight. The observation begins with a short trail of historical ironies. Once the defenders of the public school establishment against the pope's authority in Rome, Evangelical Protestants (the most prominent faction among the orthodox alliance) have not only adopted the policy positions of their nineteenth-century Catholic adversaries, they also work in collaboration with their traditional Catholic adversaries in the effort to demonopolize, and thereby weaken the power of, the public school establishment. For their part, progressivist voices on the contemporary scene defend their own cultural advantage in education in virtually the *same manner* as the Evangelical Protestants did in the nineteenth century: by appealing to public order and community good. The latter point is nicely illustrated in this way. In a speech delivered in 1888, one of the pioneers of public education on the western frontier, Reverend George Atkinson, linked the instruction of students in the "principles of rectitude" outlined in the Decalogue, Proverbs, and the aphorisms and parables of Jesus to the requirements of citizenship and national interest. This was the defense of the Protestant establishment. "If it be objected," he argued, "that this will infringe the rights of conscience, the answer can be made, that *no right of personal conscience is so sacred as the right of self-preservation of a body politic.*"[81] Nearly a century later, the National Education Association likewise linked its opposition to government support for alternative education to the "transcendent purpose of public schooling—promoting the common good."[82] A similar appeal to the common good—or to the preservation of the body politic—could just as well be (and often is) made by the defenders of the modern secular university. Such are the arguments of a contested and sometimes nervous hegemony.

9

Media and the Arts

One does not need to endure a thousand bleary-eyed evenings with Dan Rather or Tom Brokaw to understand how important a role the media of mass communications plays in our lives. Television, radio, magazines, newspapers, news magazines, the popular press, as well as music, film, theater, visual arts, popular literature, do much more than passively reflect the social and political reality of our times. Like the institutions of public education discussed in the previous chapter, these institutions actively define reality, shape the times, give meaning to the history we witness and experience as ordinary citizens. This outcome is unavoidable in many ways. In the very act of *selecting* the stories to cover, the books to publish and review, the film and music to air, and the art to exhibit, these institutions effectively define which topics are important and which issues are relevant—worthy of public consideration. Moreover, in the *substance* of the stories covered, books published and reviewed, art exhibited, and so on, the mass media act as a filter through which our perceptions of the world around us take shape. Thus, by virtue of the decisions made by those who control the mass media—seemingly innocuous decisions made day to day and year to year—those who work within these institutions cumulatively wield enormous power. In a good many situations, this power is exercised unwittingly, rooted in the best intentions to perform a task well, objectively, fairly. Increasingly, however, the effects of this power have become understood and deliberately manipulated. Is it not inevitable that the media and the arts would become a field of conflict in the contemporary culture war?

There are at least two matters to consider here. First, the contest to define reality, so central to the larger culture war, inevitably becomes a struggle to control the "instrumentality" of reality definition. This means that the battle over this symbolic territory has practically taken shape as a struggle to influence or even dominate the businesses and industries of public information, art, and entertainment—from the major television and radio networks to the National Endowment for the Arts; from the Hollywood film industry to the music recording industry, and so on. But there is more. At a more subtle and symbolic level, the tensions in this field of conflict point to a struggle over the meaning of "speech" or the meaning of "expression" that the First Amendment is supposed to protect. Underlying the conflict over this symbolic territory, in other words, are the questions, "What constitutes art in our communities?" "Whose definition of entertainment and aesthetic appreciation do we accept?" "What version of the news is fair?" And so on.

TAKING ON THE ESTABLISHMENT

We begin by considering a brief vignette of an event that occurred at a pro-life march in Washington, D.C. The day was filled with speeches from politicians, religious leaders, pro-life leaders, and other luminaries. Several hundred thousand people listened attentively, cheered, chanted, prayed, and sang songs. Such are the rituals of modern political rallies. At one point during the rally, however, a number of pro-life advocates spontaneously turned toward a television news crew filming the event from atop a nearby platform and began to chant in unison, "Tell the truth!" "Tell the truth!" Tell the truth!" What began as a rumble within a few moments had caught on within the crowd. Soon, tens of thousands of people were chanting "Tell the truth!" "Tell the truth!" "Tell the truth!" Of all the aspects of the rally covered in the newscast that evening or in the newspapers the following day, this brief and curious event was not among them.

The story highlights the conviction held by virtually everyone on the orthodox and conservative side of the new cultural divide that the media and arts establishment is unfairly prejudiced against the values they hold dear. They do not tell the truth, the voices of orthodoxy maintain, and what is worse, they do not even present opposing sides of the issues evenhandedly. Here is the National Right to Life Committee's direct mail statement: "ABC, CBS, and NBC [have] Declared War . . . on the Movement. . . .We cannot let a handful of network executives and Hollywood writers, actors and directors poison America with their godless attitudes, which are anti-religion, anti-family and anti-life." Tim LaHaye echoed this sentiment in his own mail appeal:

> It's no secret to any of us how the liberal media manages the news and helps to set the national agenda on public debate. They report the news in such a way as to promote the political goals of the left. This censorship of Christian principles and ideas covers many more issues than abortion and the homosexual lifestyle. The media slants what is reported in the areas of national defense, the budget, school prayer, and Soviet expansion in Central America, among others. The truth in all of these areas is being hidden.[1]

Of the film industry, another spokesman said, "The people in Hollywood are so far removed from the people of middle America. They have a hostility toward people who believe anything at all. They live in a hedonistic, materialistic little world."[2]

Exaggerated they may be, but the general perceptions are not totally born out of illusion. Studies of the attitudes of media and entertainment elites, as well as of television news programming and newspaper coverage of various social issues and political events, have shown a fairly strong and consistent bias toward a liberal and progressivist point of view.[3] The field over which these particular battles are waged, then, is uneven—and the contenders recognize it as such. One contender takes a position of defending territory already won; the other strives to reclaim it. There are three major ways in which traditionalists have sought to reclaim this symbolic (and institutional) territory.

One way has been in a direct assault against the media and arts establishment. Acquiring a large-circulation newspaper or a network was something that had been "a dream of conservatives for years," according to Howard Phillips of the Conservative Caucus.[4] Early in 1985, such an assault was made. After years of frustration with what it called "the liberal bias" of CBS, a group called Fairness in Media (FIM) spearheaded a move to buy out the television network. Through its leading spokesman, Senator Jesse Helms, FIM sent a direct mail letter to more than a million conservatives across the country urging them to purchase twenty shares each of common stock in the company, the end of which would be to "become Dan Rather's boss." The plan was not a ruse. Conservative spokesmen called the idea "inspired" and "realistic," and hundreds of people called FIM to find out how to participate. Officials at CBS initially brushed off the proposal but soon were engaged in rearguard action against it, hiring two law firms, an investment banking house, and several public relations firms. Its official response: "CBS intends to take all appropriate steps to maintain the independence and integrity of its news organization." At CBS, a spokeswoman added, "our sole purpose is journalism and our goal is objectivity."[5] Conservatives and others in the orthodox alliance would naturally respond, "whose standards of objectivity?" Ultimately, of course, the bid to take over the network failed but those who supported the idea were not put off. "It may take a while to accomplish [this goal]," one editorialized, "but it's a goal well worth waiting—and striving—for."[6]

The persistent effort of the orthodox alliance to hold the media establishment accountable for the content it presents is another strategy. Numerous national and local organizations are committed to this task, covering a wide range of media. Morality in Media, for example, is an interfaith organization founded in 1962 by three clergymen in order to stop traffic in pornography and to challenge "indecency in media" and to work "for a media based on love, truth and good taste." Accuracy in Media has, since 1969, sought to combat liberal bias by exposing cases where the media have not covered stories "fairly and accurately." The Parents' Music Resource Center, established in 1985, is concerned to raise the awareness of parents about the content of modern rock music, especially heavy metal music. Its specific focus is, according to one of its founders, "not the occasional sexy rock lyric . . . [but] the celebration of the most gruesome violence, coupled with explicit messages that sadomasochism is the essence of sex."[7] One of the most visible of all media watchdog groups is the American Family Association and the affiliated CLeaR-TV, or Christian Leaders for Responsible Television. Founded by the Reverend Donald Wildmon, the American Family Association membership claims ordinary believers and religious leaders from all Christian faiths, Protestant, Catholic, and Orthodox, and together they propose to combat the "excessive, gratuitous sex, violence, profanity, [and] the negative stereotyping of Christians."[8]

These organizations are joined by many others both national and local, including town and city councils around the country that share a similar concern about the content of public information and entertainment. They are effective because they are grass-roots in orientation (or at least they pose as being locally connected to the grass-roots), and they make use of proven techniques of popular political mobilization: letter writing, boycott, countermedia exposure, and the like.

As much a support structure for the various orthodox and conservative subcultures as a weapon in the culture war, communities within the orthodox alliance have created an entire network of alternative electronic media. These alternative media challenge the media and arts establishment a third way, then, through competition, offering programming that defines a fundamentally different and competing reality and vision of America. Conservative Catholics and Orthodox Jews play different roles in some of these media, but it is the Evangelicals who dominate this alternative media industry. Take film as an example. The mainstay dramas produced by Billy Graham's World Wide Pictures have always been deliberately Evangelistic in tone and purpose. More recently, however, Evangelicals have begun to create films that "uphold traditional values." For example, Florida-based Evangelist D. James Kennedy, frustrated and angry about the insensitivities of the Hollywood film establishment toward religiously observant Americans, founded a film company in the late 1980s. "We're tired of sex and blasphemy and immorality, of sadism and influencing people for ill," he said. "We believe there are people who would like to watch something other than drugs and sex. Now, I know there are various kinds of reality in this country, including the reality of the toilet. But how about the *realities of morality and courage and devotion?*"[9] Though Evangelical in nature, Kennedy's initiative has received support from Catholic and Jewish quarters as well.[10]

Even more vigorous challenges have been made by the Evangelical-dominated television and radio industry. Within the Evangelical subculture alone there were over 1,300 religious radio stations, over 200 religious television stations and 3 religious television networks broadcasting in the United States by the early 1990s.[11] The Catholic place in this industry is relatively small by comparison but it does make an important contribution. The programming goes far beyond televised religious services or radio broadcasts of sacred music to include religious talk shows, soap operas, drama, Bible studies, and news commentary. In addition to these enterprises is a billion-dollar book industry (made up, within the Evangelical orbit alone, of over 80 publishing houses and over 6,000 independent religious bookstores) that publish and market books on, for example, how to be a better Christian, how to raise children, how to cope with a mid-life crisis, not to mention a sizable literature on what is wrong about America and what you can do about it. And a multimillion dollar music industry extends far beyond the latest rendition of "Blessed Assurance" by George Beverly Shea to Hasidic and Christian rock and roll, folk, heavy metal (groups called Vengeance, Petra, or Shout singing such releases as "In Your Face"), and even rap music.

THE POLITICS OF FREE SPEECH

What makes these battles over the media and arts especially interesting is that they reveal a conflict that is several layers deeper. The first layer of conflict concerns the nature and meaning of art and music, as well as the nature and meaning of information. Inevitably this conflict leads to the more philosophical and legal disputes over the nature of "speech" and "expression" protected by the First Amendment. There is no end to the number of "headline cases" in which these sorts of issues are worked out. The fact is that each dispute contains within it all the underlying philosophical and legal tensions as well. Collectively, they make the matter a crisis over which actors on both sides of the cultural divide urgently press for resolution.

To demonstrate how this conflict is played out at these different levels, it is necessary to get down to specific cases. The object here is not to comprehensively survey and catalogue the various disputes over media and the arts in recent times. The following sampling of a few widely publicized controversies from different areas of public expression demonstrates a larger pattern of discourse among the contenders, one that ultimately carries us to the deeper issues of expression and censorship in the culture war.

The Avant-Garde and Its Discontents

It begins with the quest for novelty. This impulse is undeniably a driving force in the arts, entertainment, and news media. The quest is based on the premise that the new will somehow be better than the old, a premise that fits well with America's utilitarian demand for improvement. The expectation that the media and arts will continue to innovate keeps an audience coming back for more. Cultural tensions, of course, inhere within the quest and on occasion they erupt into full-blown controversy.

Art

Out of a budget of more than 150 million dollars a year, the National Endowment for the Arts funds literally hundreds upon hundreds of projects in theater, ballet, music, photography, film, painting, and sculpture. In the late 1980s, however, it became widely publicized that the National Endowment for the Arts had indirectly funded two controversial photographic exhibits. One project, by Andres Serrano, included, among others, a photograph of a crucifix in a jar of Serrano's urine, entitled *Piss Christ;* the other project, by Robert Mapplethorpe, included, among many others, a photograph that turned an image of the Virgin Mary into a tie rack as well as a number of homoerotic photos (such as one showing Mapplethorpe with a bullwhip implanted in his anus and another showing a man urinating in another man's mouth). All of this was well publicized. Avant-garde? To say the least! But Serrano and Mapplethorpe are, their defenders maintained, "important American artists." One critic called the photograph *Piss Christ* "a darkly beautiful photographic image."[12] Likewise, the director of the Institute of Contemporary Art in Boston concluded of Mapplethorpe's exhibit, "Mapplethorpe's work is art, and art belongs in an art museum."[13]

For those in the various orthodox communities, the controversial aspects of the Serrano and Mapplethorpe exhibits were not art at all but obscenity. "This so-called piece of art is a deplorable, despicable display of vulgarity," said one critic. "Morally reprehensible trash," said another. Of Serrano himself, a third stated, "He is not an artist, he is a jerk. Let him be a jerk on his own time and with his own resources." The American Family Association responded with full-page advertisements in newspapers asking, "Is this how you want your tax dollars spent?"[14]

These voices had a sympathetic hearing in the halls of government as well. In response to the National Endowment for the Arts funding of these projects and the likelihood that it would fund still other such projects in the future, Senator Jesse Helms introduced legislation that would forbid the endowment from supporting art that is "obscene or indecent." The National Endowment for the Arts agreed to make grants available only to those who pledge not to do anything of this nature. The endowment, a Helms ally argued in support of this proposal, should not showcase "artists whose forte is ridiculing the values . . . of Americans who are paying for it."[15] Conservative columnist Doug Bandow argued similarly, "There's no justification for taxing lower-income Americans to support glitzy art shows and theater productions frequented primarily by the wealthy."[16] Still others cited Thomas Jefferson's dictum that it is "sinful and tyrannical" to compel a person to contribute money for the propagation of opinions with which he or she disagrees.

Music

Rap is just one more innovation in youth-oriented music that began decades before with rock and roll. Serious questions were raised about the form and content of this innovation, however, with the 1989 release of *As Nasty As They Wanna Be* by the Miami-based rap group 2 Live Crew. On just one album, there were over 200 uses of the word "fuck," over 100 uses of explicit terms for male and female genitalia, over 80 descriptions of oral sex, and the word "bitch" was used over 150 times. And what about the work of groups like Mötley Crüe, which invokes images of satanism, and the rap group the Beastie Boys, who mime masturbation on stage, or N.W.A., who sing about war against the police (in "Fuck tha Police"), or Ozzy Osbourne, who sings of the "suicide solution?" Was this really music?

The arts establishment responded with a resounding "yes." Its endorsements were positive and sympathetic. Notwithstanding the violence and irreverence, one essay in the *Washington Post* described rap in particular as "a vibrant manifestation of the black oral tradition. . . .You cannot fully understand this profane style of rapping if you disregard the larger folklore of the streets."[17] A review of 2 Live Crew and rap in general in the *New York Times* claimed that this form of musical expression "reveals the tensions of the communities it speaks to. But with its humor, intelligence and fast-talking grace, it may also represent a way to transcend those tensions."[18] Even at its grossest, one critic wrote in *Time,* this entire genre of music represents "a vital expression of the resentments felt by a lot of people."[19]

Needless to say, the opinions within the orthodox communities were less enthusiastic. One American Family Association member called the work of the rap poets of 2 Live Crew as well as other exemplars of popular music, such as the heavy metal of Mötley Crüe, Twisted Sister, and the like, "mind pollution and body pollution."[20] An attorney involved in the controversy commented, "This stuff is so toxic and so dangerous to anybody, that it shouldn't be allowed to be sold to anybody or by anybody."[21] Because this album was being sold to children, he continued, the group's leader, Luther Campbell, was nothing less than "a psychological child molester."[22] Judges in Florida agreed with the sentiment, finding the lyrics to *As Nasty As They Wanna Be* to violate local obscenity laws. Police arrested Campbell for performing the music in a nightclub after the decree, as well as record store owners who continued to sell the album. In response, Campbell promised two things: a legal appeal and a new album—"this one dirtier than the last."[23]

Film

Of all the films produced by Universal Studios perhaps none has been more controversial than *The Last Temptation of Christ,* based on the 1955 best-selling novel by Nikos Kazantzakis. The intent of the film, according to its director Martin Scorsese, was to present the basic humanity of Christ who discovers—nay, chooses—his divinity. The film portrays a Jesus plagued by human doubt and subject, though not quite vulnerable, to the range of human temptations, including lust, pride, anger, power, and the fear of death. Christ, for example, is shown to fantasize about being married to Mary Magdalene and having sexual intercourse with her; later, after she has died, he imagines marrying Mary (of Mary and Martha) and then still later, committing adultery with Martha. He is also shown confessing in anguish, "I am a liar, I am a hypocrite. I am afraid of everything . . . Lucifer is inside me." In the end, however, he is shown renouncing the final temptation, the offer by Satan to reject his role of Messiah, and accepting his destiny to die for humankind.

A biblical costume epic this certainly was not. Although the film critic establishment was not entirely enamored with the technical aspects of the film, overall they gave the film high marks for its sensitivity and artistry. *USA Today* called it "an extraordinary accomplishment." The *Los Angeles Times* deemed it "an intense, utterly sincere, frequently fascinating piece of art by a director for whom, clearly, the message of Jesus' life had immediacy and meaning." The *Washington Post* called it "a work of great seriousness by one of this country's most gifted filmmakers." In the words of the *New York Daily News* the film was a work of "integrity, reverence and a good deal of cinematic beauty." And finally, the *Los Angeles Herald Examiner* called Scorsese's work "one of the most serious, literate, complex and deeply felt religious films ever made."[24]

It is not surprising that progressivist opinion in the denominations was generally sympathetic to this view. A spokesman for the National Council of Churches called the film "an honest attempt to tell the story of Jesus from a different perspective." The Episcopal bishop of New

York called the film "theologically sound."[25] And a theologian at Notre Dame was quoted as saying, "This film is . . . fairly distinguished art."[26]

To say that the conservative Catholic and Evangelical communities did not share this view of the film is to understate their position monumentally. The universal conclusion was that *The Last Temptation of Christ* was "sacrilegious." Morality in Media judged the film to be "an intentional attack on Christianity."[27] "Utter blasphemy of the worst degree," was the way Reverend Falwell put it. "Neither the label 'fiction' nor the First Amendment," he continued, "gives Universal [Studios] the right to libel, slander and ridicule the most central figure in world history."[28] Official Catholic opinion complained that the Christ portrayed in the film was "not the Christ of Scriptures and of the church."[29] But even this was an understatement in the eyes of the more orthodox Catholics and Evangelicals. Christ, they claimed, was made "an object of low fantasies." Focus on the Family concluded that Jesus was portrayed "as a confused, lustful wimp who denies his divinity and struggles with his sinful nature."[30]

Intense hostility led to sustained protest within the larger community of conservative Catholics and Evangelicals. Mother Angelica, a nun who has run the nation's largest Catholic cable network, called on protesters to drive with their headlights on leading up to opening day to signal their opposition to the film. The American Society for the Defense of Tradition, Family and Property published a full-page "open-letter" to Universal Studios in the *New York Times* with the word "Blasphemy" printed at the top. Concerned Women for America asked all MCA stockholders (MCA owns Universal) to sell the company's stock. The American Family Foundation sent out 2.5 million mailings protesting the film and anti-*Temptation* spots appeared on 700 Christian radio stations and 50 to 75 television stations. These actions spawned a massive letter-writing campaign, street protests, and picketing at film openings in cities across the country, (roughly 25,000 people staged a protest rally at Universal City on one day alone), and, of course, a nationwide boycott called by leaders in the Eastern Orthodox, Catholic, and Evangelical Protestant faiths. Moreover, one Evangelical leader, Bill Bright of Campus Crusade for Christ, offered to raise money to reimburse Universal for all copies of the film, which would then "promptly be destroyed."[31]

Publishing

Of "teen" magazines, there seems to be no end. Yet the publication of one of them, *Sassy,* caused quite a stir. Modeled after the popular

Australian teen magazine *Dolly, Sassy* would offer American teenagers the most candid presentation of teen problems and issues available. Early issues carried articles such as "Sex for Absolute Beginners," "So You Think You're Ready for Sex? Read This First," "Should I Talk During Sex?" "The Truth About Boys' Bodies," "The Dirty, Scummy Truth About Spring Break," "Laural and Leslie and Alex and Brian Are Your Basic Kids. They're dating. They go to movies and concerts. They fight over stupid things. They make up. They're sad sometimes. They're happy. AND THEY'RE GAY," among others. In times like these, editors reasoned, it is important to build up "a spirit of openness in talking to teens about sex," drugs, and other issues that they confront. Thus *Sassy* promised, according to an introductory letter, to "help you with some of the really tough decisions you have to make, such as how to know when it's the right time to say no or yes to that special guy and plenty of other things that your mother forgot to tell you." After all, the letter continued, "There are times when you really need to talk with a friend, not with parents or teachers or other people."[32]

The criticisms that followed the publication of *Sassy* carried much the tone of the other moral criticism we have seen. According to traditionalists, the magazine could only have a negative effect on the minds and morals of teenagers, for it encouraged promiscuity and discouraged respect for parental authority by usurping their role in the task of moral and sexual education. Concerned Women for America, Focus on the Family, the American Family Association, and others were incensed by the arrogance and intrusiveness of such a venture and staged a boycott of the advertisers of the new magazine. Hundreds of letters were written to these advertisers complaining of their indirect support for the undermining of morality among children and in the end, five major advertisers and several smaller ones pulled out. The editor, in an interview, admitted that the effect had been "very damaging" financially and, moreover, that the episode had had an impact on editorial policy.

Television

Every year during the ratings sweep, the major networks display their raciest and most innovative programming. In years past, television shows like "Miami Vice," "Dream Street," "Knots Landing," "thirtysomething," "A Man Called Hawk," "The Cosby Show," among many others have made strong showings within the national television audience. These, in turn, become strong draws for corporations wanting to advertise their products. Critics admit that the amount of sexual intimacy outside of marriage, violence, and profanity portrayed on some of these shows is very high, yet they also have been quick to point out that many of these shows are technically innovative and treat many issues such as homosexuality, child abuse and incest, and the ambiguities of ethical behavior in law enforcement, marriage, student culture, and the like, with great sensitivity.

Sensitivity is the last thing these television shows display, in the view of many with orthodox commitments. To the contrary, "television," claimed a letter from the American Family Association, "is undermining the Judeo-Christian values you hold dear and work hard to teach your children."[33] For this reason, leaders from CLeaR-TV visited with executives from the three major networks in order to express their concerns. According to Reverend Wildmon, "They used the same words that I used, but we certainly didn't mean the same thing by them." From this point on, the leaders decided to approach the advertisers rather than the networks. "Advertisers don't give you a cold shoulder. They want to be your friend."[34] In line with this strategy, the American Family Association and CLeaR-TV began to approach advertisers. Sponsors who did not respond positively to their concerns very often faced the threat of a boycott. PepsiCo, for example, pulled a commercial featuring pop star, nude model, and actress Madonna and their promotion of her world tour; General Mills, Ralston Purina, and Domino's Pizza pulled advertising from "Saturday Night Live"; Mazda and Noxell were also influenced in this way; and of the 400 sponsors of prime-time television in the 1989 ratings sweeps, CLeaR-TV focused on the Mennon Company and the Clorox Corporation, pledging to boycott their products for a year for their sponsorship of programs containing sex, violence, and profanity. Of this latter boycott, Roman Catholic Bishop Stanislaus Brzana of New York (one of more than one hundred bishops nationwide who endorsed CLeaR-TV) argued, "We believe our cause will benefit *not only our group but the whole country.*"[35] The work of CLeaR-TV has not been isolated. Kimberly-Clark and Tambrands pulled ads from "Married . . . with Children" after a Michigan homemaker threatened action.[36] The National Decency Forum and the American Family Association have sought to press the Federal Communications Commission, even with legal action, to enforce its "decency code."[37] And finally (though the list could go on), "dial-a-porn" companies who advertise on television have been pressured and a few shut down through legal prosecution and popular pressure by such groups as Citizens for Decency through Law, Concerned Women for America, and Morality in Media.

Decoding Art and the Avant-Garde

The preceding examples are but a few well-publicized illustrations of cultural warfare in various media and forms of public expression. The point of reviewing them was to demonstrate, across media, certain patterns of cultural conflict. Despite the variations of situation and media, one can trace a common and consistent thread of sentiment on each side of the new cultural divide.

On the progressivist side, there is a tendency to value novelty and the avant-garde for their own sake. This in itself is not controversial. What is controversial is *how* avant-garde is defined. Progressives implicitly define the "avant-garde" not so much as the presentation of classic social themes in new artistic forms, but rather as the symbolic presentation of behavior and ideas that test the limits of social acceptability. More often than not this means the embrace of what the prevailing social consensus would have called "perverse" or "irreverent," what Carol Iannone calls "the insistent and progressive artistic exploration of the forbidden frontiers of human experience." Lucy Lippard acknowledges as much in her review of the Serrano corpus in *Art in America:* "His work shows," she contends, "that the conventional notion of good taste with which we are raised and educated is based on an illusion of social order that is no longer possible (nor desirable) to believe in. We now look at art in the context of incoherence and disorder—a far more difficult task than following the prevailing rules."[38] A similar theme can be found in each of the other cases reviewed. In rap music and in television programming, the boundaries of social consensus around human relationships are tested through excessive sex and violence; in the film *The Last Temptation,* they are tested through the demythologization of ancient Christian belief; in publishing the magazine *Sassy,* the boundaries of adolescent innocence (at what age and how kids should learn about sexuality) are tested. In each case, an earlier consensus of what is "perverse" and what is "irreverent" is challenged, and as it is challenged, it inevitably disintegrates.

The issue is sharpened when considering the special case of art. Here too the underlying controversy is over how art is to be defined. In general, progressivists tend to start with the assumption that there is no objective method of determining what is art and what is obscene. Historical experience demonstrates time and again that even if a consensus declares that a work has no enduring artistic value, the consensus may change; the work could, over time, come to be viewed as art.[39] For this reason one must recognize and at all times respect and defend the autonomy of the artist and of artistic effort. Artists should not be bound by legal constraints or inhibited by social conventions, for artistic genius may yet emerge, if it is not already evident. Indeed, modern criticism does regard art "as a 'sacred wood,' a separate universe, a self-contained sovereignty" and the artist, in writer Vladimir Nabokov's words, as responsible to no one but himself.[40] One artist expressed this theme when he said, "It is extremely important that art be unjustifiable."[41]

Out of this general perspective comes the implicit understanding that a work is art if "experts" are willing to call it art and if it symbolically expresses an individual's personal quest to understand and interpret one's experience in the world.[42] Both themes were evident in the expert testimony given at the 1990 obscenity trial of the Contemporary Arts Center in Cincinnati where the question "What is art?" was posed directly in view of the Mapplethorpe retrospective. Jacquelynn Baas, director of the University Art Museum at the University of California at Berkeley, responded to the question of why one should consider Robert Mapplethorpe's work as art by declaring: "In the first place, they're great photographs. Secondly, in this work he dealt with issues that our society, modern society is grappling with . . . what it means to be a sexual being, and also race, that was an important part of the show." Robert Sobieszek, curator of the George Eastman House International Museum of Photography reiterated the same two themes. "I would say they are works of art, knowing they are by Robert Mapplethorpe, knowing his intentions. They reveal in very strong, forceful ways a major concern of a creative artist . . . a troubled portion of his life that he was trying to come to grips with. It's that search for meaning, not unlike van Gogh's."[43] Both experts declare, prima facie, the work to be art; both point out how it symbolically expresses Mapplethorpe's quest to interpret the world and his place in it.

For the orthodox and their conservative allies, expert opinion is not a reliable measure of artistic achievement and the artist's intentions are completely irrelevant to determining whether a work is art. Rather, artistic achievement is measured by the extent to which it reflects the sublime. Critic Hilton Kramer endorses this view in speaking of federal funding for art that reflects "the highest achievements of our civilization."[44] George F. Will similarly favors the view that art, at least art worthy of support, is recognized in its capacity to "elevate the public mind by bringing it into contact with beauty and even ameliorate social pathologies."[45] Art worthy of government funding, therefore, should be justifiable on the grounds that it serves this high public purpose. Congressman Henry Hyde, in reflecting about his role in the public policy process, argues that "art detached from the quest for truth and goodness is simply self-expression and ultimately self-absorption."[46] Again, what all of the voices on this side of the cultural divide hold in common—whether orthodox theists like Hyde or secular platonists like Kramer and Will—is a belief in a metaphysical reality for which art is to be a symbolic expression.

In sum, for the orthodox and their conservative allies artistic creativity is concerned to reflect a higher reality. For their opponents, art is concerned with the creation of reality itself. Art for the progressivist is, then, a statement of being. To express oneself is to declare one's existence. Hilton Kramer may be correct that the professional art world maintains a sentimental attachment to the idea that art is at its best when it is most extreme and disruptive, but he is probably wrong if he believes this to be its chief or only aim. More fundamentally, if only implicitly, the contemporary arts project is a statement about the meaning of life, namely that life is a process of self-creation. As this enterprise takes public form, however, contemporary art and the avant-garde come to represent nothing less than the besmearing of the highest ideals of the orthodox moral vision.

When all is said and done, however, the events taking place in each of the contexts mentioned earlier—the action and reaction of progressivists and cultural conservatives—represent only the first stage in the development of a deeper debate about the limits of public expression in American society.

CENSORSHIP

Progressivist Accusations

The immediate reaction of the progressivists is that those who complain about art do so because they "do not know enough about art," or simply "do not care about art."[47] All of the protest demonstrates, as the *Washington Post* put it, "the danger of a cultural outsider passing judgement on something he doesn't understand."[48] Such comments may sound elitist (and undoubtedly are), but their significance goes beyond implying that those who do not share progressive aesthetic taste are simple philistines. The real significance of such sentiments is that they reaffirm the basic characteristic of the contemporary culture war, namely the nigh complete disjunction of moral understanding between the orthodox and progressivist communities—in this case, on what constitutes art. The progressivist communities and the arts establishment display a certain arrogance in believing that their definitions of "serious artistic merit" should be accepted by all, and this leads them to categorize various cultural conservatives as "Know-Nothings," "yahoos," "neanderthals," "literary death squads," "fascists," and "cultural terrorists."[49]

The response of progressivists to this situation, however, quickly evolves beyond this. In a way, what we hear after this initial response is less of an argument than it is a symbolic call to arms, a "Banzai!" that reveals a spontaneous, unified, and passionate indignation every bit as deep as that expressed by the orthodox in reaction to tarnishing of their ideals. Irrespective of the circumstances or media, the orthodox protest evokes among progressives the cry of "censorship."

Nowhere has this alarm sounded more loudly than in the case of the protest against network television. People for the American Way, Americans for Constitutional Freedom, *Playboy,* and many others have viewed the boycotting of corporate advertisers of television programming as acts of "economic terrorism" that are tantamount to censorship. "What is more intrusive than the attempt by fundamentalist censors to dictate what we can watch in the privacy of our own homes?" asked the founder of Fundamentalists Anonymous. Donald Wildmon, whom *Playboy* called the "Tupelo Ayatollah," is nothing short of "dangerous." Said the executive director of Americans for Constitutional Freedom, "We intend to do everything to prevent him from setting himself up as a censor who can remake America in his own image."[50]

Similar accusations are leveled in every other situation where the orthodox protest the content of public media. The music industry viewed the efforts of the Parents' Music Resource Center to have albums labeled "contains explicit lyrics" as an act of censorship. Frank Zappa called it a conspiracy to extort. Outside observers viewed the orthodox influence on *Sassy*'s editorial policy (through the threat of corporate boycotts) as "horrifying," tantamount to the suppression of ideas. The varied protests against *The Last Temptation of Christ* (particularly the boycott) were viewed by many progressives as acts of censorship, born out of "intolerant narrow-mindedness," "bigotry," and "pharisaism."[51] Universal Studios responded to Bill Bright's offer to purchase all copies of the film with full-page newspaper advertisements in four cities, stating that the right to free expression was not for sale. Economic pressure (in the form of the boycott) against hotel chains that make adult films available to their patrons has been called censorship. Proposals to defund the National Endowment for the Arts were viewed as a move toward censorship. Even the refusal of printing companies to print "controversial" materials has been deemed "printer censorship."[52] And, finally, efforts to prohibit flag burning have been called political censorship.

Implicit within this accusation, of course, is the legal judgment that the constitutionally guaranteed right to freedom of speech is either threatened or actually violated by conservative protest. For this reason, the Bill of Rights is almost always invoked by progressives or by artists themselves. When, for example, Nikki Sixx of Mötley Crüe was told in an interview that there were those who objected to the band stating on stage that their "only regret is that [they] couldn't eat all the pussy [they] saw here tonight, he responded, 'I say fuck 'em. It's freedom of speech; First Amendment!' "[53] Thomas Jefferson himself might not have put it quite that way or even necessarily agreed with the application, but without fail, the legacy of Jefferson directly informs the content of the progressivist reply. Luther Campbell of 2 Live Crew echoed this sentiment when he said, "We give America what they want. Isn't there such a thing as free enterprise here? Isn't there such a thing as freedom of speech?" The record store owner in Florida arrested for selling *As Nasty As They Wanna Be* put the matter in a slightly larger context. "We tell the Lithuanians, you know, fight for freedom . . . And yet, we're trying to censor our own country. . . .We don't need nobody to censor us and they're violating our civil rights and our freedom of speech. And next—what else will it be next?"[54] And finally, a purveyor of "adult art" was perhaps the most articulate on this matter. "The fact that speech is offensive to some people," he said, "the fact that it is controversial, is exactly the sort of speech that the First Amendment was designed to protect. Speech that is acceptable to everyone, that's not controversial, doesn't need protection, because nobody is going to try to suppress it."[55]

The pounding repetition of this accusation is in accord with the general position taken by the People for the American Way, who believe that this brand of censorship is not only on the increase, it "has become more organized and more effective" with haunting implications.[56] The very language employed by cultural conservatives when they insist it is time to "clean up our culture" or to "stop subsidizing decadence" is, as several writers contend, "chillingly reminiscent of Nazi cultural metaphors."[57] Robert Brustein, writing in the *New Republic,* goes so far as to dismiss the distinction between censorship and the effort to influence the distribution of taxpayers' money (as in the effort to defund "offensive art" at the National Endowment for the Arts), insisting that defunding art is a form of censorship. He concludes that "only government—in a time when other funding has grown increasingly restrictive and programmatic—can guarantee free and innovative art. And that means acknowledging that, yes, every artist has a First Amendment right to subsidy."[58]

The progressivist response to this backlash has gone beyond rhetoric into direct political action as well. Full-page newspaper ads criticizing the censorious impulse have appeared. Individual artists, the ACLU, Playboy Enterprises, *Penthouse,* the American Booksellers Association, and many other individuals and organizations have initiated litigation against a number of organizations, such as Concerned Women for America and the American Family Association. Counterboycotts were formed, such as the one called by Fundamentalists Anonymous against Pepsi in order to "protest Pepsi's capitulation to censorship." ("No Madonna, no Pepsi," they claimed. We will make Pepsi "the choice of the fundamentalist generation"—"only losers will drink Pepsi!")[59] A number of new organizations, such as Americans for Constitutional Freedom, the National Campaign for Freedom of Expression, and the Media Coalition, also came to life as part of the progressivist reaction to these assaults.

Orthodox Counteraccusations

To the accusation of censorship, the reply of cultural conservatives is "nonsense!" *Christianity Today* editorialized that the media and arts establishment

> use freedom of speech as a means to flout standards of common public decency. We must not throw in the towel. Christians must unite in mounting a counteroffensive through our families, churches, schools, and other institutions. The legal issues surrounding public standards may be complex, but the moral imperatives are not. We must not abandon the ring of public debate to those who would use freedom of speech as an excuse to be as morally offensive as they "wanna" be.[60]

Implicit here and in much of the orthodox and conservative rhetoric is the view that communities have the right to decide for themselves what standards will be used to discriminate between art and obscenity. If, through the democratic process, standards are agreed upon, why should communities not be entitled to uphold them through official means?

Donald Wildmon also rejects the idea that he and his compatriots are somehow violating the First Amendment protections of free speech, but he takes a slightly different tack. He insists that artists do have the right to express themselves as they please but that he too has a right to speak out against them. This posture is expressed paradigmatically in his rationale for acting against Pepsi for its plans to fund the Madonna tour.

> Here is a pop singer who makes a video that's sacrilegious to the core. Here's a pop star that made a low-budget porn film. Here's a pop star who goes around in her concerts with sex oozing out, wearing a cross. Now Pepsi is saying to all the young people of the new generation, "Here is the person we want you to emulate and imitate." They can do that. They've got every right to give Madonna $10 million dollars, put it on television every night if they want to. All I'm saying is "Don't ask me to buy Pepsi if you do it."[61]

The same rationale undergirds Wildmon's approach to the television networks. "The networks can show what they want to show. The advertiser can sponsor what he wants to sponsor. And the consumer can spend his money where he wants to. [The idea] that I must spend my money with these companies to help support these programs that I find offensive [—] I don't believe that." To those who wonder aloud whether he is infringing on others' rights, he responds, "I'm not infringing on anybody's rights. I have as much right as any other individual in this society to try to shape society. I have as much right to try to influence people. . . . I'm very cognizant of other people's rights. All I'm asking is for them to be cognizant of mine."[62]

Tipper Gore of the Parents' Music Resource Center called the cry of censorship "a smoke screen," a dodge for taking corporate responsibility for their product. In asking for labels on record albums, her group claimed, they were asking for more information, not less. The group's approach, then, "was the direct opposite of censorship." Morality in Media takes the argument one step further in maintaining that "freedom of expression is not the exclusive right of producers, publishers, authors or a handful of media executives. Freedom of expression belongs . . . to the entire community. . . . [it is only a] vocal, unremitting, organized community expression [that] will bring about a media based on love, truth and good taste."[63]

The debate over censorship becomes even more interesting when the accusation of censorship is leveled at progressives by the voices of orthodoxy. At one extreme Jimmy Swaggart insists that "those of the humanistic stripe want to see all Bibles banned in America."[64] But accusations of censorship also come from more tempered voices within the conservative alliance, with much greater credibility.

The complaint that progressivists and a liberal educational establishment censor, through exclusion, material on traditional religion in the public school textbooks was noted in the last chapter. The same kind of de facto censoring occurs, it is maintained, when major magazines and newspapers, through editorial edict, refuse to review books written and published by conservative Catholics or Evangelical Protestants, or deny them the recognition they deserve by not including these works on their best-seller lists. The Evangelical writer Francis Schaeffer, for example, sold over 3 million copies of his books in the United States, and yet his books were never reviewed in the *New York Times Book Review* or *Time* and never counted on any best-seller list. The same was true of Hal Lindsey's *Late Great Planet Earth,* a book that was the top nonfiction seller in America in the 1970s—for the entire decade. The book was not reviewed by the literary establishment nor did it appear on weekly best-seller lists until it was later published by a secular publishing house. For publishing elites to ignore this literature, for whatever reasons—even if they do not believe such works constitute "serious literature or scholarship"—is, they say, to "censor." As columnist Cal Thomas put it, the "practice of treating the Christian market as a kind of 'Negro league' of publishing creates a false impression that we live in a totally secular society where persons with religious principles have nothing to say. If occasionally they do say something in print, their opinions or ideas are not worth reading or considering."[65]

It was in this spirit that the editors of the conservative magazine *Chronicles of Culture* wrote (in a subscription appeal):

> Once upon a time in America, you could say you loved your country, believed in God, and held your marriage sacred . . . and *not* be snickered at as a simple-minded innocent.
>
> Your could believe in honesty, hard work, and self-reliance;

you could speak of human *responsibilities* in the same breath as human rights . . . and *not* be derided as an insensitive fool.

You could speak out against profane books, depraved movies, and decadent art; you could express your disapproval of drug-sodden entertainers, America-hating educators, and appeasement-obsessed legislators . . . and *not* be branded as an ignorant reactionary.

And yes, once upon a time in America, you could actually believe in *morality,* both public and private, and *not* be proclaimed a hopeless naif—more to be pitied than taken seriously.

But that was before the "censorship of fashion" took control of contemporary American culture.

This insidious form of censorship is not written into our laws or statutes—but it is *woven* into the very *fabric* of our culture. It reigns supreme in literature and the arts, on television and in film, in music and on radio, in our churches, our public schools, and our universities. And above all else, it is dedicated to the propagation of one agenda—the *liberal activist* agenda for America.

The "censorship of fashion" is not only sinister and subtle, it's also ruthlessly *effective.* It employs the powerful weapons of *ridicule* and *condescension* to stifle the voices of millions of Americans, like you, who still cherish our traditional values.[66]

Assaults on the right to free speech, some orthodox leaders contend, are further evident in lawsuits against those organizations that boycott, picket, or systematically protest against the sale and distribution of "sexually explicit material" or against abortion clinics. Such lawsuits have been based on the Racketeer Influenced and Corrupt Organizations (RICO) Act. For example, *Playboy* and *Penthouse* magazines as well as Waldenbooks filed extortion and racketeering charges against the Florida chapter of the American Family Association for using pickets and boycott threats to get 1,400 stores to stop selling the magazine. Said a spokesman for the defendants, "The expansion of the use of RICO against free expression activities is extremely dangerous to the future of free speech, and *is censorship at its worst.*"[67]

The view that the media, arts, and literary establishment is intolerant of orthodox perspectives and ideals is not merely a rhetorical device for getting back at progressives but a deeply held conviction. It is the sense of institutionalized bias and even censorship against the orthodox that has inspired the rise of religiously orthodox equivalents to an anti-defamation league. The Catholic League for Civil and Religious Rights is such a group in the conservative Catholic orbit; though groups like the Rutherford Institute serve such a function within the Evangelical camp, calls for an organization deliberately identified and acting in the capacity of a Christian antidefamation league were issued in the early 1990s.[68] Given the nature of the culture war, such a development is, perhaps, inevitable.

Decoding Free Speech

Back and forth the arguments go. After a time, the details of this conflict become tediously predictable. One side claims that a work is "art"; the other claims it is not. One claims that a work has enduring aesthetic or literary appeal; the other claims it only appeals to the eccentric interests of a deviant subculture. At least on the face of it, one is tempted to agree with Justice John Marshall Harlan who concluded that "one man's vulgarity is another's lyric." Such relativism may not be desirable but it seems to be the necessary outcome of the present cultural conflict. In this light, it is entirely predictable that each side would claim that the other side is not committed to free speech but to a systematic imposition of its values and perspectives on everyone else. Alas, one person's act of "censorship" has become another's "commitment to community standards."

Thus, in the contemporary culture war, regard for rights to the freedom of speech has become a matter of "whose ox is being gored" at the moment.[69] The fact is, both sides make a big mistake when they confuse *censuring* (the legitimate mobilization of moral opprobrium) with *censoring* (the use of the state and other legal or official means to restrict speech).[70] Censuring, say through economic boycott or letter-writing campaigns, is itself a form of political speech protected by the First Amendment and employed legally all of the time whether in boycotts against South Africa, Nestle's, or California lettuce growers, or against the purveyors of sexually explicit or theologically controversial art. But the finer points of distinction are lost on many of the activists in this debate. Even when the protest is merely the expression of disapproval, what each side invariably hears are the footsteps of an approaching cadre of censors. In most cases, however, neither side presents a genuine threat to the rights of the other to free expression. The cry of censorship from both sides of the cultural divide, then, becomes an ideological weapon to silence legitimate dissent.

This being said, it must also be stated that real censorship *is* taking place and the voices of both cultural conservatism and progressivism perpetuate it in their own ways. Censorship, again, is the use of the state or other official means to restrict speech. In every case it is justified by the claim that "community standards" have been violated. The use of the police to arrest the members of 2 Live Crew in Florida and the use of law to shut down the Contemporary Arts Center in Cincinnati because they violated community standards of obscenity are, then, textbook cases of such censorship. Censorship is also perpetuated on the other side of the cultural divide. It is seen in the efforts of student groups and universities to prohibit, in the name of community standards, defamatory remarks and expressions against minorities, gays, and women. (Would progressives throw their support or legal weight behind a similar code that prohibited say, unpatriotic, irreligious, or sexually explicit "expressions" on the community campus?) Censorship is also seen, to give another example, in the suspension of Andy Rooney from his job at CBS in 1990 for making remarks against gays. On both sides of the cultural divide, the concept of "community standards" is invoked as an ideological weapon to silence unpopular voices. Understanding how the standards of one moral community can be so diametrically opposed to the standards of the other takes us back to the root of the culture war itself.

ART, EXPRESSION, AND THE SACRED

A critic quoted earlier warned of the danger of a cultural outsider passing judgment on something he does not understand. The reality of the culture war is that the cultural conservative and the progressivist are each outsiders to the other's cultural milieu. Accordingly, each regularly and often viciously passes judgment on the other. That judgment is not at all bad in itself. Such is the back and forth of democratic discourse. The danger is not in passing judgment but in the failure to understand why the other is so insulted by that judgment. *That* is the measure of their mutual outsiderness.

The orthodox, for example, demonstrate such a position when they view certain artistic work in isolation from the larger aesthetic project of an artist and label it obscene, pornographic, and prurient.[71] Who are these people, progressivists ask, to label the life work of Serrano and Mapplethorpe as vulgarity? That they cannot see the "enduring artistic achievement" of an artist's oeuvre is a gauge of their alienation from "high art" discourse. The same kind of obtuseness is found among progressivists. Consider the controversy surrounding *The Last Temptation of Christ.* A *Washington Post* editorial stated with no equivocation that audiences would not find the film blasphemous.[72] Another reviewer, from *Newsweek,* said, "One can think of hundreds of trashy, thrill-happy movies devout Christians could get upset about. Instead, they have taken to the airwaves to denounce *the one movie that could conceivably open a viewer's heart to the teachings of Jesus.*" Still another reviewer, from Newhouse Newspapers, called the film, "The most realistic biblical film ever made."[73] Who are these people, orthodox Christians ask, to proclaim universally that *The Last Temptation of Christ* was not blasphemous? For millions of Americans it certainly was, and it was a measure of progressives' outsiderness that they could not acknowledge it to be.

This kind of mutual misunderstanding reveals once more that the conflict over the media and the arts is not just a dispute among institutions and not just a disagreement over "speech" protected by the First Amendment. Ultimately the battle over this symbolic territory reveals a conflict over world views—over what standards our communities and our nation will live by; over what we consider to be "of enduring value" in our communities; over what we consider a fair representation of our times, and so on. As a bystander at the Contemporary Arts Center in Cincinnati observed during the controversy over the Mapplethorpe exhibit, "This isn't just an obscenity prosecution. This is a trial of a good part of American culture."[74]

But even more, these battles again lay bare the tensions that exist between two fundamentally different conceptions of the sacred. For those of orthodox religious commitments, the sacred is obvious enough. It is an unchanging and everlasting God who ordained through Scripture, the church, or Torah, a manner of life and of social relationship that cannot be broached without incurring the displeasure of God. On the other side of the cultural divide, the sacred is a little more difficult to discern. Perhaps Tom Wolfe had it right when he observed that art itself was the religion of the educated classes.[75] Maybe this is why Broadway producer Joseph Papp said as he observed the police coming into the Cincinnati Contemporary Arts Center to close the Mapplethorpe exhibit, "It's like an invasion. It's like they're coming into a church or coming into a synagogue, or coming into any place of worship. It's a violation."[76] Such an insight makes sense if we see art as a symbol of conscience. To place any restrictions on the arts, therefore, is to place restrictions on the conscience itself; it is to place fetters on the symbol of being. Such an insight also makes sense if we see art as a symbol of immortality—of that which will outlive us all. To place restrictions on art is to place restrictions on the (secular) hope of eternity. Perhaps this is why the procedural guarantee of freedom of expression has also acquired a sacred quality in progressivist circles.

The idea that the battle over the arts is related to the tensions between two different conceptions of the sacred is not far-fetched. How else can one explain the passion and intensity on both sides of the cultural divide were it not that each side, by its very being and expression, profanes what the other holds most sublime? If this is true, we are again reminded of the reasons that the larger culture war will not subside any time soon.

10

Law

As we have seen, the attempt to gain advantage in the contemporary cultural contest by means of superior moral reasoning is frustrated largely because the contenders themselves operate from different philosophical assumptions and by very different rules of logic and moral judgment. The advocates of opposing sides find themselves in a moral Tower of Babel, everyone speaking, even shouting, but unable to understand or to be understood. Sometimes activists resort to efforts to delegitimate their opposition and its agenda through discrediting labels and commentary. It has become clear that this is a trade in which all participants engage with matching vitality and conviction. At least on the surface of things, the result appears to be a stalemate.

Yet there is another field of conflict on which opposing sides of the cultural divide attempt to gain the advantage. It is the legal system. De Tocqueville himself observed that "there is hardly a political question in the United States which does not sooner or later turn into a judicial one."[1] This is undoubtedly more true now than in the 1830s when he made the remark. Is there any part of contemporary life in America that has not become engulfed by litigation? Certainly all of the fields of conflict reviewed here—from the various aspects of family life, to education, to free speech, not to mention health (for example, smokers' versus nonsmokers' rights), health care (such as the right to die), and social protest (such as when RICO or federal antiracketeering laws are applied to certain kinds of political activism)—are simply awash in legal imbroglio. Nevertheless, something more subtle and even more elementary is at issue than the evolution of public discourse from political disagreement to legal dispute.

PACKING THE COURTS

The most conspicuous area over which the legal system is contested is in the composition of the bench itself—judges selected by the president as federal court appointments. This is no small affair, for as history makes clear, judges not only decree what the Constitution legally requires, but what it morally implies as well. The power of selection vested in the executive branch of the government, therefore, is nothing less than a temptation to prejudice the bench in favor of those judges and attorneys whose legal philosophy and opinions are most compatible with the current administration.

A comment made in the 1980s is a telling way to begin. In an occasional paper published by the People for the American Way, the author asserted that the "new Right's court packing campaign" through the 1980s was "profoundly anti-constitutional."[2] The claim, in a broader perspective, appears disingenuous, since the temptation to prejudice the court in this way has rarely been resisted by presidents. Presidents have long attempted to fashion the federal judiciary in their own ideological cast and have in large part succeeded. Truman appointed 47 percent of the federal bench; Eisenhower, 56 percent; Kennedy, 33 percent, Johnson, 38 percent; and Carter, 40 percent. Ronald Reagan, in two terms, appointed more than 50 percent. The growth of the judiciary is a factor here. The actual number of district and appellate judges has increased more than twofold—from about 280 during the late 1940s to roughly 760 in the late 1980s.[3] So, as the number of judgeships has grown, so too has the president's influence over them. But the logic and temptation of "court packing" has extended to the Supreme Court as well. President Franklin Roosevelt, for example, went so far as to formally propose that the Court be expanded by six more Justices in order to tip the balance of opinion in favor of New Deal legislation. Although the plan finally failed, it is said that it succeeded in its effect, for it served to intimidate the existing Supreme Court into sympathy for Roosevelt's agenda. Moreover, even without expanding the number of Justices, FDR made a virtual clean sweep of the Court during his administration in the eight appointments he eventually made.

Because the personalities and judgments of the Supreme Court receive much media attention, one might imagine that it is really the composition of the Supreme Court that is most decisive for American jurisprudence. As the court of final appeal its practical and symbolic importance is undeniable. Even so, one should bear in mind that the Supreme Court typically offers its opinion on no more than 150 cases every year. By contrast, the federal district and appeals courts typically handle over 300,000 cases in the same period. The course of American life, then, would seem to be influenced as much if not more by decisions at lower levels than by the Supreme Court. The point, of course, is that the composition of the federal judiciary at all levels is tremendously significant.

Despite previous patterns and precedents of court packing at all levels, however, it is fair to say that the evolving culture war has intensified the anxiety of individuals and groups on all sides over the matter of bias of the courts. The progressive and orthodox-conservative alliances each want the plurality on the bench to reflect their interests in the culture war. The events and polemics surrounding the effort by the Reagan administration to replace Justice Lewis Powell with nominee Robert Bork in 1987 illustrate this dynamic well.

On the retirement of Justice Powell, Paul Gerwitz at the Yale Law School remarked that it was not just another vacancy but "the pivot point in the next generation of American Constitutional Law."[4] In a very different language, those on the right agreed. This Court vacancy, claimed *Christian Voice,* may be the "last chance . . . to ensure future decades will bring morality, godliness, and justice back into focus."[5] Falwell himself claimed that "we are standing at the edge of history. [Judge Bork's nomination] may be our last chance to influence this most important body."[6] To this end the Moral Majority saw to it that up to 22,000 postcards in support of Bork were delivered to the Senate Judiciary Committee. Ultimately, these efforts and others like them were paltry compared to the resources mobilized by liberal activists and organizations. Between 10 and 15 million dollars were spent by progressivist organizations (as diverse as the National Organization for Women, the National Education Association, the National Abortion Rights Action League, the NAACP, Planned Parenthood, People for the American Way, the ACLU, the AFL-CIO, Common Cause, and the like), many of which united under the new organization Alliance for Justice, in order to defeat Bork's nomination.[7] By itself, People for the American Way spent over a million dollars on television and radio advertisements, full-page newspaper advertisements, and editorials in local and national media—all to defeat the nomination of a man they described as having an "icy contempt for decades of Supreme Court jurisprudence," and who "would turn back the clock of progress."[8]

The events surrounding the Bork nomination were extreme and unprecedented by any standard. Nevertheless, they well illustrate how strategic the judiciary has come to be seen in the minds of activists on both sides of the cultural divide. It is for precisely this reason that George Bush nominated David Souter, a man with no identifiable linkages with the issues of the culture war, to replace retiring Justice William Brennan in 1990. Had Souter held an identifiable position on *Roe v. Wade* or on affirmative action, for example, both sides would have immediately mobilized in the way they did over the Bork nomination. As it was, the opposition to Souter was launched primarily by feminist groups such as the Fund for a Feminist Majority and the National Organization for Women. People for the American Way and the American Civil Liberties Union chose not to oppose the nominee for a lack of ammunition. He had left no paper trail. Bush's claim that his nomination was not motivated by politics, then, could not have been more disingenuous, for the decision could not have been more political. There would be no other way to move a nominee through confirmation hearings. Clearly, these unfolding machinations exemplify the level of tension each side has come to feel about the outcome of the battle over this important field of conflict. The political drama following Thurgood Marshall's retirement in 1991 tells a similar story.

THE RULES FOR RESOLVING PUBLIC DIFFERENCES

Court packing may be the most conspicuous area of contention in the battle over the legal system, yet at a very different level, the strife extends to the very *procedures* for working out moral disagreements in the public realm; the legal, indeed constitutional *methodology* for resolving mutual differences. The conflict at this level is rarely reported in the public media but in the long run it is far more consequential for the larger struggle for cultural domination.

Take as an example the 1988 Supreme Court case that challenged the tax-exempt status of the Roman Catholic Church for its public opposition to pro-abortion legislation. Though the Supreme Court ultimately only addressed specific technical issues that framed the case, the root of this case was whether churches have a right to speak out on moral issues in the political realm without endangering their tax-exempt status.[9] The group Abortion Rights Mobilization argued that the exemption provided the Catholic Church with an unfair subsidy for partisan political activity in the abortion dispute. In this case, as in many others, it makes a critical difference who wins. *Those who define how a contest is to be played out will have an upper hand in shaping its final outcome.* It is no surprise, then, that the struggle to define those rules has escalated and intensified.

The battle over the rules by which contending alliances work out their differences shows how the struggle for definition has shifted to the substance of law and the judiciary. The single best measure of this, I would contend, is the multiplying number of court cases dealing with the relationship between church and state in America. The Supreme Court cases dealing with the meaning of the First Amendment religion clauses were very rare prior to the 1870s. By the middle of the twentieth century the ten-year average number of church and state cases had increased to nineteen (between 1937 and 1946). By the years 1977–86, the number had nearly doubled to thirty-five.[10] In sum, at the Supreme Court level, the first three-fourths of America's history as a nation witnessed only one-fourth of the religion cases while the last fourth of American history has witnessed three-fourths of the religion cases. The same pattern in church and state litigation is seen in lower federal courts and in state courts. There has been explosive growth: now the cases number in the thousands.[11]

The Technical Issue

The numbers are impressive but the basic question lingers unanswered: what bearing do church and state disagreements have on the struggle to determine the procedures of public disagreement? How are the first sixteen words of the First Amendment—"Congress shall make no law respecting an establishment of religion nor prohibiting the free exercise thereof"—relevant to the contemporary culture war? Why is this part of the Constitution the center of legal controversy? The answer is in part sociological: articulating the rights and responsibilities of religion (in a strictly traditional and institutional sense) is not what the religion clauses are all about. The religion clauses articulate something that is broader and more generic, namely, *the interrelationship between the convictions of consciousness, the autonomy of belief and belief systems, and the powers and prerogatives of the state.* "Free exercise" means the protection under the law to live and worship according to the dictates of conscience. But are there limits to what the state will accept as permissible? If so, what are the limits and how do those limits change? Likewise, the "no establishment" provision means that the state will not link its interests with the interests of a particular faith, that it will be as neutral as possible—but is "neutrality" really achievable? If not, on which side should the state err? It is in the subtle vagaries in the interpretation of these clauses that the interests of different ideological contenders can either be enhanced or diminished.

This entire issue can be addressed by way of exploring (1) the opposing ways in which "religion" is defined by the courts and (2) the opposing ideals of the proper relationship between church and state. The questions may seem esoteric and beside the point, yet we will see that they are of decisive significance.

Defining Religion

To understand how the legal definition of religion has come to be contested, it is first necessary to sketch out the ways in which the courts have implicitly conceptualized religion. For this task it is useful to refer to the analytical tools of the social sciences. Although these definitions have never been explicitly invoked by the courts, it is clear that the courts operate within a framework that is laid out by the social sciences.

Social Scientific Definitions of Religion

For all practical purposes, social science offers two approaches to the definition of religion: the substantive approach and the functional approach. Both definitional approaches emerge out of respected intellectual traditions, but the analytical differences are marked.[12] Those who adopt the substantive model argue that religion should be defined by *what it is*—that is, by the "meaning contents of the phenomenon." Those who favor the functional model maintain that religion should be defined according to *what it does.*

In the substantive approach the differentia is the category of the "sacred" or the "holy." Yet the sacred, from this perspective, has a fairly specific meaning. The sacred is the realm of the supramundane or the transcendent—what Rudolf Otto called the *mysterium tremendum*. As such it is a reality that humans experience as "wholly other," for it evokes feelings of ineffable wonder and awe. Religion, then, is the meaning system that emanates from the sacred.

Again, what distinguishes functional approaches to religion is the concern for what it does—its role and consequences for individual and social existence. For the individual, religion provides "road maps for the soul"—a meaning system offering a sense of purpose and meaning to the life course, a stable set of moral coordinates to guide everyday life as well as mechanisms to help the individual cope with the traumatic experiences of suffering, pain, and death. At the societal level, religion functions to justify institutional arrangements, thereby generating social integration (or in Marxist terminology, legitimating the status quo). At this level, religion can also perform a prophetic function, delegitimating the status quo and calling for the establishment of a new social order. From this perspective, religion is also defined by the sacred but the sacred in this case could be any ultimate value or any orienting principle adhered to by a social group.[13]

Although analytically distinct, these approaches clearly are not mutually exclusive. The substantive approach recognizes the functionality of religion and the functional approach recognizes the special qualities of the supernatural. Nevertheless, both approaches carry different analytical consequences. Generally the substantive model delimits religion to the range of traditional theisms: Judaism, Christianity, Islam, Hinduism, and so on. The functional model is more inclusive. By defining religion according to its social function, religion has become largely synonymous with such terms as cultural system, belief system, meaning system, moral order, ideology, world view, and cosmology. For all practical purposes, even functionalists still think of religion in its traditional sense—a body of beliefs and practices emanating from a transcendent, often supernatural source—but as the approach implies, a cultural system does not have to have a deity for it to be considered religious in character. Confucianism and Theravadin Buddhism, for example, contain no supernatural referent to speak of, yet few would not include these in the larger pantheon of world religions. Other examples are less obvious, such as political ideologies, social movements, and therapeutic techniques. Scholars typically refer to these as "quasi religions" or "religion-surrogates" or "functional equivalents" of religion. Even those who are committed in principle to a more substantive approach recognize the profoundly religious nature of these phenomena and employ these terms to describe them.

It is within these parameters that American jurisprudence has sought to define religion. Yet the task of defining religion for legal purposes has not been a systematic process but one that has evolved from case to case with different judges.

Legal Definitions

It was not until the 1870s that the Supreme Court took up the question of the nature of religion spoken of in the First Amendment. From this time through the end of the nineteenth century and well into the twentieth century the courts defined religion in strictly substantive terms—religion referred to theistic notions of divinity, morality, and worship.[14] In 1890, for example, the Supreme Court Justices held that "the term 'religion' has reference to one's view of his relations to his Creator, and to the obligations they impose for reverence for his being and character, and of obedience to his will."[15]

The reason for adopting this restricted approach was simple. As Justice David Brewer wrote for the majority opinion in *Church of the Holy Trinity v. United States* (1892), "Our civilization and our institutions are emphatically Christian. . . . From the discovery of this continent to the present hour, there is a single voice making this affirmation . . . that this is a Christian nation."[16] Thus it was entirely understandable that in the cases dealing with the legality of Mormon polygamy, the Justices would legitimate their decision of opposition by referencing "the consent of the Christian world in modern times."[17]

Forty years later, the courts again approached the problem of defining religion and the strict substantive approach was again affirmed. The case was *United States v. Macintosh,* a case dealing with a Canadian immigrant and professor in the Yale Divinity School who was denied citizenship because he refused to agree to bear arms unless he were first allowed to decide whether the war was "morally justified." There, in the course of its decision, the Supreme Court maintained that

> the essence of religion is belief in a relation to God involving duties superior to those arising from any human relation. . . . One cannot speak of religious liberty, with proper appreciation of its essential and historic significance, without assuming the existence of a belief in supreme allegiance to the will of God.[18]

The assumption of a Christian nation was absent from the definition but the theistic meaning was emphatically not.

Not long after this decision, however, the courts began to expand their approach. The first indication of this came in 1941 when a federal court of appeals was presented with a case involving a conscientious objector. The individual, Mathias Kauten, sought exemption from military service because he maintained that such service would be in violation of his "religious conscience." The legal difficulty posed by his argument was that he openly admitted that his objection was not rooted in a "belief in a deity." Nevertheless, the court ruled in Kauten's favor, in part through a broadened definition of religion. As the court put it,

> Religious belief arises from a sense of the inadequacy of reason as a means of relating the individual to his fellow men and to his universe—a sense common to men in the most primitive and the most highly civilized societies. . . . It is a belief finding expression in a conscience which categorically requires the believer to disregard elementary self-interest and to accept martyrdom in preference to transgressing its tenets. . . . Conscientious objection may justly be regarded as a response of the individual to an inward mentor, call it conscience of God, that is for many persons at the present time *the equivalent of what has always been thought a religious impulse.*[19]

The significance of the decision was that it altered the central reference point in the legal understanding of religion. Where the reference point had previously been the nature of belief (in a divine being), it was now the psychological function of belief. Within four years the Supreme Court affirmed this position when it held that courts could not consider the truth of particular creeds or tenets, only the sincerity with which individuals adhered to their creed.[20]

The shift toward a functional definition of religion was affirmed yet again in the early 1960s. In 1961, for example, the Supreme Court struck down an old Maryland statute requiring all public employees to declare their belief in God. The case was *Torcaso v. Watkins* and it involved a postal worker who was unwilling to make the declaration because it violated his freedom of belief. The Court agreed, stating that Maryland law had also violated the no-establishment clause of the First Amendment because it put "the power and authority of the State of Maryland . . . on the side of one particular sort of believers—those who are willing to say they believe 'in the existence of God.' "[21] It further maintained that "neither the State nor the Federal Government can constitutionally aid all religions as against non-believers, and neither can aid those religions based on a belief in the existence of God as against those religions founded on different beliefs."[22] Of "those religions founded on different beliefs" it explicitly mentioned the Eastern religious faiths of Buddhism and Taoism, but also the functional equivalents, ethical culture and secular humanism.

In another case involving conscientious objectors in 1965, the Supreme Court again affirmed the functional approach. Until this time the Selective Service Act of 1948 only granted exemptions to objectors whose religion was directly related to their belief in a Supreme Being. The Court concluded that the words "belief in a Supreme Being" could be construed as a "belief that is sincere and meaningful [and] occupies a place in the life of its possessor parallel to that filled by the orthodox belief in God of one who clearly qualifies for the exemption."[23] In formulating this opinion, the Court referred to the work of Paul Tillich who defined the essence of religion not as a belief in God so much as an "ultimate concern," what individuals consider to be the depth of their lives, what they take seriously without reservation. In this light the Justices concluded that religion could be defined as all sincere beliefs "based upon a power or being, or upon a faith, to which all else is subordinate or upon which all else is ultimately dependent."[24]

With this series of decisions the constitutional definition of religion had expanded in a way that largely paralleled an increasingly inclusive pluralism in America. Its chief effect was to formally embrace nontheistic and, in particular, secularistic ideologies within the shelter of protection provided by the First Amendment religion clauses. On the surface the justification was both obvious and unassuming. The framers of the Bill of Rights just had not anticipated an America in which religious faith (and nonfaith) was so diversified, and where that diversity was so prominent. Therefore the courts were simply making constitutional adjustments that would serve the interests of a broader justice. As true as this may have been, the net effect carried several, then unforeseen, complications.

To this point, the functional definition of religion had been applied only to the free exercise clause. It had not been applied to the clause prohibiting the establishment of religion or religious faith. But the language of the First Amendment makes it clear that rights also carry restrictions. In order to be consistent the courts would eventually have to apply a functional definition to the establishment clause as well. But this would mean that secularistic faiths and ideologies would also be prohibited from receiving support from the state. In anticipation of this, some constitutional scholars have openly rejected the possibility, arguing for a "double standard"—a functional definition for free exercise purposes (in order to protect "the multiplying forms of recognizably legitimate religious exercise") and a substantive definition for establishment purposes.[25] Without a double standard, as Lawrence Tribe reasoned, every humane government program could then be "deemed constitutionally suspect."[26] Other constitutional scholars have dissented from this, arguing that public justice can really be served only if the rights and restrictions imposed on theistic faiths are also imposed upon "nontheistic faiths."[27] Besides, this recognition has been the practice in many European countries for decades.

A Question of Interests

How religion is defined by the legal establishment is not merely a matter of academic curiosity but an issue linked directly and practically to the interests of opposing sides of the contemporary cultural conflict. It was clearly in the interests of progressives (and secular progressives in particular) for the courts to recognize a broader functional definition of religion in the early 1960s, for it guaranteed rights that had not previously or (at least formally) been recognized. These court decisions represented a significant achievement for secularist organizations and intellectuals who had been working for nearly three decades to have humanism recognized as a religion or at least as a functional equivalent of a religion.[28] At the same time a functional definition was counter to the interests of the religiously orthodox (and the Evangelicals in particular), for the broader definition challenged Protestantism's de facto favored status in American law, education, and cultural mythology.

At this point the application of the "functional test" to the free exercise clause is an accomplished reality. Its application to establishment cases, however, has not yet been determined. But here again different interests would be served by the different possible outcomes. In fact the interests in the establishment cases are precisely the opposite of what they are in the free exercise cases. If the courts were to employ a functional definition of religion for establishment purposes it would serve the interests of the orthodox, because it would ensure that secular values and ideals would never be favored by the state over transcendent values and ideals. If, however, the courts employ a substantive definition of religion (and thus maintain a double standard), progressivist interests could be served for it would mean that secular ideologies and ideologies similarly aligned would be supported by the state and not be legally challenged. Just as the interests of the Protestant establishment had been implicitly linked with the power of the state through the nineteenth and early twentieth centuries, so too the interests of a secular establishment would also be linked.

The scenario is not merely hypothetical. A widely publicized test of this came in the 1986 "Alabama Textbook Case" (*Smith v. Board of School Commissioners*), a case that pitted a coalition of Evangelical Protestants, conservative Catholics, and other "theists" against the Mobile Board of Education, which was backed by, among others, the American Civil Liberties Union and the People for the American Way.[29] The plaintiffs attempted to document the "distortion and exclusion of religious data" from the history textbooks, "the bias against religion in the social studies texts," and the bias toward a secular humanism in the home economics texts.[30] They also attempted to show that secular humanism, both as a formal sectarian movement and as a more diffuse if not latent moral ideology, was the "functional equivalent of a religion." In short they argued that many of the textbooks used in the country's public schools were actually promoting the "religion of secular humanism" and were therefore in violation of the no-establishment provision of the First Amendment. As would be expected, the defendants rejected all of these claims.[31] This one case by itself, then, illustrates clearly the polarization of orthodox and progressivist interests and ideals over how religion should be defined for establishment purposes.[32]

Church and State

Of the emerging nation-states in the late eighteenth century and nineteenth century, the United States and the Netherlands were unique in their formulation of church-state relations. The other emerging nations established a formal bond between "throne and altar" whereby the state would provide financial and administrative support for the church (one particular church) and the church would in turn legitimate the activities of the state as well as provide certain services on its behalf, such as education, welfare, public health, and the like. In America and the Netherlands, however, no such constitutional provisions were made. Religion was formally disestablished. This, of course, did not mean that the state played no favorites. As is well known, the Reformed Church retained many privileges in Holland through the nineteenth century, as did a common Protestantism in America. Nevertheless, in the administrative structure of the state a formal division between church and state was instituted. In the language provided by Thomas Jefferson's letter to the Danbury (Connecticut) Baptist Association in 1801, the religion clause "build[s] a wall of separation between Church and State."[33]

The contemporary quarrel over church and state is not really about whether a wall of separation of church and state should exist or not. It is true that among the orthodox Evangelicals a cluster of "reconstructionists" reject it in favor of a more theocratic model of governance derived from Old Testament law. Yet their numbers are very small. The real question is what does "separation" mean? Should the "wall of separation" be unapproachable and totally unbreachable or should the wall be low and pervious? Would the interests of the state best be served by a policy of absolute mutual isolation or by one of occasional and strategic cooperation?

In judicial practice two traditions of interpretation have evolved to reflect these alternatives. The position of strict separationism maintains the former, that the wall of separation must be high and impervious, because the rights of religious minorities are always threatened when the power of faith is linked with the power of the state. In principle, therefore, the state should neither receive aid from nor provide aid to any religion, be it material, monetary, or symbolic. As Justice Hugo Black wrote in 1947 in the famous case *Everson v. Board of Education,* the government cannot "pass laws which aid one religion, aid all religion, or prefer one religion over another."[34] The opponents of this position maintain that the strict separation of church and state is a sociological impossibility. Institutions as large and encompassing as these will inevitably intersect. What, then, should govern how church and state relate to one another? The accommodationist response maintains that the state should never favor one faith over another, yet it should be free to accommodate and even assist all faiths equally. By so doing the state generates goodwill among the many communities of faith. These communities, in turn, are not only disposed to fostering a climate of civic virtue but are free to assist the government in meeting the welfare and educational needs of the people, particularly for those people who fall through the "safety net" of the existing apparatus.

Once More, a Question of Interests

All of this is relevant for a single reason: these two traditions of legal interpretation are no longer the subject of a specialized and even arcane legal discourse, but have become the currency of a larger public debate. More specifically, the categories of "accommodationism" and "strict separationism" have become the parameters of a dispute over judicial procedures within which contending sides in the contemporary culture war press their advantage. There are important exceptions to the rule but even so, because the programmatic interests of each are at stake, it is not difficult to predict which interpretive position each alliance tends to favor and why.[35] Progressivist interests (particularly within the secularist and Jewish communities) tend to favor the policy of strict separation. In the Jewish case it is because separationism tends to undermine the culturally dominant position of Christianity vis-à-vis the state. In the secularist case it is because such policies reinforce the privatization of religious faith. The interests of religious orthodoxy and cultural conservatism more generally, by contrast, tend to be aligned with accommodation. While church and state remain separate and unequal, such policies nevertheless position these two institutions more as partners rather than as antagonists. Accommodationist policies not only allow but even encourage both the presence and participation of various religious voices in defining public policy and national identity.

The play of interests and "legal ideology" are most clearly seen among the activists themselves. Although perhaps less clearly, these tendencies are also seen within the communities they represent. Consider, for example, the results of the 1987–88 Williamsburg Charter Survey on Religion and American Public Life.[36] Members of the general population and several elite groups (including ministers, priests, rabbis, media elites, and secular academics) were asked a series of questions about the relationship between church and state in this survey. The results largely substantiate this intuition. On questions of general principle, fairly sharp contrasts emerged. Respondents were posed with the choice, for example, of whether they believed that "the government should not provide any support to any religions" or that "the government should support all religions equally." Nearly nine out of ten of the academics (87 percent), mainline ministers (85 percent), and liberal rabbis (92 percent) chose the strict separationist position compared to less than half of the theologically conservative ministers (48 percent) and conservative priests (28 percent). Even the more Orthodox rabbis were less uniform on this point than their more liberal counterparts; 73 percent adopted the strict separationist position. Respondents were also posed with the choice of whether "the government should take special steps to protect the Judeo-Christian heritage" or whether "there should be a high wall of separation between church and state." Within the general population, the plurality of Evangelicals (49 percent) opted for their accommodationist position compared to only 28 percent of the mainline counterparts and 18 percent of the secularists. Among the leadership groups, 53 percent of the Evangelical ministers favored the accommodationist position compared to only 13 percent of the liberal Protestant ministers, 5 percent of the secular academics, and 13 percent of the media elites. Once more the overwhelming majority of rabbis rejected the accommodationist stance, but the more Orthodox Jewish leaders were slightly less likely.[37] At a practical level this issue engendered a similar response. Over half of the Evangelical laity (52 percent) and clergy (56 percent) and the Catholic clergy (61 percent) agreed that the "government should require that Judeo-Christian values be emphasized in public schools." Yet only minorities among secularists (18 percent), the mainline Protestant laity (28 percent) and clergy (30 percent), the liberal Catholic clergy (39 percent), academics (9 percent), and media elites (14 percent) held this position.

These patterns can also be seen in the attitudes of various sectors of the population as they bear on the concrete issues of contemporary legal dispute. At the extremes, for example, nearly nine of ten (88 percent) Evangelicals agree that "it is good for Congress to start sessions with a public prayer." Less than four in ten (37 percent) of all secularists hold this position. The comparison is less severe within religious communities, yet the gaps are still substantial. Just over two-thirds (67 percent) of the orthodox Catholics held this position compared to under half (49 percent) of their more progressive counterparts. Likewise, the gap between Evangelical and mainline Protestant was 20 percentage points. Among elites the pattern is also strong. Nearly all of the Evangelical ministers (93 percent) agreed that it is good for Congress to start sessions with a public prayer, yet less than one of every five (19 percent) of the academics agreed with this statement.[38] The identical pattern is seen in attitudes about the virtue of beginning sporting events at public high schools with a prayer.[39]

Another example appears in the government support for the public display of religious symbols. Ninety-one percent of the Evangelicals and 85 percent of the conservative Catholics (and as many of their leaders) thought it was "OK for a City Government to put up a manger scene on government property at Christmas." Sixty-eight percent of the secularists, 58 percent of the media elites, and 37 percent of the academics held this view. This was not merely a display of Christian ethnocentrism on the part of the orthodox Protestants and Catholics but a genuine commitment to the principle of accommodationism, for they displayed very nearly the same enthusiasm for the public display of Menorah candles during a Jewish holiday.[40]

Much the same could be said about a daily "moment of silence" in public schools. Among all of those asked, the greatest cleavage can be seen between an Evangelical laity and academic elites. Nearly nine out of ten (89 percent) of the former compared to only two of ten (23 percent) of the latter agreed that "public schools should set aside a moment of silence each day for students to pray if they want to." Within the general population alone there was a certain polarizing tendency, yet it was not nearly as great as this.[41] This could also be said for the religious elites. The Evangelical ministers were 25 percent more likely to take the accommodationist position than the mainline ministers; conservative Catholic priests were 11 percent more likely than their liberal counterparts; and while rabbis were overwhelmingly separationist in their views on this subject, the more Orthodox were three times more likely than their progressivist colleagues to favor the accommodationist position.[42]

Though not nearly so sharp, an ideological contrast also exists over the issue of "equal access." The majority of the general population (up to 70 percent) and elites agree that "public schools should allow student religious groups to hold voluntary meetings in school classrooms, when classes are not in session," but do so with varying intensity.[43] The same is true about the issue of government aid to religious schools. The majority of academics (74 percent), media elites (67 percent), mainline Protestant ministers (80 percent), liberal rabbis (96 percent), and secularists (in the general population—59 percent) reject the proposition and by so doing take the strict separationist position. This contrasts with under half of the Evangelicals (46 percent) and Evangelical ministers (48 percent), Orthodox rabbis (50 percent), and Catholic priests (16 percent) who take the separationist stance.[44] In selective populations the polarization even extended to the issue of religious taxation. Nearly all of the religious elites (among Protestant and Catholic elites just under nine of ten) were united in their opposition to the statement "Churches should have to pay taxes on all their property." Nevertheless, 61 percent of the secularists in the general population favored this taxation as did over four in ten (42 percent) of the academic leaders, and nearly four in ten (36 percent) of the media elites.

It is important to note that the ideological tensions over the relationship between church and state do not necessarily represent disagreement over what the role of religion in public life should be. Indeed there is remarkable agreement by all leadership groups that religions have a right to play a role. Even though many progressivists (particularly in academia and the media) "would personally like to see organized religious groups stay out of politics,"[45] roughly three-fourths of all the leadership groups agreed that "religious groups *should* have a legal right to get involved in politics."[46] They showed consistency in this opinion by recognizing the legitimacy of religiously based activism in concrete political issues, even when the issues were ones they opposed. With very few exceptions a decisive majority of all leadership groups agreed that "it is proper for religious leaders to publicly support political candidates who are running for office," that "it is proper for religious leaders to try to close pornographic bookstores," that it is "OK for the Right to Life movement to use religion in the debate on abortion," that it is "OK for Jewish groups to give money to politicians who support Israel," and that "it is proper for religious leaders to try to influence U.S. policy toward South Africa." The majority of progressivists even endorsed the right of the Moral Majority to engage in political activity.[47] Moreover, these leadership groups also generally agreed that the state should not impede religious groups from becoming involved in this way. For example, when presented with the statement, "Followers of the Reverend Sun Myung Moon should not be allowed to print a daily newspaper in Washington, D.C.," a strong majority of all leaderships disagreed.[48] Even when presented with the statement, "It should be against the law for preachers to use television shows to raise money," these elites also, though a bit more reluctantly, disagreed.[49]

The problem then is not about whether religion could have a voice in public life but about whether there should be any institutional cooperation between organized religion and the state.

The Judicial Muddle over Church and State

In an environment defined by the push and pull of conflicting interests, it is little wonder that judicial practice on church and state relations should be confused.[50] Some decisions have clearly favored the strict separationist interpretation. The first of these was *Everson v. Board of Education* in 1947, a case involving a challenge to a New Jersey statute that provided for the use of tax money to reimburse parents for the cost of transporting their children to parochial schools. The statute was upheld on a technical observation, but the language used by the Court in its decision explicitly invoked the language of strict separationism.[51] "Neither [a state nor the federal government] can pass laws which aid one religion, aid all religion or prefer one religion over another."[52] Not only did this language provide the turning point for the advancement of separationist legislation after the Second World War, but it became the principal channel marker from which virtually all subsequent church and state case law would have to set its bearing and course.

Within a year this language was tested in *McCollum v. Board of Education,* when the Court decided that a program allowing teachers from religious organizations to offer thirty minutes a week of religious instruction in the public schools during normal school hours (on a voluntary basis) was unconstitutional. The Court reaffirmed the language of *Everson,* claiming that the establishment clause erected a wall of separation between church and state "which must be kept high and impregnable."[53]

The agenda of strict separationism was extended through the 1960s in two important cases. One case, *Engel v. Vitale* (1962), concerned the use of government-written prayer in the public schools. The prayer in question had been drafted by the (New York) State Board of Regents and read as follows: "Almighty God, we acknowledge our dependence on thee, we beg Thy blessings upon us, our parents, our teachers and our Country." The Court found its recitation in the public schools unconstitutional, despite the fact that students were not forced to recite those prayers over their parent's objection. Just one year later in *Abington Township School District v. Schempp,* the Supreme Court decided that to read the Bible in the public schools as a devotional exercise was also unconstitutional, for it also represented the government's advancement of the cause of religion in the context of the public schools.[54]

Decisions of a similar interpretive bend were made in the years following. In 1968 the Supreme Court struck down a forty-year-old Arkansas statute that prohibited the teaching of theories of evolution in the public schools and universities.[55] In 1971 the Court declared two programs of public aid to private religious schools unconstitutional.[56] In 1973 it invalidated a New York program providing tuition reimbursement to low-income families and tax deductions for middle-income families with children in nonpublic schools; at the same time it declared unconstitutional a program that provided state payments to private schools to cover the expense of preparing and administering state-mandated examinations; in 1980 the Court struck down a Kentucky law that allowed for the posting of the Ten Commandments in public schools.[57] Two years later, the Court upheld the law requiring all, even those who might have religious objections (in this case, the Amish), to pay social security taxes.[58] In 1985 it rejected an Alabama statute setting aside a daily period of silence for meditation or voluntary prayer in the public schools. In 1986 it rejected the claim of an Orthodox Jewish Air Force officer that he be allowed to wear a skullcap while in uniform. And in 1987 (in *Edwards v. Aguillard*) the Supreme Court struck down a Louisiana statute requiring the balanced treatment of creation science and evolution in the public schools.[59]

Almost as frequently the Court has favored the accommodationist position in its decisions. In 1952 (*Zorach v. Clauson*) it upheld the constitutionality of "released time" religious education in New York City, where upon the written request of their parents, students were permitted to leave school premises during school hours to receive religious instruction. In 1961 it endorsed the constitutionality of Sunday closing laws.[60] In 1968 it upheld another New York statute requiring local public schools to lend secular-subject textbooks to parochial school students.[61] In the 1970 decision *Walz v. Tax Commission,* the Supreme Court upheld the constitutionality of state tax exemptions for religious property. Two years later, in *Wisconsin v. Yoder,* the Court upheld the rights of Old Order Amish to exempt their children from the requirement to attend school until they are sixteen years of age. In 1977 the Justices reaffirmed the legality of loaning textbooks to parochial school students.[62] A year later it rejected the constitutionality of a legislative ban against the clergy serving in public office.[63] In 1981 it invalidated state prohibitions against student religious groups' access to campus meeting facilities (at the university level) that were also available to other student groups.[64] In 1983 the Justices upheld the practice of the Nebraska legislature of opening each business day with a prayer delivered by a paid and permanent chaplain.[65] In 1984 it upheld the rights of a city government (Pawtucket) to erect a city-sponsored Christmas display. In 1988 the Supreme Court upheld the constitutionality of the Adolescent Family Life Act (in *Bowen v. Kendrick*), an act that permitted federal funds to flow to religious as well as nonreligious organizations promoting chastity among teenagers. Over the course of the years the courts have also reaffirmed the constitutionality of the motto "In God We Trust" on coinage as well as government-paid chaplains in the military.[66]

While by no means a comprehensive compendium of the Supreme Court cases on church and state, this review does illustrate the inconsistency that pervades Court decisions. Is there in fact a substantive distinction between "the permissible loan of textbooks to parochial school students and the impermissible loan of maps and other instructional aids"?[67] Is there a substantive difference between "public school employees providing services on parochial school premises and those same employees serving the same parochial school students in premises adjacent to the parochial school"? If in a lay persons' perception judicial practice on church and state seems vague if not chaotic, they are not alone in this view. Virtually all observers of American jurisprudence agree that since the middle of the century the decisions of the Supreme Court on this subject have been "erratic and unprincipled," "inexcusably inconsistent."[68] Justice Powell himself admitted in 1977 that "our decisions in this troubling area [of church and state] draw lines that often must seem arbitrary."[69] The evidence of case law bears out this assertion.

Yet it would be misleading to leave the impression that through the judicial inconsistencies, there has been a rough balance of decisions in favor of each interpretive tradition. Since *Everson* there has been a fairly clear judicial bias toward strict separationism. For separationists this trend represents an overdue corrective to a historical bias that placed Christian faith and practice in a favored position vis-à-vis the state. The logic of this corrective, in the view of its proponents, simply needs to be extended. For the critics on the side of accommodationism, the tilt toward separationism represents an "inversion" of the true meaning of the religion clauses. Accepted judicial wisdom, they say, has elevated "separation" to be the basis of all religion clause analysis, whereas its true end is the preservation of freedom and the expansion of tolerance. As a number of legal scholars and observers have argued, the establishment clause should be interpreted in a way that defers to the values underlying the free exercise clause.[70] As Richard Neuhaus put it, "No establishment should serve free exercise."[71]

LAW AND DOMINATION

Though the definition of religion and the debate over church and state are the principal battlegrounds over which the procedural dimension of the culture war is fought, the First Amendment issue of free speech dealt with in the last chapter also bears on these topics directly. Do street preachers have the right to proselytize? Do picketers have the right to picket stores that sell pornographic literature or hospitals and clinics that perform abortions? Do spectators at sporting events have the right to display religious signs? Do students have the right to hand out religious newspapers on school grounds or deliver a valedictory address that has religious references in it? All of these questions and others like them have been posed legally and have been addressed by the courts. Here again, the decisions have a lasting impact upon the outcome of the larger culture war.

In all of this we should not lose sight of the social factor. In this polarizing setting, nearly every case concerning church and state or religion and free speech becomes more than a legal or academic dispute—it becomes a regional if not national contest to sway popular sentiment. For the newspaper-reading and television-watching public, each case becomes high drama, perhaps no less than in Dayton, Tennessee, in the mid-1920s during the Scopes trial. In virtually every major church and state case taken up in the 1980s and after, particularly those involving the American Civil Liberties Union or People for the American Way, public relations offices or communications advisers have been engaged to organize and direct media offensives. Those on the orthodox side of the cultural divide have been far less successful at playing the mass media, but there are signs that in future cases they will be responding in kind.[72]

It is also unsurprising to see many of these cases adopted as particular causes of particular activist organizations who favor one side or another. Organizations such as the ACLU, the Christian Legal Society, People for the American Way, Rutherford Institute, the Catholic League for Religious and Civil Rights, and Concerned Women for America are regularly involved in moral litigation of this sort. The ACLU supported the plaintiffs in opposing Bible reading in the public schools (*Engel v. Vitale*). The Greek Orthodox Church threatened to withdraw from the National Council of Churches because the council opposed both Bible reading and prayer in public schools. The ACLU and the National Council of Churches were plaintiffs in the original "Pawtucket crèche" lawsuit (*Lynch v. Donnelly*). Concerned Women for America provided assistance to the plaintiffs and the People for the American Way provided assistance to the defense in the Tennessee schoolbook case (*Mozert v. Hawkins County School Board*), just as Pat Robertson's Freedom Council Foundation assisted the plaintiffs while the ACLU and People for the American Way (and, originally, the American Humanist Association) assisted the defense in the Alabama "secular humanism" case. The ACLU was an original plaintiff in the Louisiana "creationism" suit (*Edwards v. Aguillard*). Americans United for Life and the ACLU were the hidden forces behind *Bowen v. Kendrick.* And, in the *Webster v. Reproductive Health Services* decision alone, sixty-seven religious organizations submitted *amicus curiae* briefs. Not only do these organizations provide financial backing to the principals involved, and legal advice in the form of *amicus curiae* briefs, then, but they also generate tremendous national publicity through direct mail, advertisements, and editorial commentary. Their involvement, then, influences both the nature of the legal debate and the substance of the outcome. More fundamentally, their involvement inflates the political significance of each decision and thereby further simplifies and polarizes a complex substantive (and, oftentimes, technical) legal debate.

The significance of the debate bears repeating: what is ultimately at stake is the ability to define the rules by which moral conflict of this kind is to be resolved. Once again, those who define how a contest is to be played out will have the advantage of shaping its final outcome. Influencing the structure of the rules represents a critical part of the overall effort to reestablish an old or to formulate a new cultural hegemony. The depth of the current cultural conflict in conjunction with the tremendous ambiguity that characterizes church and state law can only mean that there will be more and more litigation—for such litigation will force the courts to clarify its position.[73] In all likelihood, that act of "clarification" will result in the advancement of the interests of one side of the new cultural divide and the diminishment of the interests of the other.

11

Electoral Politics

Most Americans view the work of government as the task of administrating the affairs of state. Political campaigns, then, are simply the mechanism for choosing the lawmakers to perform that formidable role. Fair enough—politicians (not to mention political scientists!) view government and elections that way, too. Nevertheless, as I argued in the Opening Observations of part IV of this book, electoral politics also carries a cultural meaning not usually discerned.[1] The argument bears repeating: the true significance of electoral politics lies not in the selection of lawmakers and administrators, but in the opportunity given to the citizens of a community and nation to embrace or reject certain symbols of national life. In the heat of an election candidates will certainly tout their own competence, experience, knowledge and grasp of issues, and conviction as against the incompetence, inexperience, stupidity, and moral diffidence of their opponent. Yet in the final analysis, candidates are selected by their parties and run principally on the basis of the symbols of collective life with which they identify in campaign rhetoric and in their official biographies. In due course, the candidate himself or herself actually becomes a symbol of community ideals. Even their individual names and faces become a kind of shorthand for articulating certain ideals of our life together—inspiring admiration and devotion in some; provoking disgust or hostility in others. In this light, elections can be seen as rituals regularly enacted through which ordinary people select the ideals of their life together—ultimately, the ideals of what

America is and should be. For this reason, the tug of war over the dominant symbols of our public culture has a somewhat subtle and indirect influence in determining the outcome of elections. The contemporary culture war defines the *moral context* within which any candidate for public office must contend in the run for public office. It provides the dominant symbols and establishes many of the parameters of campaign debate. At the same time, however, the election itself is often a dramatic enactment of the culture war itself or of a skirmish within the culture war.

A word or two of qualification: to offer this perspective on the meaning of electoral politics is not to say that every election is shaped by the tensions of the culture war equally. Because of the peculiarities of local history, a sudden shift of public attention (because of, say, an act of international terrorism or an impending economic crisis), or even idiosyncrasies of the candidates themselves (perhaps they really are incompetent, inexperienced, or stupid), the tensions of the contemporary culture war may have little play in an election. Moreover, even with those considerations aside, the play of the contemporary culture war tends not to hold equally at all levels of political office. The race for county supervisor of Albemarle County, Virginia, or for mayor of Sioux City, Iowa, or for any other local or regional office may be completely immune to these forces. Indeed, the tendency is that the higher the public office (that is, the greater the power of the position where decisions made affect the national interest), the more vulnerable those campaigns will be to the competing visions of the culture war. The grounds for this claim are quite evident in the financial allocations of political action committees or PACs and some special purpose organizations as well as the pronouncements and often endorsements of the activists themselves. The campaign contributions and influence peddling of the major actors in the culture war—on both sides of the cultural divide—go almost exclusively to the highest levels of political office, while local and regional elections are virtually ignored.

Although ideology is perhaps most consequential at such high levels of office as the Congress and the presidency, it is interesting to note that campaigns for these offices have not historically drawn candidates from the ranks of a movement "vanguard" or leadership. Perhaps this is because the activist's depth of commitment and singleness of mind typically do not make for qualities befitting political compromise. The candidacies of Jesse Jackson and Pat Robertson in the 1988 presidential elections, then, may be notable exceptions to the rule. Arguably, they may also signal that, depending on the fate of the culture war, such candidacies may become less exceptional. It will be recalled that Yehuda Levin ran for Congress and then for mayor, not with any illusion that he had a chance of winning, but to make a symbolic statement about the concerns of Orthodox Judaism. Yet even for those candidates who are not actively committed to certain cultural interests themselves, it is clear that they must play to those interests to varying degrees in their campaigns both in the hope of gaining a constituency and of discrediting their opponents.

PLAYING OFF THE INTERESTS

Examples of how candidates have played off the competing interests of the contemporary culture war could be found throughout many levels of government and in probably every election year since the 1960s. The manipulation of those interests, however, was especially apparent in the presidential campaigns of the 1980s. What follows is not comprehensive, by any means, but merely illustrative of these dynamics.

Carter and Reagan

In the 1980 contest between incumbent Jimmy Carter and former California governor Ronald Reagan, for example, these interests of the culture war had a decisive and, at least in the case of the family issue, an unanticipated effect. As seen earlier, it was the Carter administration more than any other previous administration that transformed the family from a private institution into a public policy issue: Carter's future vice-president, Senator Walter Mondale, initiated the influential 1973 Subcommittee on Children and Youth hearings on "American Families: Trends and Pressures," and Carter himself, during the New Hampshire primary, pledged to hold a White House conference on the family. But by the time of the conference and, in part because of it, Carter lost control of the issue. His own moderately progressive views were drowned out in the clamor of the extremes and the debate over the family acquired a life of its own.

Perhaps because it was no longer exclusively their issue, the family received little attention in the Democratic platform in the 1980 campaign. Only one section was devoted to family concerns and that consisted of only one sentence: "The Democratic Party supports efforts to make federal programs more sensitive to the needs of the family, *in all its diverse forms*" (emphasis added). Consistent with the progressive tone of the platform, Carter himself, though an Evangelical Christian and personally opposed to abortion, played increasingly to the interests of the progressivist vision of the family. Of the ERA he declared that it was "the last remaining need in our nation to realize the hopes and ambitions of our original founders, that people would have equal opportunity."[2]

It was Reagan and the Republican party, of course, that gained the advantage from Carter's fumbling of the family issue, largely because they could draw on the grass-roots activism of the newly mobilized (and largely Evangelical and conservative Catholic) pro-family coalition. In contrast to the Democratic platform, three sections of the Republican platform focused exclusively on the family. Both in general and in detail, these paragraphs pledged unequivocal "support for legislation protecting and defending the traditional American family against the ongoing erosion of its base in our society." Reagan's message from the stump was consistent with this theme. He pledged to seek federal judges "who respect traditional family values and the sanctity of innocent life," and declared himself to be for equal rights for women although against the ERA ("I cannot believe that there are some who think that I would in anyway restrict the freedom and rights of women").[3] He also spoke against abortion ("I notice that everybody who's for abortion has already been born").[4]

The family, of course, was by no means the only or even the most important issue of the 1980 campaign. It was simply one of a collage of symbols with which the candidates had to contend. Cynically or sincerely, each candidate articulated his broader vision for America in the language provided by opposing sides of the culture war. Thus, Reagan aligned his own candidacy with the vision and aspirations of the culturally conservative side of the cultural divide by proclaiming that "America is a land of destiny created by some divine plan"; by recognizing that there is "a great hunger in America for a spiritual revival"; by sharing its belief "that law must be based on a higher law"; by identifying with its quest to "return to traditions and values we once had."[5] At the same time, he sought orthodox support by encouraging the participation of this typically apolitical sector of the U.S. population in political discourse. As he said a month and a half before election day, "I have thought for a long time that too many of our churches have been too reluctant to speak up on behalf of what they believe is proper in government and they have been too lax in interfering in recent years with government's invasion of the family itself."[6] He was speaking, of course, to churches of orthodox commitment.

In Jimmy Carter's view, Reagan offered nothing less than a "fantasy America" built upon policies that were "outrageous and irresponsible." The Republican future, Carter argued in his acceptance speech at the Democratic National Convention, was a future of "despair," "surrender," and "risk," and that stood in sharp contrast to the Democratic future of "security, justice and peace." He aligned his own candidacy with the vision and aspirations of liberals by voicing compassion "for the troubled Americans—the poor, the jobless and afflicted," and by declaring that he was "proud to run on a progressive and sound platform." This was reaffirmed by his vice-presidential nominee Walter Mondale, who described the Republican convention as "isolated in a bubble of privilege" with only "token" representatives of women, workers, and minorities, compared to the Democratic convention which was "a mirror of all America—all of it: black and white, Asian and Hispanic, native and immigrant, male and female, young and old, urban and rural, rich and poor."[7]

Reagan and Mondale

Symbols that were prominent in the 1980 election resurfaced in the 1984 Reagan–Mondale contest. After four years, Reagan continued to press the same vision and invoke the same symbols that had first put him in the White House. "We're going forward," he proclaimed just over a month before the election, "with values that have never failed us when we lived up to them: dignity of work, love for family and neighborhood, faith in God, belief in peace through strength, and a commitment to protect the freedom which is our legacy as Americans." In line with this theme, Vice-President Bush identified the Republican platform with the "preservation of values" including "freedom, family, work and faith."[8]

By Mondale's lights, Reagan's political philosophy was not classical conservatism but a conservatism that cynically courted the Religious Right. "Both [party] platforms were prepared by Jerrys," he claimed, "ours under the leadership of Geraldine Ferraro and theirs by Jerry Falwell. There's a big difference."[9] Mondale's resentment of the novel political role of Evangelicals and other conservative religious groups and for Reagan, who continued to encourage this activism, was not well disguised. It surfaced again and again throughout the campaign. "What makes America great," he stated in a speech in Tupelo, Mississippi, "is that our faith is between ourselves, our conscience and our God, and we don't have to clear our faith by passing muster with some politician who happens to be running against us." "Politicians," he continued, "should keep their nose out of religion."[10]

Nevertheless, the ties between Reagan and the religious conservatives remained strong. For his part, he maintained his public commitment to, among other things, voluntary prayer in schools, equal access, tuition tax credits and vouchers, and traditional family values, which included strong opposition to abortion.

Mondale and the Democratic party continued to press their agenda through the emblems of progressive cultural commitments: economic justice ("jobs and employment are the center of Democratic thinking"), women's rights ("a top priority of a Democratic Administration will be ratification of the unamended equal rights amendment"), abortion rights ("reproductive freedom [is] a fundamental human right"), and so on. It was on this latter issue that the tensions of the cultural conflict flared up again. In this situation, it was between Archbishop John J. O'Connor (who stated that he did not believe a Catholic "in good conscience" could vote for a political candidate who approved of abortion or favored leaving the decision to women, and who chastened the Democratic vice-presidential candidate for "misrepresenting Roman Catholic teachings on abortion") and New York's governor Mario Cuomo, Senator Edward Kennedy, and vice-presidential candidate Geraldine Ferraro (who chided the archbishop for not respecting the separation of church and state).[11]

One might be tempted to attribute the remarkable success of the Reagan campaigns in 1980 and 1984 to the exceptional persona of Ronald Reagan himself and his ability to communicate. Liberal political commentators throughout the decade did precisely this. How else, they reasoned, could one explain the popular success of a man who was so obviously feeble-minded and philistine if not for some earthy charisma that appealed to the plebs. That being the case, the "Reagan magic" was purely idiosyncratic—not likely to be repeated again. Such a logic may be appealing but it rather misses the point. Democrats consistently maintained that Reagan's policies were antithetical to his rhetorical affirmation of "God, family, work, neighborhood, peace, and freedom." One will recall on this point that Geraldine Ferraro went so far as to question the sincerity of Reagan's Christian faith because his economic policies were, in her view, "so unfair." Protest they did, yet they could not deny Reagan's ability to establish a link between the ideals he espoused and himself. Even Mondale conceded at the end the 1984 campaign that "when the true story of this election is written, I suspect it will not be about me or Mr. Reagan—but about you [the American people]," and "the kind of people we are."[12] Or rather, the kind of people we, as Americans, *choose* to be. The competing ideals of the culture war promised to be prominent in campaigns long after 1984 and after Reagan would step down from office.

Bush and Dukakis and Others

In the 1988 presidential campaigns, the culture war was more than just a backdrop for the race. The candidacies of two Baptist ministers through the primary season, each of them a prominent leader on opposing sides of the cultural divide, brought the symbols and issues of the culture war directly to the campaign trail. Both Jesse Jackson and Pat Robertson called for moral and spiritual leadership and both invoked the language of biblical revelation in their speech. At this very general level, their rhetoric was nearly identical. For Robertson, the "American people were crying out for basic moral leadership."[13] Jackson could not have agreed more, for such leadership, he maintained, could "part the waters and lead our nation in the direction of the Promised Land."[14] The content of that moral and spiritual leadership, of course, was vastly and predictably different for the two men. For Robertson, it meant "bringing God back into the public schools," returning to "the faith of our fathers and the traditional standards of family life in America," limiting "gross pornography," stopping the slaughter of unborn children, opposing communism, and defending democracy around the world, and so on. For Jackson, it meant "meeting the needs" of the poor, "the dispossessed of this nation," and creating a coalition of "the damned, the disinherited, the disrespected, and the despised," by seeking "justice, peace and jobs."

Perhaps it was the candidacies of Jackson and Robertson that heightened the visibility of national identity as an implicit campaign issue affecting other candidates as well, especially in the campaign oratory of the two final contenders. As George Bush put it, "When a person goes into that voting booth, they're going to say, who has the values I believe in?"[15] Bush himself was acutely aware of the role of "values" (or more accurately, symbols or symbolic expressions of values) in the election and he invoked them regularly and directly. To Democratic candidate Michael Dukakis's claim that this election was not about ideology but about competence, Bush responded: "Competence makes the train run on time but doesn't know where they're going. Competence is the creed of the technocrat who makes the gears mesh but doesn't for a second understand the magic of the machine. The truth is, this election is about the beliefs we share, the values that we honor and the principles that we hold dear." But Bush went much further than this. In his acceptance speech at the Republican National Convention, for example, he put it this way:

> An election that's about ideas and values is also about philosophy. And I have one. At the bright center is the individual. And radiating out from him or her is the family, the essential unit of closeness and of love. For it's the family that communicates to our children—to the 21st century—our culture, our religious faith, our traditions and history. I am guided by certain traditions. One is that there's a God and He is good, and His love, while free, has a self-imposed cost: we must be good to one another.

Generalities they might have been, but they were generalities that fit with a particular vision of America. And Bush elaborated upon them in a litany of other symbols of the contemporary culture war recited throughout the campaign:

> Should public school teachers be required to lead our children in the pledge of allegiance? My opponent says no, and I say yes. Should society be allowed to impose the death penalty on those who commit crimes of extraordinary cruelty and violence? My opponent says no, but I say yes. And should our children have the right to say a voluntary prayer, of even observing a moment of silence in the schools? My opponent says no, but I say yes. And should free men and women have the right to own a gun to protect their home? My opponent says no, and I say yes. And is it right to believe in the sanctity of life and protect the lives of innocent children? My opponent says no, and I say yes.[16]

A slightly different litany could be heard in the televised debate with his opponent Michael Dukakis. After identifying Dukakis as "a card-carrying member of the ACLU," Bush stated that he did not agree "with a lot of the—most of the positions of the ACLU. . . . I don't want to see my 10 year old grandchild go into an X-rated movie. I like those rating systems. I don't think they're right to try to take the tax exemption away from the Catholic Church. I don't want to see 'under God' come out from our currency. Now these are all positions of the ACLU and I don't agree with them."[17]

For his own part, Dukakis (like Carter and Mondale before him) invoked the symbols of an alternate vision of America, one in which the symbols of economic justice were most prominent. "If any one tells you," Dukakis said, "that the American Dream belongs to the privileged few and not all of us, you tell them the Reagan era is over and that a new era is about to begin." He and the Democratic party "identify with and care for struggling, working families."[18] As Dukakis put it elsewhere, "This election is not about overthrowing governments in Central America; it is about creating jobs in middle America." Prominent in this vision of America were the symbols of personal liberty, the most prominent issue being abortion. On this, Dukakis affirmed the right of "the woman in the exercise of her own conscience and religious beliefs" in making that decision, contrary to Bush who, he claimed, was "prepared to brand a woman a criminal for making the decision to abort."[19]

My point in all of this has not been to provide an exhaustive review of campaign oratory. Nor has it been to suggest that the debates of the culture war are the only or even most consequential of all these elections. This brief journey through the rhetoric of the presidential campaigns of the 1980s illustrates how the contemporary cultural conflict provides the ideological context within which political campaigns must negotiate and make their claims.

Realignment in the Electorate

The contemporary culture war is not just ideological scenery. In fact, it has consequences in the voting behavior of the electorate. At the presidential level, white Evangelicals fled the Democratic party in droves in the 1980s to support the Republican candidate: 61 percent voted for Reagan in 1980; 79 percent supported Reagan in 1984; and 72 percent voted for Bush in 1988. The Catholic vote was as divided as the general Protestant vote through these years: 47 percent went for Reagan in 1980; 61 percent supported Reagan in 1984; and 49 percent voted for Bush in 1988. Here, too, are signs that the more orthodox Catholics voted conservative Republican while the more progressive Catholics voted liberal Democrat.[20]

The abandonment of traditional party loyalties by these groups since the 1980s has generated much interest on the part of professional political scientists. It was thought that Southerners—Southern Evangelicals—could be counted upon to vote with the Democratic party. So too, Northern and Midwestern Catholics were also believed to be Democratic party loyalists. As Archbishop John Whealon said, "I [was] a somewhat typical example of [the] link between U.S. Catholics and Democrats. In my childhood home, God and Jesus Christ were first, the Catholic Church second, and the Democratic Party was third."[21] Yet both Southerners generally and Southern Evangelicals in particular switched to the Republican party en masse. Likewise, Catholic voters could no longer be relied upon as a voting bloc. Political scientists have looked upon this with astonishment, as though a shift in party affiliation and voting behavior *in itself* meant something important. Their assumption is that the electorate changed in a meaningful way. In fact, the substantive change was not with these voters (who at least on cultural issues were always conservative and remain so to this day), but with the parties that presumed to represent them. Archbishop Whealon put it succinctly when he stated, "The nation needed Franklin Roosevelt and the Democrats to bring legal power to the trade unions, security for the elderly, subsidies to the farmers, and special help to the poor. But by its repeated stance in favor of abortion, the Democratic Party has abandoned the Catholic Church and fragmented a Catholic bloc. . . . Therefore, reluctantly, I am unable in conscience to remain a registered Democrat. Feeling abandoned, I hope that the Democratic Party regains its moral principles and its soul." Mae Duggan and other orthodox Catholics would agree wholeheartedly.[22]

THE EMERGENCE OF "RHETORICAL LEADERSHIP"

The objection can be anticipated. No, the identification with and use of potent cultural symbols is nothing new in American electoral politics. Certainly one can recognize this phenomenon in nearly every election in U.S. history, although it is especially pronounced in a few. A few illustrations are instructive.

In the election of 1860, for example, Abraham Lincoln and Stephen Douglas squared off over the issue of slavery. Lincoln invoked the symbols of the abolitionist movement (for whom slavery was nothing less than "a great moral, social and political evil"—a "national sin"). Douglas invoked the symbols of peace, national unity, and the preservation of the status quo. Claimed Douglas, "I care more for the great principle of self-government, the right of the people to rule, than I do for all the

Negroes in Christendom. I would not endanger the perpetuity of this Union, I would not blot out the great inalienable rights of the white man, for all the Negroes that ever existed."[23] To this, Lincoln responded, "Many of our adversaries are anxious to claim that they are specially devoted to the Union, and take pains to charge upon us hostility to the Union. . . . we put to them this one proposition: What ever endangered this Union, save and except Slavery?"[24]

The election of 1896 also witnessed lofty rhetoric. In this election, William Jennings Bryan represented the interests and ideals of Midwestern populism against William McKinley, who championed the interests of the East Coast establishment. The central issue of this election was whether to have a silver or gold standard for currency. Bryan described the crusade for a silver standard at the Democratic National Convention as nothing less than "a cause as holy as the cause of liberty—the cause of humanity." For Bryan it was "the issue of 1776 over again." "We will answer [our opponents'] demand for a gold standard," he passionately declared, "by saying to them: 'You shall not press down upon the brow of labor this crown of thorns. You shall not crucify mankind upon a cross of gold.' " Bryan's chief rhetorical antagonist in this election, Bourke Cockran, responded on behalf of McKinley and industrial labor by saying, "In the name of humanity you shall neither press a crown of thorns upon the brow of labor nor place scourge upon his back." Indeed, "when this Populist assault upon common honesty and common industry shall have been repelled, the foundations of this republic will remain undisturbed . . . resting forever upon the broad basis of American patriotism, American virtue, and American intelligence."[25]

In the 1928 election contest between Republican Herbert Hoover and (Catholic) Democrat Al Smith, the issues were national prosperity, prohibition (the continued viability of the Volstead Act), and Smith's own religious faith. Smith was repeatedly referred to as the "rum-soaked Romanist," and the "candidate of Tammany," and it was widely rumored that he would transform the East Wing of the White House into the pope's summer home. As for Hoover and the GOP, they were "the party of 'pillage and privilege,' " and the ones who had injected "bigotry, hatred, and intolerance" into the campaign.[26]

That candidates for public office would invoke and thus become themselves symbols of the contemporary culture war, then, is not terribly surprising. Nevertheless, there is *something new and exceptional about the relationship between culture and contemporary electoral politics.* Apart from the issues and symbols themselves, what is unique has to do with the context and method of leadership in late twentieth-century America. What is novel is the disposition of a democratic leadership, especially the presidency, to attempt to speak to the voting public directly—to inspire, persuade, and sway them through a popular or mass rhetoric that sets forth idealistic images of the republic and ennobling images of the American people. What is singular, in a word, is a form of national leadership predicated upon popular oratory.[27]

Through the decades of the nineteenth and early twentieth centuries, popular leadership through rhetoric was fairly uncommon.[28] Aside from the inaugural address (which *was* presented orally and intended for a broad audience), the State of the Union message, special presidential recommendations and veto messages (which were originally intended as messages to Congress), very few personally initiated addresses to the larger public (such as Washington's Farewell Address and Lincoln's Gettysburg Address) or policy speeches were ever delivered by presidents.

It was not sloth that kept these leaders from facing the American public. It was, rather, the fear held by the framers of the Constitution and their nineteenth-century successors, that mass oratory would "undermine the rational and enlightened self-interest of the citizenry which their system was designed to foster and on which it was thought to depend for its stablity."[29] A leadership premised upon popular oratory would be a form of governance vulnerable to the shifting winds of public opinion, all of which would undermine the prudential judgment integral to effective statesmanship.[30]

It was not until Woodrow Wilson that it became commonplace for presidential speeches to be directed to the people. On this his dictum was simple and new: "There is but one national voice in the country and that is the voice of the President." (In fact, Wilson was the first president since Jefferson to deliver the State of the Union address before Congress in person!)[31] And now, of course, presidents have come to believe that they are not effective leaders unless they exhort the public directly on a regular basis.[32] And so it is that the executive branch employs a large band of ghostwriters who provide the president with something to say for every possible circumstance and occasion. Importantly, the pressure to say something is not just in the mind of the president. It has become, rather, an institutionalized feature of that office's public function.

The "rhetorical presidency" is institutionalized in part because of the doctrine of presidential leadership inherited from Wilson. Equally influential have been the media of mass communications, which offer the means through which the president can reach a national audience both directly and immediately. In addition, the use of these media has entailed a fundamental change in the very medium by which the president communicates publicly: from the written to the spoken word; from a text that could be studied by a literate and politically engaged reader to a visible, dramatic performance that can be as easily switched off as switched on. Add to this the fact that television and radio journalists "filter" public speech by selecting comparatively small "sound bites." (These sound bites, incidently, are getting smaller and smaller. Between the 1968 and 1988 presidential elections, the average sound bite decreased from 42.3 seconds to only 9.8 seconds. During the same time period, "the time television networks devoted to visuals of the candidates, unaccompanied by their words, increased by 300 percent.")[33] Together these factors create tremendous pressure to capture the attention of a fleeting audience through simplified and inflated political discourse. As James Ceaser put it, under these conditions, "argument gives way to aphorism."[34]

To fail to mention the pivotal role of ideologically oriented interest groups in all of this would be remiss. Here the relationship is dialectic. On the one hand, a "rhetorical presidency" increases the prevalence and power of the ideological interest groups. This occurs for the simple reason that a leadership based upon public opinion will give rise to groups wanting to shape that opinion. It is no accident, then, that ideological PACs have increased dramatically in number, size, and budget since the 1970s.[35] The very context and requirements of national leadership under these new conditions encourages such groups to exert as much influence as possible. And presidents are vulnerable to it. On the other hand, politically oriented special purpose groups further institutionalize a "rhetorical leadership" by placing ever higher demands on the office as a condition of their support. Progressivist groups have made their financial and grass-roots support contingent upon a politician's promise of support for their concerns. Likewise on the orthodox side of the cultural divide, Catholic politicians (to give but an example) have been sent warning shots across their bows, as it were, with the indirect threat that they risk excommunication if they failed to support the Church's moral teachings, particularly on abortion. (John Cardinal O'Connor of New York was the first prominent Catholic to raise this possibility in public debate, and while he said he had no politician in mind, the excommunication of Catholics involved in the abortion business elsewhere in the country gave his words a sharpness that even he might not have intended.) Under these cultural and political conditions, it is no wonder that the number of specific promises made by presidential candidates over the course of an election campaign has been escalating dramatically since the early 1950s.[36]

It is essential to point out, at this stage, that while the pressures generated by competing factions in the culture war are especially great for the national leadership, these pressures appear to be increasingly applied to state and local elections. This is particularly true since the highly publicized *Webster v. Reproductive Health Services* decision made possible state regulation of abortions. Because of this, state and local officials have to answer to antagonists as well. Four months after *Webster,* the issue of abortion and the factions mobilized on both sides proved to be decisive for the Virginia gubernatorial race.[37] In local and regional campaigns across the country, incumbents and challengers have sought to duck for cover while the cannons of special interest lobbies are loaded and aimed. Even at these levels, leadership is fast becoming "rhetorical" in nature.

These institutionalized constraints, then, shadow more and more politicians, though it remains especially the case with the presidency and members of Congress throughout their tenure in office. Yet such forces are particularly pronounced in the election campaign. It has been observed that the modern campaign for national office is organized in such a way that "demagogy or pandering is almost necessary to stay in the running."[38] Without doubt, nowhere is the rhetoric of candidates more inflated than during the campaigns. And this is significant because the campaign has become the metaphor if not the model for practical governing. Certainly it is the campaign that sets the tone for governing rather than the other way around.

If this is all true, then the meaning of national leadership in American democracy has indeed changed. Words not only rival deeds, words become deeds; speeches become events—events that are just as real as an action taken by the state. And in this, speaking becomes a principal mode of governing. The consequences of this for the contemporary culture war are not insignificant. The most extreme consequence is that it leads to the belief that those gifted in public speech will make good government leaders. Wilson himself said that "it is natural that orators should be the leaders of a self-governing people."[39] This is what made it possible and credible for activists and ideologues like Jackson and Robertson—individuals with no experience in government—to run for the presidency, as they did in 1988. It is entirely plausible that other major activists in the contemporary culture war (at least those skilled in public oratory) will follow in their wake.[40] Note, for example, the call at the NOW national convention in Cincinnati in 1989 for a new independent feminist political party. At the very least, the consequences of a leadership predicated upon public oratory are that politicians will always be vulnerable to the power and interests of the opposing sides of the culture war. They will always and perhaps increasingly have to contend with competing symbols, ideals, and visions of the world.

POLITICIANS AND THE CULTURE WAR: WHO IS USING WHOM?

The foregoing discussion invites speculation on the broader question in electoral politics of "who is using whom." The obvious answer is to say that it is the candidates who cynically use the symbols of the culture war and thus one constituency or the other in the service of their own political ambitions. The obvious answer is also undoubtedly true to a large extent. But recognizing this does not mean that all politicians who do employ the symbols of the present cultural conflict are motivated by cynicism. They are just as likely to be sincere—the ends are the same.

A much more intriguing and perhaps plausible reply to this question, however, puts it the other way around: electoral politics play a decisive role in furthering the interests of antagonists in the culture war. In this view, the ambitions of particular politicians are virtually irrelevant. Almost anyone could fill the spot. Why? Because it is the contemporary *cultural contest that provides much of the language*—the slogans, the aphorisms—through which all candidates and parties, whoever they are, must, at least in part, define themselves. It is the contemporary culture war that establishes many of the parameters of campaign debate within which opposing candidates and parties must maneuver.

In reality, there is something of a symbiosis at play here—politicians indeed use symbols of the cultural conflict to realize their political aspirations, but at the same time the mechanisms of electoral politics provide a device through which opposing interests and visions in the culture war are advanced. It is difficult to say, yet it is possible, quite possible, that in the broader flow of American history, the latter will prove to have the greater sway.

Listening to the foolish things many politicians say during an election campaign as they manuever around the thickets and booby traps of the culture war, one almost cannot help but chuckle. But our laughter turns to nervous wonder the instant we remember that these same politicians are dealing with the most urgent issues of the day as representatives of the longest standing and most powerful democracy in the world. The contrast between a sound-bite leadership driven by the competing interests of the culture war and the wise and noble leadership one might hope for given the legacy of our democracy is distressing to say the least. Yet I think it is wrong to conclude that it is the culture war that demeans democratic discourse. The culture war is about who we are as a nation and who we will choose to become. It is then the proper subject of democratic debate, not the source of its cheapening. Politicians may be hostage to the issues, symbols, and interest groups of the culture war but it is they and the electoral organizations behind them who choose to respond the way they do and it is we, a distressingly passive electorate, who accept things as they are. The problem, of course, is that when the legacy is not upheld, when democratic discussion and debate devolves into the morass it has become, there is even less hope that the various battles of the culture war can be resolved. The fissures that divide America can only grow deeper.

Parting Observations

Of the seemingly countless skirmishes and battles within the various fields of conflict just surveyed, each dispute is rooted in events with their own unique characteristics and very often their own set of combatants. Maybe this is part of why we tend not to see the myriad controversies as being linked in any coherent way. Yet if we consider them more closely, we can see that within each conflict, however minor it may seem to be, are appeals to opposing visions of the good life and the good society. These underlying appeals to both fundamental assumptions and high ideals show that these controversies form part of a fabric: they are episodes in a larger culture war.

AMERICA ABROAD: A BRIEF WORD ON WAR

As we have seen, these opposing symbolic appeals create a cleavage that runs like the San Andreas Fault right through much of the territory making up domestic policy in America, including areas and issues not discussed here. It is also reflected in some areas of foreign policy—perhaps most urgently in America's military involvement abroad.

Few developments can change a nation—its mood, its identity, its people—like war. War always brings to light the most basic questions of national purpose: What is it about our nation—our history and place in the world—that should obligate it to fight? What national purpose is served by risking the lives of our young men and women? What compelling reason justifies the commitment of our military resources and manpower so far away from home? It is one thing for the country to wage war in order to defend its national borders. One will find little debate there. But should it intervene, as the United States has, in the affairs of other nations in the role of global policeman? That is a very different matter and one infinitely harder to justify in a democratic context. In such a situation, the fundamental questions of national identity and purpose are asked again and again with a certain relentless intensity—in marches and rallies, protest demonstrations, political pronouncements, editorials, and political oratory.

Consider the range of interventions the American military has undertaken in recent decades: Vietnam, Granada, Lebanon, Panama, and the Persian Gulf. In the controversy that raged over each, the lines of division in public debate were drawn neither over different cost/benefit analyses of national economic interest nor over different assessments of national security. Rather, the public debate always centered on differing perspectives regarding America's role in the world community, and the different public philosophies that undergirded those perspectives. Put more simply, the long, tearful, and sometimes bloody debate about Vietnam was not about the fate of a peasant society in southeast Asia, but about America. The debates about Lebanon and Panama and more recently the Persian Gulf were about America too. In each case, the opposing interests of the larger culture war have been very much present and at play.

As noted in chapter 4, it is not that the moral epistemologies of either coalition need be directly linked by one position on the war or another. (It is worth noting that some Protestant dispensationalist Fundamentalists in the orthodox coalition did link the war in the Persian Gulf to Biblical prophesies of Armageddon, with Iraq as Babylon and Saddam Hussein as the successor to Nebuchadnezzar, but this was exceptional.) Rather, it is the competing public philosophies of the culture war (which, as we have observed, sometimes hold only loose affinities to these moral positions) that are at play.

One vision holds that America's extraordinary power entails responsibility to intervene for the principles of good and fair play, through mediating disputes, deterring or thwarting the aggression of one nation against another, and holding regional tyrants at bay. For one who is confident of America's essential goodness, it would seem only appropriate that American democratic institutions be encouraged abroad. A strong military would be essential for these reasons alone; its use from time to time is simply one of the burdens of being a superpower. The chief opposing vision holds that a strong military represents a misuse of America's power and resources. As good as America may be, it has no right to impose its institutions or its way of life upon other nations. Meddling with the sovereignty of other nations and regions hints too much of an unsavory, old-style imperialism. Besides, it is a singular injustice to commit America's considerable wealth toward its military, which can only deal with the management of the world's conflict, rather than toward alleviating social and economic inequality—the source, more often than not, of such conflict.

Clearly, the circumstances of American intervention greatly influence the appeal to one vision or the other. In the case of Vietnam, for example, the latter vision came to hold sway, and eventually forced the end of the war in defeat. In the Persian Gulf, the appeal to the former was virtually impossible to resist. The respective counter-visions were articulated, however, for the duration of both conflicts: in Vietnam, by those whose distrust of communism was uncompromising (including a preponderance of Evangelicals and conservative Catholics); in the Persian Gulf, by those whose distrust of American-sponsored violence was uncompromising (including the very vocal leadership of the mainline Protestant and Catholic denominations). In this way, the opposing interests and ideals of the culture war become part of the fabric of debate about American military involvement abroad.

A PARTING NOTE

As a parting observation, it is worth highlighting a fundamental feature of the contemporary cultural conflict, noted earlier in the abstract, but now—through this brief glimpse into the matter of American military intervention abroad, as well as through our reconnaissance into the other fields of conflict—amply illustrated. It is that the opposing moral visions at the heart of the culture war and the rhetoric that sustains them acquire something of a life of their own. True, *the culture war is rooted in an ongoing realignment of American public culture and has become institutionalized chiefly through special-purpose organizations, denominations, political parties, and branches of government. The fundamental disagreements that characterize the culture war, we have seen, become even further aggravated by virtue of the technology of public discourse, the means by which disagreements are voiced in public. In the end, however, the opposing moral visions become, as one would say in the tidy though ponderous jargon of social science, a reality sui generis: a reality much larger than, and indeed autonomous from, the sum total of individuals and organizations that give expression to the conflict. These competing moral visions, and the rhetoric that sustains them, become the defining forces of public life.* Certainly there is a strong philosophical and sociological impulse toward moral and political consistency, such that people on one side of the cultural divide on one issue will remain on the same side for other issues. And yet we know at this point that the cultural divide—the overarching "binary opposition"—cuts differently on different issues, showing that an organization can maintain politically liberal positions on most issues while adopting moderate or conservative positions on others—and vice versa. These "exceptions to the rule" are common to every field of conflict, but their existence is ultimately irrelevant. However individuals or organizations align themselves on particular issues, *they become subservient to, and if unwilling must struggle against, the dominating and almost irresistible categories and logic of the opposing visions and rhetoric of the culture war.*

V

TOWARD RESOLUTION

12

Moral Pluralism and the Democratic Ideal

What will be the fate of the present clash of cultures? What will be the outcome?[1] The first part of this chapter deals with the future of the culture war as it is likely to be if things continue as they are. The second part considers the challenges the culture war poses to the democratic experiment and the public philosophy that has long sustained it.

One might be tempted to say that the tensions created by the polarizing impulses in American public culture will quickly wane. The reason typically offered is grounded in the hunch that religiously based political activism cannot be sustained for any length of time in a modern and forward-looking democracy.

Consider, for example, the dwindling public credibility of the Evangelicals. The titillating sexual scandals of the ministers Jim Bakker and Jimmy Swaggart and the failed presidential campaign of Reverend Pat Robertson, televangelists all, in the late 1980s provided clear evidence for this conjecture. The discontinuation of the *Fundamentalist Journal* in December 1989 and the folding of the most prominent orthodox political organization of that decade, the Moral Majority, four months earlier, would also seem to confirm this notion. For one observer writing in the *New Republic*, the conclusion one could draw from the mounting evidence was plain. "Rarely in modern times," he wrote, "has a movement of such reputed potential self-destructed so suddenly. Free thinkers may want to reconsider their skepticism about divine intervention."[2]

At one level the observation may be on target. The New Religious Right of the late 1970s and 1980s, arguably, is politically spent. But what was the New Religious Right? It was a particular clustering of prominent individuals and organizations in alliance with what could be called laissez-faire conservatives cemented by a particular political leadership—the Reagan administration. That being the case, it would only be a matter of time before its power abated. As sure as the years come and go, alliances weaken and administrations change; leaders get old, retire, and die.

But the end of the Religious Right should not be confused with the end of political activism on the part of the larger orthodox alliance. The former may be defunct as a "movement" but the passions that animate the latter are anything but defunct. Remember that, after all, the war is a war of moral visions.

Indeed, it is likely that the decline of the Religious Right only represents the beginning of a new stage in the evolution of the culture war. The strategy of the Evangelical wing of the orthodox alliance at the end of the 1980s and the start of the 1990s, for example, has been to move from the national stage to state and local activism. As Tim LaHaye put it, "In the nineties, the Religious Right is going to be composed of a host of independent, locally sponsored and funded organizations that work in unison." By the early 1990s, Pat Robertson's political organization had already turned in this direction. Said one of the spokesmen for Christian Coalition, "We think the Lord is going to give us this nation back one precinct at a time, one neighborhood at a time, and one state at a time. We're not going to win it all at once with some kind of millennial rush at the White House."[3] To this end, their aim is to hold "political technology training schools" around the country in order to field as many as 5,000 candidates at all levels by the end of the decade.

Another apt illustration of this tendency can be found in the organization Coalition on Revival (COR), founded in the mid-1980s. It draws support, legitimation, and intelligence from more than a hundred very prominent Evangelical leaders who comprise its steering committee. According to its introductory brochure,

> We believe the times we live in are so desperate and the culture of North America has come so close to going over the cliff . . . that any plans less aggressive and less courageous [than those specified by COR] will not turn our culture around in time to avoid a new dark age for the entire civilization. In a nutshell, we believe we must

> systematically attempt to rebuild our civilization on the biblical foundations on which we were originally built. We believe God is calling all local Christians to participate in this holy endeavor. . . . We have no other option.[4]

To this end, a five-year plan calls for the establishment of twenty-four "ministry networking committees" in sixty major cities throughout North America. They are to "function in a coordinated way as a single Spiritual Army under the leadership of local Christian 'Elders in the City Gate.' " The first priority of the national leadership, then, has been to "locate the fearless, local leaders in each of these cities, who will want to build this local Spiritual Army under their own leadership."[5]

Though the tone is very different, this tendency among politically active Evangelicals is typical of the strategy taken by Catholics, Jews, and secularists on both sides of the cultural divide. The culture war is not fading away by any means. It is, at most, decentralizing.[6]

However the culture battles actually take shape, the passions that animate the culture war remain. *The truth is that the two sides of the cultural divide peacefully coexist only so long as neither side gains actual or symbolic advantage over the other.* The opportunity to appoint a replacement to the Supreme Court (as in the case of the nomination of Robert Bork in 1987, David Souter in 1990, and Clarence Thomas in 1991), rallies and marches commemorating or celebrating the anniversary of a formative political event (such as Central America Week, or Gay Awareness Week), the introduction in Congress of a highly disputed piece of national legislation (such as the Equal Rights Amendment or the constitutional amendment banning flag burning), a controversial Court ruling (such as the decision in *Webster v. Reproductive Health Services* in July 1989 allowing individual states to impose restrictions on the practice of abortion), the showing of a controversial film (as in *The Last Temptation of Christ*) or art exhibit (as in the Mapplethorpe exhibit in various cities), and even the recurring presidential elections every four years—all of these events and many others provide concrete occasions for one side or the other to gain measurable advantage over the other. The result is a rupturing of any "peace" that might seem to exist. The culture war will undoubtedly take on many different forms and involve an ever-changing cast of personalities and organizations, but the underlying hostility promises to be protracted.

But what will come of it?

LOCATING THE ADVANTAGE

It is naive under any historical circumstances to assume that the truthful position will prevail, or that "things will work out for the best for all concerned." It is equally naive to imagine that a rationally negotiated settlement of the culture war will take place. Not only is it theoretically implausible, it is also well nigh a sociological impossibility. The principal reason is that the most vocal advocates at either end of the cultural axis are not inclined toward working for a genuinely pluralistic resolution. If anything, the opposite is closer to the truth: not only is the sociological impulse for one side to subjugate the other, each side would seem to insist on it. This is most clearly seen in the deliberate effort of both extremes to monopolize the symbols of legitimacy (patriotism, Americanism, family, First Amendment, and so on), thus excluding other groups that claim a right to the American heritage. Extremes on each side of the cultural divide, in other words, engage in a strange form of double talk: each side insists that the other has a right to exist and to exercise free speech; at the same time, the opposition is judged illegitimate by virtue of the substance of its message (for example, the opposition is "unpatriotic," "un-American," or "undemocratic") and, by implication, it should not exist and should not voice its opinion. To put this more sharply, the implication is that since the opposition is a danger to society, the social order would be better off if it did not exist or at least if it were not a significant player in public life. Yet both sides in this contest are cavalier in their use of these powerful symbols of legitimacy and illegitimacy. Inasmuch as this is true, the spirit of democratic tolerance is strained. The rhetoric used by both extremes exaggerates the power and intentions of their opposition. It also seeks to preempt American ideals and thus monopolize the symbols of legitimacy. In this, each side implicitly attempts to discredit the positions if not threaten the very existence of its opposition.

Yet all of this leaves the impression that, in reality, the contemporary cultural conflict is at a standoff: the claims of one side essentially balancing the claims of the other; the resources of one equalizing the resources of the other. If this impression has been made throughout, it is in part because this inquiry has focused principally upon understanding the nature and scope of the cultural conflict, without assessing which side may have the advantage. But at this point it is appropriate to pose that question directly. Is this culture war at an impasse or does one side have the edge over the other?

Who Has the Edge?

Rather than see decline, some observers have argued that the moral vision of the orthodox alliance, particularly as championed by the Evangelical Protestant community, is in a strong position to actually dominate American public discourse in the near future. Jeffrey Hadden and Anson Shupe, for example, have argued that "the conservative Christian movement has the potential to become solidified enough to 'take over the country.' " They predict that "by the end of this century . . . [conservative Christians] seem destined to become the single most powerful force in the United States."[7] Some might reject their projections as implausible, but the bases upon which these claims are made are compelling: the loss of confidence over liberal public philosophy, the legitimation of the "conservative cultural revolution" by the Reagan administration and neo-conservative intellectuals in the 1980s, the monopoly over religious broadcasting, the mastery over the skills of fund raising, and the growth of an increasingly conservative older sector of the population.[8] Add to this the extensive array of "parallel institutions" mentioned earlier—the schools, colleges and universities, the publishing—and the credibility of Hadden and Shupe's claim increases.

Another reason is that on many issues, such as abortion, religion and education, homosexuality, and the like, there is an indigenous passion and intensity of moral commitment that exists in some parts of the orthodox alliance that is just not found in balancing measure by their counterparts on the progressivist side. On some issues this translates into a new militancy. The anti-abortion project, Operation Rescue, and the tactics of civil disobedience it employs, signals this change. There are other signs as well. In his testimony before the Congress, the director of Chicago's Pro-Life Action League stated emphatically: "Nonviolent direct action to end abortion is preferable to bombing abortion chambers. But if access to free speech, assembly and redress of grievances are denied, the violence of abortion will inevitably be opposed by other means."[9] Even in the Coalition for Revival literature itself, there is a call to screen out of their seminars "any well-meaning Christian who simply is not willing to die for Christ at this time" in order to secure only "martyr-willing, mighty warriors."[10]

Still another reason why the orthodox moral vision maintains viability is that the state itself, though predominantly secular in character, is not monolithically secular. Numerous individuals and groups within the state are allies of orthodox interests and ideals and, from the inside, press their claims. Depending on the administration, cultural conservatives are very often found in the executive branch of government, as was certainly true during the Reagan and Bush administrations. Consider, in this regard, the powerful adversary role played by then secretary of education (and Catholic conservative) William Bennett. Also depending on the administration in power, the circulation of elites in the federal judiciary and in the Supreme Court can also have a powerful impact in favor of orthodox interests. The vision of America embodied in the judiciary will have enduring consequences long after particular members have been replaced.

All of these factors are compelling in themselves. But are they sufficient to endow conservative Christianity and the broader alliance of cultural conservatives with power to achieve an outsized share of influence in the struggle to define the American character and its future?

The institutional resources and power behind the progressivist vision are at least as strong and probably much stronger than those favoring the orthodox. One of the strongest is the constitution of the knowledge industry itself—the "reality-defining" mechanisms of contemporary American society. As is well known, the knowledge industry experienced tremendous growth in the twentieth century, especially after the Second World War. In research and development, in all levels of education (elementary, secondary, and higher education), in the media of mass communications (including national, regional, and local newspapers, magazines, the three largest commercial television networks, and the majority of all radio broadcasting, advertising, and film), in information-processing technology (particularly computer technology), and in the information services (including therapy, social work, accountancy, architecture, law, medicine, and the like), both expenditures and personnel grew prodigiously. It would be pointless to review here what has already been analyzed with great diligence by others.[11] But to give a general idea, by 1980 in the United States, the knowledge industry had come to account for some 34 percent of the Gross National Product and knowledge workers had come to comprise up to 41 percent of the economically active population.[12]

The dimensions of the knowledge sector, then, have become immense. But the real significance of this lies not in its rate of growth or its rate of innovation but in its political, moral, and intellectual character. Much of the sector is dominated by the pragmatic interests of a post-industrial economy: technological innovation, organizational efficiency, and managerial effectiveness. Perhaps the most charitable evaluation one could make about these pursuits is that they are agnostic toward orthodox interests and concerns. Yet other important sectors of the industry, as we have seen, such as the entertainment, news, and political media, and the educational establishment—both lower and higher levels—and the so-called helping professions, are demonstrably anti-orthodox. As noted earlier, surveys of the opinion of media, intellectual, and entertainment elites, studies of the curriculum of elementary and secondary school textbooks, among other sources, all make clear that it is here that progressivist ideals are most deeply institutionalized and most vigorously advocated.[13]

The secular knowledge sector is a crucial influence in determining the outcome of our cultural conflict in part because much of it has the patronage and protection of the state itself. Science and education are, in the main, appendages of the state, as are the myriad regulatory agencies dealing with health, occupational safety, welfare, communications, among others. So too, of course, is the judiciary. The knowledge industry and the modern state, then, are linked in complex and fundamental ways. Not only does this mean that the state provides much of the financial, personnel, and administrative infrastructure for the knowledge industry, but the state can limit dissent through its coercive powers. It is in the realm of education where these powers are most prominent. Since school attendance is mandatory for all children up to the eighth grade, and since the government has a monopoly on public education, children are required to be educated under the auspices of the state. The only alternatives available, as we know, are for families that have the time to give to home schooling or the money to afford private education.

The patronage and protection of the state is significant for another reason. As alluded to earlier, the state itself (to the degree that one can distinguish it from the knowledge industry), is emphatically secular in character. This has been increasingly true in two ways. The first concerns the formal relations between religion and government. Not only has the government assumed more and more jurisdiction over areas of social life previously controlled by the churches and synagogues but it has also been less and less inclined to assist religious organizations as they attempt to contribute to the public good, through, for example, religiously based education and welfare services. Second, a secular orientation is manifested in the way the modern state is organized from its highest to lowest echelons according to bureaucratic principles. Thus the *very ethos* of the modern state is unsupportive of a broad cultural system rooted in, legitimated by, and promoting (through public policy) a commitment to transcendent ideals.

The social location of popular support for religious orthodoxy, typically at the margins of contemporary American public life, a distance away from its centers of power, is another factor in the balance of the culture war. As I argued in chapter 1, the culture war is primarily a war of the middle classes. Most Orthodox Jews, conservative Catholics, and Evangelical Protestants, however, are members of the lower middle class, while secular progressives and their religious allies tend to be of the highly educated, wealthier, and relatively mobile upper middle and middle classes engaged in professional work. The social differences are seen in other ways as well. Whereas Orthodox Jews and conservative Catholics are very often found in urban centers, the largest contingent of the orthodox-minded, the Evangelicals, are from the small towns and rural areas of the South and Midwest. By contrast, liberal Catholics and Protestants are strongly represented, and in the case of more progressive Jews and secularists almost uniformly represented, in the urban centers of the Northeast, Midwest, and West Coast—Los Angeles, San Francisco, Denver, Chicago, New York, Boston, and Washington, D.C. Moreover, the orthodox tend to be, on average, a slightly older population and disproportionately female, whereas progressivists, and secularists in particular, tend to be younger and disproportionately male.[14]

Perhaps even more telling is the social location of the centers of cultural activism. Clearly the majority of all organizations, whether orthodox or progressivist, are located in Washington and New York. These cities, along with Boston, Chicago, Los Angeles, and San Francisco, comprise the political nucleus of national life and the regions from which the larger cultural warfare emanates. Nevertheless, the representation of cultural conservatives is far less concentrated in these cities. For example, in a survey of more than 400 public affairs organizations taken from the *Encyclopedia of Associations,* just more than half (56 percent) of those committed to conservative causes were located in these national and regional urban centers, compared to 83 percent of the liberal groups. The remainder from both camps were located in small cities and towns. Nearly as revealing, 18 percent of the conservative associations were located in the South, compared to 3 percent of the liberal associations.[15] The point is very simple. It is considerably more difficult to alter the ethos of national public life for those operating in large measure from the periphery of social power than for those whose efforts are concentrated in the center. In this way, too, the larger progressivist vision has an advantage.

Lest it be imagined that because of these formidable societal tendencies, history will ultimately favor the progressivist vision of America—that the defeat of the conservative vision is nearly a foregone conclusion—one must consider some other influences and tendencies that favor the orthodox side of the cultural divide. The first is that specific challenges to the dominant reality-defining institutions (such as television, film, music) very often work. The boycotting of the products of companies that sponsor television shows considered morally objectionable by such groups as the American Family Association or CLeaR-TV, as we have seen, have influenced advertising and programming. The protest of the Parents' Music Resource Center against what they felt was gratuitous violence and illicit sexuality succeeded in getting numerous record companies to place a warning label on record album jackets. And the picketing of such films as *The Last Temptation of Christ* by conservative Catholics and Evangelicals have likewise affected box-office profits. The orthodox alliance, then, is capable of providing an effective challenge to a secular and progressively inclined media.

Another factor favoring the orthodox is that institutions promoting a progressivist vision for America are equally vulnerable to the pressures of reorganization and redirection as the orthodox institutions. There are some indications of rightward movement on the part of such mainline Protestant denominations as the United Methodist Church and the Presbyterian Church, U.S.A., on such issues as abortion, homosexuality, and the like. The enfeebling of the once robust National Council of Churches is another illustration of change and redirection in organizations committed to progressive social action. As with the orthodox, these organizations and the vision they promote also depend heavily upon public acceptance and legitimation: they are compromised when they do not have it.

In addition to these factors, the conservative vision of America can be reinforced by the failures of a liberal social policy in providing quality education, in ensuring public safety, in protecting the social order, in generating economic prosperity, and so on. For all of these reasons, then, the orthodox side of the cultural divide is more powerful than might first be imagined.

A Plausible Denouement

Which side will finally gain advantage in this culture war? The outcome may be mixed. That is, it will depend upon the way specific controversies evolve within particular fields of conflict—family and family policy, law, mass media, public education, electoral politics, and so on. Within these contexts, outcomes will depend upon effective strategies, the allocation of resources, and the accidents of historical opportunity. For the time being, however, general conclusions about the broader direction of the culture war may not be possible.

Yet before the question of outcomes is abandoned altogether, we should explore another aspect of the conflict within public culture, for it too will have repercussions. This concerns the long-term vitality of moral commitments.

One is tempted to argue, for example, that as long as cultural conservatives maintain alternate institutional mechanisms for promoting their distinct cultural perspective, the conflict will persist unabated. And yet this is not necessarily the case. The Italian social philosopher Antonio Gramsci, discussed in chapter 2, has argued that "organic" or progressively oriented intellectuals succeed in their bid to replace the older cultural hegemony in part by *assimilating* "traditional" intellectuals.[16] What this means, if Gramsci is correct, is that the moral and political vision of opposition defended by traditional intellectuals is transformed through compromise and moderation. In the end, the very substance of the traditional antagonism is neutralized.

There are indications that this process has already begun to take shape in the various orthodox communities. In the Orthodox Jewish community, for example, this is seen in the emergence of "Modern Orthodoxy" as distinct from the traditional Hasidim. On the surface what distinguishes the Modern Orthodox community is its posture toward the observance of Halakah (traditional Jewish law). The Modern Orthodox reject the idea that strict observance of ritual duties and prohibitions is a sign of religious purity. True faith, rather, is born out of a proper relationship with God and with other human beings. What their right-wing counterparts view as a negligence toward Jewish law, therefore, they tend to view as flexibility. But more significantly, the Modern Orthodox are distinguished by their nonseparatist approach toward non-Orthodox and non-Jewish culture. The Modern Orthodox are openly syncretistic, drawing on many aspects of contemporary experience that are believed to enhance the practice of faith. They are willing, for example, to make compromises with ritual observance in order to receive a secular education, to pursue a career in the secular professions, and so on. What this means in the long run is that Orthodoxy itself is being reconstructed in terms that are more compatible with the spirit of the times. In this light it is not surprising to find within some quarters of Modern Orthodoxy the rather novel tendency to take seriously, if not actually adopt, progressivist positions on such issues as the changing role of women, changing sexual mores, abortion, and the like.

Much the same process can be seen within orthodox Protestantism. My study of the Evangelical leadership in the early 1980s showed that the process of assimilation was well under way. This was particularly true among the younger cohort of elites who had largely abandoned the separatism of their Fundamentalist forebears in favor of a more progressive cultural and political orientation.[17] Take, for example, the traditional ethic of self-sacrifice and self-mortification. For previous generations such asceticism served the purposes of living a more spiritual life. Among the younger cohort of elites, this has given way to a quest for self-expression and self-realization. Eight out of ten agreed that "a good Christian will strive to be a 'well-rounded person,'" and nearly two-thirds (62 percent) agreed that "for the Christian, realizing your full potential as a human being is just as important as putting others before you." With regard to the politics of family life, a significant percentage of the younger generation had largely abandoned a commitment to the "traditional" model of family life in favor of a socially androgynous model, where men and women play out similar if not identical roles in both public and domestic life. The majority rejected the idea that "it is best if the wife stays at home and the husband works to support the family," as well as the idea that "a married woman should not work if she has a husband capable of supporting her." On public issues such as gun control, welfare, the death penalty, the draft, defense spending, nuclear power, and American relations with the Soviet Union, the attitudes and opinions of the younger generation of Evangelical leaders did not differ appreciably from their secular counterparts. It was only on the issues of abortion, the Equal Rights Amendment, and homosexuality where the majority did not take a more liberal position. And yet the majority rejected the belligerence of such groups as the Moral Majority as an appropriate manner of political engagement.

This process of an accommodation to the spirit of the times can be seen at a more subtle cultural level too. As numerous observers have made clear, the knowledge sector has altered the intellectual character of American public culture.[18] How has it accomplished this? One of the central characteristics of modern rationality is its autonomy or self-groundedness. Arguments must stand on their own logic. They must be self-sufficient. Arguments based upon an external authority, such as the church or tradition, and arguments based upon inherited office, property, or force or violence are therefore ruled illegitimate from the start. Thus, the exclamation of the believer that homosexuality is a sin is insufficient; pronouncements from ecclesiastical authorities that abortion is murder are not enough; proclamations from religious ideologues declaring secular humanism the unofficial religion of the state are inadequate. Given the assumptions of modern rationality, these kinds of authority are the fraudulent substitute for "serious" argumentation. By contrast, the only legitimate grounds of argumentation are the tools of logic and empirical evidence.

The point is that at a deeper level of public discourse, the knowledge sector has largely defined the rules for public argumentation and that very often the voices of orthodoxy have agreed to play by them. Every time an Evangelical pastor makes an appeal to "medical and psychological proof" to establish that homosexuality is harmful to the well-being of the homosexual and makes no other appeal; every time a conservative Catholic priest relies exclusively on scientific evidence to demonstrate that the fetus is a living, human being; every time the religiously orthodox invoke psychological studies or achievement tests—and nothing else—to establish their claim that children are better off if their mothers stay at home rather than pursue a professional career outside of the home, the orthodox alliance tacitly submits to the linguistic domination of its more progressive opposition.

The evidence suggests that Gramsci might be right. There is the distinct possibility that orthodox communities may become so assimilated to a progressive political (and linguistic) culture that they will not be capable of offering any effective opposition to the world view that currently plagues them. To put it in different words, if the orthodox alliance is not able to sustain an enduring opposition, it may be because the orthodox communities are themselves involved in a process of re-symbolizing the "historic faiths" in terms that are more compatible with the assumptions of a secular and progressive public culture. Nevertheless, this process is very slow and opposition to a clearly defined enemy (which all groups within the orthodox alliance have) can thwart the process.

THE CHALLENGES POSED TO THE AMERICAN DEMOCRATIC IDEAL

While few would dispute that the broader social forces of modern life discussed so far will have enormous consequences for the evolution of American public culture, only the vulgar sociological determinist would maintain that these will be the only factors in determining the outcome. There is a way in which the assertion of human will also makes its impress on the outcome of public affairs. Cultural conflict may be about the struggle for domination, but the conflict can be channeled and made equitable through the creation and institutionalization of a relatively autonomous public philosophy. *Agreement around a renewed public philosophy could establish a context of public discourse, not to mention the legal and political apparatus, to sustain a genuine and peaceable pluralism—even in the face of what appears to be the monumental compulsion of history.*

There is, of course, a legacy of such public philosophizing in America—a well-established mechanism for coping with cultural conflict. Its central ideal has been the simultaneous commitment to both diversity and unity; pluralism and consensus. The Latin motto *e pluribus unum* (one out of many), found on the Great Seal is perhaps America's most potent symbol of national identity. And yet while the American experiment has been unique in the modern world for its celebration and application of this ideal, the ideal is as old as classical philosophy itself. It is seen in the teachings of Zeno and the Greek stoics (and in the policies of Alexander, who united Greeks and Persians under a single system), in Cicero's conception of *res publica,* in the instructions of Paul, in which the Church would be "neither Greek nor Jew, . . . barbarian, Scythian, bond nor free." It was in the revival of classical philosophy in the late eighteenth century that these ideas would be reaffirmed and rearticulated in the writings of Madison, Jefferson, Mason, and Washington. Indeed, it was to be the basis of the "new order of the ages"—the *novus ordo seclorum*—of which America was to become the embodiment.

But the times and circumstances have changed in ways that classical philosophy and the founders of the American republic could have never anticipated. The question then arises, Is a public philosophy that builds on this ideal really tenable at the end of the twentieth century? More pointedly, in what way can the democratic ideal of *e pluribus unum* remain genuinely workable when pluralism would seem to *expand indefinitely* and when the traditional sources of moral and legal consensus are no longer either credible or dependable? The issue is by no means new, yet the requirement for a coherent answer becomes increasingly urgent, particularly as the culture war unfolds. In our own generation, it is in the debate over *moral pluralism* and its expansion that the dilemma concerning diversity and unity becomes most sharply crystallized.

The Problem of Moral Pluralism

The dilemma we face is two-pronged and can be posed as a series of questions. Are there any limits to pluralism? Is there anything, in other words, that we will not view as acceptable behavior or lifestyle? Should there be any such limits? And on what grounds can a community justify the imposition of limits to pluralism? What compelling reasons, acceptable to all, are there for establishing boundaries between what is acceptable and what is not?

The dilemma is crystallized by an instructive incident from U.S. legal history. In the closing decades of the nineteenth century a number of cases dealt with the legality of polygamy in the United States. One of the most interesting of these involved a man by the name of George Reynolds, a Mormon (in fact, the private secretary to Brigham Young) who had been convicted of polygamy and sentenced to one year in prison in October 1874.[19] After several appeals, Reynolds's case was eventually reviewed by the Supreme Court. His case was based upon a simple logic: he had the right to practice polygamy because it was allowed and even encouraged by his religion and the First Amendment guaranteed the free exercise of his religious faith. His argument further implied a challenge to the state's endorsement of monogamy. Since the law only allowed monogamy, and monogamy was a tenet of Christianity and Judaism, was there not, in the government's favoring of the Judeo-Christian practice of monogamy, a flagrant violation of the Constitution's establishment clause? The Supreme Court responded to Reynolds's argument in this way:

> Laws are made for the government of actions, and while they cannot interfere with mere religious belief and opinions, they may with practices. Suppose one believed that human sacrifices were a necessary part of religious worship, would it be seriously contended that the civil government under which he lived could not interfere to prevent a sacrifice? . . . So here, as a law of the United States, it is provided that plural marriages shall not be allowed. Can a man

> excuse his practices to the contrary because of his religious belief? To permit this would be to make the professed doctrines of religious belief superior to the law of the land, and in effect to permit every citizen to become a law unto himself. Government could exist only in name under such circumstances.[20]

Reynolds's claim was soundly rejected.

Twelve years later, the Supreme Court again rejected Mormon claims to the "right" to practice polygamy arguing that

> it was never intended or supposed that the [First] [A]mendment could be invoked as a protection against the legislation for the punishment of acts inimicable to the peace, good order and morals of society. . . . However free the exercise of religion may be, it must be subordinate to the criminal laws of the country passed with reference to actions regarded by general consent as properly the subjects of punitive legislation.[21]

Needless to say, the "general consent" invoked in this decision reflected nothing less than the state's imprimatur upon the Jewish and Christian (and non-Mormon) moral tradition.

Though the kind of dilemma posed by the Mormon polygamy cases was faced over a century ago, it has reasserted itself on the contemporary scene with even greater passion. The paradigmatic case is the abortion issue where the logic is recapitulated almost verbatim, as has been seen, within the ranks of the pro-choice lobby. As the Religious Coalition on Abortion Rights has repeatedly maintained, "If abortion is a religious issue. . . . And religious theologies differ. . . . And each denomination counsels its members according to its own theology. . . . Wouldn't a law prohibiting abortion violate religious liberty? Exactly."[22] And not only would this prohibition violate the free exercise clause of the First Amendment, but it would also violate the establishment clause for it would, as a statement from the Disciples of Christ put it, "legislate a specific religious opinion or belief concerning abortion upon all Americans."[23] When, therefore, this progressive religious coalition argues that "the issue of abortion is a crucial test of religious liberty—one of the cornerstones of our democracy," it is in effect arguing that the right to abort is itself a measure of the proper functioning of modern democracy.[24]

The case of abortion is an important illustration, but in the end, just one illustration. The same logic has been applied to homosexuality.

According to the National Gay and Lesbian Task Force, "In our diverse culture, no one religious group, regardless of its strength or numbers, should impose its teachings or beliefs on persons who do not share those beliefs. To codify into law the teachings of any one religion erodes religious freedoms of all and ignores the fact that the interfaith religious community has not reached consensus on private, adult, consensual sexual behavior. A founding principle of our government is separation of church and state which is [therefore] violated by codifying the teachings of any one religion."[25] The ACLU has argued similarly in an official memorandum sent to members of the California State Assembly's Education Committee. "The ACLU regrets to inform you of our opposition to SB2394 concerning sex education in public schools. It is our position that teaching that monogamous, heterosexual intercourse within marriage is a traditional American value is an unconstitutional establishment of a religious doctrine in public schools. There are various religions which hold contrary beliefs with respect to marriage and monogamy. We believe SB2394 violates the First Amendment."[26]

Though the constitutional justification is slightly different, the logic of legal rights is employed to press the expansion of moral pluralism in still other areas, as well. In the case of pornography, it is the right of free speech. In the case of progressive programs of sex education in the public schools, it is the right to education and informed choice. The exercise of these rights also becomes a measure of democratic pluralism and tolerance.[27] It is quite possible that the erosion of consensus could evolve much further than it has already. Its logic can be applied with facility at a national level to still other moral issues such as active euthanasia, the use of fetal tissue in the development of new medical technologies, pederasty, and so on.[28] Indeed, the advocates of these changes already use the logic of legally protected individual rights to justify their practice. By its very nature, the libertarian impulse in progressive moral philosophy is to "invent rights, ever more rights. . . ."[29]

To argue that the "right to abort," or the "right to engage in homosexual relations," and so on are expressions of the rights of conscience (protected under the First Amendment), and to argue conversely that restrictions against those activities are expressions of the establishment of religion (prohibited by the First Amendment)—these may or may not be convincing legal arguments, acceptable in a court of law. They have proven, however, to be powerful tools of popular persuasion. Because of arguments like these, the concept of "general consent" as a basis for restricting acts considered "inimicable to the peace, good order and morals of society" comes to sound increasingly hollow, distant—implausible. "What consent?" one would inevitably ask. The reply: there is little if any "general consent" that remains. Such codes of morality in our society "have long since gone the way of feudalism and witch-burning."[30]

The reaction to all of this is predictable. It was foreshadowed in 1925 by the Fundamentalist from Tennessee (quoted in chapter 5) who declared, "People are free in this country to worship God as they please but they are not free to do everything that the devil wants done."[31] Nearly seven decades later, a Christian Voice pamphlet argued the point with similar frustration: "The acceptance of these perversions as 'moral alternatives' has eaten away at the moral fiber and the morals of America as a whole."[32] Another Fundamentalist publication articulated this complaint even more explicitly and bitterly: " 'Tolerance,' as the word is commonly used (or abused) today, usually means that we should 'tolerate' evil, 'tolerate' sin, 'tolerate' apostasy, 'tolerate' treason. . . . Under the cloak of 'TOLERANCE' and 'DEMOCRACY,' anti-Christian and anti-American propagandists are undermining the very foundation upon which this great republic was built."[33]

A strong tendency on the progressivist side of the cultural divide, then, is to defend moral pluralism as a social good and to encourage a corresponding expansion of toleration. The tendency on the other side is to reject moral pluralism as a social evil and to do whatever possible to inhibit its further expansion. Such fundamental disagreements poignantly signify a loss of the *unum,* the "center," the moral consensus in American public philosophy.

Two pressing questions arise at this point. The first addresses those who embrace the progressivist impulse. Here the question is not whether moral pluralism is a good or an evil but whether it is, when taken to its logical extremes, sociologically feasible or morally desirable. If not, where and how are limits to be placed on pluralism? It is one thing in a society where there is a basic moral consensus for one to say that "I happen to be a Jew," for another to say, "I happen to be Christian," and for still another to say, "I happen to be a Buddhist." Theological or confessional pluralism does not necessarily create any serious social dislocation. But the situation is quite different in a society that does not share an underlying moral agreement. Except in the realm of the absurd, it is difficult to imagine the same kind of conversation applied to various moral behaviors. For example, says one, "Personally I'm into ritual animal sacrifice." "Oh really," says another, "I happen to be into man-boy love relationships," "That's great," responds a third, "but my preference is . . . ," and so on.

Yet what may seem absurd in this hypothetical dialogue acquires the patina of reality in the bitter satire of one anti-abortionist who claimed, "Personally, I'm opposed to the bombing of abortion clinics, but I don't want to impose my morality on anyone else."[34] In his ridicule, those pro-choice advocates as well as other like-minded progressives who legitimate their position according to the moral logic of "Personally, I'm opposed," are taken to task. If progressives are serious about the "right to choice," viewed by their opponents to be nothing less than murder, why should they not allow pro-life advocates to exercise their personal moral freedom—their "rights"—by choosing to destroy an abortion clinic? Arguably, the pro-life advocate may take the moral high ground by asserting that the destruction of property is far less repugnant an act than the "widespread destruction of human life."

Applied to moral behavior, then, the logic of rights and personal choice cuts in two directions. It can justify the expansion of moral diversity, legitimating that which had previously been considered wrong, evil, harmful to society, or destructive to life. On much the same grounds it can also justify an opposition to that expansion, in ways that may be recognized as wrong but considered necessary for the health of society and for the preservation of life. Taken to these opposite ends, pluralism becomes a euphemism for unrestrained moral relativism.

The second question addresses those who embrace the orthodox vision. Here the issue is more straightforward. Is it sociologically feasible to reimpose through public policy a moral ethos that is essentially frozen in the late nineteenth century? Given the classic American ideals of public justice, is this end even morally desirable? The political problem facing those who answer "Yes" is, as Thomas Aquinas put it, that "the law cannot command all virtues and forbid all vices." Authority imposed from the top down without regard for the sensitivities of those dominated is, in other words, a recipe for oppression and, in turn, widespread popular discontent.

From Public Compact to Competing Interests

To restate the problem, what are the limits of pluralism, if any? And upon what enduring grounds can a democratic society justify the imposition of limits? To put it more directly: Can a republic carry on over time without a common agreement as to what constitutes the "good" or the "right" (and, therefore, what should be enjoined and what should be eschewed)?

Without a common agreement about what is good or what is right (or at least about the rules for determining the good and the right), all that remain are the particularistic claims about what is good and what is right articulated by varying and opposing factions. The question then becomes, "Which particularism will reign?" Each side of the contemporary cultural divide correctly perceives this when it claims that the opposition wants "to turn their own personal beliefs into law"—"to impose their moral, spiritual, and religious environment upon everyone." When this is the case, all that remain are competing interests, the power to promote those interests, and the ideological constructions to legitimate those interests.

In this situation the conjectures of the brute "Minski" in the Marquis de Sade's anti-epic novel *Juliette* are validated. To the accusation that he had been "abominably unjust" in raping, sodomizing, and murdering more than two dozen boys, girls, men, and women, he responded with chilling lucidity:

> Similar to the concepts of virtue and vice, [the concepts of justice and injustice] are purely local and geographical; that which is vicious in Paris turns up, as we know, a virtue in Peking, and it is quite the same thing here: that which is just in Isfahan they call unjust in Copenhagen. Amidst these manifold variations do we discover anything constant? Only this: . . . self interest . . . is the single rule for defining just and unjust.
>
> Justice has no real existence, it is the deity of every passion. . . . So let us abandon our belief in this fiction, it no more exists than does the God of whom fools believe it the image: there is no God in this world, neither is there virtue, neither is there justice; there is nothing good, useful, or necessary but our passions, nothing merits to be respected but their effects.[35]

Effects, Sade explains, brought about through the exercise of power.

Sade's view is not entirely a caricature. This view is precisely the message of the debate over curricular revisions in the university. The politicization of higher learning has meant that, as there can be no virtue, there can also be no objective truth. "Objectivity" is in the eye of the beholder since, as all sides seem to agree—no one is free from bias. Indeed, as some say, the very quest for greater understanding is, at one level or another, tainted by interests. This is also the message of the debate over "art." Cultural conservatives maintain that contemporary art is primarily concerned with the politics of individual autonomy. This is the reason why it finds such sympathetic support among a wide range of cultural progressivists and why its net public effect is to "shock the traditional bourgeoisie." Against this, the orthodox alliance reasons, art must contain an improving power or public purpose, a "purpose transcending the mere satisfaction of self-expression." Progressivists and leaders in the arts establishment immediately reply that the purposes to which their opponents speak are themselves political in that they legitimate existing social arrangements. The politicization of "expression" in this way, then, presupposes a relativism about the content of art and the public meaning of art, the resolution of which is the assertion of power by one side over the other. The loss of agreement in the realm of law, family policy, and human life, as well, points to just the same effect.

The dilemma, then, reasserts itself: moral pluralism has expanded and seems to promise to expand further. At the same time, traditional sources of an underlying cultural, political, and legal consensus are less and less credible to vast segments of the population and therefore less and less functional for the republic as a whole. What is more, each side of the cultural divide uses the mechanisms for working through fundamental differences (that is, through law, communications, and language) in ways that only widen the gulf between the principals. Through this, the communities on both sides of the cultural divide have become little more than competing interest groups (with different conceptions of the public good, of public virtue, and of public justice, not to mention different conceptions of national identity and purpose) which struggle to attain the power to establish those conceptions as the givens—the "oughts"—of the larger public culture.

Democratic Experiments, Past and Present

When the content of public life—the prevailing vision of the good and the just—is decided principally through the competition of power and interests, there is reason to pause and wonder. Can a liberal democracy remain not just superficially functional but healthy and robust without an elementary and somewhat universal agreement in the public realm about the criteria for distinguishing the social good from the socially destructive or about the rules of reason for making equitable public policy?

The reply of most moral and political philosophers to this question tends to be simply, "probably not." The nub of disagreement in these circles is over just how dismal the situation is.

There are some who describe the current state of affairs in the most fearsome of terms. According to Alasdair MacIntyre, for example, the loss of the languages of public morality has precipitated the advent of a "new dark ages." Indeed, he writes, "The barbarians are not waiting beyond the frontiers; they have been governing us for quite some time. And it is our lack of consciousness of this that constitutes part of our predicament."[36] Similarly cheerless views have been made by others, such as Allan Bloom, who see in these developments and in the inability to respond to them, the collapse of the high traditions of Western civilization.

Many others, however, believe that this view overstates the problem. Serious deficiencies exist in American public philosophy, to be sure, but such pessimism is both exaggerated and unwarranted.[37] Richard Madsen, for example, maintains that Americans do share a broad consensus about the relationship between the individual rights to pursue selfish interests and the social responsibility to contribute to the public good. Yet he concedes that ultimately this is a "contentless consensus"—a matter of form over substance. People share a consensus on the principles of public life but fail to agree on the practical everyday and political meaning of those principles.[38] Others believe even this assessment is too gloomy. Such pessimism, critics such as Jeffrey Stout say, underestimates the level of agreement on the good that exists in our society and overestimates the depth of discourse necessary for us to reason coherently with each other on most issues. This consensus may be provisional and it may exist in superficialities—"overlapping moral platitudes too numerous to mention." Nevertheless the consensus is real and significant. Among other things it points substantively to the recognition that we should not kill each other over our disagreements—"the realization that it would be a bad thing, that it would make life worse for all of us, to press too hard or too far for agreement on all details in a given vision of the good."[39] There are other substantive points of agreement as well. Thus, as weak as the philosophical foundations of American democracy may be, the new dark ages are not necessarily upon us and neither does history necessarily trace a downward spiral toward ruin.

Within a social scientific frame of reference, it is risky if not inappropriate to jump in on these discussions. A few observations, however, may not be too impertinent. Take first the issue of violence. Physical violence is notably absent from the contemporary culture war (notwithstanding accusations, for example, that Planned Parenthood leaders are "baby killers" and pro-life activists in Operation Rescue are "terrorists"). It is true that abortion clinics have been bombed on occasion. Laboratories used for animal experimentation have been trashed. Gay activists infected with the AIDS virus have spat in the faces of police officers. It will also be recalled that gays firebombed Chuck McIlhenny's church and house and harassed him ceaselessly with death threats. But these as well as other expressions of violent rage (such as flag burning, bomb threats to theaters, and the like) have been, on the whole, rather rare. America, after all, is neither Belfast nor Beirut. (Not yet anyway.) In some ways, it is difficult to imagine that the American culture war could ever evolve to these extremes. Still, some escalation in the violence is possible, particularly if the aims of particular political actors seem to them interminably frustrated. Violence may appear to them to be the only recourse for making progress against their opposition. At present, however, the conflict remains at a level of intensity that is high enough to mobilize resources and to sharpen rhetorical antagonism but not high enough to trigger widespread acts of rage. If this is so, it is in large part because rival activists have in fact agreed to reject overt violence and to pursue their objectives within the boundaries of legitimate political action.

Consider also a more sociological matter. While it may be true that there is no substantial agreement on the "good" and the "just," there are other sources of social cohesion and solidarity that cannot be ignored in discussions such as these. There are, for example, massive and constraining qualities of everyday life, qualities that resist changes in the given routines of social life and in the order of social relationships.

But the question remains, is all of this or any of this adequate? However much latent solidarity may exist among antagonists, however resistant people and communities might be to change, and however much agreement there may be on moral platitudes "too numerous to mention," is it enough to keep a liberal democracy not just superficially functional but vital over the long term?

It is fair to say that the experiment that is America is not on the brink of collapse, as the voices on each side of the cultural divide would have us believe. But the clash of opposing voices in our public culture do point to matters of considerable moral weight. The contemporary culture war is certainly a symptom of the loss of the languages of public morality in American society. Many of the battles of the culture war also represent a strain upon the course of democratic practice, a strain that could conceivably evolve into a serious threat to these traditions if the contenders become yet more polarized. These things being the case, the contemporary culture war also embodies both a challenge to understand more fully that which most deeply divides moral communities and an opportunity to reappropriate and invigorate the traditions of democratic experience.

EPILOGUE

Democratic Possibilities

Although the debate over the magnitude of peril facing democratic discourse thrusts and parries forward, virtually all agree that public moral discourse in America is shallow and fragmentary, detached from the long and rich traditions from which particular positions are rooted. Very few, if any, therefore, deny the political and social importance to press for a new, common rationality, a new *unum* wherein public virtue and public civility can be revitalized. But practically speaking, how is this to happen?

No one is so naive to believe that under present circumstances the consensus pursued could be or even should be some form of consensus of values and beliefs. The divisions, at this level, are firm and unyielding. If any consensus is achievable it could and should first be about *how* to contend over the moral differences that divide—a public agreement over *how* to publicly disagree. When consensus is realized at this plane, genuine disagreement becomes an accomplishment; authentic debate becomes a virtue.[1]

AGREEMENT WITHIN DISAGREEMENT

The point warrants clarification. To pursue an "agreement within disagreement" is not to settle for an arid proceduralism, where the highest shared ideals are contained in the technical dicta of a bureaucratic rationality. Take, as an example, the agreement that contending factions will not kill each other over their differences. Such an agreement is no small accomplishment in the context of world history. It means that the ultimate forms of power and restraint cannot be used to advance particular interests. Yet alone this agreement does not lead to any other positive public end. It does not presuppose a mutual respect for moral differences, it does not encourage serious public argument, nor does it raise the quality of public debate. It does not bring about any substantive resolution to the pressing demands of public policy disputes nor does it provide the mechanisms for deciding upon a national agenda. The "agreement within disagreement," then, must be more substantive than the bland utilitarianism of bureaucratic procedure. There must also be the recognition that civil conflict can and should eventually lead to more substantive forms of political agreement.

How is this possible? Despite his own seemingly intractable pessimism, Alasdair MacIntyre himself has suggested that one of the critical ways in which rival and incompatible positions on moral issues can be rationally resolved is by recognizing that different positions are not autonomous but are rooted within different traditions of rational justification. By comprehending those "living traditions" (including the historical and social context within which those traditions exist, its central concepts, and its first principles, the manner in which its wisdom has accumulated, and its leading advocates, both past and present), "the problem of diversity is not abolished, but it is transformed in a way that renders it amenable of solution."[2]

The suggestion is useful, but alone, probably ineffectual. One reason is that the comprehension of the living traditions of moral justification is an achievement attainable by full-time intellectuals, perhaps exclusively. Lower-level cultural workers, the activists who occupy the trenches of cultural warfare, much less ordinary citizens, either do not have the time or the economic incentive (since their job is to win) to decode the traditions they oppose. Indeed, as Robert Bellah and his associates have shown in their book *Habits of the Heart,* most Americans do not have the time or inclination to even comprehend their own moral traditions fully.[3] Is it conceivable that they would take the time or generate the empathy to understand another's?

A second reason the solution may be ineffectual is that *it ignores the problem of power.* It fails to take into account the reality that some traditions are linked to structures of social and political authority which are themselves capable of undermining the legitimacy and presence of opposing traditions.

PRACTICAL STEPS

If rational resolutions to the moral issues that threaten to polarize American society are possible, other strategies would also have to be agreed upon. If a just settlement of the incommensurable differences that exist in social and political life is viable, other conditions or civic practices would have to be established and maintained.

The first of these relates to *changing the environment of public discourse.* The chief environment in which public discussion presently takes place (the new communications technologies discussed in chapter 6) is notably conducive to reaching mass audiences but it is not at all conducive to rational deliberation. The reason is plain. Genuine debate, whether public or private, is always a dialectic; always a direct and immediate exchange. Positions taken and accusations made can be challenged directly by rebuttal, counterpropositions, cross-examination, and, inevitably, the presentation of evidence. Genuine debate is always most effective when the same audience is there to witness all of the exchange and to receive all of the information. Needless to say, extremist rhetoric is extremely difficult to maintain in this discursive environment. The very context of genuine debate predisposes actors to rhetorical moderation and forbearance. But it is impossible to generate these dynamics in television commercials, in political print advertisements and proclamations, and issue-oriented direct mail. Newspaper editorials and certain television programming do allow for some debate but the technical constraints of these media (space for newspapers and time for television programs) tend to seriously limit the depth of debate. Because there is no dialectic, because there is no mechanism for ensuring accountability, the newer communications technologies provide an environment that predisposes actors to rhetorical excess.

The other chief environment of public discourse in our day is the courtroom. When a battle in the contemporary culture war becomes a real-life drama of ordinary people opposing each other on an issue, litigation seems inevitable. All too often, however, litigation is pursued as the first step rather than the last resort in resolving these matters. Yet the moment that a public dispute turns to the courts, the discourse surrounding that dispute is fundamentally transformed. Attorneys, of course, are paid to win, not to do what is right. What is more, a great deal of money and a great number of reputations are at stake. Add to this the role of the media in reporting these events and polarization is virtually guaranteed.

Without a change in the environments of public discourse, therefore, demagoguery and rhetorical intolerance will prevail.

A second condition that would seem essential for rationally resolving morally grounded differences in the public realm would be the *rejection by all factions of the impulse of public quiescence.* This might seem an odd thought, when many Americans groan for the day when the activists would just shut up. Nevertheless, democracy depends upon the contribution of many voices. But there is a tendency among those Americans in the middle of these debates to hesitate from speaking at all. This is a tendency that has expression on both sides of the cultural divide in ways unique to their world views.

For those who lean toward orthodox commitments, quiescence takes form in private resignation—an acceptance of the privatization of religious faith. The danger is this: when religious faith (of whatever political orientation) is public, it reaffirms the existence of ideals and standards that are independent of personal subjectivity, ideals and standards that are publicly known and must be publicly reckoned with. When totally personalized, religious faith cannot perform that critical function of being a guard against either political anarchy or political tyranny.

Among those who lean toward progressivist commitments, public quiescence tends to take form as a radical subjectivism. To claim that there is no meaning to life except that which the individual chooses to bestow upon it, that there is no justice except the justice that exists in the realization of particular individual interests, that virtue is entirely personal and perspectival, is to deny that there is a public realm to which we all belong. In one of its most insidious expressions, this view contends that the issue of truth and order in common life is no longer an interesting question, and thus it is time to change the subject. Granted, this view is a rallying cry of a vocal minority on the progressivist side of the cultural divide, but the case needs to be made against it for it is ultimately parasitical. The kind of liberal society enjoyed by the radical subjectivists cannot be generated or sustained on subjectivist grounds. They must depend on others whose beliefs sustain the moral order.

Either way, without a common belief that public standards do exist and without a commitment to determine what they are, there is no basis for making public compromises, there is not even the will to make the effort. We must avoid the temptation, in either form, to be "idiots"—a word, which in one of its original meanings, described the totally private person who is oblivious to the importance of and need for public-minded civility.[4]

A third condition is the *recognition of the "sacred" within different moral communities.* The "sacred" is that which communities love and revere as nothing else. The "sacred" expresses that which is non-negotiable and defines the limits of what they will tolerate. Walter Lippmann once wrote that "the toleration of differences is only possible on the assumption that there is no vital threat to the community." The problem in contemporary public discourse is that what one faction views as a vital threat, another views as entirely legitimate; what one moral community views as a *de*-sacralization, the other views as a constitutional right. Nevertheless, if rational resolution is at all possible, all parties need to recognize that their own particular action can be so offensive to their opposition—so far beyond what, from the perspective of the opposition's moral tradition, is reasonably tolerable—that it spurs the opposition to a reaction that really does present a vital threat to the community, namely the use of violence. In other words, a common recognition of what constitutes a "vital threat" for the opposition predisposes all factions to pursue their respective agendas in the public realm with a measure of prudence and caution.

If the third condition is a recognition of the "sacred" in moral commitments of the others, the fourth condition is a *recognition of the inherent weaknesses, even dangers, in their own moral commitments.*

On the *progressivist side* of the cultural divide, the weakness comes as a reticence to talk about the limits or boundaries of the acceptable and the unacceptable—and in this, a general unwillingness to articulate the constituent elements of the public order. This posture can be seen, for example, in the unwillingness of the guardians of *haute culture* to define any limits to artistic expression, so long as it is produced or performed by someone they are willing to call an artist. It can be seen in a certain libertarian impulse to permit most any kind of sexual activity so long as it is private and among consenting individuals. It can be further seen in the unwillingness of the most vocal pro-choice advocates to articulate any conditions or circumstances under which abortion should be restricted, despite the fact that the overwhelming majority of Americans (while certainly wanting legal abortions in some cases) do not like the idea of abortion on demand. So too it can be seen in the failure of flag burners, direct mail writers, talk-show hosts, certain journalists, and other staunch advocates of free speech to articulate the ways in which their personal rights and professional obligations might be constrained by certain codes of *civic* responsibility or community obligation. The list could go on. The libertarian emphasis on rights and personal autonomy can only lead to the conclusion that constraints are arbitrary. Thus, the very ideal of "limits" must be relegated to the realm of personal inclination; of decisions individuals make about their *own* lives. In any case, the argument goes, such limits certainly cannot or should not be imposed upon public and collective life for to do so would place the very traditions of personal freedom in America in jeopardy.

The problem, of course, is that collective life by definition ceases to exist without some agreed upon standards defining what the community or nation will embrace and what it will eschew and in both cases, why. So where are these standards to come from? What moral languages and images can be drawn upon to articulate the obligations of community life? Here progressivists face two problems.

The first problem is that the most vocal and often the most bellicose voices of religious orthodoxy have coopted the language of obligation and moral concern. Just because one opposes censorship, as Garry Wills put it, does not mean that one agrees with pornographers. So too, just because one opposes a ban on all abortion does not mean one favors abortion in all circumstances; and just because one opposes gender discrimination does not mean that one opposes the nuclear family; and just because one favors the empowerment of women and minorities does not mean one has abandoned meritocratic standards. There are moral arguments to be made and moral strategies to be designed that lead to an articulation of a progressive vision of the common good, one that entails rights and responsibilities. The illustration can be elevated to a general principle applying to many areas of social life. Yet within the contemporary public discourse, one risks being branded a "right-winger" by even invoking moral criteria. Indeed, the very word "morality" has become a right-wing word. It should not be.

The second problem is that when progressivists have had the courage to break out of that bind to talk about "our obligations toward one another" or the "boundaries of community life," they often do so in languages that do not resonate with anyone but those who breathe the rarified air of the university campus. The great debates between liberals and communitarians over the nature of justice, of rights and equality, of the good, and so on, for example, are almost always pitched in an economic or philosophical language that is virtually impenetrable for even the broadly read nonexpert. So too the idea proposed by another school of progressivist thought, that our sense of moral obligation in modern secular society derives principally from the concrete circumstances of our everyday lives—that community is possible because of the moral meanings we socially create and recreate in the tedium of daily living—is yet another example of how inaccessible the intellectual languages of moral obligation are.[5]

These two cases illustrate something else too; that is, the strong tendency within a good part of progressivist thinking to ignore religion. The basic anthropological reality is that most human societies have been religious—transcendent faiths, in other words, have been the source of the moral obligation that underlies collective life. Yet like the word "morality," the concept of religion or transcendence is also very often dismissed by secular progressivists as "right-wing." Here too they are way off the mark. The point is that the failure to articulate the constitutive elements of public order—of limits, and so on—and the tendency to reject the possibility of transcendence as a source of communal renewal are two fundamental aspects of a progressivist public philosophy that will alienate not only their opposition but the mainstream of American society.

On the *orthodox side* of the new cultural divide, the weakness, indeed danger, is just the opposite—it lies in their eagerness to set limits. One may have many complaints about the different models of social life that the orthodox would envision. But the problem from the perspective of public discourse is not with their desire for order or even the kind of order they desire. Rather, it is with an assumption made in one of their principle methods. To establish the "good" society, it is essential to establish and maintain laws that reflect the good. The assumption is that—to speak concretely—if *Roe v. Wade* is reversed, if obscenity laws are enforced, if sodomy laws are upheld, and prayer is legally permitted in the public schools, all will be well because these laws, once again, reflect the "good."

The problem in this view is the failure to see that the establishment of a moral order (one that is even halfway pleasant to live in) requires popular consent. There cannot be morality without virtue; and there cannot be collective order without community, without the voluntary yet binding social relationships within which meanings are taken for granted. If moral society is their objective, the goal of the orthodox should be the cultivation of virtue, rather than simply the maintenance of law. To this end, the orthodox could seek new ways to enact their moral ideal in the context of community life.

Among the weaknesses in both orthodox and progressivist alliances, then, is an implicit yet imperious disregard for the goal of a *common life.*

AN AMERICAN LEGACY

In offering these musings I am not at all suggesting that alliances compromise on matters of principle. Pluralism is not the bland arithmetic mean of what everyone in a society believes, nor tolerance the obligation to make one's deepest beliefs tolerable to others. We are dealing with the sacred after all. By its very nature, the principles that derive from it are non-negotiable. A principled pluralism and a principled toleration is what common life in contemporary America should be all about. But this is only possible if all contenders, however much they disagree with each other on principle, do not kill each other over these differences, do not desecrate what the other holds sublime, and do not eschew principled discourse with the other.

In the end, the possibility that public discourse could accommodate to these conditions, adopt these civic practices, or come to any kind of common understanding might be unrealistic. As Bea Blair, whom we met in the prologue put it, "I don't like debating because I don't think it gets anywhere. . . . And I don't think [my opponents] are much interested in it either because it's really not very productive." Alas, the centrifugal forces that would maintain the present state of affairs or that would even further polarize public discourse are quite real and imposing. Such an end would require the assertion of will against the compulsions of history; the subjugation of technological imperative to higher principles of human community.

Though perhaps a bit fanciful, the idea that public discourse could accommodate to conditions such as these remains a vital possibility.[6] America, it is said, has always been a nation by intention and ideas. As historians have made very clear, our founders faced similarly imposing historical odds in forging the public philosophy that established the American experiment in democracy in the first place. Not to endeavor again would betray that legacy.

Notes

CHAPTER 1: CULTURAL CONFLICT IN AMERICA

1. See J. Dolan, "Catholic Attitudes Toward Protestants," in *Uncivil Religion*, ed. R. N. Bellah and F. E. Greenspahn (New York: Crossroad, 1987), pp. 72–85, for a brief review of Catholic resentment toward Protestantism and the reasons why it was relatively muted.
2. See T. M. Keefe, "The Catholic Issue in the *Chicago Tribune* Before the Civil War," *Mid-America* 57 (October 1975): 227–45.
3. These figures come from R. A. Billington, "Tentative Bibliography of Anti-Catholic Propaganda," *Catholic Historical Review* 18 (1932): 492–513. Among the newspapers and magazines were *The Protestant Vindicator, The Anti-Romanist, The Protestant Banner, Priestcraft Unmasked, The Native American, The Reformation Defended Against the Errors of the Times, The American Protestant Magazine, The Spirit of the XIX Century,* and *The North American Protestant Magazine* or, as it was also called, *The Anti-Jesuit.* Among the books published were such evocative titles as *Jesuit Juggling: Forty Popish Frauds Detected and Disclosed* (1834), *The Papal Conspiracy Exposed and Protestantism Defended in the Light of Reason, History and Scripture* (1855), *Popery Stripped of Its Garb* (1836), *The Papacy: the Anti-Christ of Scripture* (1854), and *Book of Tracts on Romanism: Containing the Origin and Progress, Cruelties, Frauds, Superstitions, Miracles and Ceremonies of the Church of Rome* (1844).
4. Through the 1840s and 1850s the Committee for the Inspection of Convents was established and operated by the Commonwealth of Massachusetts. See R. A. Billington, *The Protestant Crusade* (Gloucester, Mass.: Peter Smith,

1963); and T. Maynard, *The Story of American Catholicism* (New York: Macmillan, 1942).

5. Horatio Alger, *Adrift in New York, and the World Before Him,* ed. William Coyle (New York: Odyssey Press, 1966); *Ben, the Luggage Boy, or Among the Wharves* (Boston: Loring, 1870); *Paul the Peddler, or The Adventures of a Young Street Merchant* (Boston: Loring, 1871).
6. This literature is summarized in some depth in M. N. Dobkowski, "American Anti-Semitism," *American Quarterly* 29 (Summer 1977): 166–81. See also Louis Harap, *The Image of the Jew in American Literature: From Early Republic to Mass Immigration,* 1st ed. (Philadelphia: Jewish Publication Society of America, 1974).
7. A number of important sources explore the nature of anti-Semitism at the end of the nineteenth and the beginning of the twentieth centuries. See, for example, O. Handlin, "American Views of the Jews," *American Jewish Historical Society* 40 (June 1951): 323–45; J. Higham, "Social Discrimination Against Jews," *American Jewish Historical Society* 47 (September 1957):1–33; Higham, "Anti-Semitism in the Gilded Age," *Mississippi Valley Historical Review* 43 (March 1957): 559–78; and C. Stember, ed., *Jews in the Mind of America* (New York: Basic Books, 1966).
8. R. Hofstadter and M. Wallace, eds., *American Violence* (New York: Vintage Books, 1971), p. 302.
9. An account of these experiences is given in G. Sessions, "Myth, Mormonism, and Murder in the South," *South Atlantic Quarterly* 75 (Spring 1976): 212–25. See also T. O'Dea, *The Mormons* (Chicago: University of Chicago Press, 1957); and D. B. Davis, "Some Themes of Counter-Subversion," *Mississippi Valley Historical Review* 47 (1960): 205–25.
10. Interestingly, while neutrality increased and antipathy declined, close identification among various denominations (as measured by "feelings of warmth") did not increase. These findings are a part of the University of Michigan surveys on American Presidential Politics. The "feeling thermometer" they employed was a 100 point scale along which respondents were asked to locate themselves according to coldness and warmth they felt for different groups. Coldness was measured as a score between 1 and 40, neutrality between 41 and 69, and warmth between 70 and 100. For the general population, coldness toward Catholics decreased from 13 percent of the population in 1966 to 9.9 percent in 1984. (Comparable figures were not available for Protestants and Catholics, but for blacks, the figure dropped from 15 percent to 11 percent.) Those neutral toward Catholics grew from 39 percent in 1966 to 46 percent in 1984; those neutral toward Protestants rose from 27 percent in 1966 to 47 percent in 1976; and for Jews, from 47 percent in 1966 to 56 percent in 1984. Protestants and Jews were omitted from the 1984 survey.

11. The earlier figures were taken from a 1958 Gallup Poll while the more current figures come from J. D. Hunter and O. Guinness, eds., *The Williamsburg Charter Survey on Religion and Public Life,* a survey conducted in December 1987 (Washington, D.C.: Williamsburg Charter Foundation, 1988).
12. The single most comprehensive summary of the data on non-Jewish beliefs about Jews from the 1930s to the mid-1960s is Stember, "The Recent History of Public Attitudes," in his *Jews in the Mind of America,* pp. 310–36. For the data produced between the mid-1960s and the early 1980s, see G. Rosenfield, "The Polls: Attitudes Toward American Jews," *Public Opinion Quarterly* 46 (1982): 431–43. Studies that should be reviewed in their own right and that collectively support this general thesis are C. Glock and R. Stark, *Christian Beliefs and Anti-Semitism* (New York: Harper & Row, 1966); G. Selznick and S. Steinberg, *The Tenacity of Prejudice* (New York: Harper & Row, 1969); H. Quinley and C. Glock, *Anti-Semitism in America* (New York: Free Press, 1979); and G. Martire and R. Clark, *Anti-Semitism in the United States* (New York: Praeger, 1982).
13. See the "Nationwide Attitudes Survey—September 1986, a Confidential Report Presented to the Anti-Defamation League of B'nai B'rith," by Tarrance, Hill, Newport, and Ryan. The report received a great deal of media play as well. See Bruce Bursma, "Anti-Semitism Fading for Some," *Chicago Tribune,* 9 January 1987; and Marjorie Hyer, "Poll Finds No Rise in Anti-Semitism: Most Evangelicals Reject Jewish Stereotypes," *Washington Post,* 10 January 1987, p. G8.
14. See J. L. Sullivan, J. Piereson and G. Marcus, *Political Tolerance and American Democracy* (Chicago: University of Chicago Press, 1982), for a summary of some of these data. The General Social Survey performed annually by the National Opinion Research Center has asked questions about the free speech rights of atheists, communists, and homosexuals since 1972 and even since that time the overall trend has been toward greater toleration. In 1973, for example, 41 percent of the American population agreed that a communist should be allowed to teach in public schools. By 1987 this had increased to 49 percent. Likewise, in 1973, 49 percent of the general population agreed that a homosexual should be allowed to teach but by 1987, that percentage had increased to 58. (From the author's reanalysis of the General Social Survey.)
15. Kate DeSmet, "Shotgun Approach: Congress of Fundamentalists Labels Catholic Church 'Mother of Harlots,'" *Detroit News,* 20 August 1983. The anti-Catholic and anti-Semitic invectives of the pentecostal televangelist Jimmy Swaggart have been especially pronounced. He has called Catholics "poor pitiful individuals that think they have enriched themselves by kissing the Pope's ring" (reported by the Associated Press, 9 March 1985) and has claimed that "a large segment of the Jewish community within the enter-

tainment industry . . . is doing everything in its power to *destroy* the very element that has *produced* . . . freedom" (reported in *The Evangelist,* July 1985; emphasis in the original).

16. The term "progressive" is somewhat imprecise but it is suggestive. The word is not totally satisfactory because of its association with the political movement and ideology. It also connotes a positive development which many would find debatable. Yet the search for alternate terms leads to other problems. The antonyms of orthodoxy—heterodoxy or heresy—connote too much. "Revisionism" is problematic, too, as it implies a departure from truth. The problem is not truth versus falsehood but between different interpretations of truth—interpretations that differ because the criteria (or authority) established to measure correct interpretation differ.
17. Secularists are represented in such organizations as the American Humanist Association (founded in 1941), the Council for Democratic and Secular Humanism (founded 1980), the National Service Conference of the American Ethical Union (founded 1929), Gay and Lesbian Atheists (founded 1978), Libertarians for Gay and Lesbian Concerns (founded 1981), and the Association of Libertarian Feminists (founded 1975).
18. Their agreement is confirmed in the Religion and Power Survey in James Davison Hunter, John Jarvis, and John Herrmann, "Cultural Elites and Political Values," unpublished paper, University of Virginia, 1988.
19. Robert Wuthnow's book, *The Restructuring of American Religion* (Princeton, N.J.: Princeton University Press, 1988) is the most exhaustive statement on the developments described in this book to date. Those familiar with Wuthnow's treatment should see my book not just as a validation of his general argument but as an extension of it as well. Where Wuthnow focuses upon Protestantism, I focus on the interfaith dimensions of the problem. Where he views the tensions as those that exist between "religious liberals" and "religious conservatives," I view the tensions as both deeper and more significant.
20. See Mark Noll's essay, "The Eclipse of Old Hostilities," in *Uncivil Religion,* ed. Bellah and Greenspahn, p. 99.
21. "The Webster Decision," *Nightline,* ABC-TV broadcast, July 3, 1989.
22. There is little doubt that the controversy over abortion is a central part of the larger conflict. Indeed, it has crystallized the antagonism between the orthodox and progressive as no other issue has. Yet once again, the moral propriety and legality of abortion is just one of many issues over which this war is being fought. David Broder, "Trivial Pursuits," editorial, *Washington Post,* 17 June 1990, p. D7.
23. This comment was made by photographer Jock Sturgis, taken from a transcript of "48 Hours," CBS News, 27 June 1990.
24. Ibid.
25. From an anonymous video store owner interviewed on "48 Hours," ibid.

CHAPTER 2: THE ANATOMY OF CULTURAL CONFLICT

1. John Dewey, in his book *A Common Faith* (New Haven, Conn.: Yale University Press, 1934), argued for the universality of humanism and yet he pitched his plea as a new religious faith. *The Humanist Manifesto I & II* do much the same (particularly in the first manifesto where humanism is defined as the highest expression of religious faith). But the most convincing evidence of this is the sectarian tone of any issue of *Free Inquiry* and of *The Humanist.*
2. This is the way Richard Neuhaus put it in "Religion and Public Life: The Continuing Conversation," *Christian Century* 107, 21 (11–18 July 1990): 672.
3. The best summary of the legitimating role of religion in public life remains Peter Berger's *The Sacred Canopy* (New York: Doubleday, 1967), esp. chapter 2.
4. Empirical evidence would suggest that this is a fairly rarefied discourse as well. Most public opinion surveys show a tremendous gap between elite opinion and the opinion of the general population.
5. Most of Gramsci's writings on the subject of intellectuals and cultural hegemony come from Q. Hoare and G. N. Smith, eds., *Selections from the Prison Notebooks of Antonio Gramsci* (New York: International Publishers, 1971). A useful and coherent summary of this work is found in L. Salamini, *The Sociology of Political Praxis* (London: Routledge and Kegan Paul, 1981). See also J. Femia, "Hegemony and Consciousness in the Thought of Antonio Gramsci," *Political Studies* 12, 1 (1975): 29–48; and T. Bates, "Gramsci and the Theory of Hegemony," *Journal of the History of Ideas* 36 (April–May 1975): 351–66).
6. Gramsci was a Marxist revisionist primarily concerned with explaining why the socialist revolution did not occur as anticipated and the conditions under which the urban proletariat would achieve class consciousness. Gramsci became the first Marxist thinker to adopt a nonreductionist approach to the superstructure and to develop a general theory of intellectuals and intellectual work in advanced capitalism. For Gramsci, the concept of the intellectual could not be defined by the behavior intrinsic to ideational activity. The reason is that there is a minimum of creative intellectual activity in all labor, however degraded it may be. "All men are intellectuals," he proclaimed, referring to the fact that everyone has particular tastes, has a particular aesthetic preference, and has a particular view of the world. Nevertheless, "not all men have in society the function of intellectuals." For Gramsci, then, intellectuals were functionaries of the superstructure. What is more, intellectuals in this sense do not themselves constitute a class but are simply "strata" produced *within each* social class. In other words, all social classes produce intellectuals who defend the interests of their class and assert its hegemonic interests. In the past, intellectuals of the dominant classes

have always been able to maintain their hegemony because the ideologies of the masses never had the capacity to become universal and integral conceptions of the world. Gramsci felt that Marxism was the most integral conception of the world aimed at raising the consciousness of the masses. Because it allowed for a new organic and dialectical relationship between intellectuals and the masses, he optimistically believed the grounds were laid for a new and effective challenge to the dominant powers. Gramsci's analysis of the role of intellectuals in modern societies would have emerged as a lasting contribution were it not for his unshakeable commitment to the idea and reality of the proletarian revolution. Thus modified, Gramsci provides powerful analytical tools for the study of contemporary cultural conflict.

7. For Gramsci this dynamic played itself out with interesting but not falsifying variation in the bourgeois revolutions in France, Italy, England, and Germany. See Salamini, *Sociology of Political Praxis*, pp. 109–13, for a summary of his review.
8. The most elaborate documentation of the ideals of American exceptionalism in the nineteenth century can be found in E. Tuveson, *Redeemer Nation* (Chicago: University of Chicago Press, 1968).
9. S. M. Lipset, "American Exceptionalism Reaffirmed," *Tocqueville Review* 10 (1990): 13 makes a similar point.
10. Ibid.
11. David Shenk, "Mobilizing the Campus Voice," *CV: The College Magazine* 1, 4 (1989): 50.
12. John F. Baker, "A War That Must Be Won," *Publisher's Weekly*, 1 June 1990, p. 8.
13. From an endorsement for the Alabama Family Alliance, by James Dobson, president of the national organization Focus on the Family.
14. This is particularly true among conservative activists because of their embattled position in the social structure. Quoted in Richard Viguerie, *The New Right: We're Ready to Lead* (Falls Church, Va.: Viguerie Company, 1980).

CHAPTER 3: THE CHANGING STRUCTURE OF AMERICAN PLURALISM

1. Perhaps the first history of religion in America was published by Robert Baird in 1844 (*Religion in America* [New York: Harper and Brothers]). In chapter 7 of book III, Baird himself makes this point: "Any doubts that the Constitution of the United States may suggest as to the Christian character of the National Government will be dissipated by a statement of facts." Here he lists dozens of ways in which the government reflects a Christian character despite its being formally separated from any establishment.
2. These figures come from T. Maynard, *The Story of American Catholicism* (New

York: Macmillan, 1942), p. 277; and G. Shaughnessy, *Has the Immigrant Kept the Faith?* (New York: Arno Press, 1969), chs. 8–10.

3. The estimates are a bit dodgy. In the *American Jewish Yearbook, 1899–1900* (Philadelphia: Jewish Publication Society of America, 1899) it was estimated that there were 6,000 Jews in 1826 and in 1840 there were 15,000. Comparable data for the later years mentioned can be found in the 1916 *Census of Religious Bodies* (Washington, D.C.:, Department of Commerce, 1916). Many of these figures are based on the number of family households.
4. Charles S. Liebman cites figures that put the Jewish immigration into the United States between 1881 and 1885 alone at 50,000. See his "Orthodoxy in American Jewish Life," in *Dimensions of Orthodox Judaism,* ed. R. P. Bulka (New York: KTAV Publishing, 1983), p. 39.
5. D. Ravitch, *The Great School Wars* (New York: Basic Books, 1973).
6. W. Herberg, *Protestant, Catholic, Jew* (New York: Harper and Row, 1955).
7. See T. Smith, "Immigrant Social Aspirations and American Education," *American Quarterly* 21 (Fall 1969): 523–43; T. Smith, "Religion and Ethnicity in America," *American Historical Review* 83 (December 1978): 1155–85; and R. Miller and T. Marzik, eds., *Immigrants and Religion in Urban America* (Philadelphia: Temple University Press, 1977).
8. Schechter quoted in Smith, "Religion and Ethnicity in America," p. 118.
9. Many scholars have commented on this metaphor. See, for example, E. L. Tuveson, *Redeemer Nation* (Chicago: University of Chicago Press, 1968). But the work of Timothy Smith is among the most careful and insightful on this point. See his "Religion and Ethnicity in America"; "Biblical Ideals in American Christian and Jewish Philanthropy" *American Jewish History* 74 (September 1984): 3–26; "New Approaches to the History of Immigration" *American Historical Review* 71 (July 1966): 1265–79; and "Immigrant Social Aspirations and American Education."
10. These figures are derived from G. Gallup, *Religion in America* (Princeton, N.J.: Princeton Religion Research Center, 1985).
11. Figures on the growth of Mormonism are derived from successive volumes of the *Yearbook of American and Canadian Churches* (Nashville: Abingdon Press, annual).
12. Numerous studies point to the patterns of upward mobility of Catholics. Andrew Greeley has gone even further by arguing that Catholics have become nearly comparable to Protestants in educational attainment and occupational prestige and have pulled ahead of Protestants in income. See A. M. Greeley, *Ethnicity, Denomination, and Inequality* (Beverly Hills, Calif.: Sage, 1976).
13. These data came from Richard Ostling, "Americans Facing Toward Mecca," *Time,* 23 May 1988, pp. 49–50. For comparative figures see Terry Muck, "The Mosque Next Door," *Christianity Today,* 19 February 1988, pp. 15–17; and the *Yearbook of American and Canadian Churches.*

14. Ibid.
15. Gallup, *Religion in America,* p. 34.
16. See R. Wuthnow, "Religious Movements and Counter-Movements," in *New Religious Movements and Rapid Social Change,* ed. J. A. Beckford (Paris: UNESCO, 1987).
17. The best summary statistics for this phenomenon are found in Wuthnow, "Religious Movements." On the impact of the new religious consciousness in San Francisco, Wuthnow's "Bay Area" surveys are tremendously revealing. See R. Wuthnow, *The Consciousness Reformation* (Los Angeles and Berkeley, University of California Press, 1976). On its impact in Boulder, see Fergus M. Bordewich, "Colorado's Thriving Cults," *New York Times Magazine,* 1 May 1988, pp. 37–43.
18. These figures are taken from Gallup, *Religion in America.* The most recent data are from J. D. Hunter, *The Williamsburg Charter Survey on Religion and American Public Life* (Washington, D.C.: Williamsburg Charter Foundation, 1988).
19. Robert Wuthnow's accumulation of evidence on the expansion of higher education is very convincing on this point. He shows, for example, that the proportion of college-age individuals attending and completing university training grew from 22.3 percent in 1960 to 35.2 percent in 1970. What is more, expenditures on higher education expanded from $2.2 billion in 1950 to $5.6 billion in 1960 to $23.4 billion in 1970. R. Wuthnow, *The Restructuring of American Religion* (Princeton, N.J.: Princeton University Press, 1988), p. 155.
20. G. P. Fogarty, *The Vatican and the American Hierarchy* (Stuttgart: Anton Hiersemann, 1982), p. 144.
21. This passage was quoted from J. A. Hardon, *American Judaism* (Chicago: Loyola University Press, 1971), p. 104.
22. I rely heavily upon the account given by Fogarty, *The Vatican and the American Hierarchy,* pp. 177–94. See also M. M. Reher, "Leo XIII and 'Americanism,' " *Theological Studies* 34 (1973): 679–89.
23. See G. P. Fogarty, "Dissent at Catholic University: The Case of Henry Poels," *America* (11 October 1986): 180–84.
24. See N. Glazer, *American Judaism* (Chicago: University of Chicago Press, 1957), p. 38.
25. A good brief summary of the Conservative movement can be found in B. Martin, "Conservative Judaism and Reconstructionism," in *Movements and Issues in American Judaism,* ed. B. Martin (Westport, Conn.: Greenwood Press, 1978), pp. 103–57. A more expanded history can be found in M. Sklare, *Conservative Judaism: An American Religious Movement* (New York: Schocken, 1972).
26. Later orthodox Catholic groups included the Catholic Traditionalist Movement (1964), Catholics United for the Faith (1968), Charismatic Renewal

Services (1971), and the Catholic League for Civil and Religious Rights (1973), and on the progressivist side were the higher echelons of the Catholic leadership (including the American Catholic Bishops) as well as Dignity, Catholics for ERA, and so on.

27. G. Lenski, *The Religious Factor* (Garden City: Anchor Doubleday, 1961).
28. R. Stark and C. Glock, *American Piety: The Nature of Religious Commitment* (Los Angeles and Berkeley: University of California Press, 1968).
29. The most comprehensive review of this evidence can be found in Wuthnow, *The Restructuring of American Religion,* chapter 5, "The Declining Significance of Denominationalism." What I review here are only samples from this literature.
30. Ibid., p. 92.
31. Indeed, negative feelings toward Episcopalians, Lutherans, Methodists, Presbyterians, and Baptists were almost nonexistent and negative opinions of the more sectarian denominations such as the Mormons and the Pentecostals were only slightly more visible (up to one-fifth of the population held such views). See ibid., pp. 91–92.
32. A Gallup Poll in 1955 showed, for example, that only one of every twenty-five adults (or 4 percent) no longer adhered to the faith of their childhood. Almost thirty years later, one of every three adults belonged to a faith other than the one in which they had been reared. Among Presbyterians, Methodists, and Episcopalians the ratios were even higher. Interestingly, these patterns even hold for Jews and Catholics: roughly one out of six had switched to another faith. These Gallup figures are reported in ibid., p. 88.
33. Ibid.
34. From the author's reanalysis of the 1987 General Social Survey. The question about abortion was the most sweeping, asking for approval or disapproval of abortion "under any circumstances." The Baptists were, as expected, significantly more conservative politically than the Unitarians, Episcopalians, and the United Church of Christ. But again, I would argue that this is a function of the theological and political demography of the membership of these denominations.
35. These figures are taken from Wuthnow, *The Restructuring of American Religion,* p. 84.
36. The dates given for the YMCA and the Salvation Army are the years that these organizations were established in the United States.
37. A more comprehensive list can be found in the *Catholic Almanac* (Huntington, Ind.: Our Sunday Visitor, Inc., 1987), pp. 564–71.
38. A more comprehensive list can be found in the *American Jewish Yearbook* (Philadelphia: American Jewish Committee, 1986), pp. 366 ff.
39. On how these organizations have become increasingly powerful, see A. Hertzke, *Representing God in Washington: The Role of Religious Lobbies in the American Polity,* Ph.D. diss., University of Wisconsin, 1986.

40. All of these figures are taken from Wuthnow, *The Restructuring of American Religion,* pp. 112–13.
41. Umbrella organizations are somewhat limited in number but are fairly well known. Among them are the National Council of Churches (1950) reconstituted from the earlier Federal Council of Churches (1908), the Consultation on Church Union (1962), the Interchurch Center (1948), the National Association of Evangelicals (1942), the American Council of Christian Churches (1941), the Independent Fundamentalist Churches of America (1930), the Independent Fundamentalist Bible Churches (1965), the National Association of Holiness Churches (1971). These also include the agencies working across religious faiths, such as the National Ecumenical Coalition (1976), the National Conference of Christians and Jews (1928), the International Jewish Committee on Interreligious Consultations, and the American Forum for Jewish-Christian Cooperation (1980). Years in parentheses indicate year of foundation, here and throughout the text and notes.
42. This category would include hundreds of professional associations as diverse as the Fellowship of Christian Firefighters, the Association of Orthodox Jewish Scientists, the Christian Association of Psychological Studies, the Catholic Association of Foresters, the National Association of Orthodox Jewish Teachers, the National Catholic Bandmasters' Association, the Christian Pharmacists' Fellowship, the Jewish Lawyers' Guild, Cowboys for Christ, and the like. It would also include "protectionist" societies, societies oriented toward safeguarding particular religious and moral beliefs. Among these would be the Catholic League for Religious and Civil Rights (1973), the Anti-Defamation League of B'nai B'rith (1913), Jews for Jews (1970), Project Yedid (1980), the Spiritual Counterfeits Project (1975), the Cult Awareness Network (1974) and the Voice of Liberty Association (1961). Beyond these it would include an enormous religious media industry: nearly 1,400 radio stations, more than 220 television stations, more than 500 religious newspapers and periodicals, and more than 2,000 religious titles per year. Finally it would include educational organizations: more than 500 Orthodox Jewish day schools, more than 16,000 Evangelical Christian elementary, junior and senior high schools, and just under 10,000 Catholic parochial schools, more than 100 Evangelical, 238 Catholic, and 30 Jewish colleges and universities.
43. Here again it is nearly impossible to catalogue the variety. To illustrate, by 1988 there were about 25 religiously oriented organizations dealing with the issue of abortion, at least 17 dealing with the relationship between church and state, about 6 focusing on pornography, well over 50 concerned with women's or men's rights, roughly 22 treating the issues surrounding homosexuality, about 10 focusing on the role of the media, approximately 36 dealing with the issues of war and peace, and more than 100 concerned with the promotion of general value systems. An analysis of these organi-

zations can be found in Hertzke, *Representing God in Washington: The Role of Religious Lobbies in the American Polity.*

44. A close reading of the *Encyclopedia of Associations* (Detroit: Gale Research Co., 1988) reveals that the average group in these metropolitan areas tends to have a staff of ten to twelve and a budget of several hundred thousand dollars per year. Some, however, have two to three times the staff and a budget of up to 10 million dollars. See also Edward Zuckerman, *Almanac of Federal PACs, 1986* (Washington, D.C.: Amward Publications, 1986), esp. chapter 4 on special interest groups PACs.
45. According to the *Encyclopedia of Associations* the Moral Majority (or Liberty Federation), founded in 1979, claimed a membership of 72,000 ministers and 4 million lay people in 1988. It has chapters in all fifty states. Christian Voice (founded 1978) claims to represent 41,000 ministers from forty-five denominations as well as sixty congressional members. And the Religious Roundtable (founded 1978) claims to have 100,000 members and 330 state or local groups.
46. From the *Encyclopedia of Associations,* listing no. 15261.
47. Ibid., listing 13975.
48. Ibid., listing 16925.
49. Lutherans Concerned (1974) has 1,000 members and 20 local groups; Presbyterians for Lesbian/Gay Concerns (1974) has 500 members and 30 local or regional groups; Friends for Lesbian and Gay Concerns (1973—Quaker) has 500 members and 10 local groups; United Church Coalition for Lesbian/Gay Concerns (1973—United Church of Christ) has 400 members; Unitarian Universalist Lesbian/Gay Caucus (1971) has 1,000 members and 20 local groups; and the "denomination" for homosexuals and lesbians, the Universal Fellowship of Metropolitan Community Churches (1970) claims 27,000 members and nearly 300 local or regional groups.
50. Women's rights organizations include the Episcopal Women's Caucus (1971), the United Methodist Churches' General Commission on the Status and Role of Women (1972), Council on Women and the Church (1973) and United Presbyterian Women (1959) of the Presbyterian Church, U.S.A, the Unitarian Universalist Women's Federation (1963), and the United Church of Christ Coordination Center for Women in Church and Society (1980).
51. Peace groups include the Methodist Peace Fellowship (1950), the Lutheran Peace Fellowship (1941), Disciples Peace Fellowship (1935), Episcopal Peace Fellowship (1939), Presbyterian Peace Fellowship (1983) and the Quaker/Mennonite organization, New Call to Peacemaking (1975).
52. One measure of the hostility between the orthodox and the progressivists within a denomination is represented by the fact that in 1988, the Presbyterian Church, U.S.A. (PCUSA) broke off communion with the Evangelical Presbyterian Church (EPC) because of accusations that the EPC was engaged

in activities intended to promote defection from the PCUSA. This was reported in *Christianity Today* 32 (12 August 1988): 64–65.

53. These figures were reported in "Presbyterian Gadfly Expands Its Influence," *Christianity Today* 32 (18 February 1988): 42.
54. Theodore Jennings, Jr., "The 'Houston Declaration' is Heretical," *Christian Century* 105 (20 April 1988): 399–401.
55. The Fellowship of Concerned Churchmen (1973) and the Foundation for Anglican Traditions both serve on behalf of maintaining traditional Anglican Christianity. Both oppose the ordination of women priests and the use of the new prayer book. In *Christian Century* 106 (June 21–28, 1989): 615–616, it was reported that in Fort Worth, Texas, in that month, 600 lay and clergy delegates of the Evangelical Catholic Mission voted to establish the "Episcopal Synod of America." This represented efforts to establish a "church within a church" on the part of traditionalists who wanted to stay in the Episcopal Church while providing them with an ecclesiastical framework for maintaining their opposition to the church's ordination of women and the erosion of episcopal and biblical authority within the denomination. Also within the Episcopal Church is the 11,000 member Episcopalians United, and the National Organization of Episcopalians for Life, a pro-life lobby.
56. Certainly the split that occurred in the Lutheran Church–Missouri Synod in 1976 when a "conservative" faction captured control of the denomination and forced several "liberal" seminary professors to resign, is indicative of these fissures. The formation of the Evangelical Lutheran Church in America only institutionalized this division further. There is also a pro-life group, Lutherans for Life.
57. Details of this major denominational dispute can be found in Nancy Tatom Ammerman's *Baptist Battles* (New Brunswick, N.J.: Rutgers University Press, 1990).
58. Michael Cuneo, in "Soldiers of Orthodoxy: Revivalist Catholicism and the Battle for the North American Church," unpublished paper, 1988, Department of Religion, Dalhousie University, provides an overview of these organizational developments in North American Catholicism. His analysis extends to Canada as well as the United States. Another look into the orthodox Catholic response can be found in M. T. Iglesias's brief study of Catholics United for the Faith (CUF): "CUF and Dissent," *America* 156 (11 April 1987): 303–7.
59. Although the periodicals *Challenge* and *Interim* are based in Winnepeg, Manitoba, and in Toronto, Ontario, respectively, they are read by American traditionalists as well.
60. Heilman provides data to show that the Orthodox Jewish community is not monolithic. Modern Orthodoxy would find itself on the progressivist side of many issues. It is the traditionally Orthodox that are most aligned with

political and moral conservatism. Some in the Conservative Jewish camp would also align themselves in this way. See S. Heilman, "Orthodox Jews: An Open or Closed Group?" in *Uncivil Religion,* ed. R. N. Bellah and F. E. Greenspahn (New York: Crossroad, 1987), p. 130.

61. See Allen Roth, "Orthodox Jews Becoming a Major Force for Conservatism," *New York Tribune,* 24 October 1984. The picture accompanying this story shows a sizable crowd of Hasidic Jews in the balcony of City Hall chambers protesting the reintroduction of the Gay Rights Bill in the City Council.
62. See "First for Orthodoxy: Washington Bureau for Government Affairs to Open," in *Coalition Tammuz* (June 1988).
63. It is important to recall, however, that public culture is largely constituted by the activities and pronouncements of elites. The key players, then, are not so much the "rank and file" or the ordinary passive supporters of a cause, but the activists or leadership. It is the ideological constructions of elites that are most consequential and, importantly, it is here where the ideological affinities are most clearly crystallized.
64. The survey part of the Religion and Power Project funded by the Lilly Endowment was conducted under the direction of the author by the Opinion Research Corporation of Princeton, N.J. A sample of roughly 1,300 religious leaders was drawn from the 1985 edition of *Who's Who in Religion.* After deaths and nonforwarded mail were discounted, a total number of 791 individuals responded, represented a 61 percent response rate. Protestantism, Catholicism, and Judaism were dichotomized into *theologically* liberal and conservative camps in line with the present argument. The divisions took the following form: conservative Protestants were operationalized as those who identified themselves as either an Evangelical or a Fundamentalist; liberal Protestants comprised the remainder. Conservative Catholics were defined as those who identified their theological inclinations on the conservative side (4, 5, 6, and 7) of a seven-point liberal–conservative continuum while liberal Catholics identified their theology on the liberal side of the continuum (values 1, 2, and 3). The Orthodox Jews identified themselves as such in the survey just as Conservative and Reform Jews identified themselves this way.
65. The question for this series of behaviors reads as follows: "Please indicate how you personally feel about each of the following. Do you believe each is morally wrong, morally acceptable, or not a moral issue?" On premarital sexuality, the actual figures were as follows: Protestants: orthodox—97 percent, progressive—59 percent; Catholics: orthodox—97 percent, progressive—82 percent; Jews: orthodox—72 percent, progressive—31 percent. Chi square, significant at .000 level. On premarital cohabitation: Protestants: orthodox—95 percent, progressive—58 percent; Catholics: orthodox—93 percent, progressive—82 percent; Jews: orthodox—74 percent, progressive—33 percent. Chi square, significant at .000 level.

66. The pattern on pornography holds for Catholics but not as dramatically as it does for Jews and Protestants. Catholics were a bit more uniform in their opinion here. The actual figures were as follows: Protestants: orthodox—95 percent, progressive—47 percent; Catholics: orthodox—87 percent, progressive—75 percent; Jews: orthodox—64 percent, progressive—15 percent. Chi square, significant at .000 level.
67. On this question the actual figures were as follows: Protestants: orthodox—68 percent, progressive—23 percent; Catholics: orthodox—57 percent, progressive—32 percent; Jews: orthodox—45 percent, progressive—8 percent. Chi square, significant at .000 level.
68. The pattern of response was similar when asked about authority in the home—the theologically orthodox of each faith were more apt to agree that "the husband should have the 'final say' in the family's decision making." The actual figures were as follows: Protestants: orthodox—53 percent, progressive—10 percent; Catholics: orthodox—27 percent, progressive—8 percent; Jews: orthodox—13 percent, progressive—4 percent. Chi square, significant at .000 level. One of the more important tests of this authority concerns the decision to bear children. Is it "all right for a woman to refuse to have children, even against the desires of her husband to have children?" The majority of progressive leaders in Protestantism and Judaism agreed that it was all right compared to minorities in the orthodox side of these faiths. The figures for agreement with this item were as follows: Protestants: orthodox—49 percent, progressive—70 percent; Catholics: orthodox—8 percent, progressive—27 percent; Jews: orthodox—23 percent, progressive—63 percent. Chi square, significant at .000 level. Progressive Catholic leaders (18 percent) were more likely to agree with this statement than orthodox Catholic leaders (11 percent) and yet the majority of both camps disagreed with the statement. Few in either the orthodox or progressive camps in Protestantism, Catholicism, and Judaism maintained an unqualified traditionalism in family affairs. For example, only a very small number held that a married woman should not work if she has a husband who could support her, and just as few in either camp would agree that "women should take care of running their home and leave the running of the country up to men." (The first statement read: "It is all right for a married woman to earn money in business or industry, even if she has a husband capable of supporting her?" Among all groups the number disagreeing with this statement was under 5 percent. The same is true with the second statement with the exception of conservative Protestant leaders, 18 percent of whom agreed that women should take care of running their home and leave the running of the country up to men.) Yet they disagreed sharply when responding to the question of priorities. More than eight out of ten of the orthodox leaders in these faiths agreed that "a woman should put her husband and children ahead of her career" compared to only four out of ten of the progressive

Protestant and Jewish leaders and six out of ten of the liberal Catholic leaders. (The actual figures were as follows: Protestants: orthodox—86 percent, progressive—40 percent; Catholics: orthodox—83 percent, progressive—63 percent; Jews: orthodox—80 percent, progressive—46 percent. Chi square, significant at .000 level.) This general disposition extended to attitudes about the mother's relationship with her children. Leaders on the progressive side of the theological continuum in all faiths were more inclined than their theologically conservative counterparts to agree that "a working mother can establish just as warm and secure a relationship with her children as a mother who does not work." Accordingly, they were disproportionately more likely (twice as likely among Protestants) to disagree that "a preschool child is likely to suffer if his or her mother works." (For the first question about mother-child relationships, the figures were Protestants: orthodox—57 percent, progressive—81 percent; Catholics: orthodox—65 percent, progressive—77; Jews: orthodox—56 percent, progressive—82 percent. Chi square, significant at the .000 level. For the second question, the figures (for those disagreeing) were Protestants: orthodox—32 percent, progressive—65 percent; Catholics: orthodox—41 percent, progressive—48 percent; Jews: orthodox—46 percent, progressive—76 percent. Chi square, significant at the .000 level.)

69. Roughly eight out of ten of the progressives in Protestantism (80 percent), Catholicism (78 percent), and Judaism (88 percent) favored the passage of the ERA compared to much smaller numbers on the orthodox side (Protestants—31 percent; Catholics—42 percent; Jews—54 percent). On abortion, progressives of all three faiths were significantly less likely to condemn abortion as morally wrong, particularly within Protestantism and Judaism. (The actual figures were as follows: Protestants: orthodox—93 percent, progressive—41 percent; Catholics: orthodox—100 percent, progressive—93 percent; Jews: orthodox—40 percent, progressive—8 percent. Chi square, significant at .000 level.) So too the orthodox and progressive wings of these faiths were deeply split over the issue of homosexuality and lesbianism—the former were between two and three times more likely to denounce the practice of homosexuality and lesbianism as morally wrong than the latter. Nine of ten Evangelicals, and eight of every ten Catholic and Jewish leaders condemned homosexuality as morally wrong compared to fewer than five of every ten mainline Protestant and liberal Catholic leaders and fewer than three of every ten of the liberal Jewish leaders. The actual figures on the question on homosexuality read as follows: Protestants: orthodox—96 percent, progressive—45 percent; Catholics: orthodox—81 percent, progressive—49 percent; Jews: orthodox—80 percent, progressive—25 percent. Chi square, significant at .000 level. The responses to the question on lesbianism were, within a percentage point, identical.

70. Once again, for reasons relating to the political and ethnic history of the

Jewish community in America (such as their longstanding political liberalism), the pattern is generally less distinct among Jewish elites than among Protestant or Catholic elites, but the divisions there are still quite remarkable. (On political party preference, the percent of those who identified themselves as Democrats were Protestants: orthodox—25 percent, progressive—53 percent; Catholics: orthodox—46 percent, progressive—77 percent; Jews: orthodox—38 percent, progressive—57 percent. Chi square, significant at .000 level.

71. Those describing themselves as somewhat liberal, very liberal, or far left were as follows: Protestants: orthodox—11 percent, progressive—60 percent; Catholics: orthodox—12 percent, progressive—77 percent; Jews: orthodox—36 percent, progressive—67 percent. Chi square, significant at .000 level.

72. There was basic agreement among all parties on the basic functions of the welfare state—that "the government has the responsibility to meet the basic needs of its citizens, even in the case of sickness, poverty, unemployment and old age," and that "the government should have a high commitment to curbing the economic and environmental abuses of big business." At least eight out of ten of all religious leaders regardless of theological orientation, agreed with these statements. (The only exception was the opinion of Evangelical leaders on the issues of governmental responsibility, 54 percent agreed.) While there is basic agreement all the way around, there still are differences in the intensity with which the various factions agree. Catholic and Protestant leaders on the progressive side were significantly more likely to "strongly agree" with these statements. There was also a certain agreement that "the government should work to substantially reduce the income gap between the rich and the poor." The difference between liberal (76 percent) and conservative (43 percent) Protestants is thirty-three percentage points and between liberal (78 percent) and conservative (59 percent) Jews, it is nineteen percentage points. Among Catholics, however, the difference is only two percentage points (92 percent to 90 percent). Beyond this, the agreement came to an end. As one might predict, the more progressively oriented leaders in Catholicism and Protestantism were up to twice as likely as the orthodox to agree that "big business in America is generally unfair to working people." Though not as striking the same general pattern held for Jews as well (The actual figures were as follows: Protestants: orthodox—27 percent, progressive—48 percent; Catholics: orthodox—39 percent, progressive—69 percent; Jews: orthodox—36 percent, progressive—42 percent. Chi square, significant at .000 level.) Similarly, progressives in each tradition were up to twice as inclined as their theologically orthodox counterparts to disagree with the statement, "economic growth is a better way to improve the lot of the poor than the redistribution of existing wealth." (The actual figures of those disagreeing with that statement were Protestants:

orthodox—14 percent, progressive—44 percent; Catholics: orthodox—23 percent, progressive—50 percent; Jews: orthodox—24 percent, progressive—33 percent. Chi square, significant at .000 level.) A similar statement was made about the application of this principle to the Third World: "Capitalist development is more likely than socialist development to improve the material standard of living of people in the contemporary Third World." The ideological gap between the orthodox and progressive ranged between twenty-four percentage points (Catholic) and thirty-four percentage points (Protestant), with Jews in between, at twenty-eight points of difference. When finally presented with the statement "The U.S. would be better off if it moved toward socialism," less than half of all the religiocultural factions agreed, yet the pattern once again held true to form: progressives of all traditions were up to three or four times more likely to agree than their orthodox rivals. (The figures of those agreeing with that statement about socialism were Protestants: orthodox—7 percent, progressive—33 percent; Catholics: orthodox—13 percent, progressive—46 percent; Jews: orthodox—8 percent, progressive—25 percent. Chi square, significant at .000 level.)

73. For example, when asked whether they thought "U.S.-based multinational corporations help or hurt poor countries in the Third World," the orthodox were substantially more prone to believe that they helped—at a ratio of 2 to 1 in Protestantism and 3 to 1 in Catholicism. (The percentages of those responding "helped" were Protestants: orthodox—76 percent, progressive—38 percent; Catholics: orthodox—53 percent, progressive—16 percent; Jews: orthodox—76 percent, progressive—53 percent. Chi square, significant at .000 level.) On the political rather than economic side of this concern the pattern again holds true. When asked whether they favored or opposed the U.S. policy of "selling arms and giving military aid to countries which are against the Soviet Union," the orthodox of these three faiths were more inclined to favor it by dramatic margins. The differences between the orthodox and progressive in Protestantism were, respectively, 73 percent and 35 percent; within Catholicism, 52 percent and 22 percent; and within Judaism, 92 percent and 61 percent. The chi square was significant at the .000 level. This was also the case when these leaders were asked about the anti-Sandinista contras of Nicaragua. Only in the case of Evangelicals did a decisive majority actually favor the policy of supporting the contras, yet the ratio of those favoring to opposing the policy (according to theological disposition) within the other traditions was equally strong. (Those favoring the policy were as follows: Protestants: orthodox—62 percent, progressive—14 percent; Catholics: orthodox—39 percent, progressive—5 percent; Jews: orthodox—45 percent, progressive—18 percent. Chi square, significant at .000 level.) So too, when asked about the relative "importance of Central

American countries (such as El Salvador and Nicaragua) to the defense interests of the United States," nearly two to one of the orthodox in all traditions were more likely to respond with "very or fairly important."

The now predictable configurations were generally borne out on numerous other issues. The favorable responses for economic sanctions against South Africa for its policies of apartheid were as follows: Protestants: orthodox—52 percent, progressive—87 percent; Catholics: orthodox—83 percent, progressive—90 percent; Jews: orthodox—47 percent, progressive—78 percent. Chi square, significant at .000 level.) The creation of a Palestinian homeland in Israel brought favorable responses as follows: Protestants: orthodox—42 percent, progressive—82 percent; Catholics: orthodox—87 percent, progressive—85 percent; Jews: orthodox—3 percent, progressive—20 percent. Chi square, significant at .000 level.) Europe's neutrality in the East–West conflict: (The responses favorable toward the idea of Europe's neutrality were Protestants: orthodox—26 percent, progressive—47 percent; Catholics: orthodox—20 percent, progressive—46 percent; Jews: orthodox—18 percent, progressive—27 percent. Religious leaders were also asked whether they favored or opposed keeping U.S. troops in Europe as part of the NATO commitment. The differences were not so dramatic but they were in line with predictions: Protestants: orthodox—95 percent, progressive—80 percent; Catholics: orthodox—84 percent, progressive—70 percent; Jews: orthodox—95 percent, progressive—88 percent. Chi square, significant at .000 level.) The policy of a "freeze" in the construction and deployment of nuclear weapons was another issue. When asked about a nuclear freeze for both the United States and the Soviet Union, the differences flattened out considerably. When asked whether they favored the implementation of the policy by the United States even if the Soviet Union did not pursue it, striking divisions between the orthodox and progressive camps reemerged (The actual figures of those favoring a freeze for both super powers were Protestants: orthodox—78 percent, progressive—95 percent; Catholics: orthodox—95 percent, progressive—98 percent; Jews: orthodox—92 percent, progressive—90 percent. Favoring the policy for the United States alone [regardless of what the Soviet Union does] the split resurfaced. Those in favor were Protestants: orthodox—16 percent, progressive—52 percent; Catholics: orthodox—35 percent, progressive—70 percent; Jews: orthodox—10 percent, progressive—29 percent. Chi square, significant at .000 level.) (The question for this and the other issues reviewed in this last section asked if the respondent favored or opposed the policy.)

74. The attempt to dichotomize these religious leaders according to either an orthodox or progressive theological inclination is admittedly forced. Dichotomies may be more prone to develop in organizations but among individuals

the distinction would seem artificial and perhaps unfair. Among individuals intuition would suggest a continuum with orthodoxy and progressivism being the two extreme poles. Undoubtedly this is true. Even so, at least today there appears to be an increasing polarization among denominational and para-denominational organizations. What is more, there may be a tendency for the leadership to align themselves dichotomously as well. Would the differences between orthodox and progressive camps in each religious tradition have been as prominent if this were not the case? Though a dichotomy may not adequately reflect reality, as an analytical exercise it has still proven to be extremely instructive. The evidence pointing to a restructuring of ideological affinities within America's religious leadership would seem overwhelming.

75. A reanalysis of the 1982 Roper Survey of Theologians (Protestant and Catholic) showed that when analyzing the variation of opinion on such issues as the spending priorities of the government, the evaluation of business practices, defense policy, moral behaviors (from homosexuality to abortion), and nuclear policy, belief orthodoxy on average accounted for 45 percent of the variation across tradition and an average of 33 percent of the variation within traditions. See J. D. Hunter, J. Tucker, and S. Finkel, "Religious Elites and Political Values," unpublished paper, University of Virginia, 1989.

76. P. L. Berger, "A Market Model for the Analysis of Ecumenicity," *Sociology and Social Research* 30 (Spring 1963): 77–93; S. Cavert, *The American Churches and the Ecumenical Movement 1900–1968,* (New York: Associated Press, 1968); and T. Parsons, "Religion in Postindustrial America: The Problem of Secularization," *Social Research* 41 (1974): 193–225.

77. In addition to information provided by the Catholic League, I was greatly assisted by a scholarly treatment of the League by J. Varacalli, "To Empower Catholics: The Catholic League for Religious and Civil Rights as a Mediating Structure," *Nassau Review* 5, 4 (1988): 45–61.

78. *Hard Questions for the Catholic League* (Milwaukee, Wisc.: Catholic League for Religious and Civil Rights, 1982, p. 2.

79. This survey was conducted by the author during the first two weeks of October 1986. The organizations included were drawn from the *Encyclopedia of Associations:* The Catholic League for Religious and Civil Rights, Liberty Federation, the Roundtable, Morality in Media, Eagle Forum, Prison Fellowship, the National Right to Life Committee, the American Catholic Conference, the American Catholic Committee, the American Coalition for Traditional Values, Christian Voice, the American Society for the Defense of Tradition, Family, and Property, Coalitions for America, Christian Citizen's Crusade, Conservative Caucus, the Foundation for Religious Action in the Social and Civil Order, the Jewish Right, the National Pro-Family Coalition, the National Traditionalist Caucus, the Order of the Cross Society,

Parents' Alliance to Protect Our Children, the Ethics and Public Policy Center, the Institute for Religion and Democracy, Religious Heritage of America, Rock is Stoning Kids, Students for America, United Parents Under God, American Life Lobby, Christian Action Council, Human Life International, Association for Public Justice, Voice of Liberty Association, Methodists for Life, Catholics United for Life, Human Life Center, Pro-Family Forum, Center on Religion and Society, American Pro-Life Council, the National Federation for Decency, Americans for Life, Concerned Women for America, Fund for an American Renaissance, We the People, the Ad hoc Committee for the Defense of Life, the National League of Catholic Laymen, the American Council for Coordinated Action, and the Black Silent Majority. In all but a few cases, I undertook a telephone interview with a representative of these organizations. In some instances, though, enough information was provided in the description of the organization in the *Encyclopedia of Associations*.

80. The American Family Association is located in Tupelo, Mississippi, and Donald Wildmon is its executive director.
81. See the organization's listing in the *Encyclopedia of Associations*. Much in keeping with this effort, yet organizationally separate, is a journal founded in 1987 entitled *Touchstone: A Journal of Ecumenical Orthodoxy*.
82. Consult the *Encyclopedia of Associations* for the relevant data on staff, budget, membership, and other measures of communicative power.
83. Annette Daum, "Turning Point," *Interreligious Currents* (A Publication of the Department of Interreligious Affairs, Union of American Hebrew Congregations) 1, 2 (Spring 1983): 1.
84. Telephone interview with an unidentified staff member of the Washington Interreligious Services Council, 13 October 1988.
85. Tim LaHaye, *The Race for the 21st Century* (Nashville, Tenn.: Thomas Nelson, 1986) p. 109.
86. Franky Schaeffer, *Bad News for Modern Man* (Westchester, Ill.: Crossway Books, 1984). Emphasis is in the original.
87. At the very least, conservative Catholics and Jews are reconsidering their traditional posture toward Evangelicals—asking hypothetically, as one featured article in *The Jewish News* (Phil Jacobs, "Have We Been Misreading Jerry Falwell?" March 21, 1986, p. 16) did. The general conclusion was "Yes, the Jewish community has overreacted and Falwell may be a genuine ally of the Jews."
88. Telephone interview with Rabbi Kanett, director of the Washington, D.C. office of Agudath Israel, 13 October, 1988.
89. Telephone interview with John Pantuso of the Catholic League, 13 October 1988.
90. Haberman quoted in *The Religion and Society Report* 5, 7 (July 1988): 5.

CHAPTER 4: COMPETING MORAL VISIONS

1. One might just as well use the term "public theology" in this context. In the late 1960s, sociologist Robert Bellah coined the term "civil religion" to describe these general, quasi-religious visions of public life. For Bellah and for those who employed the term in the years to follow, however, civil religion meant something very specific. It was "the religion of the republic," a vague but complex public myth whose symbolism was rooted explicitly in the biblical tradition—derivative of all biblical faiths but embodying none in particular—that served to legitimate national life. Few have come to doubt its existence but many have debated whether it is a positive or a negative cultural force. For its proponents, this "civil religion" was a social glue that helped to bind the country together. For its critics, it was a tool cynically used in the rhetoric of politicians, a hollow ritual exhibited during times of national celebration and grieving, and an idolatrous form of religious nationalism that Fundamentalists were particularly prone to espouse. What all of those who have used the term at least implicitly maintain is that nations (and America in particular) have just one civil religion. In truth, however, every religiocultural tradition can and usually does construct its own mechanisms for legitimating national life. My preference is to call these "public theologies." A complimentary view is offered by R. Wuthnow, "Divided We Fall: America's Two Civil Religions," *Christian Century* 105 (20 April 1988): 395–99.
2. Rus Walton, *One Nation Under God* (Old Tappan, N.J.: Fleming H. Revell, 1975), p. 24.
3. Peter Marshall and David Manuel, *The Light and the Glory* (Old Tappan, N.J.: Fleming H. Revell, 1977). Taken from the dust-jacket and developed throughout all 384 pages of the book.
4. George Otis, *The Solution to Crisis-America* (Old Tappan, N.J.: Fleming H. Revell, 1972), p. 53.
5. From the Constitution and By-Laws of the Christian Citizens Crusade, Inc.—Article IV, number 4.
6. John W. Whitehead, *The Separation Illusion* (Milford, Mich.: Mott Media, 1977), p. 13.
7. Tim LaHaye, *The Battle for the Mind* (Old Tappan, N.J.: Fleming H. Revell, 1980), p. 37.
8. Ed McAteer, "Is There Not A Cause," a brochure published by the Religious Roundtable.
9. LaHaye, *The Battle for the Mind,* p. 39.
10. Whitehead, *The Separation Illusion,* pp. 23, 18.
11. John Eidsmoe, "Creation, Evolution and Constitutional Interpretation," *Concerned Women for America* 9, 9 (September 1987): 7.

12. See C. Taylor, "Religion in a Free Society," in *Articles of Faith, Articles of Peace: The First Amendment Religion Clauses and the American Public Philosophy*, ed. J. D. Hunter and O. Guinness (Washington, D.C.: Brookings Institution, 1990), pp. 93–113.
13. Michael Novak, *The Spirit of Democratic Capitalism* (New York: Simon and Schuster, 1982). In 1945, Reverend Carl MacIntyre wrote that "the Bible teaches private enterprise and the capitalistic system, not as a by-product or as some side line, but as the very foundation structure of society in which men are to live and render an account of themselves to God . . . in the maintenance of the system of private enterprise [is] the very life and liberty of the church itself." Carl MacIntyre, *The Rise of the Tyrant* (Collingswood, N.J.: Christian Beacon Press, 1945), pp. xiii, xv.
14. Jerry Falwell, *Wisdom for Living* (Wheaton, Ill.: Victor, 1982), pp. 102, 131. Likewise, the Christian Citizens' Crusade holds that "the American system of private enterprise [was established] in accordance with the clear teachings of Scripture." Without it, "our form of government, our way of life . . . could not exist." From the Constitution and By-Laws of the Christian Citizens Crusade, Inc.—Article IV, number 5.
15. Jerry Falwell, *Listen America!* (New York: Doubleday, 1980), p. 13.
16. Pat Robertson, *The Secret Kingdom: A Promise of Hope and Freedom in a World of Turmoil* (Nashville, Tenn.: Thomas Nelson, 1982), pp. 151–52.
17. This was reported by Russell Chandler, "God as Capitalist: Seminar Promotes Religion and Riches," *Los Angeles Times*, 1 June 1981, p. 3.
18. Ronald Nash makes precisely this argument in "The Christian Choice Between Capitalism and Socialism" in *Liberation Theology*, ed. Ronald Nash (Grand Rapids, Mich.: Baker Books, 1987).
19. This argument is made in great detail in R. J. Rushdoony, *The Politics of Guilt and Pity* (Fairfax, Va.: Thoburn Press, 1978), chapter 8, "Liberty and Property."
20. Reported by Chandler, "God as Capitalist: Seminar Promotes Religion and Riches."
21. Gilder is quoted in an interview from *Christianity Today* in Wuthnow, "Divided We Fall: America's Two Civil Religions."
22. Rushdoony, *Politics of Guilt and Pity*, p. 130. Chapter 5, "The Meaning of Justice," is very eloquent on this point.
23. From the pamphlet "Christian Voice: Preserving a Free Society," Christian Voice, brochure.
24. LaHaye, *The Battle for the Mind*, p. 37.
25. Students for America statement of principle, from a brochure.
26. Pat Robertson, *America's Dates with Destiny* (Nashville, Tenn.: Thomas Nelson, 1986), p. 297.
27. Reported in *Broadcasting Washington, D.C.*, 10 February 1986.
28. Falwell, *Listen America*, p. 17.

29. Mary Peek, "What Every Teacher Should Know about the New Right" (Washington, D.C.: National Education Association Task Force on Academic Freedom, n.d.), p. 7.
30. See the insightful essay by G. Wills, "The Secularist Prejudice," *Christian Century* 107 (24 October 1990): 969–70.
31. Paul D. Simmons, "A Theological Response to Fundamentalism on the Abortion Issue" (Washington, D.C.: Religious Coalition for Abortion Rights Education Fund, n.d.).
32. See Taylor, "Religion in a Free Society," pp. 93–113.
33. This remark was made by bell hooks, quoted in *Common Ground—Different Planes: The Women of Color Partnership Program Newsletter* (April 1988).
34. Norman Lear, "The Search for Stable Values," in *Values, Pluralism and Public Education* (Washington, D.C.: People for the American Way, 1987), p. 42.
35. Brochure, People for the American Way, Washington, D.C.
36. "RCAR Has No Pictures in This Brochure," Religious Coalition for Abortion Rights, brochure.
37. Aaron Anderson and David Anderson, "A Minimum Wage for a Minimum Justice," *Christianity and Crisis* 48 (6 June 1988): 195–96. In a direct mail advertisement, the journal claimed: "Justice for the oppressed, and hope for the suffering. It's a simple message at the core of the Christian faith."
38. From a newsletter published by the Religious Network for Equality for Women, sent to the author in June 1988.
39. Membership brochure published by Clergy and Laity Concerned.
40. Brochure announcing Peace with Justice Week, 1988.
41. "What Does the Lord Require of You?" National Impact, brochure.
42. This survey was introduced in the last chapter in note 64.
43. The question read, "Do you think the United States has a special role to play in the world today or is it pretty much like other countries?" Nine out of ten of the religious leaders in all categories (with the exception of the liberal Protestants for whom eight out of ten) chose the former.
44. The question read, "Do you think the United States should aspire to remain a world power or should it aspire to become a neutral country like Switzerland or Sweden?" Between 86 and 100 percent of all religious elites chose the former.
45. The actual figures of those saying "not very much" or "none at all" were as follows: Protestants: orthodox—21 percent, progressive—50 percent; Catholics: orthodox—25 percent, progressive—60 percent; Jews: orthodox—21 percent, progressive—45 percent. Chi square, significant at .000 level.
46. The majority of liberal Jews (71 percent) also agreed that the United States was "a force for good" but the gap between progressive and orthodox was still twenty-one percentage points.
47. The question read, "As a nation, do you think we treat people in the Third

World fairly or unfairly?" The actual figures of those saying that America treats the Third World "unfairly" were as follows: Protestants: orthodox—27 percent, progressive—71 percent; Catholics: orthodox—50 percent, progressive—87 percent; Jews: orthodox—19 percent, progressive—39 percent. Chi square, significant at .000 level.

48. The question read, "How would you characterize the competition between the U.S. and the Soviet Union? Is it fundamentally a struggle in power politics or is it fundamentally a moral struggle?" The actual figures of those saying that it was a moral struggle, were as follows: Protestants: orthodox—43 percent, progressive—14 percent; Catholics: orthodox—39 percent, progressive—14 percent; Jews: orthodox—46 percent, progressive—21 percent. Chi square significant at .000 level.
49. This is the 1988 Roper Study of Theologians. Catholics were included in this survey but not easily divisible into orthodox and progressive camps. For this reason, the results for Evangelical and liberal Protestants are reported.
50. R. Wuthnow conceptualizes the debate in this way in his book *The Restructuring of American Religion* (Princeton, N.J.: Princeton University Press, 1988).
51. References to these "communities of faith" can be found in virtually all of the literature produced by these coalitions.
52. For an elaboration of these points, see R. Merleman, *Making Something of Ourselves: On Culture and Politics in the United States* (Los Angeles and Berkeley: University of California Press, 1984), p. 30. See also the essay by R. N. Bellah, "Competing Visions of the Role of Religion in American Society," in *Uncivil Religion,* ed. R. N. Bellah and F. E. Greenspahn (New York: Crossroad, 1987), p. 221.
53. Within orthodox Protestantism, see J. D. Hunter, *American Evangelicalism: Conservative Religion and the Quandary of Modernity* (New Brunswick, N.J.: Rutgers University Press, 1983). Within Orthodox Judaism, see S. Heilman, "The Many Faces of Orthodoxy," *Modern Judaism* 2, 1 (1982): 23–51; and S. Heilman, "The Many Faces of Orthodoxy, Part II," *Modern Judaism* 2, 2 (1982): 171–98.
54. Almost any issue of *Free Inquiry* and *The Humanist* reflects a particularly venomous opinion of orthodoxy, particularly of Evangelical Christianity. As for the general secularist public, J. D. Hunter, *The Williamsburg Charter Survey on Religion and American Public Life* (Washington, D.C.: Williamsburg Charter Foundation, 1988), demonstrates the greatest popular hostility toward orthodoxy of all Americans who reside in this sector of the population.
55. See J. J. C. Smart, *Our Place in the Universe* (Oxford, Blackwell, 1989), for a cogent statement and summary of this view.
56. Rosemary Radford Ruether in an essay in *Homosexuality in the Priesthood and the Religious Life,* ed. Jeannine Gramick (New York: Crossroad, 1989) quoted in "Homosexuality and the Churches," by Richard John Neuhaus, *First Things* 1 (May 1990): 68.

57. As stated in a booklet published by People for the American Way, "Cohabitation is just one of the ways that people are adapting to the changes, the stresses and complexities of modern life. It will neither replace marriage nor occur in every person's path through life. However, those who do choose it should be free to do so without government-inspired fear, guilt or discrimination against them." Bob Frishman, *American Families: Responding to the Pro-Family Movement* (Washington, D.C.: People for the American Way, 1984), p. 32.
58. See the discussion of Merleman's concept of "tight-boundedness" in Bellah, "Competing Visions of the Role of Religion."
59. Perhaps the best discussion of the concept of isomorphism is made by George Thomas in his book *Revivalism and Cultural Change* (Chicago: University of Chicago Press, 1989).
60. Falwell, *Listen America,* p. 167.
61. From a brochure, "Please Don't Pretend," published by the Christian Action Council, Washington, D.C.
62. This comes from a Religious Coalition for Abortion Rights brochure titled, "A Theological Response to Fundamentalism on the Abortion Issue," p. 9. The brochure contends, "No one would deny the continuum of human development from fertilization to maturity and adulthood. That does not lead to the assumption, however, that every stage in the continuum merits the same value as 'life' or constitutes the same human entity."
63. Ibid., p. 11.
64. These quotations come from the Religious Coalition for Abortion Rights pamphlet entitled, "Abortion: Why Religious Organizations in the United States Want to Keep It Legal." This is also the position of the Americans United for the Separation of Church and State, as articulated in a friend-of-the-court brief filed with the Supreme Court on the famous *Webster v. Reproductive Health Services* case of 1989. Referring to the Missouri law's assertion that personhood begins at conception, the brief states, "Such an inherently theological, but controversial, determination violates a core purpose of the establishment clause of the First Amendment—that is, the absolute prohibition against government preference of one religious sect or denomination over another and the placing of the state's imprimatur on a particular religious dogma." Reported in *Christian Century* 106, 14 (26 April 1989): p. 440.
65. Falwell, *Listen America,* p. 181.
66. The executive secretary of the Presbyterians for Lesbian and Gay Concerns, James Anderson, put this view forward in a telephone interview, 13 October 1988, when he said that "people can develop good, loving relationships with other people regardless of sexual orientation."
67. Telephone interview with Edward Young, the former secretary for Integrity, the Episcopalian gay and lesbian group, 3 October 1988. Second quo-

tation from a letter written by a Ph.D. candidate at Union Theological Seminary, published in *Christianity and Crisis* 48 (1 February 1988): 22.

68. A. MacIntyre focuses on the issues of war, abortion, and justice and freedom. See *After Virtue* (Notre Dame, Ind.: University of Notre Dame Press, 1984), pp. 6–8.

CHAPTER 5: THE DISCOURSE OF ADVERSARIES

1. M. Shipley, *The War on Modern Science* (New York: Alfred A. Knopf, 1927), p. 3.
2. Anticlericalism and general opposition to religious institutions and sensibilities were both extreme and violent in France after the Revolution and the Jacobin seizure of power. Americans who heard about the terrors of French republicanism in the 1790s (associated with and sometimes attributable to the success of the doctrinaire secularism of the Enlightenment) feared that the French experience might be replicated in America. Many (including George Washington and John Adams) voiced fears of a conspiracy emanating from France designed to undermine the American democratic experiment. By the end of the eighteenth century these concerns developed into a popular Evangelical outcry, in the form of belief in the "conspiracy" of the Illuminati. This secret Masonic organization was reputed to oppose religion and clerical authority and many believed that the Illuminati were committed to a plan to transform America, through evil machinations, into a secular state. In the mid-1770s an anticlerical Enlightenment organization called the Illuminati had been formed in Bavaria. The number of its members never exceeded a few thousand and within ten years it had been officially suppressed by the local government. But rumor attributed far more power to the organization than it ever held in reality. Fears of a conspiracy by the Illuminati and its supporters in the United States contributed to the passage of the Alien and Sedition Act, designed to protect the country against both the foreign and domestic supporters of Jacobinism. The language of the act gave the president the authority to deport all aliens "he shall judge dangerous to the peace and safety of the United States, or shall have reasonable grounds to suspect are concerned in any treasonable or *secret machinations* against the government" (emphasis mine). Quoted in S. M. Lipset and E. Raab, *The Politics of Unreason* (Chicago: University of Chicago Press, 1970), p. 37. Belief in the Illuminati plot found its most fertile ground among the New England clergy. The plot's most prominent detractors included Timothy Dwight, president of Yale. They accused Jeffersonian Republicans of being "the dupes and accomplices of this . . . pernicious organization." One Federalist even claimed that Thomas Jefferson himself was "the real Jacobin, the very child of modern illumination, the foe of man, and the

enemy of his country." Supporters in Europe and America were called "wicked and artful men," "impious conspirators," "the enemies of human happiness," and were accused of "corrupting the principles and morals of our youth," of promoting promiscuity, of "propagating falsehoods," of conspiring to gain "control of all such cultural agencies as the schools, literary societies, newspapers, writers, booksellers, and postmasters"; of spreading "infidelity, impiety and immorality," of secretly plotting "to root out and effectually destroy Religion and Civil Government." These epithets were made by a variety of New England clergymen in sermons and tracts. These are quoted in V. Stauffer, *New England and the Bavarian Illuminati* (New York: Columbia University Press, 1918), p. 283. See also Lipset and Raab, *The Politics of Unreason*, pp. 35–39.)

3. Specific fears of the Illuminati faded away, but hostility to liberal religion and irreligion did not. In the wake of the Second Great Awakening, these fears evolved into animosity toward Freemasonry. The Masons, a secret organization, was founded in the early eighteenth century in Britain, and spread to Europe and North America. A superb history of anti-masonry can be found in P. Goodman, *Towards a Christian Republic* (New York: Oxford University Press, 1966). I draw from this book heavily. While Masonry borrowed symbols and rituals from a variety of ancient sources, it owed most of its identity to the spirit of the Enlightenment. The Masons' essential doctrines reflected what they considered to be the best of the modern sensibility: a commitment to the principles of natural religion—a nonsectarian and deistic faith that had distilled the moral essence of revealed religion but had abandoned obscurantist theologies. Thus God, the Great Architect, was a benevolent power whom one could understand and approach through reason and the practice of charity, tolerance, and brotherhood. Masons also believed that science had the capacity to promote human happiness and to advance the cause of civilization. By the first quarter of the nineteenth century, there were well over 1,000 local lodges and about 100,000 members drawn from a variety of denominations. Masonic membership was dominated, however, by the Episcopalians, Unitarians, and Universalists. At the heart of anti-Masonic opinion was an Evangelical resentment. Ronald Formisano observed, in a study of the formation of political parties in Michigan, that a "Unitarian-Orthodox division often was the essence of Masonic-Antimasonic polarity." See R. P. Formisano, *The Birth of Mass Political Parties in Michigan, 1827–1861* (Princeton, N.J.: Princeton University Press, 1971). For Evangelicals, Masonry was associated with "deism, radicalism and terrorism" and was the force behind the French Revolution and the Jacobin assault on Christian faith. Yet, opposition to Masonry would have probably remained at a fairly low intensity had it not been for the kidnapping, disappearance, and alleged murder of William Morgan in 1826. Morgan had been a member of a Masonic order in western New York. But over time he

became disaffected with the organization and decided to violate his oath of silence by publishing an exposé of the secrets of Freemasonry. Though it was never proven, his misfortune was widely attributed to the Masons as an act of revenge for his treason. The event "dramatically demonstrated" to Evangelicals "that when men no longer feared God, whatever their formal religious professions, they lost all restraint." Goodman, *Towards a Christian Republic,* p. 79. Morgan's disappearance immediately precipitated a national movement to destroy Freemasonry. By 1830, the anti-Masons not only claimed to have begun 124 papers dedicated to educating the public about the evils of Masonry but could also boast of their own distinct and powerful political party. Lipset and Raab's research shows that Masonic power was concentrated in the northeastern states. By 1928 anti-Masonic politicians had been elected to numerous positions (from governor to state senators and assemblymen) to the state governments of Vermont, Massachusetts, New York, Pennsylvania, and Rhode Island. See Lipset and Raab, *The Politics of Unreason,* p. 41. At heart, anti-Masonic opinion recalled the fears of the Illuminati plot. Masonry was said to be "corrupt," for it "encouraged sensuality, overeating, drinking, ribaldry, indecency and disrespect for women," its oaths were "blasphemous" and its rituals "barbaric," and it was committed to "spreading infidelity, despotism and misery throughout the earth." One Massachusetts minister claimed, in 1832, that Freemasonry was "the darkest and deepest plot that was ever formed in this wicked world against the true God, the true religion and the temporal and eternal interests of mankind." These views are quoted in Goodman, *Towards a Christian Republic,* chapter 4.

4. A hostility toward traditional religious faith was plainly in evidence by the founding of the American republic. The fiercest critics of orthodox religion were the disciples of the "cult of reason" in France and in the United States. For a useful summary of Enlightenment rationality in the United States from the late eighteenth century through the first three decades of the nineteenth century, see J. Corrigan, "The Enlightenment," in *The Encyclopedia of the American Religious Experience,* vol. 2, ed. Charles H. Lippy and Peter W. Williams (New York: Charles Scribners and Sons, 1988), pp. 1089–1102. Thomas Paine, author of *Common Sense* and *The Age of Reason,* went to great lengths to debunk revealed religion in general and biblical revelation in particular. He claimed, for example, that the Pentateuch was not written by Moses but by "very ignorant and stupid pretenders" centuries later, that the Hebrew prophets were either "impostors or overrated eccentrics" and that Christianity was "the strangest system of religion ever set up" because it committed a murder upon Jesus in order to redeem mankind for the sin of having eaten an apple. See H. M. Morais, *Deism in Eighteenth Century America* (New York: Columbia University Press, 1934), p. 125. Labeled "a filthy little atheist" (in fact, Paine was a deist), Paine was the most famous

detractor of orthodoxy and perhaps the most committed to undermining clerical authority, but he was certainly not alone. Elihu Palmer, Joseph Priestly, Thomas Cooper, Ethan Allen, among many others also launched vigorous, even bigoted attacks on the "superstitions" of the past. Popular support for an enlightened faith was slim then, since the deists tended to appeal to a better educated, more cosmopolitan, and sometimes slightly eccentric following. Compared to the Evangelicals, they had relatively little institutional power as well: they were primarily a loose group of unaffiliated deists, the "religiously irreligious," Unitarians, Universalists, liberal Congregationalists, Episcopalians, and Masons. Deistic and freethinking societies such as the Druidical Society of Newburgh founded in about 1788, the Universal Society of Philadelphia founded in 1791, the Deistical Society of New York in 1794, the Society of Theophilanthropy founded in both Baltimore and New York in 1808, and a few periodicals such as the *Temple of Reason,* the *Theophilanthropist,* the *Rights of Man, Prospect, or View of the Moral World, Western Examiner,* and the *Inspector* also promoted Enlightenment ideas. Although small in number and fairly weak in power, this loose coalition did offer a distinct and conspicuous cultural voice through the early nineteenth century. Their distinctiveness was largely defined by relentless ridicule of Christianity. Elihu Palmer called the Christian scheme of salvation, "nonsense and irrationality," and the Bible, "a book, whose indecency and immorality shock all common sense and common honesty." G. Koch, *Republican Religion: The American Revolution and the Cult of Reason* (New York: Henry Holt, 1933), p. 64. The *Temple of Reason,* 17 January 1801, p. 84, called the epistles of Paul "pompous and declamatory bombast," "harangues," and "the enthusiastic ravings of a madman." The social problem with "Christian superstition" was that it "creates intolerance, and persecutors, who are much more injurious to society than the most abandoned debauchers." *Temple of Reason,* 24 January 1801, p. 91. In the 29 November 1800 issue, the periodical editorialized: "We see the priests praying for the power of the Inquisition against the *Temple of Reason*—we hear the female bigot [the Church] giving vent to her rage, and in the true spirit of Christian superstition, invoking all powers of hell on the devoted head of him, who ventures to differ from her in opinion. Such is the folly, such is the madness, such is the wickedness of those, who are blinded by superstition. It is a consolation, however, in these latter days, that the tender and friendly hand of philosophy is removing the veil from the eyes of this superstition" (p. 29). Christian ministers and missionaries were regarded as "moral vermin" and "mental imbeciles," accused of everything from swindling people to sleeping with slaves. D. Doepke, "The Western Examiner: A Chronicle of Atheism in the West," *The Bulletin* 30 (1973). The *Temple of Reason,* 13 December 1800, editorialized, "Our experience tells us that the greatest rogues are geneally concealed under the robe of religion; and that those who repeat the most prayers are pretty expert at cheating their neighbors, and that they who are most devout in public are the greatest reprobates in private" (p. 41).

5. S. Warren, *American Freethought 1860–1914,* (New York: Columbia University Press, 1943), p. 213.
6. The Catholic Church took a "wait and see" position on the subject of evolution, but the 13 July 1925 edition of the *New York Times* (p. 17) reported that prominent Catholics could be found on both sides of the issue.
7. From a resolution of the Fourth Annual Convention of the World Christian Fundamentalists Association, 1 July 1922.
8. Emphasis in the original. The author was Reverend Charles F. Bluske, of Asheville, North Carolina. His concern was to "expos[e] the fallacies of the evolution hoax." Quoted in M. Shipley, *The War on Modern Science* (New York: Alfred A. Knopf, 1927), p. 100.
9. Ibid., p. 40.
10. Ibid., p. 240.
11. Quoted in James D. Bernard, "The Baptists," *American Mercury* 7, 26 (February 1926): 136.
12. J. W. Butler, "Fights Evolution to Uphold Bible," *New York Times,* 5 July 1925, pp. 1–4.
13. Reverend Earl Dretzschmar quoted in Shipley, *The War on Modern Science,* p. 162.
14. L. P. Ribuffo, *The Old Christian Right* (Philadelphia: Temple University Press, 1983), p. 92.
15. Ibid., p. 85.
16. Carl MacIntyre, *Twentieth Century Reformation* (Collingswood, N.J.: Christian Beacon Press, 1944), chapter 1.
17. See Warren, *American Freethought,* for a review of free thought in the 1800s.
18. J. E. Kleber, " 'Pagan Bob' on the Comstock: Robert G. Ingersoll Visits Virginia City," *Nevada Historical Society Quarterly* 22 (Winter 1979): 243–253.
19. Robert G. Ingersoll, "Thomas Paine: With His Name Left Out, the History of Liberty Cannot be Written," in *The Gods and Other Lectures* (Washington, D.C.: C. P. Farrell, 1878), pp. 157–58.
20. Ibid., p. 158.
21. The years following World War I were years of general discontent among American intellectuals. Some attributed it to the war, some to the decline of capitalism, others to the growing mass culture of modern democracy, but whatever the cause many took it out on the rural and generally religious culture of conservative Protestantism in particular, and the South in general. See H. F. May, *The Discontent of the Intellectuals: A Problem of the Twenties* (Chicago: Rand McNally, 1963).
22. These were taken from Shipley, *The War on Modern Science,* from the Introduction and pp. 369, 373.

23. Ibid., p. 3.
24. Ibid., p. 28. Shipley also commented, "This final objective is subjugation of our state and national governments, a virtual union of church and state under sectarian—Fundamentalist—domination" (p. 26), and, "The Fundamentalists are determined to overthrow our (secular) civil and political institutions and substitute for the government founded by the Fathers of the Republic a theocracy" (p. 26).
25. Ibid., p. 15.
26. Ibid., p. 369.
27. From C. Bode, ed., *The Young Mencken: The Best of His Work* (New York: Dial, 1973), pp. 369–70.
28. From Mencken's *Prejudices: Fifth Series,* quoted in May, *The Discontent of the Intellectuals,* pp. 26, 27.
29. Obadiah Holmes, "The Threat of Millennialism," *Christian Century* 39 (28 April 1921): 10; and (5 May 1921): 16–17; "The Capitalists and the Premillenarians," *Christian Century* 38 (14 April 1921): 3.
30. Harry F. Ward, "Fascist Trends in American Churches," *Christian Century* 70 (15 April 1953): 490–92.
31. Editorial, "Blueprint for Discord," *Christian Century* 71 (30 June 1954): 782–83; and Ralph L. Roy, "Ministry of Disruption," *Christian Century* 70 (8 April 1953): 410–14.
32. Address by A. Bartlett Gramatti, president of Yale University, to incoming freshmen, August 3, 1981. *The Dallas Morning News,* 6 May 1981.
33. ACLU direct mail appeal, quoted in "Iowa Fall Out," *Wall Street Journal,* 18 February 1988.
34. A version of this section appears in J. D. Hunter, "The Liberal Reaction to the New Christian Right," in *The New Christian Right: Mobilization and Legitimation,* ed. R. Liebman and R. Wuthnow (New York: Aldine, 1983).
35. From a speech by Reverend Timothy Healy, president of Georgetown University, September 1981, Washington, D.C.
36. Quoted in an editorial by Frank Creel, "A Liberal Sandpaper Job on the Rev. Jerry Falwell," *New York Tribune,* 20 October 1984.
37. Paul D. Simmons, "A Theological Response to Fundamentalism on the Abortion Issue" (Washington, D.C.: Religious Coalition for Abortion Rights Education Fund), p. 14.
38. ACLU mailing, New York, no date. ADA brochure, Washington, D.C., no date. People for the American Way pamphlet, Washington, D.C., "Q & A."
39. Public broadcasts of Jimmy Swaggart, 13 and 14 January 1987, reported in Mike Zahn, "TV Evangelists Targeted in Ads," [Milwaukee] *Journal,* 14 April 1987.
40. Ed McAteer, "The Intellectual Barbarians," Religious Roundtable, Memphis, Tenn., no date.

41. Tim LaHaye, *The Battle for the Mind* (Old Tappan, N.J.: Fleming H. Revell, 1980) p. 57.
42. *The Voice of Liberty Newsletter* 22, 1 (March 1982).
43. From a direct mail solicitation, Planned Parenthood, Washington, D.C., no date, and one from the Catholic League for Religious and Civil Rights, Milwaukee, Wis., no date.
44. An attorney for the American Jewish Committee (AJC) commented, "There is a danger . . . that [the religious right] may succeed in legitimating and legalizing the notion that the Constitution and the political process may be used to institutionalize Christianity in the nation." "AJC Speakers Fearful of Efforts to Institutionalize Christianity," *Washington Post,* 22 May 1981. People for the American Way proposal for funding (Washington, D.C., no date), and "Interreligious Currents," 3, 1 (1984): 1.
45. Reverend Charles Bergstrom, introduction "The Witch Hunt Against Secular Humanism," People for the American Way, Washington, D.C., no date. Mary Peek, "What Every Teacher Should Know About the New Right" (Washington, D.C.: NEA Task Force on Academic Freedom, no date).
46. From People for the American Way report, "Secular Humanism Attacks on Public Schools: 1982–1987," quoted in *Springfield News and Leader,* 14 March 1987.
47. "Preserving Liberty: The First Five Years, 1980–1985" People for the American Way, Washington, D.C., no date, p. 16. In a press release dated 5 October 1986, the ACLU said that the right labeled "everything about contemporary life they object to" as "secular humanism."
48. David Bollier, "The Witch Hunt Against Secular Humanism," People for the American Way, Washington, D.C., no date.
49. Pro-choice groups are particularly troubled by the power of the Catholic Church in defense of the pro-life cause. The Religious Coalition for Abortion Rights alluded to it in a brochure: "Laws proposed by anti-choice organizations would . . . establish religion by making one—and only one—theological view about 'personhood' the only law of the land." In another of the group's brochures, entitled "Theology and Politics," John Swomley makes this argument explicit: "The Roman Catholic bishops of the United States continue to campaign for passage of an amendment to the Federal constitution which would write Catholic doctrine into constitutional law," p. 1.
50. Falwell made this complaint repeatedly through the 1980s, as did others. See, for example, William P. Hoar, "Bashing Christians for Fun and Profit," in *Conservative Digest,* reprinted as an insert in the *Newsletter of Concerned Women for America* 9, 2 (February 1987).
51. Don Feder, "Christian Candidates Raise Secularist Hackles," reprinted in *Biblical Scoreboard,* 1986. Leo Ribuffo, "Liberals and That Old-Time Religion," *Nation,* 29 November 1980, pp. 572–73, makes the same point.

52. Letter to the editor, Ted Paul, "Outcry on Religion Too Selective," *Buffalo News,* 20 June 1986.
53. Falwell quotation from the introduction, Richard Viguerie, *The New Right: We're Ready to Lead* (Falls Church, Va.: Viguerie Company, 1981). Karen Mulhauser, direct mail appeal, National Abortion Rights Action League, n.d.
54. LaHaye, *The Battle for the Mind,* p. 142. Flo Conway and Jim Siegelman, "Holy Terror," *Playboy* (June 1982): 126.
55. From the Presidential Biblical Scoreboard, "The American Paradox: Christian Majority—Christians CAN Regain Control from the Liberal Minority," (Spring 1988): 6. From a statement of John Buchanan, 18 March 1988, cited in press clipping, People for the American Way. The entire sentence was, "In making these charges [about what Falwell called "the Civil Rights Sodom and Gomorrah Act"], Rev. Falwell is bearing false witness against the overwhelming majority of Congress and those who share in the national consensus on civil rights and the growing consensus on women's rights."
56. From a National Abortion Rights Action League direct mail appeal.
57. LaHaye, *The Battle for the Mind,* p. 183.
58. See John H. Simpson, "Moral Issues and Status Politics," in *The New Christian Right: Mobilization and Legitimation,* ed. Robert Liebman and Robert Wuthnow (New York: Aldine, 1983), pp. 187–205.
59. Robertson quoted in an editorial by Anthony Podesta, "Robertson: Radical Posing as Friendly TV Evangelist," *West Palm Beach* [Fla.] *Post,* 9 July 1986.
60. Editorial, Anthony Podesta, "Robertson's Radicalism: Sticky Views of the Teflon Televangelist," *Levittown-Bristol Courier Times,* 11 July 1986.
61. The Americans for Democratic Action comment was reported in an editorial by Joseph Sobran, " 'Epidemic of Intolerance,' " *Southtown Economist,* 21 August 1981. The reference to the ACLU came from the *Biblical Scorecard,* 1986 national edition.
62. LaHaye, *The Battle for the Mind,* p. 138.
63. Bob Frishman, *American Families: Responding to the Pro-Family Movement* (Washington, D.C.: People for the American Way, 1984), pp. 11–12.
64. Quoted from a proposal for funding for Friends of the American Way.
65. The language is ubiquitous on nearly every front. In the case of abortion, a NARAL brochure notes: "The well-financed anti-abortion minority in this country is determined to destroy our individual liberty and to impose on us their specific religious belief."
66. Kenneth Connors, "Public Issues and Private Morality," *Christian Century* 97 (22 October 1980): p. 1002.
67. Brochure, People for the American Way, Washington, D.C., no date.
68. Cal Thomas quoted in "Forum Focuses on Religion's Role in Politics," *Philadelphia Inquirer,* 3 December 1987.
69. *Newsletter of Concerned Women for America* 11, 2 (February 1989): 6. Consider

the remark made by Falwell when he charged Senator Paul Simon with "a complete lack of tolerance toward those who differ with [him]" (June 1986 issue of the "Liberty Report").

70. Direct mail from NARAL, Washington, D.C., no date, and from CCMRC, no date.
71. Norman Cousins, "The Threat of Intolerance," *Saturday Review* 8 (January 1981): p. 8. ACLU ad, *New York Times*, November 23, 1980, p. A 10.
72. "A Citizen's Guide to the Right Wing," Americans for Democratic Action. Washington, D.C., no date.
73. Direct mail appeal, National Abortion Rights Action League.
74. "Preserving Liberty: The First Five Years, 1980–1985," People for the American Way, Washington, D.C., no date.
75. Mich Heiland, "Moral Caretakers May Bury Us All," *Arlington* [Tex.] *Daily News*, 13 April 1986.
76. Paul Simmons, "Pro-Family, He Finds Himself Rated Anti in Eyes of Unseeing Fanatics," *Los Angeles Times*, 10 June 1981.
77. "The 'New Right' Post-Election: With Emphasis on the Religious New Right," Americans for Democratic Action, Washington, D.C., no date. "Assault on the Bill of Rights: The Jewish Stake '84," *Interreligious Currents* 3 (Fall 1984): 1.
78. Edward Morgan, "What They're Saying About the New Right," *NEA Advocate* 14 (January–February 1980): 7.
79. Anthony Podesta, "The American Way," in *Values, Pluralism and Education* (Washington, D.C.: People for the American Way, 1987).
80. "Extremism in the Name of God," *Chicago Tribune*, 27 September 1981.
81. Anthony Podesta, "Swaggart: America's Farrakhan of the Right," *Baltimore Sun*, 24 November 1986.
82. "Ultraright Lashes Back After Goldwater Attack," *Chicago Tribune*, 16 September 1981.
83. This came from a small tract by Bill Bright, "Your Five Duties as a Christian Citizen," published by Christians Concerned for More Responsible Citizenship.
84. Biblical Scorecard, 1986 edition, p. 6. "Candidates Biblical Scoreboard," Christian Voice, 1986 National edition.
85. "Feminists Take Aim at Idaho Potato Farmers to Push Pro-Death Agenda," in news digest, *Newsletter of Concerned Women for America* 12, 5 (May 1990): 9.
86. "Let's Set the Record Straight," published by the Moral Majority, Lynchburg, Va., no date.
87. Jimmy Swaggart, quoted in *Broadcasting*, 10 February 1986.
88. John W. Whitehead, *The Stealing of America* (Westchester, Ill.: Crossway Books, 1983); John W. Whitehead, *The Second American Revolution* (Elgin, Ill.: David C. Cook, 1982), p. 146. In an even earlier book, much the same

claims are made: see his *The Separation Illusion* (Milford, Mich. Mott Media, 1977).

89. Methodists for Life brochure, no date.
90. Simmons, "A Theological Response to Fundamentalism on the Abortion Issue," p. 1. Walt Michalsky, "The Masquerade of Fundamentalism," *Humanist* 41 (July–August 1981): 15–52.
91. From public broadcasts of Jimmy Swaggart, 13 and 14 January 1987, reported in Zahn, "TV Evangelists Targeted in Ads." Fund-raising appeal from Jerry Falwell for the I Love America PAC, no date.
92. Another example was "The Falwell Game" advertised throughout the gay community in 1986. See Eugene Curtin, "The Gays' 'Falwell Game' is a Mean, Gloomy Business," *New York Tribune,* 4 April 1986. This article was based upon an article entitled "Hey kids! Let's All Play the Falwell Game," *Seattle Gay News,* 17 January 1986. The object of the game was to "squander Jerry Falwell's millions" by encouraging "players" to call his toll-free number repeatedly so that "there would be no calls getting through at all." "Dedicated players" call the number and pledge "to become a faith partner, with the intent of not paying." In return the caller would be sent a free Bible. By March of that year, the "Old-Time Gospel Hour" was getting roughly 50,000 harassing calls a month, costing the ministry about $2 million in phone calls, Bibles, other written materials, and postage, according to an Associated Press story, "Harassing Calls, 'Crisis' Plague Falwell Ministry," *Dallas Morning News,* 31 March 1986.
93. This was an editorial cartoon published in 1986 and syndicated by United Feature. It was published originally in the *Dayton Daily News.*
94. Montagu quoted in Philip Hilts, "Creationism gets New Life in Nation's Public Schools," *Washington Post,* 25 July 1981.
95. Isaac Asimov, "The Blind Who Would Lead," *MacLeans,* 2 February 1981, p. 6.
96. Telephone interview with Rabbi Yehuda Levin, June 15, 1990, Michael Waldstein, quoted in the *National Catholic Register,* 26 January 1986.
97. Morehead Kennedy, *Ayatollah in the Cathedral* (New York: Hill and Wang, 1986). Calling this to my attention was the *Religion and Society Report.*
98. David Bird, "Moral Majority Assails Attack on It by the President of Yale," *New York Times,* 2 September 1981. The minister was Reverend Dan C. Fore, pastor of Staten Island Bible Church. The last statement was specifically directed toward People for the American Way, but the claim is often made about progressivists in general. Hoar, "Bashing Christians for Fun and Profit."
99. See J. D. Hunter, "The Liberal Reaction to the Christian Right," pp. 149–163; and J. Garvey, "Made for Each Other: The Fundamentalist-Humanist Complex," *Commonweal* 108 (16 January 1981): 6–8.

CHAPTER 6: THE TECHNOLOGY OF PUBLIC DISCOURSE

1. Quoted by Robin Toner, "200,000 Demonstrate Against Abortion," *New York Times,* 29 April 1990, p. 26. At the same march, a student leader from Columbia University argued to his audience, "Today we want to show this country that we are not a bunch of religious fanatics who want to force women to have babies. We are intelligent, rational people and despite what many might think, our cause is alive and well." Quoted by Calvin Sims, "Columbia Students Join Rally Against Abortion," ibid., p. 26. A young mother from Winters, California, who was protesting the content of her child's textbooks, echoed a similar complaint, "We have heard that rhetoric over and over. First of all they have called us right-wing, then fundamentalist, then, radical Christians, whatever. They've called us everything but what we are; parents, concerned parents."
2. George Marsden provides a telling illustration of this process in the particular case of the creation versus evolution debate in his essay, "A Case of the Excluded Middle: Creation Versus Evolution in America," in *Uncivil Religion,* ed. R. N. Bellah and F. E. Greenspahn (New York: Crossroad, 1984).
3. Emphasis added. This statement was made by Sue Purrington, executive director of the Chicago chapter of the National Organization for Women. Patricia Ireland (vice-president of NOW) dismissed them as well. "Their only agenda is antiabortion work. There is no support in terms of creating the social support systems for women who indeed want to have a child—no work for improving women's wages, or decent housing or child care." *Chicago Tribune,* 12 November 1989, section 1, p. 1.
4. See H. Stout, *The New England Soul* (New York: Oxford University Press, 1986), pp. 3–4.
5. A. de Tocqueville, *Democracy in America* (New York: Vintage, 1954), p. 58.
6. N. Postman, *Amusing Ourselves to Death: Public Discourse in the Age of Show Business* (New York: Viking, 1985), p. 37; and Census of the United States, (Washington, D.C.: Government Printing Office, 1850), p. 65.
7. Postman, *Amusing Ourselves to Death,* p. 38.
8. Adell-Marie Stan, "Pat Hussey and Barbara Ferraro Battle On," *Conscience* 7 (May–June 1986): 1.
9. Brochure, People for the American Way, Washington, D.C., no date.
10. The most comprehensive summary of these data is provided by J. K. Hadden and A. Shupe, *Televangelism: Power and Politics on God's Frontier* (New York: Henry Holt, 1988), chapter 8.
11. Dom Bonafede, "Part Science, Part Art, Part Hokum, Direct Mail Now a Key Campaign Tool," *National Journal,* 31 July 1982, p. 1332.
12. Ibid., p. 1334.
13. Tina Rosenburg, "Diminishing Returns: The False Promise of Direct Mail," *Washington Monthly* 15, 4 (June 1983): 34.

14. The study was conducted by *Congressional Quarterly,* reported in Christopher Buchanan, "New Right: 'Many Times More Effective' Now," *Congressional Quarterly Weekly Reports,* 24 December 1977, p. 2649–53.
15. Rosenburg, "Diminishing Returns," p. 34.
16. G. Easterbrook, "Junk-Mail Politics," *The New Republic* (25 April 1988): 21.
17. Quoted in S. Blumenthal, *The Permanent Campaign: Inside the World of Elite Political Operatives* (Boston: Beacon Press, 1980), p. 227.
18. Bonafede, "Part Science, Part Art, Part Hokum, Direct Mail Now a Key Campaign Tool," p. 1333.
19. Richard Viguerie, for example, had the names of more than 30 million conservative-leaning individuals by 1977 and mailed out 76 million letters. See Larry Sabato, *The Rise of Political Consultants* (New York: Basic Books, 1981), esp. chapter 4, "Direct Mail: The Poisoned Pen of Politics."
20. See Susan Rouder, "Mobilization by Mail," *Citizen Participation* 2 (September–October 1980): 3. Another study from 1976 was cited in Sabato, *The Rise of Political Consultants,* p. 220.
21. Roger Craver, president of the largest progressively oriented direct mail firm, Craver, Mathews, and Smith, of Washington, D.C., quoted in Bonafede, "Part Science, Part Art, Part Hokum, Direct Mail Now a Key Campaign Tool," p. 1333.
22. Robert Smith of Craver, Mathews, and Smith, quoted in Sabato, *The Rise of Political Consultants,* p. 241.
23. Robert Smith of Craver, Mathews, and Smith, quoted in Easterbrook, "Junk-Mail Politics," pp. 17–21. John Buckley, executive director of the Fund for a Conservative Majority in 1977, claimed that "in some cases, the shriller you are the more success you have in raising funds." Buchanan, "New Right: 'Many Times More Effective' Now," pp. 2649–53.
24. This is language actually used in a Jesse Helms NCPAC solicitation. See Rosenburg, "Diminishing Returns," p. 34.
25. Direct mail solicitation, Moral Majority, no date. Roger Craver of Craver, Mathews, and Smith, quoted in E. J. Dionne, "The Mail-Order Campaigners," *New York Times,* 7 September 1980.
26. Robert Smith of Craver, Mathews, and Smith, quoted in Easterbrook, "Junk-Mail Politics," pp. 17–21.
27. Robert Smith, quoted in ibid., pp. 17–21.
28. Ibid.
29. Robert Smith, quoted in Sabato, *The Rise of Political Consultants,* p. 241.
30. Jim Martin, quoted in ibid., p. 241.
31. Ibid.
32. Ibid., p. 244.
33. Bonafede, "Part Science, Part Art, Part Hokum, Direct Mail Now a Key Campaign Tool," p. 1336.
34. Postman, *Amusing Ourselves to Death,* p. 43.

35. Personal correspondence, Reverend Dr. Michael McIntyre, original acting director of People for the American Way, 18 August 1983.
36. On the power of political advertisements, see, for example, Michael Oreskes, "TV Is a Player in Crucial Race for California," *New York Times,* 29 April 1990, p. 22.
37. See "Now, for Sizing Up Number at the Rally," *New York Times,* 29 April 1990, p. 26.

CHAPTER 7: FAMILY

1. David Blankenhorn, "American Family Dilemmas," paper presented at conference titled "What Do Families Do?" at Stanford University, November 1989.
2. Quoted in Arthur W. Calhoun, *A Social History of the American Family from Colonial Times to the Present* (New York: Barnes and Noble, 1945), pp. 301–305.
3. Daniel Patrick Moynihan was probably the first to call for a national family policy in his influential article in *America* in 1965. D. P. Moynihan, "A Family Policy for the Nation," *America* (18 September 1965): 280–83. The entire February issue of *Journal of Marriage and the Family* was devoted to the issue of government policy toward the family. For a brief review of this literature see J. Dempsey, *The Family and Public Policy* (Baltimore: Brooks, 1981).
4. Kenneth Keniston and the Carnegie Council on Children, *All Our Children: The American Family Under Pressure* (New York: Harcourt Brace Jovanovich, 1977), pp. 76, 216–20.
5. Ibid., p. 78.
6. See B. Berger and P. L. Berger, *The War Over the Family* (New York: Anchor Doubleday, 1984).
7. Dempsey, *The Family and Public Policy,* pp. 89–90.
8. James Kilpatrick column, *Washington Post,* 14 June 1980.
9. For example, at the Baltimore Conference on Families, the following recommendation was made: "We support policies which preserve and protect basic legal and human rights of all family members. To guarantee these rights we support . . . ratification of the ERA . . . [and] Elimination of discrimination and encouragement of respect for differences based on sex, race, ethnic origin, creed, socio-economic status, age, disability, diversity of family type and size, sexual preference or biological ties." Of the 583 ballots cast, 250 were strongly in favor; 42 moderately in favor; 58 moderately opposed, and 233 strongly opposed.
10. See Lynn Langway, Lucy Howard, and Donna Foote, "Family Politics," *Newsweek,* 28 January 1980, pp. 78–79.

11. Edith Pendleton in the *Nashville Banner* (1 March 1980) cited in Dempsey, *The Family and Public Policy,* p. 85.
12. From an editorial in the *Washington Post,* 31 May 1980, cited in ibid., pp. 85–86.
13. David Gerke in the *New Mexican,* cited in ibid., p. 86.
14. From Diane Ravitch, "In the Family's Way," *New Republic,* 28 June 1980; pp. 18–24.
15. Tim LaHaye, *The Battle for the Family* (Old Tappan, N.J.: Fleming H. Revell, 1982), pp. 210–11. In fairness, LaHaye also states that there is no "Christian wife who wouldn't find pleasure in a husband who returned each night with these same characteristics" (p. 210).
16. Taken from C. Degler, *At Odds* (New York: Oxford University Press, 1980), p. 471. Emphasis added.
17. *Phyllis Schlafly Report* 5, 7 (February 1972): 3, 4.
18. Quoted in Jane Mansbridge, *Why We Lost the ERA* (Chicago: University of Chicago Press, 1986), p. 104.
19. This argument was made by LaHaye, *Battle for the Family,* in the chapter on feminism (p. 139). Phyllis Schlafly's organization, STOP ERA, argued similarly in an undated brochure: "What does the word 'sex' [in the language of the ERA] mean? The sex you are, male or female, or the sex you engage in, homosexual, bisexual, heterosexual, sex with children . . . or whatever? . . . One thing is for sure: Militant homosexuals from all over America have made the ERA issue a hot priority. Why? To be able finally to get homosexual marriage licenses, to adopt children and raise them to emulate their homosexual 'parents,' and to obtain pension and medical benefits for odd-couple 'spouses.' "
20. See Gaylell Binion, "The Case for an Equal Rights Act," *Center Magazine* 16, 6 (November–December 1983): 2–7, and the lively debate that followed in the same issue.
21. Quoted in "Women's Work—And Wages," in *Newsweek,* 9 July 1984, pp. 22–23.
22. See the remarks made by Gerald McEntee, president of the American Federation of State, County and Municipal Employees, quoted in "Pay Men, Women Equally for 'Comparable' Work?" *U.S. News and World Report,* 24 December 1984, p. 47; and Ellen Wilson Fielding, "Feminism and Freedom," *Crisis* (December 1988): 8.
23. Richard Ostling, "Farewell to Thee's and He's," *Time,* 7 May 1990, p. 117.
24. The Reverend Alvin F. Kimel, Jr., "A New Language for God?" *Reports from Episcopalians United* 2 (1990): 14.
25. This figure is derived from the U.S. Department of Health, Education, and Welfare, *Digest of Educational Statistics* (Washington, D.C.: Government Printing Office, 1970), p. 70; ibid., 1974, p. 80; and 1979, p. 96.
26. The general figure is taken from William L. Baumgaertner, ed., *Fact Book*

on Theological Education (Vandalia, Ohio: Association of Theological Schools, 1985–86). The figure is derived from member schools. The number of women in the mainline seminaries is even greater, as suggested by women's enrollment in the seminaries of several mainline denominations. In the United Methodist seminaries, women comprised 29 percent of the total enrollment, in the Episcopal seminaries the figure was 34 percent, and in the United Church of Christ the figure was as high as 44 percent. Indeed a 1986 *New York Times* article reported that half of all seminarians at the Harvard Divinity School were women. See Ari Goldman, "As Call Comes, More Women Answer," *New York Times,* 19 October 1986. In the more conservative theological seminaries, women's representation is only slightly less than the national average. This is suggested by the enrollment figures of women in Southern Baptist seminaries, which was 20 percent in 1985. See the 1985–86 *Fact Book on Theological Education,* p. 87.

27. In 1985, for example, Women for Faith and Family, an organization of Catholic women, sent a petition, "Affirmation of Catholic Women," to the National Council of Catholic Bishops charged with writing the Pastoral Letter on Women. The affirmation was signed by more than 4,000 Catholic women. This statement was published in *Catholicism in Crisis* (April 1985): 39.
28. See chapter 8, "Motherhood and Morality in America," in K. Luker, *Abortion and the Politics of Motherhood* (Los Angeles and Berkeley: University of California Press, 1984) for an elaboration of this argument.
29. From an *amicus* brief on behalf of the defense in the *Webster* case published in the *New York Times,* 23 April 1989, section 4.
30. From "Early Childhood Education: An Attempt to Further Socialize America," *Newsletter of Concerned Women for America* 11, 7 (July 1989): 11. "Children," as Jerry Falwell put it, "deserve a well-educated, imaginative and full-time mother." Quoted in B. Frishman, *American Families: Responding to the Pro-Family Movement* (Washington, D.C.: People for the American Way, 1984), p. 34.
31. Both statements quoted in *Citizen* 2, 6 (June 1988): 14.
32. See Rosemary Radford Ruether's essay in *Homosexuality in the Priesthood and the Religious Life,* ed. Jeannine Gramick (New York: Crossroad, 1989), quoted by Richard John Neuhaus, "Homosexuality and the Churches," *First Things* 1, 3 (May 1990): 65.
33. From the Opening Statement of the National Gay and Lesbian Task Force's *Federal Legislative Report* (January–December 1989).
34. Quoted in the *Washington Post,* 25 January 1990, p. 1.
35. Terry Hall, from a review of "Essays on the Crucial Questions," by Joseph Sobran, in *Catholicism in Crisis* (July 1983): 46–47.
36. All the quotes in this paragraph came from a direct mail solicitation sent out in early 1990 for the National Gay and Lesbian Task Force, Washington,

D.C., under the name of its executive director, Urvashi Vaid. Emphasis in the original.

37. Quoted in Walter Isaacson, "Should Gays Have Marriage Rights?" *Time,* 20 November 1989, p. 102.
38. This quote is from Paula Ettelbrick, legal director of Lambda Legal Defense and Education Fund, quoted in ibid, p. 102.
39. From a packet distributed by the National Gay and Lesbian Task Force on Sodomy Law, Washington, D.C., no date.
40. Quoted in Robin Toner, "Senate, 92 to 4, Wants U.S. Data on Hate Crimes Spawned by Bias," *New York Times,* 9 February 1990, p. A17.
41. From a direct mail memorandum to National Gay and Lesbian Task Force members from Urvashi Vaid, Washington, D.C., dated 8 February 1990.
42. See Jacob Weisberg, "Gays in Arms," *New Republic,* 19 February 1990, p. 20.
43. Quoted in Neuhaus, "Homosexuality and the Churches," p. 67.
44. Letter to the Editor, *The Review* [Baltimore], 1 August 1980.
45. Quoted in Neuhaus, "Homosexuality and the Churches," p. 67.
46. Editorial, "A New Generation," in *Crisis* (October 1988): 2.
47. A celebrated case was the ordination of J. Robert Williams, a self-avowed and practicing homosexual, by Right Reverend John S. Spong, bishop of the Diocese of Newark, in December 1989. Episcopalians United responded with a nationwide call for the bishop's formal censure.
48. See James G. Wolf, ed., *Gay Priests* (New York: Harper & Row, 1989).
49. These are listed in a document on Sodomy Law Reform produced by the National Gay and Lesbian Task Force. They include among others, the Presbyterian Church, U.S.A. (1970), Philadelphia Yearly Meeting of Friends (1973), American Friends Service Committee (1976), Unitarian Universalist Association (1970), United Church of Christ (1969), Episcopal Church Convention, Diocese of New York (1974), Protestant Episcopal Church in the USA (1976), Lutheran Church in America (1970), American Lutheran Church (1977), United Methodist Church (1976), National Federation of Roman Catholic Priests' Councils (1974), National Council of Churches of Christ (1973), American Jewish Congress (1973), and Union of American Hebrew Congregations (1977).
50. See Randall Frame, "The Issue That Won't Go Away," *Christianity Today* 34 (5 March 1990): 28.
51. The quote is from Beverly LaHaye of Concerned Women for America, as an endorsement of the book *AIDS and Young People,* advertized in the *Newsletter of Concerned Women for America* 10, 10 (October 1988): 21.
52. See William A. Henry III, "Forcing Gays Out of the Closet," *Time,* 29 January 1990, p. 67.
53. See Berger and Berger, *The War Over the Family* p. 27. As Tim LaHaye put it in his *Battle for the Family,* "Today thousands of the brainwashed victims

of our humanistically controlled society are trading the love of unborn children for 'me-ism' and their own 'personal rights' " (p. 23). Second quote from NGLTF brochure, Washington, D.C., undated.

54. The first statement is taken from Calhoun, *A Social History of the American Family from Colonial Times to the Present,* p. 72; the second is taken from Lyndon B. Johnson, "Remarks of the President at Howard University," Washington, D.C., 4 June 1965.
55. Quoted in Nadine Brozan, "White House Conference on the Family: A Schism Develops," *New York Times,* 7 January 1980, p. D8.

CHAPTER 8: EDUCATION

1. Robert Simonds quoted in *Attacks on the Freedom to Learn, 1986–87,* People for the American Way, p. 9. The ACLU quote comes from a direct mail solicitation. No date provided.
2. The two best histories of public education as a field of conflict and change are D. Ravitch, *The Great School Wars, 1805–1973: The Public Schools as a Battleground for Social Change* (New York: Basic Books, 1973), and L. Jorgenson, *The State and the Non-Public School, 1825–1925* (Columbia, MO.: University of Missouri Press, 1987).
3. V. P. Lannie and B. C. Diethorn, "For the Honor and Glory of God: The Philadelphia Bible Riots of 1844," *History of Education Quarterly* 8 (Spring 1968): 46–51.
4. Quoted in Jorgenson, *The State and the Non-Public School,* p. 107ff.
5. Ibid.
6. Ibid.
7. Between 1965 and 1985, for example, the number of Catholic elementary and secondary schools fell 28 percent and student enrollments declined 54 percent. This decline has been due in large part to the loss of a distinct Catholic identity resulting from two developments. The first is the pluralization and liberalization of the Catholic tradition since Vatican II. Consensus over the traditional benchmarks of Catholic identity was lost. The second development is the tremendous social mobility of Catholic communities after the Second World War—a move away from the cities and to the more wealthy suburbs; away from the communities and institutions earlier generations had built as a preserve for religious and ethnic life. The consequence of both trends has been the melding of the thought, behavior, and values of ordinary Catholics with those of the mainstream of American society. See J. D. Hunter, "Evangelical Schools in Growth; Catholic Schools in Decline," *Wall Street Journal,* 8 March 1988, p. 34.
8. Quoted in Franklin and Betty Parker, "Behind Textbook Censorship," *National Journal* [A Publication of Phi Kappa Phi] (Fall 1988): 37.

9. From Robert L. Simonds, *Communicating a Christian World View in the Classroom,* a teachers' manual published in Costa Mesa, California, by the National Association of Christian Educators, p. 6.
10. Mel and Norma Gabler (founders of a conservative organization called Educational Research Analysts) are reported as saying that one may find "the godless religion of secular humanism" wherever one finds "evolutionary dogma, self-autonomy, situation ethics, Christianity negated, sexual freedom, total reading freedom, death education, internationalism and socialism." Quoted in *Attacks on the Freedom to Learn, 1986–87,* p. 20.
11. Telephone interview with Mae Duggan of Citizens for Educational Freedom and the Thos. J. White Educational Foundation, 7 June 1989. According to Duggan, "it is the Evangelicals who are new to the opposition to secular humanism."
12. Hitchcock, 1982, pp. 106–9. From a direct mail solicitation of the Catholic League.
13. *Catholic League Newsletter* 13, 4. Father Virgil Blum was invoking the terms first used by Jerome Lefkowitz.
14. "Position Paper on Public Policy Issues—National Legislative Agenda—1987," Agudath Israel of America, Washington, D.C., 1987.
15. "The 700 Club," Christian Broadcasting Network, 13 May 1984.
16. People for the American Way research document, "Jimmy Swaggart: Voice of Intolerance," Washington, D.C., undated. His original statement was made in February 1985.
17. Percentages from the author's reanalysis of J. D. Hunter, *The Williamsburg Charter Survey on Religion and American Public Life* (Washington, D.C.: Williamsburg Charter Foundation, 1988).
18. This particular decision, Bright suggested, precipitated a series of "plagues" that included "the assassinations of President Kennedy, Senator Robert F. Kennedy and the Rev. Dr. Martin Luther King Jr., acceleration of the Vietnam War, escalation of crime, disintegration of families, racial conflict, teenage pregnancies and venereal disease." Marjorie Hunter, "Evangelist Calls for Restoration of Prayer in U.S. Public Schools," *New York Times,* 31 July 1980, p. A14.
19. *America: To Pray or Not To Pray?* (Washington, D.C.: Concerned Women for America, 1988). The book was offered free to those who made a minimum contribution of twenty-five dollars to the organization. The quotation is from a direct mail solicitation advertising this book. Emphasis added.
20. For the first quote see Bill Sidebottom, "This Teachers' Union Agenda Has Little to Do with Education," *Focus on the Family Citizen* 29, 9 (September 1988): 10–11. Sally D. Reed, *NEA: Propaganda Front for the Radical Left* (Alexandria, Va.: National Council for Better Education, n.d.). For a precis of the book see its review in *Educational Freedom* 22, 1 (Fall–Winter 1988–89): 53. The final quote was taken from this review.

21. "The 700 Club," Christian Broadcasting Network, 20 November 1984.
22. The statement was attributed to Mary Futrell by Sidebottom, "This Teachers' Union Agenda Has Little to Do with Education," p. 11.
23. The statement was made by Robert Pawson, a member of the NEA and the founder of "Teachers Saving Children," an organization that "bases its working philosophy on the Judeo-Christian ethic." It was for the reason that Pawson gives that three Michigan teachers (two Protestant and one Catholic) protested the NEA using their money for lobbying purposes. Their case was eventually dealt with by the Equal Employment Opportunity Commission, which ruled that the three did not have to pay union NEA dues because of their religious convictions.
24. Paul Vitz, "Religion and Traditional Values in Public School Textbooks: An Empirical Study," a report submitted to the National Institute of Education, Washington, D.C., 1985, and "Religion and Traditional Values in Public School Textbooks," *Public Interest,* Summer 1986, pp. 72–90.
25. Quoted in *Attacks on the Freedom to Learn, 1986–87,* p. 20.
26. Mel Gabler quoted in B. Frishman, *American Families: Responding to the Pro-Family Movement* (Washington, D.C.: People for the American Way, 1984), p. 102.
27. J. Hitchcock, *What Is Secular Humanism? Why Humanism Is Secular and How It Is Changing Our World* (Ann Arbor, Mich.: Servant Books, 1982), pp. 106–9.
28. From Reverend Paul Marx, "Sex Education: Successful Anywhere?" *Fidelity* (April 1983): 29.
29. Paraphrased from an editorial in the *Wall Street Journal* (12 April 1982) in R.V. Young, "Sex Education as Education," *Fidelity* (July 1982): 10.
30. Hitchcock, *What Is Secular Humanism?,* pp. 106–9.
31. R.V. Young, "Sex Education as Education," p. 11.
32. Jack Novik, legal director for the ACLU, quoted in an ACLU news release dated 5 October 1986.
33. Frishman, *American Families,* p. 98.
34. ACLU, direct mailing, undated.
35. *Dushane Fund Reports* 10, 4 (1987): 7.
36. Frishman, *American Families,* p. 95.
37. Ibid.
38. *Attacks on the Freedom to Learn, 1986–87,* p. 21. The point is reiterated in the introduction: The "cumulative attack . . . strikes at the heart of public education: methods, materials, and ideas designed to teach basic skills, critical thinking, responsibility, and tolerance."
39. Leslie C. Francis and Decker Anstrom, "Right Wing Attacks on Support Threaten Public Schools," *Los Angeles Times,* April 23, 1983, p. 23.
40. See Reed, *NEA: Propaganda Front for the Radical Left,* or material published by Americans for Educational Choice, the Citizens for Educational Freedom,

the National Association for the Legal Support of Alternative Schools, or the National Association for Parental Rights in Education.

41. From an interview with a Baptist layman, quoted in Paul Parsons, *Inside America's Christian Schools* (Macon, Ga.: Mercer University Press, 1987), p. 22.
42. Citizens for Educational Freedom brochure, "Children: Our Hope for the Future; Our Most Precious Resource," St. Louis, Mo.
43. Telephone interview with Mae Duggan of Citizens for Educational Freedom and the Thos. J. White Educational Foundation, 7 June 1989. See also "Children: Our Hope for the Future; Our Most Precious Resource."
44. This is seen, for example, in the Christian character of the 1988 National Home School Convention. The substance of the sessions and of the resolutions adopted by 95 percent of those in attendance, was overtly Christian. The Home School Legal Defense Association (mentioned later) takes on the "obligation . . . to defend the interests of all parents," yet still describes itself as "an openly Christian organization." See *Home School Court Report* 5, 1 (Winter 1989).
45. Brian D. Ray, "The Kitchen Classroom: Is Home Schooling Making the Grade," *Christianity Today* 32 (12 August 1988): 23.
46. See the very helpful essay by Patricia M. Lines, "An Overview of Home Instruction," *Phi Delta Kappan* 68 (March 1987): 510–17, as well as Ray, "The Kitchen Classroom: Is Home Schooling Making the Grade," pp. 23–25. These figures were also confirmed in a telephone interview with Michael Farris, director of the Home School Legal Defense Association, 12 June 1989. This figure probably reaches to 1 million if one takes migrant worker children into consideration.
47. From *Statistical Abstract of the United States, 1988,* 108th ed. (Washington, D.C.: Department of Commerce, Bureau of the Census, 1988), p. 121, table 193.
48. Hunter, *The Williamsburg Charter Survey.*
49. R. P. Bulka, "Orthodoxy Today: An Analysis of the Achievements and the Problems," in *Dimensions of Orthodox Judaism,* ed. R. P. Bulka (New York: KTAV Publishing House, 1983).
50. Telephone interview with Michael Farris, 12 June 1989.
51. "Question and Answer" brochure produced by the Citizens for Educational Freedom, no date. "Children: Our Hope for the Future; Our Most Precious Resource," St. Louis, Mo.
52. Taken from a draft of the report, "Problems with the Administration's Voucher Proposal for Chapter 1: The Equity and Choice Act," prepared for the Subcommittee on Elementary, Secondary, and Vocational Education of the Committee on Education and Labor, Washington, D.C., 1986, p. 14.
53. Discussion paper, "Choice in Public Schools," National Education Association, Washington, D.C., February 1989, p. 7.

54. This policy statement came from the NEA's Office of Government Relations, June 1985.
55. "Rallies Opposing Gay Students Disrupt Campuses," *New York Times,* 6 May 1990, pp. 51–52.
56. Chester Finn, "The Campus: 'An Island of Repression in a Sea of Freedom,'" *Commentary* 88, 3 (September 1989): 18.
57. Ernest Earnest, *Academic Procession: An Informal History of the American College 1636–1953* (New York: Bobbs-Merrill, 1953), pp. 84–85.
58. From the American Sociological Association publication *Footnotes* 12 (March 1984). Emphasis added.
59. "Joint Statement on Accuracy in Academia," 12 November 1985, drafted and signed by the American Council on Education, the American Association of University Professors, the National Association of State Universities and Land Grant Colleges, the Association of Governing Boards of Universities and Colleges, the Association of Catholic Colleges and Universities, the Association of Urban Universities, the Council of Graduate Schools, the American Psychological Association, and several others.
60. Telephone interview with Leslie Carbone of Accuracy in Academia, 25 June 1990.
61. Joseph Murphy, chancellor of City University of New York, quoted in *Chronicle of Higher Education* 31 (December 1985): 21.
62. Dinesh D'Souza, "Illiberal Education," *Atlantic Monthly* (March 1991): 51–79.
63. Writing in the *Chronicle of Higher Education* 35 (3 May 1989): 81–83, William Damon (professor of psychology and chairman of the Education Department at Clark University) argued, "I would like to see colleges engage all incoming students in mandatory racial-education programs. . . . It is important to make such programs mandatory so that they can reach students who otherwise might not be inclined to participate."
64. A superb review of this development and its implications is found in Finn, "The Campus: 'An Island of Repression in a Sea of Freedom,'" *Commentary* 88, 3 (September 1989): 17–23. Material reviewed here borrows extensively from the Finn piece.
65. The university spokeswoman was Jan Davidson and she is quoted by Charles Krauthamner in "Annals of Political Correctness," *Washington Post,* February 8, 1991, p. A19.
66. Finn, "The Campus," p. 17.
67. Kersti Yllo, "Revisions: How the New Scholarship on Women and Gender Transforms the College Curriculum," *American Behavioral Scientist* 32, 6 (July–August 1989): 659.
68. This point is made in D'Souza, "Illiberal Education," pp. 51–79. I draw extensively from this article.

69. Statement made by Michael Harris, professor of History at Wesleyan University, quoted in D'Souza, "Illiberal Education," p. 54.
70. These observations were taken from the American Psychological Association's *Council Policy Reference Book,* revised through the council's 1988 legislative year, from the files of the American Sociological Association in Washington, D.C.
71. Thomas Short, "A 'New Racism' on Campus?" *Commentary* 86, 2 (1988): 50. See Roger Rosenblatt's review of Roger Kimball's *Tenured Radicals: How Politics Has Corrupted Our Higher Education* in "The Universities: A Bitter Attack," *New York Times Book Review,* 22 April 1990.
72. The Stanford story was widely publicized. Bennett's own remarks are taken from the adaptation of a speech delivered at Stanford and reprinted in *National Review,* 27 May 1988, pp. 37–39.
73. The statement was made by John E. Becker of Fairleigh Dickinson University. He is quoted in "Opening Academia Without Closing It Down," *New York Times,* 10 December 1990.
74. Cyrus Veeser, "Great Books and Bayonets," *Harpers* 277 (October 1988): 20–21.
75. Sydney Hook, "An Open Letter to the Stanford University Faculty Senate," *Partisan Review* 55, 4 (1988): 664–74. In a more conciliatory tone, Nell Irvin Painter, a history professor at Princeton, said, "I wish that those who take potshots at what they see as a new 'political correctness' would give a thought to what American universities used to be like. Then perhaps they would hesitate before assailing the attempt to forge a pedagogy appropriate for newly diversified student bodies and faculties." Quoted in "Opening Academia Without Closing it Down," *New York Times* 10 December 1990.
76. See Paul William Kingston, "Bloom's Appeal to the American Mind," *Tocqueville Review* 9 (1987–88): 407–11. Kingston poignantly concludes: "To put the matter starkly, Bloom's appeal reflects his denunciation of Mick Jagger, not his view on Heidegger, his aversion to equality between the sexes, not his Straussian philosophy, and his celebration of elite cultural unity, not his enshrinement of philosophers' disinterested reason as the highest expression of humanity" (p. 408).
77. Fox Butterfield, "The Right Breeds a College Press Network," *New York Times,* 24 October 1990, p. A1. Perhaps the biggest financial supporter is the John M. Olin Foundation in New York. The Madison Foundation for Educational Affairs, through its Collegiate Network, also helps organize and fund the papers.
78. For a sampling of this literature, see E. Michael Jones, "Is Notre Dame Still Catholic?" *Fidelity* (June 1984): 18–26 and (September 1984): 25–34; Dick Goldkamp, "God, Sex Revolution and the Single Girl at St. Louis University," *Fidelity* (June 1984): 12–28; Editorial: "God and Mammon at Notre Dame," *Fidelity* (July 1982): 7; Ralph McInerny, "Purge at Wadhams Hall," *Cathol-*

icism in Crisis (February 1983): 22–24; "Editorial: Catholic U?" *Fidelity* (May 1985): 4–7.

79. "A Proposal for the Fulfillment of Catholic Liberal Education," Thomas Aquinas College, Santa Paula, Calif., 1981.
80. William Bentley Ball quoted in editorial, "The Bob Jones Decision: A Dangerous Precedent," *Christianity Today* 27 (2 September 1983): 14.
81. George Atkinson, "The Culture Most Valuable to Prepare Law-Abiding and Law-Respecting Citizens," in *NEA Proceedings* (1989): 115–21. Emphasis added.
82. Discussion paper, "Choice in Public Schools," p. 9.

CHAPTER 9: MEDIA AND THE ARTS

1. National Right to Life Committee, Washington, D.C., direct mail appeal, Spring 1990. LaHaye's direct mail appeal was sent out about May 1988.
2. Helle Bering-Jensen, "A Hell-Bent Crusade Against Pornography," *Insight,* 2 July 1990, p. 12.
3. Three studies, Lichter et al., *The Media Elite;* Research and Forecasts, *The Connecticut Mutual Life Report on Values in the 80s,* 1982; and my own "Religion and Power Survey" funded by the Lilly Endowment, documented these tendencies. Reports from the Center for Media and Public Affairs, Washington, D.C., summarize content analysis of television news programs and newspaper reporting for a wide range of issues (such as abortion) or political events (such as campaigns).
4. Quoted in Thomas Edsall and David Vise, "CBS Fight a Litmus Test for Conservatives."
5. Patrick Buchanan, "CBS: 'Conservative Broadcasting System,' " *Human Events,* 16 February 1985, p. 137.
6. "How Conservatives Can Get Control of CBS," *Human Events,* 26 January 1985, p. 76.
7. Morality in Media brochure, New York, no date. Accuracy in Media brochure, Washington, D.C., no date. Tipper Gore, "Curbing the Sexploitation Industry," *New York Times,* 14 March 1988, p. A19.
8. Don Winbush, "Bringing Satan to Heel," *Time,* 19 June 1989, pp. 54–55.
9. Quoted in Mike Yorkey, "A New Wind Blows Through Hollywood," *Citizen* 3, 5 (May 1989): 10 (emphasis added).
10. For example, when he learned of the Kennedy plan, the film critic Michael Medved of Public Broadcasting Service (PBS) immediately wrote Kennedy a letter of congratulation. "I want to let you know how pleased I was to hear of your plans to produce mainstream movies that promote family and religious values. While I am not a Christian myself, I am an observant Jew and active in my local synagogue in California. Along with many of my

fellow congregants, I share precisely the frustrations and the hopes for movies which you expressed in your article. . . . If there is any way that I can be helpful to you in the months ahead, please let me know. In any event, I wanted to inform you immediately that there is at least one national movie critic who is already sympathetic to your efforts." Quoted in ibid., p. 10.

11. Jeffrey K. Hadden and Anson Shupe, *Televangelism: Power and Politics on God's Frontier* (New York: Henry Holt, 1988), p. 292.
12. Lucy Lippard, "Andres Serrano: The Spirit and the Letter," *Art in America* 78 (April 1990): 238–45.
13. Transcript of ABC's "Nightline," 10 April 1990.
14. Carole S. Vance, "The War on Culture," *Art in America* 77 (September 1989): 39–43. American Family Association quote from direct mailing.
15. The observation was made by Representative Dick Armey, quoted in Alex Heard, "Mapplethorpe of My Eye," *New Republic,* 21 August 1989, p. 11.
16. Quoted in Robert Hughes, "Whose Art Is It, Anyway?" *Time,* 4 June 1990, p. 47.
17. David Mills, "The Obscenity Case: Criminalizing Black Culture," *Washington Post,* 17 June 1990, p. G1.
18. Jon Pareles, "Rap: Slick, Nasty and—Maybe Hopeful," *New York Times,* 17 June 1990, section 4, pp. 1, 5.
19. Richard Corliss, "X-Rated," *Time,* 7 May 1990, p. 94.
20. Bering-Jensen, "A Hell-Bent Crusade Against Pornography," p. 15.
21. Transcript of "48 Hours," CBS News, 27 June 1990.
22. Ibid.
23. Ibid.
24. All quoted in Tom Breen, "Film Found Artistic, but Not Blasphemous," *Washington Times,* 15 August 1988.
25. John Leo, "A Holy Furor," *Time,* 15 August 1988, p. 36.
26. The statement is attributed to the Rev. Michael Himes, quoted in a direct mail solicitation from *Fidelity.*
27. Reported in Leo, "A Holy Furor," p. 34. The conservative Catholic *Crisis* reported that even the movie critic Michael Medved agreed that the film was "only the latest and most flagrant example of Hollywood's consistent hostility toward organized religion." *Crisis* (November 1988): 4. Perhaps this is because he is an observant Jew.
28. Leo, "A Holy Furor," p. 34.
29. "U.S. Catholic Bishops Denounce Movie," *Daily Progress,* 20 August 1988, p. B4.
30. From a Focus on the Family mass mailing, dated September 1988, Pomona, Calif.
31. Advertisement, *New York Times,* 12 August 1988, p. A7.
32. From an interview, "Magazine Publisher and CWA Face Off on *Sassy,*" pub-

lished in *Newsletter of Concerned Women for America* 11 (August 1989): 22–23.

33. Direct mail appeal signed by Reverend Donald Wildmon of the American Family Association, Tupelo, Miss., Spring 1989.
34. Wildmon quoted in Winbush, "Bringing Satan to Heel," p. 54.
35. "Boycott Targets TV Sponsors," *Christianity Today* 33 (18 August 1989): 49 (emphasis added).
36. Reported in "Complicity Is Not Cost-Free," *Playboy* 36 (November 1989): 45.
37. Reported in *Focus on the Family Citizen* 2, 2 (February 1988): 11.
38. Carol Iannone, "From 'Lolita' to 'Piss Christ,' " *Commentary* 89 (January 1990): 52–54. Lippard, "Andres Serrano: The Spirit and the Letter," p. 245.
39. Richard Posner makes this point in "Art for Law's Sake," *American Scholar* 58 (Autumn 1989): 513–20. It is endorsed by critic Robert Brustein, "The First Amendment and the NEA," *New Republic,* 11 September 1989, p. 27.
40. Iannone, "From 'Lolita' to 'Piss Christ,' " pp. 52–54.
41. Robert Rauschenberg quoted in George Will, "The Helms Bludgeon," *Washington Post,* 3 August 1987, p. A27.
42. On the first theme consider the following: "Kathleen Sullivan of the Harvard Law School [has] testified [that] a work cannot legally be defined as obscene if it has serious artistic merit, and NEA grants are by definition made to works that fellow artists have validated." John F. Barber, "A War That Must Be Won," editorial, *Publishers Weekly,* 1 June 1990, p. 1.
43. Baas and Sobieszek quoted in Jayne Merkel, "Art on Trial," *Art in America* 78 (December 1990): 47. Later in his testimony, Sobieszek reiterated the view that there are no qualities that inhere in an object that make it art but that art exists when experts define it as such. When asked, "What determines what is a work of art?" he responded: "I think it's the culture at large—museums, critics, galleries."
44. Quoted in Brustein, "The First Amendment and the NEA," p. 28.
45. Will, "The Helms Bludgeon."
46. Henry J. Hyde, "The Culture War," *National Review,* 30 April 1990, pp. 25–27.
47. The first comment was made by Susan Wyatt, executive director of Artists' Space, taken from a transcript of "Mapplethorpe: Obscene in Cincinnati?" on ABC's "Nightline," 10 April 1990; the second comment is attributed to photographer Jock Sturgis, taken from a transcript of "48 Hours," CBS News, 27 June 1990.
48. Mills, "The Obscenity Case: Criminalizing Black Culture."
49. Of course, it is the arrogance of the orthodox in their particular views of art that lead them to accuse the arts establishment of being "smut peddlers."

50. Founder of Fundamentalists Anonymous quoted in "Pepsi: Soda-Pop of Puritans," *Playboy* 36 (September 1989): 42. Director of Americans for Constitutional Freedom quoted in an ACF press release, New York, 1 June 1989.
51. See Peter Bien, "Scorsese's Spiritual Jesus," *New York Times,* 11 August 1988, and a *Washington Post* editorial, "Satanism in Hollywood," 12 August 1988.
52. See, for example, Madalynne Reuter, "Small Firms Claim Printer Censorship Is Growing," *Publishers Weekly,* 29 June 1990, p. 10.
53. Cited in Tipper Gore, *Raising PG Kids in an X Rated Society* (New York: Bantam, 1988), p. 61.
54. Transcript, "48 Hours," CBS News, 27 June 1990.
55. This observation is attributed to Phil Harvey, the founder and president of Adam and Eve adult mail-order company, taken from the transcript, ibid.
56. *Attacks on the Freedom to Learn: 1986–87 Report* (Washington, D.C.: People for the American Way, 1987), p. 9.
57. All of these quotes are found in Vance, "The War on Culture," pp. 39–43. Robert Brustein also sees within the backlash to the NEA the specter of totalitarianism in "The First Amendment and the NEA," p. 28. There he says, "Totalitarianism's campaign against 'degenerate modern art,' and its insistence that art be 'the handmaiden of sublimity and beauty, and thus promote whatever is natural and healthy,' is well-known. The memory of it is still fresh."
58. Brustein, "The First Amendment and the NEA," p. 29.
59. Quoted in "Pepsi: Soda-Pop of Puritans," p. 42.
60. Timothy K. Jones, editorial: "Put Up Your Dukes," *Christianity Today* 34 (17 December 1990): 14.
61. Interview by Winbush, "Bringing Satan to Heel," pp. 54–55.
62. Ibid.
63. See Gore, *Raising PG Kids in an X Rated Society,* p. 10. "You Can Help Turn the Tide of Pornography," brochure, Morality in Media, New York, no date.
64. Reported in Mike Zahn, "TV Evangelist Targeted in Ads," *Journal* (Milwaukee, Wis.), 14 April 1987.
65. Cal Thomas, *Book Burning* (Westchester, Ill.: Crossway Books, 1983), p. 105.
66. *Chronicles of Culture* subscription appeal. Emphasis in original. In this same spirit, Father Virgil Blum of the Catholic League for Religious and Civil Rights complained that the views of the league had been "suppressed" and "censored" by a press "dominated and controlled by Secularists." Direct mail solicitation by the Catholic League, Milwaukee, Wis., no date.
67. News item in *Christianity Today* 33 (15 December 1989): 50. Emphasis added.
68. See Ken Sidey, "Open Season on Christians?" *Christianity Today* 34 (23 April 1990): 34–36.
69. Historically, of course, some Fundamentalists have shown reckless disregard for the rights of minority perspectives and values, and such disregard continues to the present. But a similar insensitivity can be found among those

who believe themselves to be champions of liberal toleration. For example, when the *New York Times* criticizes rap music for its sexism and homophobia but completely ignores the vulgarity, it shows this disregard. See Pareles, "Rap: Slick, Nasty and—Maybe Hopeful." When the head of Americans for Constitutional Freedom (ACT) claims that boycotts for liberal causes are legitimate but illegitimate for conservative causes, it also displays this disregard. The 1 June 1989 press release of ACT states: "Wildmon's weapon in his fight for censorship is the boycott. Teicher [the executive director of ACT] acknowledged that the boycott can be a legitimate means of protest when it is used, as it was during the civil rights movement, to fight for expanded rights. 'But, let's not be fooled. What Wildmon is doing is not democratic. The boycotts of civil rights movements expanded freedom. Wildmon's boycotts restrict freedom by cutting access to television shows, movies, books and magazines that are protected by the First Amendment. The television boycott will try to kill popular programs by intimidating their sponsors. These are the same tactics Senator Joseph McCarthy made infamous in the 1950s' " (pp. 5–6).

70. Garry Wills made this point eloquently in his essay, "In Praise of Censure," *Time,* 31 July 1989, pp. 71–72.
71. This was precisely the argument of Lippard in "Andres Serrano: The Spirit and the Letter," pp. 238–45.
72. Breen, "Film Found Artistic, but Not Blasphemous." An article published in the *Post* surveyed the world of film criticism and found that "movie critics across the United States concurred that . . . *The Last Temptation of Christ* . . . is far from blasphemous."
73. Emphasis added. Breen, "Film Found Artistic, But Not Blasphemous."
74. From the transcript of ABC "Nightline," 10 April 1990.
75. "Today educated people look upon traditional religious ties—Catholic, Episcopal, Presbyterian, Methodist, Baptist, Jewish—as matters of social pedigree. It is only art that they look upon religiously." Tom Wolfe, "The Worship of Art: Notes on the New God," *Harpers* 269 (October 1984): 61.
76. ABC "Nightline," 10 April 1990.

CHAPTER 10: LAW

1. See Alexis de Tocqueville, *Democracy in America,* J. P. Mayer, ed. (Garden City: Doubleday, 1969), p. 270.
2. Herman Schwartz, "The New Right's Court Packing Campaign," occasional paper, People for the American Way, Washington, D.C., no date, p. 23.
3. Alan Parker, "The Reagan Judicial Legacy," *Trial* 21 (October 1985): 11.
4. Quoted in George J. Church, "The Court's Pivot Man," *Time,* 6 July 1987, p. 10.

5. Schwartz, p. 119.
6. Ibid.
7. See Suzanne Garment, "The War Against Robert H. Bork," *Commentary* 85, 1 (January 1988): 17–26. See also the lengthy response to this treatment in *Commentary* 85, 5 (May 1988). In addition to this, see Schwartz for a review of the effort on the part of ideological groups to pack the courts.
8. The fist quotation is from *Forum,* the newsletter of the People for the American Way Action Fund (Spring 1990), p. 6. The second came from a People for the American Way brochure, "If We Take Our Freedoms for Granted, Others Will Take Our Freedoms Away," Washington, D.C., no date.
9. The case was *U.S. Catholic Conference v. Abortion Rights Mobilization (ARM)* 824 F.2d 156 (1987). The case was initiated by several pro-choice groups and individuals but led by ARM, when they sued the Internal Revenue Service and the Treasury Department for not revoking the Catholic Church's tax-exempt status because of the church's pro-life activism. The technical issues the Court addressed were twofold: first, does ARM have the legal standing to sue the government; and second, can the church be forced to hand over sensitive documents without the right to first challenge the underlying lawsuit.
10. These figures came from successive years of the *United States Court Reporter* (Washington, D.C.: U.S. Government Printing Office). Between 1947 and 1956 the number was sixteen; between 1957 and 1966 it was fourteen; between 1967 and 1976 it was thirty-four. These numbers include cases appealed to the Supreme Court on the basis of the establishment or free exercise clauses of the First Amendment, even if decided by the Court on other grounds, and cases decided by the Court on the basis of those clauses even if originally appealed on other grounds. It does not include religion clause appeals rejected by the Supreme Court.
11. Dean Kelley has made this observation on the basis of his research in *The Law of Church and State* (Westport, Conn.: Greenwood Press, forthcoming). A large part of this growth in cases is explained by the passage of the Fourteenth Amendment applying federal law to the states. Nevertheless, the expansion of such cases well after the passage of the Fourteenth Amendment stands as a testimony to the contention that the battle over procedures has intensified.
12. The substantive approach derives from the theoretical tradition of the German phenomenology—the tradition of the *religionswissenschaften* (most notably developed by such intellectuals as Max Weber, Rudolf Otto, Gerardus Van der Leeuw, Joachim Wach, and Peter Berger). The functionalist approach derives from French and British structuralism—as found in the works of Emile Durkheim, Branislaw Malinowski, A. R. Radcliffe-Brown, Talcott Parsons, Milton Yinger, Robert Bellah, Thomas Luckmann, and Mary Douglas—and German sociological materialism (Marx, Engels, and most recently, Michael Harrington). For the recent debate in social science

see P. Berger, *The Sacred Canopy* (New York: Doubleday, 1967), appendix I; Dobbelaere and Lauwers, "Definition of Religion—A Sociological Critique,"; P. Berger, "Some Second Thoughts on Substantive versus Functional Definitions of Religion," *Journal for the Scientific Study of Religion* 13 (June 1974): 125–33; and A. Weigert, "Functional, Substantive, or Political? A Comment on Berger's Second Thoughts on Defining Religions," *Journal for the Scientific Study of Religion* 13 (December 1974): 483–86.

13. This approach, of course, is entirely compatible with Paul Tillich's (1958) definition of religion as the "ultimate concern" of a social group or society as well as the Supreme Court's usage of a "functional test" in determining what religion is.
14. The review of the changing nature of the legal definitions in J. H. Choper, "Defining 'Religion' in the First Amendment," *University of Illinois Law Review* 3 (1982): 579–613; and in Whitehead," *The Second American Revolution,* provided useful guides for the following discussion. Lawrence Tribe wrote, "At least through the nineteenth century, religion was given a fairly narrow reading . . . 'religion' referred to theistic notions respecting divinity, morality, and worship." L. Tribe, *American Constitutional Law* (Mineola, N.Y.: Foundations, 1978), p. 826.
15. *Davis v. Beason,* 133 U.S. 33, 341–343 (1890).
16. *Church of the Holy Trinity v. United States,* 143 U.S. 457, 472 (1892).
17. *David v. Beason,* 133 U.S. 33, 341–343 (1890).
18. *United States v. Macintosh,* 283 U.S. 605, 633–34 (1931).
19. *United States v. Kauten,* 133 F. 2d 703, 708 (2d Cir. 1943). Emphasis added.
20. The case was *United States v. Ballard,* 322 U.S. 78, 86 (1944). It involved a Mr. Guy Ballard (alias Saint Germain, Jesus, George Washington, and Godfre Ray King) and members of his family who claimed to be Divine Messengers. As leaders of the I Am movement, they solicited funds "by means of false and fraudulent representations, pretenses and promises" (p. 79).
21. *Torcaso v. Watkins,* 367 U.S. 488, 490 (1961).
22. *Torcaso v. Watkins,* 367 U.S. 495 (1961).
23. *United States v. Seeger,* 380 U.S. 163, 166 (1965).
24. *United States v. Seeger,* 380 U.S. 176 (1965).
25. Tribe, *American Constitutional Law,* note 78, p. 827.
26. Ibid., p. 828. The other justification offered is that the First Amendment only mentions the word "religion" once, with regard to the establishment clause. That it was not mentioned with regard to the free exercise clause allows for a broader interpretation.
27. See Choper, "Defining 'Religion' in the First Amendment," pp. 610–13.
28. In his book, *A Common Faith* (New Haven, Conn.: Yale University Press, 1934), the American philosopher John Dewey insisted that his secular and humanistic beliefs constituted a religious faith. Likewise, the *Humanist Man-*

ifesto I (1933) was replete with references and inferences that humanism is a religion. Indeed, in this document it was implied that humanism was the highest realization of man's religious aspirations.

> Today man's larger understanding of the universe, his scientific achievements, and his deeper appreciation of brotherhood, have created a situation which requires a new statement of the means and purposes of religion. Such a vital, fearless, and frank religion capable of furnishing adequate social goals and personal satisfactions may appear to many people as a complete break with the past. While this age does owe a vast debt to traditional religions, it is none the less obvious that any religion that can hope to be a synthesizing and dynamic force for today must be shaped for the needs of this age. To establish such a religion is a major necessity of the present. It is a responsibility which rests upon this generation. . . . Religion consists of those actions, purposes, and experiences which are humanly significant. Nothing human is alien to the religious. It includes labor, art, science, philosophy, love, friendship, recreation—all that is in its degree expressive of intelligently satisfying human living. The distinction between the sacred and the secular can no longer be maintained.

Beyond this, Ethical Culture has since 1887 described itself as a "religious fellowship" as has the Fellowship of Religious Humanists (since 1963).

29. The inclusion of theists in this description is not arbitrary, for the case was defined as a class action suit on behalf of "all theists." Other support for the Board of Education came from the pro bono assistance of Hogan and Hartson, a large law firm from Washington, D.C.
30. *Smith v. Board of School Commissioners.* 827 F.2d 90. I was one of the expert witnesses called to testify in this case. In addition to examining the social studies textbooks for their treatment of the role of religion in American society, I also wrote a theoretical document entitled, "Humanism and Social Theory: Is Secular Humanism a Religion?" A popularized version of this was J. D. Hunter, "America's Fourth Faith: A Sociological Perspective on Secular Humanism," *This World* 19 (1987): 101–10.
31. The most interesting of the repudiations was made by an expert witness, Paul Kurtz, an apologist for the secular humanist movement, who claimed that secular humanism was not a religion—in open contradiction to contentions he had made earlier, advocating that it was in fact a religion. In chapter 13 of his 1983 book, *In Defense of Secular Humanism* (Buffalo, N.Y.: Prometheus Books), based on an article originally published in *The Humanist* (November–December 1964), Paul Kurtz writes:

> "Religion" for the humanist refers primarily to a *quality in human experience.* It is centered around man and his concerns. It is, as Tillich suggests, the expression of our "ultimate concern," the basic ideal ends to which a person is committed—the confession of which may call forth a stutter, a smile, or a blush. Thus we have a "religious experience" when we are aware of our basic values and aims.
>
> In what way does this differ from philosophical awareness? Philosophy is

> cognitive and rational, religion affective and attitudinal. Science describes for us; religion profoundly moves us. A philosophical position is converted into a religious position only when the philosophy is given the strength of passionate devotion and conviction. Religion thus goes beyond thought to stir our irrational natures. Under this definition the communist would be religious in his devotion to the aims of dialectical materialism, as would the Epicurean, the Buddhist, the Taoist in their devotion to other ideals. Here faith does not involve belief in the alleged reality of an unseen being, which is independent of, or contrary to, reason and experience; but it is a conviction that an ideal can be achieved. Religion in this sense is a serious and compelling commitment to a way of life; it gives direction and form to our energies and activities.
>
> There are thus two main characteristics of this humanistic definition of religion: (1) its reference to *fundamental* and *basic* ideals and values, and (2) its reference to *attitudes* and *feelings*. One's values, however, are not held in isolation from one's general cognitive beliefs about the world and one's place within it. Indeed, one's world view, whether naturalistic or theistic has some effect upon the general attitudes and responses that one takes toward the world in general and other human beings. Yet it is the prescriptiveness and the expressiveness that a system of beliefs may arouse that is the distinctive religious quality of experience. So far as persons are aware of their basic values, and as these have some controlling emotive power in their lives, they may be said to be "religious." When someone becomes concerned attitudinally with his ultimate principles, he is functioning religiously. (p. 116, emphasis in original)

Both in his 1986 testimony and in an issue of *Free Inquiry* (Winter 1985–86) Kurtz argues the opposite view, that humanism is not a religion.

32. *Washington Post* columnist Colman McCarthy, who typically aligns himself with progressivist causes, found himself unable to support the detractors of the plaintiffs and Judge Brevard Hand's decision in *Smith.* In the *Washington Post* 5 April 1987, p. F2, McCarthy wrote: "There's one hitch on all this: the actual 111-page decision of Judge Hand. It is not another spray of right-wing dye meant to color the debate with the biases of backwoods Bible-toters. A careful reading of the decision, as against a skimming of news accounts of it, reveals that Mobile families had a fair grievance: That what was taught in classrooms about religion was impeding the teachings of mothers and fathers at home about religion. What's wrong with that complaint?"
33. Koch, Adrienne, and William Peden, eds. *The Life and Selected Writings of Thomas Jefferson* (New York: Random House, 1944), p. 381.
34. *Everson v. Board of Education,* 330 U.S. 1 (1947).
35. To be sure, on some of these cases, orthodox and progressivist forces line up on the same side. In 1983, for example, both the reverends Jesse Jackson and Jerry Falwell came to the defense of seven Christian Fundamentalists, who were jailed in Nebraska because the Christian school their children attended had defied state laws regarding the certification of teachers. In the same year, Rev. Joseph Lowery, the leader of the Southern Christian Leadership Conference, along with other liberal and conservative religious leaders came to the defense of Rev. Sun Myung Moon, who had been convicted

of income tax evasion in connection with the finances of his Unification Church. So too religious leaders of many confessions supported the free exercise rights of Captain Simcha, an ordained rabbi and clinical psychologist at March Air Force Base who wanted to wear his yarmulke while in uniform (in *Goldman v. Weinberger,* 106 S. Ct. 1310 [1986]). In many, if not most cases, however, the legal dispute finds the orthodox favoring legal principle while progressives support total separation. Part of the muddying impulse comes from religious and theological heritage on this issue. The mainline Protestant and Catholic positions are not always so strongly separationist because, like their orthodox counterparts, they represent a distinctly religious voice in public discourse and have an interest in not remaining sequestered in the private sphere. At the same time, the historical position of the Baptists (even orthodox Baptists) has been to favor strict separationism. In the eighteenth century, Baptists were at a distinct disadvantage against the Congregationalists in New England and the Episcopalians in the South. Separationism meant a freer competition with their rivals. Though the original rationale no longer applies, Baptists have remained committed to that tradition.

36. J. D. Hunter, *The Williamsburg Charter Survey on Religion and American Public Life* (Washington, D.C.: Williamsburg Charter Foundation, 1988). The following review of the Williamsburg Charter Survey data was based upon the author's reanalysis.
37. Among all rabbis, 15 percent of the more Orthodox (measured by the professed observance of kosher rules) favored the accommodationist position compared to none of the liberal rabbis.
38. The majority of mainline ministers agreed with this statement but not nearly so unanimously—70 percent. Conservative and liberal Catholic priests were comparable at 83 percent. The majority of rabbis rejected this statement yet with different intensity—43 percent of the Orthodox agreed while only 32 percent of the liberals agreed.
39. Eighty-three percent of the Evangelicals agreed that "it is a good thing for sporting events at public high schools to begin with a public prayer" compared to 62 percent of the mainline Protestants and 34 percent of the secularists. Among Catholics, 61 percent of the orthodox believed it was a good thing compared to 46 percent of the liberal Catholics. Among the leadership, 84 percent of the Evangelical leaders agreed compared to 48 percent of the mainline Protestant ministers, 23 percent of the secular media elites, and 12 percent of the academic elites. Among Catholics, 64 percent of the conservatives compared to 56 percent of the more progressive agreed with the statement; and again, rabbis disproportionately opted for the separatist position yet by different margins. Nearly one of every five of the observant rabbis agreed compared to only 4 percent of the liberal rabbis.

40. Eighty-seven percent of the Evangelicals, 85 percent of their ministers, 81 percent of all Catholics, and 89 percent of their priests agreed that "it's OK for a City Government to put up candles on government property for a Jewish religious celebration." On the other hand, 66 percent of the secularists agreed with this statement. Jews remained consistently separationist on this issue but in a pattern that has become predictable. Nearly 20 percent of the more observant rabbis agreed that a manger scene and Menorah candles could be put up on government property, compared to only 4 percent of the less observant.
41. Compared to the 89 percent of the Evangelicals who agreed with this statement were 78 percent of the mainline Protestants, and 60 percent of the secularists.
42. The actual figures on the question about a moment of silence were as follows: Protestants: orthodox—89 percent, progressive—78 percent; Catholics: orthodox—86 percent, progressive—75 percent; Jews: Orthodox—28 percent, progressive—8 percent. Chi square, significant at .000 level.
43. Over three-fourths (77 percent) of the Evangelicals favored equal access; two-thirds (66 percent) of the mainline Protestants favored it. Liberal and conservative Catholics favored it comparably at about 72 percent, and just over two-thirds of the secularists favored the policy. Among elites there was a similar pattern: Protestants: orthodox—79 percent, progressive—70 percent; Catholics: orthodox and progressive both at 83 percent; and Jews: Orthodox—32 percent, progressive—16 percent. Chi square, significant at .000 level.
44. Of course, the Catholic hierarchy has a long history of support for this policy and therefore it is not surprising that there is no difference of opinion among orthodox and progressive Catholic priests (both at 16 percent) and Catholic laity (both at 40 percent).
45. Seventy-two percent of the academics and 57 percent of the media elites agreed with that statement.
46. The actual figures for these leadership groups were as follows: academics, 75 percent; media elites, 71 percent; orthodox Protestant clergy, 85 percent; mainline Protestant clergy, 78 percent; orthodox Catholic priests, 88 percent; progressive Catholic priests, 70 percent; Orthodox rabbis, 77 percent, and progressive rabbis, 56 percent.
47. Although there is clearly no love lost between progressives and the Moral Majority, roughly two-thirds (66 percent) of the academics, 63 percent of the media elites, 51 percent of the progressive ministers and priests, and 47 percent of the progressive rabbis disagreed that "the Moral Majority should stay out of politics."
48. The actual figures for these leadership groups were as follows: academics, 97 percent; media elites, 91 percent; orthodox Protestant clergy, 68 percent,

mainline Protestant clergy, 72 percent; orthodox Catholic priests, 70 percent; progressive Catholic priests, 83 percent; and Orthodox and progressive rabbis, 81 percent each.

49. The actual figures for these leadership groups were as follows: academics, 87 percent; media elites, 81 percent; orthodox Protestant clergy, 69 percent; mainline Protestant clergy, 75 percent; orthodox and progressive Catholic priests, 73 percent each; progressive Catholic priests, 83 percent; and Orthodox rabbis, 80 percent, and progressive rabbis, 66 percent.
50. The review that follows has drawn heavily from D. L. Beschle, "The Conservative as Liberal: The Religion Clauses, Liberal Neutrality and the Approach of Justice O'Connor," *Notre Dame Law Review* 62 (1987): 151–91.
51. The statute was upheld because the Court classified the benefits that parochial students and their parents enjoyed as part and parcel of the benefits provided to all citizens of New Jersey, regardless of their particular religious affiliation.
52. *Everson v. Board of Education,* 330 U.S. 1 (1947).
53. *McCollum v. Board of Education,* 333 U.S. 203 at 212 (1948).
54. *Engel v. Vitale,* 370 U.S. 421 (1962): *Abington Township School District v. Schempp,* 374 U.S. 203 (1963).
55. *Epperson v. Arkansas,* 393 U.S. 97 (1968).
56. *Lemon v. Kurtzman,* 403 U.S. 602 (1971). In one of these programs the state of Rhode Island paid teachers in parochial elementary schools a supplement to their salary; Pennsylvania reimbursed parochial schools for the cost of books and teacher salaries in mathematics, foreign languages, the physical sciences, and physical education.
57. *Stone v. Graham,* 449 U.S. 39 (1980).
58. *United States v. Lee,* 455 U.S. 252 (1982).
59. *Goldman v. Weinberger,* 106 S. Ct. 1310 (1986); *Edwards v. Aguillard,* 482 U.S. 578 (1987).
60. *Zorach v. Clauson,* 343 U.S. 306 (1952); *Braunfeld v. Brown,* 366 U.S. 599 (1961); *McGowan v. Maryland,* 366 U.S. 420 (1961).
61. *Board of Education v. Allen,* 392 U.S. 236 (1968).
62. *Walz v. Tax Commission,* 397 U.S. 664 (1970); *Wisconsin v. Yoder,* 406 U.S. 205 (1972); *Wolman v. Walter,* 433 U.S. 229 (1977).
63. *McDaniel v. Paty,* 435 U.S. 618 (1978).
64. *Widmar v. Vincent,* 454 U.S. 263 (1981).
65. *Marsh v. Chambers,* 463 U.S. 783 (1983).
66. *Lynch v. Donnelly,* 104 S. Ct. 1355 (1984); *Bowen v. Kendrick,* 487 U.S. 589 (1988).
67. See Beschle, "The Conservative as Liberal: The Religion Clauses, Liberal Neutrality, and the Approach of Justice O'Connor." Beschle goes on to say that "the very fact that the Court has framed two separate sets of rules has led to an obvious tension between them—to strengthen the mandate that

government not aid religion may be to weaken the principle that it may not interfere with religious practice. This tension has given critics of the application of one clause ammunition to attack the Court drawn from the Court's own treatment of the other clause." (p. 164).

68. L. Levy, *The Establishment Clause* (New York: Macmillan, 1986), p. 163.
69. See Justice Lewis Powell's separate opinion on *Wolman v. Walter,* 433 U.S. 272 (1977).
70. Fink, "The Establishment Clause According to the Supreme Court: The Mysterious Eclipse of Free Exercise Values," pp. 207–62. See also D. Dreisbach, *Real Threat and Mere Shadow: Religious Freedom and the First Amendment* (Westchester, Ill.: Crossway, 1987).
71. R. J. Neuhaus, "The Pfefferian Inversion," paper presented at the Williamsburg Charter Conference on Religion and American Public Life, University of Virginia, Charlottesville, Va., April 1988.
72. In most cases the attorneys representing orthodox interests have not had the organizational mechanisms that the ACLU or the People for the American Way have had for promoting to a large audience their perspective on the cases. Concerned Women for America (which supported the plaintiffs in *Mozert v. Hawkins County School Board*) possesses those mechanisms. The orthodox admit, in private, that they sense that the media bias is so strongly "liberal" and therefore opposed to their interests that the most they can hope to accomplish is "a correction of some of the distortions of the truth." From a telephone interview with a spokesperson from the legal division of Concerned Women for America, 14 October 1988.
73. Dean Kelley also cites an increasingly dense population and a culture of litigiousness as still other reasons why we can expect more litigation on this issue (personal communication).

CHAPTER 11: ELECTORAL POLITICS

1. Some interesting developments are taking place within political science. See, for example, the work of Paul Kleppner, *The Cross of Culture* (New York: Free Press, 1970).
2. Quoted in the *New York Times,* 19 October 1980.
3. Paraphrased in part from a Reagan news conference in Los Angeles, and reported in Howell Raines, "Reagan Reiterates Warning on Schools," *New York Times,* 14 October 1980, p. D22.
4. Reagan said this in his debate with candidate John Anderson, quoted in Adam Clymer, "In TV Debate, Reagan Counts on Presence—and Absence," *New York Times,* 21 September 1980, p. E1.

5. All of these statements were made in the Reagan–Anderson debate reported in ibid.
6. Ibid.
7. These statements by Carter and Mondale were made on the last night of the Democratic National Convention and reported in the Hedrick Smith, "Mondale on Ticket," and "Transcript of Mondale's Address Accepting Renomination for Vice Presidency," *New York Times,* 15 August 1980, pp. A1, B4.
8. Quoted in *New York Times,* 27 September 1984 "We Will Lift America Up."
9. From a speech in Cleveland, Ohio, reported in "Mondale Moves to Shore Up Base," *New York Times,* 26 September 1984, p. D23.
10. From a speech in Tupelo, Mississippi, reported in Bernard Weintraub, "Mondale Defends Himself on Religion Issue in South," *New York Times,* 14 September 1984, p. A18.
11. "Archbishop Contends Abortion is Key Issue," *New York Times,* June 25, 1984, p. D13.
12. Compare J. K. White's analysis in his book, *The New Politics of Old Values* (Hanover, N.H.: University of New England Press, 1988), p. 2. See Paul Erickson, *Reagan Speaks: The Making of an American Myth* (New York: New York University Press, 1985), p. 115.
13. See the campaign video, "Pat Robertson: Who Is This Man?" Eagle Media Group, 1988. The Robertson quotes in this paragraph are from John Donovan, *Pat Robertson: The Authorized Biography* (New York: Macmillan, 1988): esp. chapter 9, "The Body Politic."
14. The Jackson quotes in this paragraph are from Roger Hatch and Frank Watkins, eds., *Reverend Jesse L. Jackson: Straight from the Heart* (Philadelphia: Fortress Press, 1987), p. 4.
15. From the Bush–Dukakis television debate, reported in E. J. Dionne, Jr., "Bush and Dukakis with Anger Debate Leadership and Issues from Abortion to Iran-Contra," *New York Times,* 26 September 1988, p. A1.
16. From Bush's nomination acceptance speech, reported in R. W. Apple, Jr., "Bush, in Rousing Finale, Vows More Jobs but Never a Tax Rise; Backs Quayle Despite Dispute," *New York Times,* 19 August 1988.
17. From the Bush–Dukakis television debate, reported in Dionne, "Bush and Dukakis with Anger," p. A1.
18. The first statement is from the Dukakis acceptance speech at the Democratic National Convention. The second is from the Bush–Dukakis debate, reported in Dionne, "Bush and Dukakis with Anger," p. A1.
19. Dukakis nomination acceptance speech at the Democratic National Convention.
20. The key measure here for Catholics is belief orthodoxy as defined in this book, not measures of piety such as church attendance. The patterns do not show up at all on the basis of church attendance.

21. Archbishop John F. Whealon, "The Democratic and Republican Platforms," *Crisis* (October 1988): 36–37.
22. Ibid., p. 37. See Peter Occhiogrosso, "Born Again Politics: Why a Catholic Housewife is Organizing the Midwest for Pat Robertson," *Crisis* (February 1988): 19–24.
23. See Gerald Capers, *Stephen A. Douglas: Defender of the Union* (Boston: Little, Brown, 1959), p. 187.
24. See Don E. Fehrenbacher, *Abraham Lincoln: Speeches and Writings, 1859–1865* (New York: Library of America, 1984), p. 137.
25. The Cockran speech is contained in Robert McElroy, ed., *In the Name of Liberty: Selected Speeches of Bourke Cockran* (New York: Putnam, 1925). The Bryan speech is contained in *The Annals of America, Vol. 12: Populism, Imperialism, and Reform* (Chicago: Encyclopedia Britannica Company, 1976).
26. See Allan J. Lichtman, *Prejudice and the Old Politics: The Presidential Election of 1928* (Chapel Hill: University of North Carolina Press, 1979), and Henry Pringle, *Alfred E. Smith: A Critical Study* (New York: Macy Macius Publishers, 1927).
27. This entire section of the chapter draws very heavily and directly from the insightful and eloquent work in J. W. Ceaser et al., "The Rise of the Rhetorical Presidency," *Presidential Studies Quarterly* 11 (Spring 1981): 158–171; J. K. Tulis, *The Rhetorical Presidency* (Princeton, N.J.: Princeton University Press, 1987); and J. W. Ceaser, "The Rhetorical Presidency Revisited," in *Modern Presidents and the Presidency,* ed. Marc Landy (Lexington, Mass.: Lexington Books, 1985). Conversations with Jim Ceaser of the Department of Government and Foreign Affairs at the University of Virginia have also contributed to the argument presented here.
28. The speaking tour of Andrew Johnson in the summer before the 1866 elections was the only real exception. Yet Ceaser et al., in "The Rise of the Rhetorical Presidency," argue that this campaign strategy not only failed, it was considered highly irregular (p. 234).
29. Ibid., p. 237.
30. Ibid.
31. Ibid., p. 234.
32. Ibid., p. 234.
33. Kiku Adatto, "The Incredible Shrinking Sound Bite," *New Republic,* 28 May 1990, pp. 20–23.
34. See Ceaser et al., "The Rise of the Rhetorical Presidency," p. 242. The consequence of this was summed up by Patrick Buchanan. Editorializing in the *Washington Times,* Buchanan stated that the "modern media—with its insatiable appetite for drama, conflict and controversy—have made the passive presidency a museum piece" (13 March 1989).
35. The extensive data reported in L. Sabato, *PAC Power: Inside The World of*

Political Action Committees (New York: Grove Press, 1985) document this point adequately up through the mid-1980s.

36. An empirical study documenting this trend was reported in Ceaser et al., "The Rise of the Rhetorical Presidency," p. 245.
37. The major polling agencies missed the boat on this one. See Fred Barnes, "Abortive Issue," *New Republic,* 4 December 1989, who reports on the CBS/*New York Times* exit poll. This pattern was shown in a poll conducted by the Center for Survey Research at the University of Virginia just before the November 1989 election. The abortion issue overrode party loyalty, race, and every other factor in its influence on people's vote. There was, according to pollster Steven Finkel, "substantial cross-over voting based on people's abortion views; this [was] especially noticeable in the numbers of pro-choice Republicans who currently prefer [the Democratic candidate]. From a press release from the Center for Survey Research, 4 November 1989, pp. 10–11.
38. See Ceaser, "The Rhetorical Presidency Revisited," p. 32.
39. Wilson quoted in Ceaser et al., "The Rise of the Rhetorical Presidency," p. 239.
40. Tim LaHaye, in the October 1988 issue of *Capital Report,* made a call to this effect in stating, "It's time more Christians realize they can serve both their God and their country by running for some of the 97,000 elective offices in this nation" (p. 3).

CHAPTER 12: MORAL PLURALISM AND THE DEMOCRATIC IDEAL

1. The question may be moot if there is, by chance, a national economic collapse. Seymour Martin Lipset is probably correct in arguing that the politics of culture and status characterize times of plenty, while times of poverty are marked by the politics of social class. Thus a deep recession, an economic stagnation, even depression might moderate hostilities considerably.
2. Sean Wilentz, "God and Man at Lynchburg," *The New Republic,* April 25, 1988, p. 30.
3. LaHaye quoted in Kim Lawton, "Whatever Happened to the Religious Right?" *Christianity Today* 33 (15 December 1989): 44. See "Robertson Regroups 'Invisible Army' into New Coalition," *Christianity Today* 34 (23 April 1990): 35.
4. Indeed, the COR steering committee reads like a Who's Who in the Evangelical world. Harold O. J. Brown, Robert Dugan (of the Washington Office of the National Association of Evangelicals), Duane Gish, D. James Kennedy, Tim LaHaye, Beverly LaHaye, Harold Lindsell, Ed McAteer, Josh McDowell, Bob Mumford, Gary North, J. I. Packer, R. J. Rushdooney, Edith Schaeffer, Franky Schaeffer, Congressman Mark Siljander, John Perkins,

Brother Andrew, and Donald Wildmon are only a few of the names listed. The quotation is from a COR letter and brochure dated 26 February 1990.

5. Ibid.
6. In the late 1980s, Concerned Women for America, for example, changed much of its organizational strategy by placing priority on the development of local prayer/action chapters. The National Organization for Women has also been very effective at mobilizing at the local level. According to John Buchanan, chairman of People for the American Way, "It is certainly easier to do battle with a nationally televised prominent person . . . than it is to fight state-by-state and locality-by-locality battles . . . but this is where I think the battles are going to be." Quoted in Lawton, "Whatever Happened to the Religious Right?" p. 46.
7. Jeffrey K. Hadden and Anson Shupe, *Televangelism: Power and Politics on God's Frontier* (New York: Henry Holt, 1988), pp. 286, 19.
8. Ibid., pp. 286–97.
9. This passion also translates into an indigenous grass-roots organization, namely churches, parishes, and synagogues, which can be enormously effective in mobilizing mass support. One study showed, for example, that over 95 percent of the pro-life activists were religiously active compared to only 2 percent of the pro-choice activists. See Kristin Luker, *Abortion and the Politics of Motherhood* (Berkeley: University of California Press, 1984).
10. From the COR brochure and letter, 26 February 1990.
11. See, for example, Fritz Machlup, *The Production and Distribution of Knowledge in the United States* (Princeton, N.J.: Princeton University Press, 1962), and Michael Rogers Rubin and Mary Taylor Huber, *The Knowledge Industry in the United States, 1960–1980* (Princeton, N.J.: Princeton University Press, 1986).
12. Rubin and Huber, *The Knowledge Industry in the United States, 1960–1980,* chapters 1 and 10.
13. Fairly comprehensive evidence for this can be found in the "Connecticut Mutual Life Report on Values in the 80s," conducted by Research and Forecasts in 1981. The opinions of the general population on a wide variety of social, political, and moral issues were compared to the opinions of nine categories of elites (in religion, business, voluntary associations, military, education, government, the news media, science, and law and justice). Another important study showing these patterns can be found in S. R. Lichter, S. Rothman, and L. Lichter, *The Media Elite* (Bethesda, Md.: Adler & Adler, 1986).
14. One review of these data can be found in James Davison Hunter, *American Evangelicalism: Conservative Religion and the Quandary of Modernity* (New Brunswick, N.J.: Rutgers University Press, 1983), chapter 5. See also the Gallup Reports on Religion in America (Princeton, N.J.: American Institute of Public Opinion, annual).

15. The survey was conducted by the author based upon the 1988 edition of the *Encyclopedia of Associations*. The organizations used in this survey were selected if they promoted an identifiably liberal or conservative point of view on domestic policy issues relating to the culture war.
16. In his *Prison Notebooks* Gramsci states, "One of the most important characteristics of any group that is developing towards dominance is its struggle to assimilate and to conquer 'ideologically' the traditional intellectuals, but this assimilation and conquest is made quicker and more efficacious the more the group in question succeeds in simultaneously elaborating its own organic intellectuals" (p. 10). The illustration he uses is the French Revolution, where the conflicts between the organic intellectuals of the bourgeoisie and the church led to various compromises and eventually to the Dreyfus affair, which signaled the final victory of anti-clerical forces against the powerful alliance between the clergy and monarchy. Antonio Gramsci, Selections from the *Prison Notebooks of Antonio Gramsci,* 1st ed. (New York: International Publishers, 1971). See also L. Salamini, *The Sociology of Political Praxis: An Introduction to Gramsci's Theory* (London: Routledge and Kegan Paul, 1981), p. 110.
17. See James Davison Hunter, *Evangelicalism: The Coming Generation* (Chicago: University of Chicago Press, 1987).
18. One of the most powerful arguments for this idea is made by A. Gouldner, *The Future of Intellectuals and the Rise of the New Class* (New York: Oxford University Press, 1979).
19. N. Anderson, *Desert Saints* (Chicago: University of Chicago Press, 1942), pp. 290–91.
20. *Reynolds v. United States,* 98 U.S. 145, 166–167 (1879).
21. *Davis v. Beason,* 133 U.S. 33, 342–43 (1890).
22. From a Religious Coalition on Abortion Rights pamphlet, "Abortion: Why Religious Organizations in the United States Want to Keep It Legal," Washington, D.C., no date.
23. Ibid.
24. This is the closing epigram of ibid.
25. From an organizing packet for state and local activists for the National Day of Mourning for the Right to Privacy, 30 June 1989, a protest against the Supreme Court decision in *Bowers v. Hardwick.*
26. "Reductio Ad Absurdum," *Crisis* (November 1988): 7.
27. Thus the opposition to these behaviors is a measure of intolerance and hostility toward democratic pluralism. This is to say that anyone publicly opposing these things displays both "intolerance" and a "flagrant disregard for personal liberty." See Bob Frishman, *American Families* (Washington, D.C.: People for the American Way, 1984), p. 78.
28. One of the most fascinating popular apologies for moral pluralism came in

the form of a series of thirty-second "public affairs announcements" run by the People for the American Way in the mid-1980s. In each, a dozen or so people were interviewed about their preferences in eggs, music, and sports. In each case each interviewee expressed a different opinion. For example, in the commercial that played off sports we heard:

> "All sports have something to recommend them. but, uh, actually I enjoy swimming."
> "I really like basketball."
> "People think that because I'm tall, I should like basketball. But I hate it."
> "I like to watch baseball, if there's beer."
> "Boxing."
> "Surfing."
> "Football's the real sport."
> "Too bloody."
> "So violent."
> "Now you're talking my language."

The tag that followed this and all of the other announcements read: "Freedom of thought: The right to have and express your own opinions. That's the American Way." Though the explicit message concerned the "freedom of thought," the visual and discursive message was more encompassing. Because the references are made to actual behavior ("I enjoy swimming," "I love western omelets," "I love the discothèque"), the commercials become, at the very least, opaque apologies for a broader conception of pluralism.

29. Attributed to Martin Peretz of the *New Republic,* in Focus on the Family's *Citizen* 3 (February 1989): p. 11.
30. This statement is from the organizing packet for the National Day of Mourning for the Right to Privacy, 30 June 1989.
31. J. W. Butler, "Fights Evolution to Uphold Bible," *New York Times,* 5 July 1925, pp. 1–4.
32. From Christian Voice pamphlet, "Christian Voice: Preserving a Free Society."
33. "No Time to Compromise," an editorial in *Independent Voice* 35, 7 (no date).
34. Robert L. Houbeck quoted in R. J. Neuhaus, "The Abortion Debate: The Next Twelve Years," *The Religion and Society Special Report* (July 1985): B5.
35. This is from the Marquis de Sade's *Juliette* (New York: Grove, 1968), part 4, pp. 605–7.
36. A. MacIntyre, *After Virtue* (Notre Dame, Ind.: University of Notre Dame Press, 1984) p. 263.
37. This is paraphrased from Jeffrey Stout, *Ethics After Babel* (Boston: Beacon, 1988), from his insightful chapter 9, "Virtue Among the Ruins."
38. See Richard Madsen, "Contentless Consensus: The Political Discourse of a

Segmented Society," in Alan Wolfe, *The Recentering of American Society* (Berkeley and Los Angeles: University of California Press, 1991).

39. Stout, *Ethics After Babel,* p. 212.

EPILOGUE: DEMOCRATIC POSSIBILITIES

1. Cf. George Weigel, "The Requirements and Limits of Civility: How We Contend," paper presented at the Williamsburg Charter Conference, "Commitment and Civility: The First Amendment Religion Clauses and American Public Life," 11–14 April 1988, Williamsburg, Virginia; Steven M. Tipton, "The Church as a School for Virtue," *Daedalus* 117 (Spring 1988): 163–175; and *The Williamsburg Charter* (Washington, D.C.: the Williamsburg Charter Foundation, 1988).
2. A. MacIntyre, *Whose Justice? Which Rationality?* (Notre Dame, Ind.: University of Notre Dame Press, 1988).
3. This is perhaps the central argument of R. Bellah et al., *Habits of the Heart* (Berkeley and Los Angeles: University of California Press, 1985).
4. The word comes from the Greek prefix *idios,* meaning personal, private, separate—as in idiomatic, idiosyncrasy, and idiom. The idiot was the private, ill-informed person, one off on his or her own.
5. Alan Wolfe makes the most recent and forceful case for this position in his important book, *Whose Keeper? Social Science and Moral Obligation* (Berkeley and Los Angeles: University of California Press, 1989).
6. The possibility is kept alive by such efforts as the Williamsburg Charter Project. The Williamsburg Charter was an officially recognized commemoration of the bicentennial of the U.S. Constitution (see the *Journal of Law and Religion,* July 1991). Published in 1988, it celebrates religious liberty, sets out the place of such liberty in American public life, and reaffirms the place of such liberty for people of all faiths or none. In doing so it reforges a vital but controversial part of the American public philosophy, or the common vision for the common good. Here lies its importance for the culture wars. Moving beyond historical commemoration to reaffirmation today, it brings American first principles to bear on the knottiest problems of the universities, the public school classrooms, and the law courts. The most practical outcome of the Williamsburg Charter is a new curriculum on religious liberty in a pluralistic society. It has been introduced in many public schools and is making an important contribution to the education reform movement and to the maintenance of a responsible, civil society. See *Living with Our Deepest Differences: Religious Liberty in a Pluralistic Society* (First Liberty Institute at George Mason University, 1990).

Selected Bibliography

ANDERSON, NELS. *Desert Saints: The Mormon Frontier in Utah.* Chicago: University of Chicago Press, 1942.

BAIRD, ROBERT. *Religion in America: Or an Account of the Origin, Progress, Relation to the State, and Present Condition of the Evangelical Churches in the United States with Notices of the Non-Evangelical Denominations.* New York: Harper and Brother, 1844.

BATES, THOMAS R. "Gramsci and the Theory of Hegemony." *Journal of the History of Ideas* 36 (April–May 1975): 351–66.

BELLAH, ROBERT N. "Competing Visions of the Role of a Religion in American Society." In *Uncivil Religion,* ed. Robert N. Bellah and Frederick E. Greenspahn. New York: Crossroad, 1987.

BERGER, BRIGITTE, and PETER L. BERGER. *The War over the Family.* New York: Anchor Doubleday, 1984.

BERGER, PETER L. "A Market Model for the Analysis of Ecumenicity." *Sociology and Social Research* 30 (Spring 1963): 77–93.

———. *The Sacred Canopy.* New York: Doubleday, 1967.

———. "Some Second Thoughts on Substantive versus Functional Definitions of Religion." *Journal for the Scientific Study of Religion* 13 (June 1974): 125–33.

———. "Religion and the American Future." In *The Third Century,* ed. Seymour M. Lipset. Chicago: University of Chicago Press, 1979.

———. "The Worldview of the New Class: Secularity and its Discontents." In *The New Class?,* ed. B. Bruce-Briggs. New Brunswick, N.J.: Transaction Books, 1979.

———. "American Religion: Conservative Upsurge; Liberal Prospects." In *Liberal Protestantism,* ed. Robert Michaelsen and Wade Clark Roof. New York: Pilgrim, 1986.

BESCHLE, DONALD L. "The Conservative as Liberal: The Religion Clauses, Liberal Neutrality and the Approach of Justice O'Connor." *Notre Dame Law Review* 62 (1987): 151–91.

BILLINGTON, RAY ALLEN. "Tentative Bibliography of Anti-Catholic Propaganda in the United States, 1800–1860." *Catholic Historical Review* 18 (1932): 492–513.

———. *The Protestant Crusade,* 1800–1860. Gloucester, Mass.: Peter Smith, 1963.

BLUMENTHAL, SIDNEY. *The Permanent Campaign: Inside the World of Elite Political Operatives.* Boston: Beacon Press, 1980.

BODE, CARL, ed. *The Young Mencken: The Best of His Work.* New York: Dial Press, 1973.

BULKA, REUVEN P. "Orthodoxy Today: An Analysis of the Achievements and the Problems." In *Dimensions of Orthodox Judaism,* ed. Reuven P. Bulka. New York: KTAV Publishing House, 1983.

CAVERT, SAMUEL. *The American Churches and the Ecumenical Movement, 1900–1968.* New York: Associated Press, 1968.

CEASER, JAMES W. "The Rhetorical Presidency Revisited." In *Modern Presidents and the Presidency,* ed. Marc Landy. Lexington, Mass.: Lexington Books, 1985.

CEASER, JAMES W., GLEN THUROW, JEFFREY TULIS, and JOSEPH BESSETTE. "The Rise of the Rhetorical Presidency." *Presidential Studies Quarterly* 11 (Spring 1981): 158–71.

CHOPER, JESSE H. "Defining 'Religion' in the First Amendment." *University of Illinois Law Review* 3 (1982): 579–613.

CONNOVER, PAMELA JOHNSTON, and VIRGINIA GRAY. *Feminism and the New Right: Conflict over the American Family.* New York: Praeger, 1983.

CORRIGAN, JOHN. "The Enlightenment." In *Encyclopedia of American Religious Experience,* vol. 2, ed. Charles H. Lippy and Peter W. Williams. New York: Charles Scribners and Sons, 1988.

CUNEO, MICHAEL W. "Soldiers of Orthodoxy: Revivalist Catholicism and the Battle for the North American Church." Unpublished paper, Department of Comparative Religion, Dalhousie University, 1988.

DAUM, ANNETTE. "Turning Point." *Interreligious Currents* 1, 2 (Spring 1983): 1.

DAVIS, DAVID BRION. "Some Themes of Counter-Subversion: An Analysis of Anti-Masonic, Anti-Catholic and Anti-Mormon Literature." *Mississippi Valley Historical Review* 47 (1960): 205–25.

DEGLER, CARL. *At Odds.* New York: Oxford University Press, 1980.

DEMPSEY, JOHN. *The Family and Public Policy.* Baltimore: Brookes Publishing, 1981.

DEWEY, JOHN. *A Common Faith.* New Haven, Conn.: Yale University Press, 1934.

DOBBELAERE, KAREL, and JAN LAUWERS. "Definition of Religion—A Sociological Critique." *Social Compass* 74 (1973): 535–51.

DOBKOWSKI, MICHAEL N. *The Image of the Jew in American Literature.* Philadelphia: Jewish Publication Society of America, 1974.

———. "American Anti-Semitism: A Reinterpretation." *American Quarterly* 29 (Summer 1977): 166–81.

DOEPKE, DALE. "The Western Examiner: A Chronicle of Atheism in the West." *The Bulletin* 30 (1973): 29–43.

DOLAN, JAY. "Catholic Attitudes Toward Protestants." In *Uncivil Religion,* ed. Robert N. Bellah and Frederick E. Greenspahn. New York: Crossroad, 1987.

DREISBACH, DANIEL. *Real Threat and Mere Shadow: Religious Freedom and the First Amendment.* Westchester, Ill.: Crossway, 1987.

ERICKSON, PAUL. *Reagan Speaks: The Making of an American Myth.* New York: New York University Press, 1985.

FEMIA, JOSEPH. "Hegemony and Consciousness in the Thought of Antonio Gramsci." *Political Studies* 12, 1 (1975): 29–48.

FINK, NANCY H. "The Establishment Clause According to the Supreme Court: The Mysterious Eclipse of Free Exercise Values." *Catholic University Law Review* 27 (1978): 207–62.

FINLEY, M. I. *The Ancient Greeks.* New York: Viking, 1963.

FOGARTY, GERALD P. *The Vatican and the American Hierarchy.* Stuttgart: Anton Hiersemann, 1982.

———. "Dissent at Catholic University: The Case of Henry Poels." *America* (11 October 1986): 180–84.

FORMISANO, RONALD P. *The Birth of Mass Political Parties in Michigan, 1827–1861.* Princeton, N.J.: Princeton University Press, 1971.

FRISHMAN, BOB. *American Families: Responding to the Pro-Family Movement.* Washington, D.C.: People for the American Way, 1984.

GALLUP, GEORGE, JR. *Religion in America: 50 Years.* Princeton, N.J.: Princeton Religion Research Center, 1985.

GARVEY, JOHN. "Made for Each Other: The Fundamentalist-Humanist Complex." *Commonweal* 108 (16 January 1981): 6–8.

GLAZER, NATHAN. *American Judaism.* Chicago: University of Chicago Press, 1957.

GLOCK, CHARLES, and RODNEY STARK. *Christian Beliefs and Anti-Semitism.* New York: Harper and Row, 1966.

GOODMAN, PAUL. *Towards a Christian Republic: Antimasonry and the Great Transition in New England, 1826–1836.* New York: Oxford University Press, 1988.

GOULDNER, ALVIN. *The Future of Intellectuals and the Rise of the New Class.* New York: Oxford University Press, 1979.

GREELEY, ANDREW M. *Ethnicity, Denomination and Equality.* Beverly Hills, Calif.: Sage, 1976.

HADDEN, JEFFREY K., and ANSON SHUPE. *Televangelism: Power and Politics on God's Frontier.* New York: Henry Holt, 1988.

HANDLIN, OSCAR. "American Views of the Jews at the Opening of the Twentieth Century." *American Jewish Historical Society* 40 (June 1951): 323–45.

HARDON, JOHN A. *American Judaism.* Chicago: Loyola University Press, 1971.

HEILMAN, SAMUEL. "The Many Faces of Orthodoxy." *Modern Judaism* 2 (1982): 23–51.

———. "The Many Faces of Orthodoxy, Part II." *Modern Judaism* 2 (1982): 171–98.

———. "Orthodox Jews: An Open or Closed Group?" In *Uncivil Religion,* ed. Robert N. Bellah and Frederick E. Greenspahn. New York: Crossroad, 1987.

HERBERG, WILL. *Protestant, Catholic, Jew.* New York: Harper & Row, 1955.

HERTZKE, ALLEN. "Representing God in Washington: The Role of Religious Lobbies in the American Polity." Ph.D. diss., University of Wisconsin, 1986.

HIGHAM, JOHN. "Anti-Semitism in the Gilded Age: A Reinterpretation." *Mississippi Valley Historical Review* 43 (March 1957): 559–78.

———. "Social Discrimination Against Jews in America, 1830–1930." *American Jewish Historical Society* 47 (September 1957): 1–33.

HITCHCOCK, JAMES. *What Is Secular Humanism? Why Humanism Is Secular and How It Is Changing Our World.* Ann Arbor, Mich.: Servant Books, 1982.

HOARE, QUINTIN, and GEOFFREY NOWELL SMITH, eds. *Selections from the Prison Notebooks of Antonio Gramsci.* New York: International Publishers, 1971.

HOFSTADTER, RICHARD, and MICHAEL WALLACE, eds. *American Violence.* New York: Vintage Books, 1971.

HUNTER, JAMES DAVISON. "The New Class and the Young Evangelicals." *Review of Religious Research* 22 (December 1980): 155–69.

———. "The Liberal Reaction to the New Christian Right." In *The New Christian Right: Mobilization and Legitimation,* ed. Robert Liebman and Robert Wuthnow. New York: Aldine, 1983.

———. *American Evangelicalism: Conservative Religion and the Quandary of Modernity.* New Brunswick, N.J., Rutgers University Press, 1983.

———. "American Protestantism: Sorting Out the Present, Looking Toward the Future." *This World* 17 (1987): 53–76.

———. "America's Fourth Faith: A Sociological Perspective on Secular Humanism." *This World* 19 (1987): 101–10.

———. *Evangelicalism: The Coming Generation.* Chicago: University of Chicago Press, 1987.

———. *The Williamsburg Charter Survey on Religion and American Public Life.* Washington, D.C.: Williamsburg Charter Foundation, 1988.

———. "Evangelical Schools in Growth; Catholic Schools in Decline." *Wall Street Journal,* 8 March 1988, p. 34.

HUNTER, JAMES DAVISON, and OS GUINNESS, eds. *Articles of Faith, Articles of Peace: The First Amendment Religion Clauses and the American Public Philosophy.* Washington, D.C.: Brookings Institution, 1990.

HUNTER, JAMES DAVISON, JAMES TUCKER, and STEVEN E. FINKEL. "Religious Elites and Political Values." Unpublished paper, University of Virginia, 1989.

IGLESIAS, M. TIMOTHY. "CUF and Dissent: A Case Study in Religious Conservatism." *America* 156 (11 April 1987): 303–7.

JORGENSON, LLOYD. *The State and the Non-Public School, 1825–1925.* Columbia: University of Missouri Press, 1987.

KEEFE, THOMAS M. "The Catholic Issue in the *Chicago Tribune* Before the Civil War." *Mid-America* 57 (October 1975): 227–45.

KLEBER, JOHN E. " 'Pagan Bob' on the Comstock: Robert G. Ingersoll Visits Virginia City." *Nevada Historical Society Quarterly* 22 (Winter 1979): 243–53.

KOCH, GUSTAV A. *Republican Religion: The American Revolution and the Cult of Reason.* New York: Henry Holt, 1933.

KURTZ, PAUL. *In Defense of Secular Humanism.* Buffalo, N.Y.: Prometheus Books, 1983.

———. "On the Misuse of Language: A Response to Paul Beattie." *Free Inquiry* 6 (1986): 20–22.

LANNIE, VINCENT P., and BERNARD C. DIETHORN. "For the Honor and Glory of God: The Philadelphia Bible Riots of 1844." *History of Education Quarterly* 8 (Spring 1968): 44–106.

LENSKI, GERHARD. *The Religious Factor.* Garden City: Anchor Doubleday, 1961.

LEVY, LEONARD. *The Establishment Clause.* New York: Macmillan, 1986.

LICHTER, S. ROBERT, STANLEY ROTHMAN, and LINDA LICHTER. *The Media Elite.* Bethesda, Md.: Adler and Adler, 1986.

LIEBMAN, CHARLES S. "Orthodoxy in American Jewish Life." In *Dimensions of Orthodox Judaism,* ed. Reuven P. Bulka. New York: KTAV Publishing, 1983.

LIEBMAN, ROBERT, and ROBERT WUTHNOW, eds. *The New Christian Right: Mobilization and Legitimation.* New York: Aldine, 1983.

LIPSET, S. M. "American Exceptionalism Reaffirmed." *Tocqueville Review* 10 (1990): 3–35.

LIPSET, S. M., and E. RAAB. *The Politics of Unreason.* Chicago: University of Chicago Press, 1970.

LUKER, KRISTIN. *Abortion and the Politics of Motherhood.* Los Angeles: University of California Press, 1984.

MACINTYRE, ALASDAIR. *After Virtue.* Notre Dame, Ind.: University of Notre Dame Press, 1984.

———. *Whose Justice? Which Rationality?* Notre Dame, Ind.: University of Notre Dame Press, 1988.

MADSEN, RICHARD. "Contentless Consensus: The Political Discourse of a Segmented Society." In *America at Century's End,* ed. Alan Wolfe. Los Angeles and Berkeley: University of California Press, 1991.

MARSDEN, GEORGE. "A Case of the Excluded Middle: Creation Versus Evolution in America." In *Uncivil Religion,* ed. Robert N. Bellah and Frederick E. Greenspahn. New York: Crossroad, 1987.

MARTIN, BERNARD. "Conservative Judaism and Reconstructionism." In *Movements and Issues in American Judaism,* ed. Martin Bernard. Westport, Conn.: Greenwood Press, 1978.

MARTIRE, GREGORY, and RUTH CLARK. *Anti-Semitism in the United States: A Study of Prejudice in the 1980s.* New York: Praeger, 1982.

MAY, HENRY F. *The Discontent of the Intellectuals: A Problem of the Twenties.* Chicago: Rand McNally, 1963.

MAYNARD, THEODORE. *The Story of American Catholicism.* New York: Macmillan, 1942.

MERLEMAN, RICHARD. *Making Something of Ourselves: On Culture and Politics in the United States.* Los Angeles and Berkeley: University of California Press, 1984.

MILLER, RANDALL, and TOM MARZIK, eds. *Immigrants and Religion in America.* Philadelphia: Temple University Press, 1977.

MORAIS, HERBERT M. *Deism in Eighteenth-Century America.* New York: Columbia University Press, 1934.

NASH, RONALD H., ed. *Liberation Theology.* Milford, Mich.: Mott Media, 1984.

NEUHAUS, RICHARD. *The Naked Public Square.* Grand Rapids, Mich.: Eerdmans, 1984.

NOLL, MARK. "The Eclipse of Old Hostilities between and the Potential for New Strife among Catholics and Protestants Since Vatican II." In *Uncivil Religion,* ed. Robert N. Bellah and Frederick E. Greenspahn. New York: Crossroad, 1987.

O'DEA, THOMAS. *The Mormons.* Chicago: University of Chicago Press, 1957.

PARSONS, PAUL. *Inside America's Christian Schools.* Macon, Ga.: Mercer University Press, 1987.

PARSONS, TALCOTT. "Religion in Postindustrial America: The Problem of Secularization." *Social Research* 41 (1974): 193–225.

PEARCE, W. BARNETT, STEPHEN W. LITTLEJOHN, and ALISON ALEXANDER. "The Quixotic Quest for Civility: Patterns of Interaction Between the New Christian Right and Secular Humanists." In *Secularization and Fundamentalism Reconsidered,* ed. Jeffrey Hadden and Anson Shupe. New York: Paragon House, 1989.

POSTMAN, NEIL. *Amusing Ourselves to Death: Public Discourse in the Age of Show Business.* New York: Viking, 1985.

QUINLEY, HAROLD, and CHARLES GLOCK. *Anti-Semitism in America.* New York: Free Press, 1979.

RAVITCH, DIANE. *The Great School Wars: The Public Schools as a Battleground for Social Change.* New York: Basic Books, 1973.

REHER, MARGARET M. "Leo XIII and 'Americanism.'" *Theological Studies* 34 (1973): 679–89.

RIBUFFO, LEO P. "Liberals and That Old-Time Religion." *Nation,* 29 November 1980, pp. 572–73.

———. *The Old Christian Right.* Philadelphia: Temple University Press, 1983.

ROSENFELD, GERALDINE. "The Polls: Attitudes Toward American Jews." *Public Opinion Quarterly* 46 (1982): 431–43.

SABATO, LARRY. *The Rise of Political Consultants.* New York: Basic Books, 1981.

———. *PAC Power: Inside the World of Political Action Committees.* New York: Norton, 1985.

SADE, MARQUIS DE. *Juliette,* 6 vols. Translated by Austryn Wainhouse. New York: Grove Press, 1968.

SALAMINI, LEONARDO. *The Sociology of Political Praxis: An Introduction to Gramsci's Theory.* London: Routledge and Kegan Paul, 1981.

SCHWARTZ, HERMAN. *Packing the Courts.* New York: Scribners, 1988.

SELZNICK, GERTRUDE, and STEPHEN STEINBERG. *The Tenacity of Prejudice: Anti-Semitism in Contemporary America.* New York: Harper and Row, 1969.

SESSIONS, GENE. "Myth, Mormonism, and Murder in the South." *South Atlantic Quarterly* 75 (Spring 1976): 212–25.

SHAUGHNESSY, GERALD. *Has the Immigrant Kept the Faith? A Study of Immigration and Catholic Growth in the United States, 1790–1920.* 1925. Reprint New York: Arno Press, 1969.

SHIPLEY, MAYNARD. *The War on Modern Science.* New York: Alfred A. Knopf, 1927.

SIMMS, ADAM. "A Battle in the Air: Detroit's Jews Answer Father Coughlin." *Michigan Jewish History* 18, 2 (1978): 7–13.

SKLARE, MARSHALL. *Conservative Judaism: An American Religious Movement.* New York: Schocken, 1972.

SMART, J. J. C. *Our Place in the Universe.* Oxford: Blackwell, 1989.

SMITH, TIMOTHY. "New Approaches to the History of Immigration in Twentieth-Century America." *American Historical Review* 71 (July 1966): 1265–79.

———. "Immigrant Social Aspirations and American Education, 1800–1930." *American Quarterly* 21 (Fall 1969): 523–43.

———. "Religion and Ethnicity in America." *American Historical Review* 83 (December 1978): 1155–85.

———. "Biblical Ideals in American Christian and Jewish Philanthropy, 1880–1920." *American Jewish History* 74 (September 1984): 3–26.

STARK, RODNEY, and CHARLES GLOCK. *American Piety: The Nature of Religious Commitment.* Los Angeles and Berkeley: University of California Press, 1968.

STAUFFER, VERNON. *New England and the Bavarian Illuminati.* New York: Columbia University Press, 1918.

STEINER, GILBERT. *The Futility of Family Policy.* Washington, D.C.: Brookings Institution, 1981.

STEMBER, CHARLES, ed. *Jews in the Mind of America.* New York: Basic Books, 1966.

STOUT, HARRY. *The New England Soul.* New York: Oxford University Press, 1986.

STOUT, JEFFREY. *Ethics after Babel: The Languages of Morals and Their Discontents.* Boston: Beacon Press, 1988.

SULLIVAN, JOHN L., JAMES PIERESON, and GEORGE MARCUS. *Political Tolerance and American Democracy*. Chicago: University of Chicago Press, 1982.

TAYLOR, CHARLES. "Religion in a Free Society." In *Articles of Faith, Articles of Peace: The First Amendment Religion Clauses and the American Public Philosophy*, ed. J. D. Hunter and Os Guinness. Washington, D.C.: Brookings Institution, 1990.

THOMAS, GEORGE. *Revivalism and Cultural Change*. Chicago: University of Chicago Press, 1989.

TIPTON, STEVEN M. "The Church as a School for Virtue." *Daedalus* 117 (Spring 1988): 163–175.

TOCQUEVILLE, ALEXIS DE. *Democracy in America*. New York: Vintage, 1954.

TRIBE, LAURENCE H. *American Constitutional Law*. Mineola, N.Y.: Foundation Press, 1978.

TULIS, JEFFREY K. *The Rhetorical Presidency*. Princeton, N.J.: Princeton University Press, 1987.

TUVESON, ERNEST LEE. *Redeemer Nation*. Chicago: University of Chicago Press, 1968.

VAN DER LEEUW, GERARDUS. *Religion in Essence and Manifestation*. New York: Harper Torchbooks, 1963.

VARACALLI, JOSEPH. "To Empower Catholics: The Catholic League for Religious and Civil Rights as a Mediating Structure." *Nassau Review* 5, 4 (1988): 45–61.

VITZ, PAUL. "Religion and Traditional Values in Public School Textbooks: An Empirical Study." Report to the National Institute of Education, Washington, D.C., 1985.

———. "Religion and Traditional Values in Public School Textbooks." *Public Interest* 84 (Summer 1986): 79–90.

WACH, JOACHIM. *The Sociology of Religion*. Chicago: University of Chicago Press, 1970.

WARREN, SIDNEY. *American Freethought, 1860–1914*. New York: Columbia University Press, 1943.

WEIGERT, ANDREW. "Functional, Substantive, or Political? A Comment on Berger's Second Thoughts on Defining Religions." *Journal for the Scientific Study of Religion* 13 (December 1974): 483–86.

WHITE, JOHN KENNETH. *The New Politics of Old Values*. Hanover, N.H.: University of New England Press, 1988.

WOLFE, ALAN. *Whose Keeper? Social Science and Moral Obligation*. Los Angeles and Berkeley: University of California Press, 1989.

WUTHNOW, ROBERT. *The Consciousness Reformation*. Los Angeles and Berkeley: University of California Press, 1976.

———. *Experimentation in American Religion*. Los Angeles and Berkeley: University of California Press, 1978.

———. "Religious Movements and Counter-Movements." In *New Religious Movements and Rapid Social Change*, ed. James A. Beckford. Paris: UNESCO, 1987.

———. *The Restructuring of American Religion*. Princeton, N.J.: Princeton University Press, 1988.

———. "Divided We Fall: America's Two Civil Religions." *Christian Century* 105 (20 April 1988): 395–99.

Index